CORRELATION
AND
REGRESSION

Applications for Industrial Organizational Psychology and Management

SECOND EDITION

PHILIP BOBKO

Sage Publications
International Educational and Professional Publisher
Thousand Oaks ▪ London ▪ New Delhi

For information:

Sage Publications, Inc.
2455 Teller Road
Thousand Oaks, California 91320
E-mail: order@sagepub.com

Sage Publications Ltd.
6 Bonhill Street
London EC2A 4PU
United Kingdom

Sage Publications India Pvt. Ltd.
M-32 Market
Greater Kailash I
New Delhi 110 048 India

Printed in the United States of America

Library of Congress Cataloging-in-Publication Data

Bobko, Philip.
    Correlation and regression: Applications for industrial organizational
psychology and management/ by Philip Bobko.—2nd ed.
        p.   cm.—(Organizational research methods)
    ISBN 0-7619-2303-9
    1. Personnel management—Statistical methods. 2. Psychology, Industrial—
Statistical methods. 3. Industrial management—Statistical methods. I. Title.
II. Organizational research methods series.
HF5549 .B758 2001
658—dc21   00-051816

This book is printed on acid-free paper.

01   02   03   04   05   06   7   6   5   4   3   2   1

Acquiring Editor:	Marquita Flemming
Editorial Assistant:	MaryAnn Vail
Production Editor:	Sanford Robinson
Editorial Assistant:	Cindy Bear
Typesetter:	Technical Typesetting, Inc.
Cover Designer:	Michelle Lee

DEDICATION

To my darling wife, Barbara, my dear son, Christopher, and loving memories of my mom.

Barb, you came into my life and taught me that love was joyous, boundless, and infinite. Chris, you came into our lives and taught me those lessons all over again. Life becomes beautiful when I get to share it with you.

CONTENTS

PREFACE

In textbooks, you will very often find a preface which indicates how to read that particular book, the author's underlying educational philosophy, the author's intentions, prerequisite knowledge (in the case of *this* book, an introductory course in statistics), the symbols used, and so forth. If you are one of those students who compulsively reads prefaces, I say, "Welcome!" However, since I believe that the above issues and explanations are so important to all readers, I have placed them in the first half of Chapter I (with the second half of that chapter being devoted to a brief review/reminder about introductory statistics). So, look for explanations about *what* the book covers, and *how* to read the book, in Chapter I. (In fact, you can't miss them, as they pretty much take up the entire first half of that chapter!)

The current edition of this book was revised under the terrific auspices of Sage Publications, Inc. What is different in this revision? Well, many of the basic facts in elementary statistics simply haven't changed in the last five years, nor were they expected to. Therefore, many of the initial explanations in each chapter have remained unchanged (see Chapter I regarding the layered structure to each chapter). On the other hand, a few advanced extensions of the basic issues have occurred since the first edition and some of these extensions have been incorporated in asides and footnotes (see Chapter I for the meaning of an "aside"). Also, in a variety of instances, I have updated the empirical examples of applications of correlation and regression. This was fun, as it kept me on my toes − reading the content of current literature for particular applications (of course, being editor of the Journal of Applied Psychology during some of the intervening time helped me in that regard, too!). I hope you will like the mixture of "classic" cites and really up-to-date applications.

Let me conclude by saying that I have tried to write a book, and its revision, which conveys the personal enjoyment that I get in explaining statistics to students. I have tried to impart a folksy and common-sensical style of writing without losing either the required precision in statistics or the fact that the application of statistics isn't always as straightforward as some people might believe. Over the past five years, a variety of folks (students and faculty) have written notes and email messages to me indicating that they appreciated the clarity of the exposition and the perspectives brought to bear in the first edition of this book. These encouragements from readers have been heartwarming, and I have tried to keep the original tone and perspectives in the revision. I truly hope that you learn a lot from this book *and*, at the same time, enjoy what you're learning!

ACKNOWLEDGEMENTS

I do want to take the opportunity in this preface to thank many individuals. First, and foremost, I thank my wife, Barb, and my son, Chris, for their continuous emotional support of my efforts. The simultaneous hard work and joy of writing this book was always wonderfully enveloped by the context of their love. I couldn't have written this book without them.

I wish to thank my current editors at Sage Publications – Marquita Flemming and Sanford Robinson. They are wonderful examples of how editors can work positively and responsively with others to get a book to print and to help insure that the book is a quality product. I also wish to thank Frank Burrows, the initial editor for the first edition, for his continual warmth and understanding, as well as his shared belief in my vision for the book. Thank you, my editors!

Of course, this book and its revision were "simmering" in my mind for many years and, for that reason, I thank all of the students and faculty who have sat through my statistics courses and have helped me learn what types of explanations seem to work best. I thank the faculty, researchers, and students who read and provided thorough, thoughtful, and constructive commentary on particular chapters: Adrienne Colella, Janet Gebelt, Michael Gordon, David Harrison, Mark Huselid, John Mathieu, Karen Newman, Bernard Nickels, Craig Russell, Robert Sadacca, and Hilda Wing. I also thank Craig Pinder for his early encouragement in getting me to actually start this project and Larry Williams, series editor, for his strong support of this revision. I want to thank (again) Janet Gebelt for her assistance with the development of the problem sets, Barbara Bobko for her typing assistance, and Christopher Bobko for his assistance with the development of the figures in this book. Because of all of the terrific help mentioned above, I feel compelled to note that any remaining imperfections in the book are mine (unless I can find somebody else to blame them on). Go Tiger(s)!

AN INTRODUCTION, AN OVERVIEW, AND SOME REMINDERS

AN INTRODUCTION AND OVERVIEW

Welcome to correlation and regression! Although composing this book was very hard work at times, I have also had a lot of fun writing down my thoughts about how to understand regression and correlation in productive ways. I hope that some of that fun and excitement is imparted to you, the reader, as you go through the book.

While writing this book, I tried to adopt an approach that would convey the enjoyment I have had in explaining statistics to students both in the classroom and in my office. Such explanations usually involve the use of a blackboard, lots of writing and erasing, lots of gesticulations with hands and arms, and lots of interactions with students. However, in a textbook one is constrained to write in a somewhat linear fashion, and it's much harder to point to the place on the blackboard where something appeared 10 minutes ago.

I have tried to impart as much of this nonlinearity in the book as possible. One theme in this book is that life is pretzel-shaped, not linear. Also, I have tried to write the book in everyday language. One reviewer of some draft chapters mentioned that reading the manuscript was like having a conversation with the author. I hope that you, too, find the book to be both folksy and commonsensical. I truly believe that one can have these attributes in a statistics book and still make mathematically accurate statements. A dry, pedantic style and accuracy are not necessarily correlated attributes!

Another intent was to focus on research examples and "real-world" experiences in introducing each of the topics. One fundamental assumption of this book is that *the application of correlational and regression techniques is not necessarily straightforward*. In fact, it's often messy and requires thinking about the techniques in creative ways (i.e., ways consistent with the particular situation at hand). In real applications, uses of correlation and regression almost always have some unique twist. Thus, only if we truly understand the reasoning behind each of the techniques will we be able to use and exploit statistics in future situations.

In a related comment, I note that applications of statistics almost always involve value judgments (i.e., statistics usually cannot be done using only a cookbook approach). One has to choose what statistic to compute and how to interpret the result.[1] Although statistics can help us systematically sort out our options, the ultimate choices still become informed value decisions. Let me describe an example that happened during a briefing I once attended. After a 10-year effort to develop and collect data on a new selection test battery, some of the individuals involved were trying to reach consensus on which set of tests to include in the organization's selection battery. Obviously, decision makers in this organization wanted to maximize performance, so researchers conducted regressions to determine which tests best predicted performance. However, the decision makers also wanted to make sure that the tests they used helped decide *which* job in the company applicants were best suited for (i.e., they wanted tests that maximized classification efficiency). Finally, the organization also wanted to choose tests that minimized negative impact on minority and women applicants. The researchers conducted many regressions for each of these three criteria and, no surprise, found that the choice of tests depended on what they wanted to accomplish. So the decision was still value-based, in spite of the fancy statistical algorithms invoked. On the other hand, knowledge of regression, and how (correlationally speaking) the different analytic techniques ended up with different tests, was very useful information in the value decision. This book will not always give you *the* way to do something. Hopefully, it will assist you in thinking about the dimensions of the problem and how to best choose among the alternative data analytic options.

THE STRUCTURE OF THIS BOOK

An Outline

There are 10 chapters in the book, including the chapter you are reading now. I suggest you read the chapters in numerical order (with some possible exceptions to be noted below). The book is conceptually divided into two sections. Chapters II through V are concerned with *correlation*; Chapters VI through X talk about *regression* equations. Here's a brief outline of the next 9 chapters.

Chapter II. A Review of the Correlation Coefficient and Its Properties

This chapter reviews the use of a Pearson product moment correlation as a point estimate of an underlying relationship between two variables. Why do

---

[1] For example, see the discussion in Chapter VI of how our field ended up with the type of least squares regression usually invoked in research reports.

we need correlations? What are they? Why are they so important in research? Can personnel researchers speak without them? Special cases of correlations (phi, point-biserial, etc.) are indicated. Both well-known and rare (but useful) properties of the correlation coefficient are considered.

Chapter III. Testing Correlations for Statistical Significance

This chapter provides null hypothesis testing procedures for all types of correlations, using t-tests, z-transformations, and chi-square tests. Examples of hypothesis testing from literature on motivation, job security, test fairness, performance appraisal, etc., are presented. Hypothesis testing for the comparison between two correlations (both dependent and independent samples) is also addressed.

Chapter IV. Applications of Pearson Correlation to Measurement Theory

Classical test theory, reliability, and validity are considered as common applications of correlations. Examples are presented involving test construction, performance appraisal, and the measurement of constructs in organizational behavior. This chapter demonstrates how researchers might index the precision with which they measure conceptually difficult constructs. It also considers and proves some very famous results in psychometric theory.

Chapter V. Range Restriction

Range restriction is presented as an application problem in correlational analyses. The phenomenon is documented with an equal employment opportunity court case on test validation. Correction factors are analyzed.

Chapter VI. "Simple," Two-Variable Regression

The basic regression model (with examples) is presented, as well as nonstandard models (e.g., constrained regression). By using just one predictor, many of the fundamental issues surrounding regression can be presented (with solutions). Topics include the estimation of regression weights, hypothesis testing, and residual analyses. With the use of an analysis of variance approach, the relationship between regression and correlation is noted.

Chapter VII. Three Applications of Bivariate Regression: Utility Analysis, Regression to the Mean, Partial Correlation

To enhance an understanding of regression, several applications of bivariate regression are introduced. First, utility analysis is considered by demonstrating that the fundamental equation within this topic in industrial and organizational psychology is really a regression equation.

Second, regression to the mean is considered. For example, if only poor performers are selected for remedial training, then their scores would be expected to increase statistically even if the training program had no effect. We consider what to do in these cases (i.e., how to account for regression effects).

Third, partial correlation is presented as a correlation between regression residuals. There are several implications here for model building and theory testing. Also, partial and semipartial correlations help introduce the terminology for multiple regression.

Chapter VIII. Multiple (Mostly Trivariate) Regression

This chapter covers the basics of multiple (two or more predictors) regression. Many research examples are noted. Topics are an extension of those in Chapter VI and include the estimation of parameters, tests of statistical significance, the use of analysis of variance tables, the multiple correlation coefficient, the effects of multicollinearity, and the notion of a variable's unique contribution to prediction.

Chapter IX. Expanding the Regression Repertoire: Polynomial and Interaction Terms

Polynomial variables are considered as a way to increase the flexibility of multiple regression. Quadratic regression examples are presented. These regressions are also considered as vehicles for underscoring concerns about collinearity in the predictors.

The second section of this chapter considers the use of moderator variables and the search for statistically significant interactions. Interaction is presented as an extension of the multiple regression model. Examples include the use of interactions for identifying unfair tests, identifying theoretical moderator variables, and checking the equivalence of prediction functions. Statistical controversies are described and discussed.

Chapter X. More About Regression, and Beyond

The initial topic in this chapter is validity shrinkage. The role of maximization in regression is discussed, and correction factors for shrinkage are presented and examined. Statistical knowledge about these correction factors is exploited in the search for sample size requirements. Then, suppressor variables are considered as cases where collinearity in regression can give rise to unanticipated weighting functions. Finally, the use of coding and indicator variables is discussed. This allows for a direct demonstration of why analysis of variance (ANOVA) is special case of regression. A quick statement about what might come next (in a course on multivariate data analysis) is also given.

Here are some hints about how to read the book in general. As noted above, the chapters are designed to be read in numerical order. I believe that all of them can be read by a student who has had at least a one-semester course in basic statistics. To indicate the type of material I am assuming, a short review and reminder is presented in the second half of this first chapter. Because of the layered nature of the chapters (see below) and the footnotes, those of you with even greater levels of previous coursework will also benefit substantially from this book.

About the only area where derivations get messy (i.e., involve some tedious algebra) is in Chapter IV. This chapter has been designed so that the proofs are placed at the end of the chapter. Chapter IV can therefore be read without going through these proofs. (However, I *do* hope you will try to follow them. They are not difficult, and they will really help cement your understanding of the use of correlations in measurement.)

Chapter VII contains three applications of bivariate (two-variable) regression. The first two sections of this chapter (on utility analysis and regression to the mean) can be skipped, although I don't recommend it for any student in the social sciences. But whatever you do, don't skip the third section of Chapter VII (on partial correlations). Knowledge of partial correlations is critical in understanding how statistics in multiple regression (e.g., beta weights, the multiple correlation coefficient) should be interpreted.

Here are some hints about how to read each chapter. The intent was to write each chapter using spiraling levels of difficulty. That is, within each chapter, I start with a simple example or problem that motivates the chapter's topic. Then, a more advanced example or problem is presented, followed by some of the statistical results about the topic. After all that, other problems are noted that might be encountered when applying the technique (e.g., Why won't this always work?), followed by even more advanced statistical results concerning the topic. The intent is to layer the material within each chapter by starting with an intuitive understanding and progressing through the underlying statistics. Thus, within each chapter there is an intentionally large, progressive range of complexity. The further the student reads, the more detailed and intertwined the chapter becomes. (Note that I say "intertwined" here and not "confusing"!) As noted earlier, life is pretzel-shaped, and statistics reflects that reality.

Each chapter also has various footnotes and asides. These devices help link the linear requirements of textbook writing with the conversational, nonlinear style that you are used to in lectures and one-on-one discussions with instructors. The footnotes are important. Indeed, they have been expressly placed within the text (rather than as endnotes) to highlight their importance. Asides are like footnotes but remain in the flow of the text. When you figure out the conceptual distinction between footnotes and asides, let me know—my students haven't yet figured it out (and I'm not sure I know, either!).

You will also find a listing of chapter objectives at the beginning of each chapter, as well as some sample problems. The purpose of the problems is not to make you go through a large number of arithmetic calculations, although you must use your calculator in order to solve some of the problems. In most cases, though, I want you to think about the content of each chapter and its implications. Indeed, some of the problems have no numbers (and possibly no absolute answers). In problems that do require the manipulation of numbers, I tried to keep hand calculations at a minimum. Where calculations are potentially tedious, some partial answers have been provided in order to reduce the workload.

Can you already tell I enjoyed writing this book (in a perverse sort of way)? I hope you enjoy reading it (in a not-perverse sort of way!).

A BRIEF REVIEW AND REMINDER

Just so we're all on the same wavelength, here is a brief review of statistical knowledge that you will need to successfully read the chapters in this book. This review is not intended to be a replacement for an introductory course in statistics. Rather, it's more appropriate to think of it as a reminder of what you already know.

Notation

We will follow traditional notation: Greek letters will be used for population parameters, and Arabic letters for sample statistics. For example, μ_X is the population mean for the variable X, and $\overline{X}$ denotes a sample mean. Further, σ_X will represent the population standard deviation, while s_X will denote its sample counterpart. Of course, this also means that σ_X^2 will symbolize the population variance of X, and s_X^2 will represent a sample variance. (To look ahead, when we get to correlations, r and ρ will denote sample and population correlations, respectively.) Also, in a few chapters, I will use the symbol $\approx$ to mean "is approximately equal to." The letter n will always denote the sample size.

One more piece of notation should be included at this point: use of Σ. We will make liberal use of the summation sign throughout the book. I will almost always ignore the subscripts on Σ and assume they will be clear from the context. For example, the sample mean will be written $\overline{X} = (\Sigma X)/n$ rather than $\overline{X} = (\Sigma_{i=1}^{n} X_i)/n$. The removal of subscripts also makes equations less intimidating and will help when we look at the overall form of each equation from an intuitive perspective.

Standardization

Many social scientists like to standardize data. That is, rather than deal with a variable like X, with sample mean $\bar{X}$ and standard deviation s_x, they prefer to transform each data point so that the resulting data has mean 0 and standard deviation 1. This is easily accomplished by taking each score (X), subtracting the mean $(\bar{X})$ from it, and dividing the result by s_X. More formally,

I.A
$$z = \frac{X - \bar{X}}{s_X}$$

Note that Equation I.A follows tradition by labeling the result z. Thus, standardized scores are often called "z-scores."[2]

Now, why do researchers sometimes standardize their data? Because many scales in the social sciences use arbitrary numerical values. For example, one job satisfaction scale might take on the values -2, -1, 0, 1, 2, whereas another researcher might describe a 7-point scale and score it 1, 2, 3,..., 7. In this example, a score of 2 has a very different meaning depending on which scale you use. So, in order to compare results across studies, scales are standardized to the common reference point of a mean of 0 and standard deviation of 1.0.

When we discuss standardization later in this book, it will be noted that z-scores are really linear transformations of X-scores. That is, Equation I.A can be written as $z = a + bX$, where $b = 1/s_X$ and $a = -\bar{X}/s_X$. As we shall see in Chapter II, one of the beauties of the Pearson correlation coefficient is that the correlation between two variables (say, X and Y) is invariant to linear changes in either X or Y. Thus, it doesn't matter whether you standardize the data or not: the correlation remains the same (and therefore, magnitudes of correlations can be compared across studies). On the other hand,[3] the magnitudes of regression weights *will* be affected by whether or not the data are standardized. So, when possible, formulas for regression weights will be discussed in terms of correlations, means, and standard deviations. Thus, you will see which part of the weight is unaffected by standardization (e.g., portions using correlations) and which part of the weight is affected (e.g., portions involving standard deviations).

Hypothesis Testing

The traditional role and structure of hypothesis testing in management and psychology is very complex. Let me just remind you of a few things in simplified ways.

[2] The equation for z really works! That is, z-scores will have a mean of 0 and a standard deviation of 1 no matter what the original X scores were. If you don't believe it, take any set of numbers (e.g., 1, 4, 5, 12) and try it!

[3] The phrase "on the other hand" will be used many times in this book!

We will usually have a null and an alternative hypothesis. For example, take a peek ahead to the middle column of Table II.1 in Chapter II. That table displays scores for 13 individuals on a selection test (X). These scores range from 5.9 to 182, and they have a mean of $\overline{X} = 54.65$ and a standard deviation of $s_X = 48.82$. Suppose that in years past the average selection test performance was historically about 65.00. Suppose further that the organization is concerned that the quality of the applicant population might be changing. In this case, we let the null hypothesis be $H_0: \mu = 65$, and the alternative hypothesis is $H_a: \mu \neq 65$.[4] (*Note:* Remember that in traditional hypothesis testing, one usually constructs a procedure geared to rejecting H_0.)

Now, do you remember how hypothesis testing proceeded? Good! In this case, the statistic of focus is the sample mean ($\overline{X} = 54.65$). The underlying question is, Does the sample statistic of 54.65 provide sufficient evidence to reject the population null value of 65.00? To answer this question, statisticians have derived a *"sampling distribution" for $\overline{X}$; i.e., a theoretical distribution depicting all the values of $\overline{X}$ you would obtain if H_0 were true and if you generated new samples over and over and computed $\overline{X}$ for each of them.*

The sampling distribution for $\overline{X}$ is a beautifully shaped distribution centered at the null value of 65.00. That is, if H_0 were indeed true, then you'd expect sample values of $\overline{X}$ to center around 65. Because of chance occurrences due to the nature of random sampling, some values of $\overline{X}$ might be higher and some might be lower, but the mean of all these sample means would still be 65. Further, the standard deviation of this distribution of $\overline{X}$'s is estimated to be $s_X / \sqrt{n} = 48.82 / \sqrt{13} = 13.54$. For reasons discussed below, I label this standard deviation the "appropriate standard deviation" (ASD). Pictorially, we have Figure 1.1.

In this case of sample means, the name for this type of distribution is a "*t*-distribution."[5] At this point, we have to decide if our sample value of

---

[4] Suppose the organization is concerned only with the possibility that applicant quality is *declining*. Then, I tweak your memory cells by reminding you that the alternative hypothesis would be the implicitly one-sided $H_a: \mu < 65$.

[5] Note that I am using $s_X / \sqrt{n}$ to compute the standard deviation of the sampling distribution of the statistic $\overline{X}$. If the population standard deviation σ_X were known, then the standard deviation of the $\overline{X}$'s would be $\sigma_X / \sqrt{n}$ and the sampling distribution would be a "normal distribution."

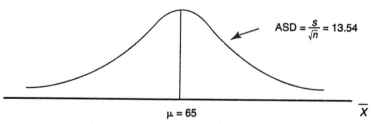

FIGURE 1.1 Shape of the sampling distribution for $\overline{X}$ when the sample size is 13 and the population mean is 65.

$\overline{X} = 54.65$ is unusual—i.e., is it so far from the assumed center value of 65 that we question the truth of our assumed mean (and therefore reject H_0); or is 54.65 in the range of what we'd expect to find from sample to sample even if H_0: $\mu = 65$ were true?

Values along the X-axis of this distribution are listed in the traditional t-tables of critical values found in your old statistics book (and in the Appendix, Table A.1, of this book). However, these t-values are *not* expressed in terms of the original units of the problem (e.g., in this case, they are not expressed in terms of absolute scores on the selection test.) Rather, the values in the table are always related to the question, *How many standard deviations is your sample statistic from the hypothesized center?* So, to conduct the test of H_0: $\mu = 65$, we note that the sample mean of 54.65 is $(54.65 - 65) = -10.35$ *units* from the hypothesized center. Since the appropriate standard deviation in the figure is equal to 13.54, the sample mean is $-10.35/13.54 = -.764$ *standard deviations* from the hypothesized mean. Is this unusual? Well, our field has adopted a definition of "unusualness" that means "occurring, by random change, less than 5% of the time." (*Note*: This is the "alpha level," or "probability level," of the test. It's usual to see probability levels of $p = .05$. Other probability levels used in the social sciences include $p = .10, .01,$ and $.001.)$

So, the t-tables in the Appendix tell you how many standard deviations you need to go from the mean in order for your particular sample statistic to be unusual (e.g., to have occurred with less than 5% probability). Also, don't forget that t-tables require something called "degrees of freedom" (df), which in this case is $n - 1 = 13 - 1 = 12$. Thus, for the two-sided test at $p = .05$ (i.e., putting $2\frac{1}{2}\%$ unusualness at each end of the distribution), we needed to go 2.179 appropriate standard deviations in either direction from the mean of 65 (check out the row for df = 12 in Table A.1 and see if you agree!). The value of 2.179 is labeled the "critical value" of the test. Now, we went only .764 appropriate standard deviations to the left of the mean. So, our sample value of $\overline{X} = 54.65$ isn't unusual enough, and we fail to reject H_0: $\mu = 65$.

Phew! I hope that was clear. Don't forget that this procedure took several weeks to teach you in your introductory statistics class. *There are some straightforward points to remember from the above example*:

First, we will be using probability levels in this book (usually $p = .05$ or $.01$). Second, the values listed in the Appendix will give us the critical values for our hypothesis tests.[6] Third, the general form of the test statistic will almost always (but not always) be

I.B
$$\frac{\text{Statistic} - \text{null hypothesis value}}{\text{ASD}}$$

---

[6] While the Appendix contains critical values for t- and F-distributions, we will also have occasion to need critical values for normal distributions. Note that the normal critical values are obtained by using the t critical values when the degrees of freedom is infinity.

For example, in our exemplary test above, the statistic was 54.65 and the null value was 65.00. When conducting a test on a single mean, the ASD is $s/\sqrt{n}$. Thus, we computed

$$\frac{\bar{X} - \mu}{s/\sqrt{n}} = \frac{54.65 - 65.00}{48.82/\sqrt{13}} = -.764$$

and found out that our sample mean was only .764 ASDs from the hypothesized mean.

The general form of Equation I.B is very useful to remember. For example, if you're testing whether two means (μ_1 and μ_2) are equal, the statistic of choice becomes $\bar{X}_1 - \bar{X}_2$, the null value is 0, and I simply need to tell you what the ASD is for the statistic $\bar{X}_1 - \bar{X}_2$.[7] Oh! I also need to tell you what the shape of the sampling distribution is. In this case, it's still a t-distribution (but the degrees of freedom is now $n_1 + n_2 - 2$). Thus, I might write

$$\frac{\left(\bar{X}_1 - \bar{X}_2\right) - 0}{\text{ASD}} \sim t_{n_1 + n_2 - 2}$$

I want to introduce a piece of notation here. The $\sim$ can be read as "is distributed as." Thus, the above formula states that the ratio on the left is distributed as a t-ratio with ($n_1 + n_2 - 2$) degrees of freedom.

Later in the book (e.g., Chapter VI), you'll see that Equation I.B is even used to test regression weights. In this case, the statistic is the sample regression weight and the null value is usually 0 (i.e., you want to reject H_0 and demonstrate that the weight is nonzero). The formula for the ASD for a regression weight is a bit messy, but not difficult to use or interpret. And the entire ratio for testing a regression weight also has an underlying t-distribution.

I couldn't resist the opportunity to remind you of two more aspects of statistical thinking before we tackle correlation and regression. These issues surround the notion of power and confidence intervals.

Power   As noted earlier, H_0 is usually constructed so that one tries to reject it in favor of H_a. Statistical "power" is the probability that H_0 will be rejected when H_0 is indeed false. We shall see that many things affect the power of the test. The t-test example conducted above should convince you of at least one determinant of power: the same size (n). That is, the ASD was $s_X/\sqrt{n}$. Because the ASD is in the denominator of Equation I.B, the factor $\sqrt{n}$ is in the denominator of the denominator! Thus, as n goes up, the entire ratio in Equation I.B becomes greater (by a factor of $\sqrt{n}$). Thus, all other things equal, the sample

---

[7] In case you have forgotten, when the two means come from independent samples, it's $\sqrt{s_1^2/n_1 + s_2^2/n_2}$, where s_i^2 are the variances and n_i are the sample sizes for the two groups of data.

t-statistic will have a greater chance of being larger than the critical t-value as the sample size is increased.[8]

Confidence intervals   To understand the notion of confidence intervals, note that the sample mean of $\bar{X} = 54.65$ is our best single guess about the true mean of selection scores. The sample mean is labeled a "point estimate." However, statisticians don't want to get stuck with such a specific value. After all, suppose the true mean is really 54.66. Then, in some sense, our best guess (of 54.65) will be wrong. So, rather than provide a single number as an estimate, the idea is to report a *range* of scores and hope that the true mean falls within that range. The range is called a "confidence interval" and is usually calculated to guarantee that it overlaps the true population value 95% (or 99%) of the time. To do this operationally, you simply work the hypothesis-testing values in reverse. That is, start with the best single guess ($\bar{X} = 54.65$) and add and subtract a particular amount to and from this value. The amount you add and subtract is $t \times \text{ASD}$, where the value of t is the critical value based on $p = .05$ if you want a 95% confidence interval (or $p = .01$ if you desire a 99% confidence interval). So, in the example above, the 95% confidence interval is

$54.65 \pm t \times \text{ASD}$ or
$54.65 \pm 2.179 \times 13.54$ or
54.65 ± 29.50

Thus, the confidence interval for the mean population selection score ranges from 25.15 to 84.15. Technically speaking, intervals constructed in this way (using samples of size 13) will include the true population mean 95% of the time. We will return to these issues in Chapter VI. Since regression equations are often used to predict events, it is quite commonplace to use confidence intervals and report a range in which you predict behavior to occur.

Well, that's the very brief reminder about your previous statistics course. If this review doesn't make sense, buy your introductory book back and review it! All I intended to do at this point was to get your statistical juices flowing again and introduce you to the notation used in this book. Now, it's time for correlation and regression!

---

[8] For example, suppose we added another 100 subjects to the study (i.e., n is now $100 + 13 = 113$). Then, the ASD is $48.82 / \sqrt{133} = 4.59$, and the value of 54.65 is $(54.65 - 65.00)/4.59 = -2.25$ standard deviations from the hypothesized mean. At $p = .05$, this is a significant result and H_0 is rejected!

A REVIEW OF THE CORRELATION COEFFICIENT AND ITS PROPERTIES

After reading this chapter, you should be able to:

- Explain what a correlation coefficient measures.
- Recognize a scatterplot and understand the direction or sign of the relationship.
- Understand the formula for the Pearson correlation, including where the important information is and the purpose of the denominator.
- Provide at least two situations where r is not appropriate for describing a relationship.
- Given any particular value of r and the raw data, multiply one or both scales by 38.2 and still know the value of the correlation.
- Give examples of how outliers can increase or decrease a correlation.
- Critique the following statement: "The correlation of .82 demonstrates that good supervisors cause increased worker productivity."
- Explain why range restriction generally reduces the magnitude of r.
- Discuss how different levels of analysis can affect r.
- Recognize factors that are important in interpreting the magnitude of r.
- Explain what r^2 measures.
- Define and distinguish among the various correlation coefficients discussed in this chapter.
- Suggest situations appropriate for the use of each type of correlation discussed in this chapter.

This chapter reviews the concept of a Pearson product moment correlation coefficient. While we will also consider other indices of relationship between two variables, the Pearson coefficient is ubiquitous in its use. It is so frequently used that in the social sciences it's often called "*the* correlation coefficient." In fact, many individuals (myself included) hold the belief that researchers in human resources management and industrial and organizational psychology cannot write an entire paragraph without using the Pearson correlation coefficient at least once! (The correlation coefficient is better than cash. Don't leave your office without it.)

The investigation of whether or not two variables are related (and the degree of any existing relationship) is a crucial component of the way social scientists think about theory development and its application. To understand this, consider the following sample of questions taken from a cursory survey of recently published journal articles:

1 In an interview setting, will interviewers with favorable preinterview evaluations of an applicant's qualifications tend to spend less time interviewing, and more time recruiting, the applicant during the interview?

2 Will individuals who have high positive mood at work (indexed by positive affectivity) be less likely to be absent than individuals with low positive mood at work?

3 In the banking industry, will there be a positive relationship between the racial diversity (across employees) of each firm and firm level performance?

4 Will self-ratings of performance correlate higher with supervisory ratings of performance when self-raters are provided with large amounts of comparative information than when they have less information?

5 Will corporate strategies marked by attempts at innovation be more likely to exist in uncertain environments as compared to more certain environments?

6 In a sample of Russian executives, will higher levels of perceived strategic uncertainty be associated with higher levels of environmental scanning frequency?

7 Will managerial style (in this case, a willingness to support the subordinate's self-determination) correlate with the subordinate's perceived trust in the organization?

8 Will greater perceptions of role conflict and role ambiguity be related to increased perceptions of job insecurity?

9 Will noncognitive tests (e.g., self-report personality scales) administered using a computer platform result in the same rank ordering of applicants as when the same tests are administered via paper and pencil?

In sum, questions about the existence of hypothesized relationships pervade management and applied psychological research. The above review provides examples of correlational hypotheses in strategic management, organizational behavior, and personnel psychology.[1] Pick up any book or journal in one of these

---

[1] If you're interested, the empirical answers to these questions are (1) yes for time spent recruiting and no for time spent questioning, (2) yes, (3) yes, but only for firms with a growth strategy, (4) yes, (5) yes, (6) yes, but only when information is perceived to be accessible, (7) sometimes, (8) yes, (9) yes. If you're *really* interested, you can read the research in, respectively, Phillips and Dipboye (1989), Pelled and Xin (1999), Richard (2000), Farh and Dobbins (1989), Miller (1988), May, Stewart, and Sweo (2000), Deci, Connell, and Ryan (1989), Ashford, Lee, and Bobko (1989), and Potosky and Bobko (1997).

areas and you will see more (e.g., Is there a relationship between selection tests and subsequent job performance? Between a person's gender and his or her salary? Between scores on an intelligence test given at 5-year intervals? Between satisfaction and turnover?).

GOOD OLD *r*

O.K. The above was intended to convince you that an index of relationship is very important to practitioners and applied social scientists. We're now moving on to a quick review of the computation of a correlation coefficient.

As you may know from an introductory statistics course, the correlation coefficient was conceived by two British researchers (Karl Pearson and Sir Francis Galton) who, given their research in genetics, were interested in relating all sorts of body measurements to each other [e.g., head length, height of knee, length of middle finger (seriously!); Galton, 1888; or see Hull, 1928, for a more complete discussion of the origin of the correlation coefficient].

Essentially, their thinking went as follows: when two variables are analyzed simultaneously, the data can be considered in the paired form (X, Y). In turn, each data pair can be plotted in two-dimensional space. The resulting picture of the relationship across all data points in the sample is called a "scatterplot."

As a further reminder, don't forget that scatterplots are easy to construct. For example, look ahead to Table II.1. Here we have 13 pairs of (X, Y) data, where X is a selection test and Y is a measure of subsequent job performance. To construct a scatterplot, draw an X-axis (usually horizontal) and a Y-axis (usually vertical). For each data pair, go along the X-axis as far as the X-score indicates and then go up as far as the Y-score indicates. Place a dot (or some other mark) at that point on the graph; this dot then represents that particular person's paired data. The collection of dots for all data points is the scatterplot. Figure 2.1 presents the scatterplot for the data in Table II.1.

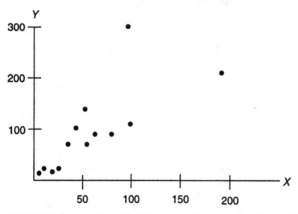

FIGURE 2.1   A scatterplot of the air traffic controller data in Table II.1.

Now, we can return to our attempt to numerically index the correlation. Note that Figure 2.1 shows a positive relationship between X and Y, such that individuals scoring higher on the selection test tend to perform better on the job. However, not all correlations in the social sciences are positive. For example, there may be no relationship between two variables, or there may even be a negative relationship between two variables (e.g., commitment to your company and number of days a year spent looking for jobs with other companies). In order to capture this extended range of possibilities, I'm sure Frank and Karl had the five scatterplots in Figure 2.2 in mind (or at least I do).

The idea is to construct a summary statistic from the (X, Y) data that satisfies several criteria. First, the index should range between -1 and $+1$. Second, if all the points lie on a straight line with positive (or negative) slope, then the statistic should be positive (or negative) 1.0—see Figures 2.2*a* and 2.2*e*. Third, if there is no relationship between X and Y (e.g., Figure 2.2*c*), then the statistic should be 0. Any other scatterplot should generate a statistic that is between 0 and 1.0 in magnitude and has the same sign as the implied slope in the scatterplot (e.g., see Figures 2.2*b* and 2.2*d*).

Now there are many formulas that will satisfy the above criteria. The accepted symbol for a sample value of the correlation is r, and the statistic that has been adopted can be written as

II.A
$$r_{XY} = \frac{\Sigma(X - \bar{X})(Y - \bar{Y})}{\sqrt{\Sigma(X - \bar{X})^2 \Sigma(Y - \bar{Y})^2}}$$

where the summations are taken over all pairs of data. Equivalently, it can be shown (by a little algebraic rearranging) that r can be expressed as

$$r_{XY} = \frac{\Sigma XY - (\Sigma X)(\Sigma Y)/n}{\sqrt{\left[\Sigma X^2 - (\Sigma X)^2/n\right]\left[\Sigma Y^2 - (\Sigma Y)^2/n\right]}}$$

where n is the sample size (i.e., the number of *pairs* of observations).

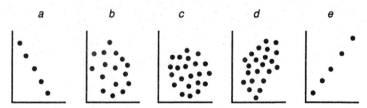

FIGURE 2.2 Five heuristic scatterplots.

The two formulas for r_{XY} are mathematically equivalent. The second is often called the "computational formula" and tends to be easier to use if you have to compute the value of r by hand. The first formula is often labeled the "conceptual formula." Indeed, let's just reflect on Equation II.A for a while:

1 *The symbol r_{XY} denotes the correlation coefficient between the variable X and the variable Y.* Throughout this text, I will drop the subscripts (unless needed for clarity) and refer to the correlation simply as r (or good old r).

2 *The symbol r was chosen for one of two reasons.* Either the word "correlation" begins with a silent r or, more seriously, r stands for "relationship." (Or perhaps Karl wanted a P and Sir Francis wanted a G, so they chose a neutral letter.)

3 *The formula really works!* For example, if the points all fall on a straight line with positive slope, the value of r is exactly $+1.0$. Try it! Take the following three data pairs for the (X, Y) pairs: (0, 2.5), (1, 6.0), (2, 9.5). A scatterplot will reveal that these data fall on a straight line. Both the numerator and denominator of Equation II.A have the value of 7.0. Thus, $r = 1.0$.

4 *There are two multiplicative factors in the denominator of Equation II.A.* If you divide each by the factor $n - 1$, you will obtain the standard deviations for X and Y (s_X and s_Y). That is,

$$s_X = \sqrt{\frac{\Sigma(X - \bar{X})^2}{n - 1}} \quad \text{and} \quad s_Y = \sqrt{\frac{\Sigma(Y - \bar{Y})^2}{n - 1}}$$

Essentially, having these standard deviations downstairs in the formula guarantees two things: (a) r is a unitless quantity (see Property 2 below), and (b) the absolute value of r never goes above 1.0.[2]

5 *Our good old r is formally referred to as the "Pearson product moment correlation."* So much for Galton. Also, the word "product" refers to the fact that most of the informational value in Equation II.A is contained in the summation of the cross-product $\Sigma(X - \bar{X})(Y - \bar{Y})$. Finally, the word "moment" does not refer to the time it takes to compute r. Rather, it is a word used in mathematics to describe types of averages (and r is sort of the average value of the cross-product: i.e., $\Sigma(X - \bar{X})(Y - \bar{Y})/n$).

6 Note that the formula for r is symmetric with respect to what you call X and what you call Y. That is, it doesn't matter which of the two variables you label X (or Y). The implication is that $r_{XY} = r_{YX}$. So, if I reverse the subscripts throughout this chapter, don't worry; it doesn't matter (if it does later in this book, I'll let you know).

All of the researchers described in the opening paragraphs of this chapter computed values of r between their variables of interest. Some individuals hypothesized (or wanted to find!) large values of r (e.g., in the prediction of job

[2] If you divide the *numerator* of Equation II.A by $n - 1$, you will obtain the "covariance" between X and Y. The covariance is also a measure of the relationship between X and Y. However, the covariance doesn't range from -1 to $+1$ and is dependent on the choice of scale (see Property 2 later in this chapter). That's why most social science researchers prefer the correlation coefficient.

performance; in the prediction of corporate strategy). Other individuals hypothe-sized values of *r* to be 0 (e.g., between gender and performance ratings). Regardless, they all computed *r*, reported its magnitude, discussed its magnitude (see Property 7 below), and often "tested *r* for significance" (see Chapter III).

king a Break: A Numerical Example

This example is provided for those of you who like to try out each equation and feel that the contrived ($n = 3$) data point example in the previous section isn't enough. Table II.1 provides data for the following hypothetical context.

Suppose the Federal Aviation Association wishes to hire more air traffic controllers. The job of these controllers is to keep planes apart by a certain distance (e.g., 3 miles). They do this by watching radar screens and talking to pilots. Suppose further (and it is indeed true) that the training of air traffic controllers is a very long and expensive process. We want to develop a test that will predict performance so that we won't have too many washouts during training. In turn, overall training costs could be reduced. Let the selection test (X) be a simple computerized simulation where the applicant, after a day or so of familiarization, is asked to manuever objects ("planes") around a video screen (e.g., direct the objects and "land" them by placing them in certain positions or "airports" on the screen). The test score (X) indicates how many objects the person can handle until any two planes get too close together (which is called a "separation conflict"). For example, the first applicant in Table II.1 managed to manuever 35 objects until a separation conflict occurred.

O.K. That's the test (X) we use. For Y, suppose we wait for the 2-year training program to be completed and measure how well the person actually did. That is, at the end of training, we give each person another simulation. Presum-ably, each person is now more capable because of the training. However, the

TABLE II.1   SIMULATOR TEST DATA AND PERFORMANCE DATA FOR 13 HYPOTHETICAL APPLICANTS FOR AIR TRAFFIC CONTROL JOBS

Applicant	Test, X	Performance, Y
1	35.0	105.0
2	45.0	75.0
3	69.0	85.0
4	182.0	208.0
5	48.7	146.1
6	100.0	100.0
7	25.0	75.0
8	98.0	300.0
9	52.0	88.0
10	8.0	16.0
11	22.8	19.2
12	5.9	13.9
13	19.0	17.0

simulation we give is a more realistic one: each airplane now has its own flight characteristics, there are restricted airspaces, airports are not all at the same altitude, winds exist and may shift direction, etc. The performance score (Y) is once again the number of planes a trained person can manuever until a separation conflict occurs. For example, after training, the first applicant could manuever and land 105 planes before a separation conflict occurred.

We now want to compute the Pearson product moment correlation (this sounds more scientific, but I really mean good old r) between the last two columns of data in Table II.1. This will give us a statistical index that numerically describes the relationship in the scatterplot we have already seen in Figure 2.1. If the correlation has a large, positive value, then we will have some evidence that we should select people (for the training program) who score high on the initial test (X).

Using Table II.1, my calculations are

$$\Sigma X = 710.4 \quad \Sigma X^2 = 67,419.34$$
$$\Sigma Y = 1248.2 \quad \Sigma Y^2 = 202,960.06$$
$$\Sigma XY = 104,707.85$$

and, skipping a few steps, I get

$$r_{XY} = \frac{36,498.5}{(169.1)(288.3)} = .75$$

Do you agree?

As we will see, there are many facets yet to be considered in interpreting the value of $r = .75$ (and we'll return to this particular example in Chapters IV and IX), but on the surface this seems to be a very large, positive value. As such, the test (X) might be considered to be an excellent initial screening device for letting people into a lengthy and expensive training program. In turn, the number of individuals who fail to pass training could be reduced.

PROPERTIES OF (AND COMMENTS ON) THE CORRELATION COEFFICIENT

1. Linearity and r

It is often stated that *r measures how close the points in a scatterplot are to a straight line*. This is what I call an almost true fact (ATF). For example, a glance at the five scatterplots in Figure 2.2 indicates that as the scatterplot looks more like a straight line (i.e., the football-shaped plot becomes narrower), the magnitude of r increases.[3]

[3] Rather than use a football metaphor, Craig Russell (personal communication) teaches scatterplots as "hot dogs on sticks." Correlations near 1.0 look like skinny, regular franks, while correlations approach 0 as the hot dogs become fatter (like those I'm used to getting at the ball park) or even evolve into meatballs. Indeed, the orientation of the stick is somewhat like the regression lines we will consider beginning in Chapter VI.

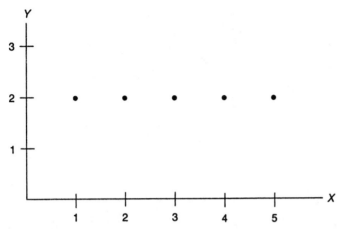

FIGURE 2.3 A scatterplot showing that Pearson's r doesn't always measure how close points are to a straight line.

However, this fact is *not* true if all the points fall on a straight line that is either perfectly horizontal or perfectly vertical. For example, suppose the (X, Y) data are (1,2), (2,2), (3,2), (4,2), and (5,2) as in Figure 2.3. Note that the line that goes through the points is indeed straight. However, since all values of Y_i are identical, the values of $Y_i - \overline{Y}$ will be 0 for all data points. In turn, both the numerator and denominator of Equation II.A will be 0! In this case (and in the vertical line case also), the correlation is undefined. (In these situations, computer packages often indicate that r cannot be computed.) In general, however, the opening statement in this paragraph is accurate, and we shall provide further support for it when we consider the interpretation of r (and r^2) in Property 7 below.

2. Scale Transformations and *r*

Another fact is that r *is unaffected by* (*or invariant to*) *linear transformations of the data*. This is a true fact! By "linear transformations," we mean any transformation (on Y and/or X) of the form $a + bX$ and/or $c + dY$, as long as b and d are not 0 (otherwise, all the transformed scores would be a constant and that's a "no-no"—see Property 1).

Why is this fact important? Suppose you were correlating job performance (Y) with job satisfaction (X) and you measured satisfaction using the "smiley-face" scale in Figure 2.4 a.[4] Note that not happy is scored 1 and very happy is scored 5.

---

[4] A version of this scale is actually used in the measurement of job satisfaction. The "faces scale" was developed by Kunin (1955). A female version of the scale has been studied by Dunham and Herman (1975).

Not happy   Very happy

X: 1   2   3   4   5

FIGURE 2.4a   A scale of job satisfaction scored from 1 to 5.

Not happy   Very happy

X*:   -2   -1   0   +1   +2

FIGURE 2.4b   A scale of job satisfaction scored from -2 to +2.

I know some researchers who would use this same visual scale but would choose to score it as in Figure 2.4b (we'll call the new scale X^*). The beauty of the Pearson correlation is that both researchers would get the same value for r (between satisfaction and performance), even though they used different scoring schemes (because one scheme is a linear transform of the other; i.e., $X^* = -3.0 + 1.0X$). So, correlational results will not be affected by any such arbitrariness in how numbers are assigned to points on a scale. This is nice.

Also, as reviewed in Chapter I, I'm sure you are aware by now that many social science researchers prefer to standardize their data. The logic is that because most scales in behavioral research are arbitrary, researchers adopt a common point of reference (i.e., z-scores, with a mean of 0 and a variance of 1) so that they can compare their results with each other.

Well, transformation to z-scores can be written as

$$z_X = \frac{X - \bar{X}}{s_X} = \frac{-\bar{X}}{s_X} + \frac{1}{s_X}X$$

That is, standard scores (z-scores) are linear transformations of the data $a + bX$, where $a = -\bar{X}/s_X$ and $b = 1/s_X$. So, the correlation coefficient between performance and satisfaction, or any other two variables, is the same whether or not one standardizes the data.

By the way, while the above fact is true, it is not amazing. That is, the formula for r (see Equation II.A) was *constructed* to be invariant to linear scale changes. For example, it doesn't matter what the means on X and Y are in the data—the formula indicates that they're always subtracted from the original X (and Y) scores. Further, remember that the denominator of Equation II.A is essentially the product of the standard deviations for X and Y (s_X and s_Y). Thus, no matter what the value of the standard deviations, they are always "divided out" of the result. Pretty tricky, eh?

A related fact is that *r is a unitless quantity*. Note that the numerator of Equation II.A carries the units of X times the units of Y (our old friend the cross-product). However, downstairs in this formula is the product of the two standard deviations that carry their respective units with them. Thus, the products of the units cancel each other out and r is left unitless. This is another way of saying that correlation coefficients can be compared across studies even though the scaling of social science variables may differ from study to study.

3. Extreme Values on *X* or *Y* (Outliers)

Another property of correlations states that *the magnitude of r can be greatly affected by outlying values*. Put another way, we can say that r is not robust to outliers.

If you remember your statistics course (I have heard it called "sadistics"!), this property was also true for means and standard deviations: for example, the mean of the scores {1,2,3,4,5} is 3 (right in the middle), but changing the largest score of 5 to an extremely large value of 50 increases the mean drastically (to 12), such that almost all the data are below the mean.

Now, similar effects occur for the correlation. For example, consider the fictitious scatterplot in Figure 2.5. Let's assume that these data represent 20 midlevel managers who have been selected for promotion based on their assessment center scores (X). Assume Y is a measure of subsequent performance on the job (the raw data for this example are given in Table II.2). The correlation in this data is $r = .14$ and is not particularly large (and the scatterplot makes it look even smaller).

FIGURE 2.5 Hypothetical assessment center data without outlier.

TABLE II.2 FICTITIOUS DATA FOR 21 MIDLEVEL MANAGERS

Manager	Assessment center score, X	Performance rating, Y	
1	1	9	For $n = 20$:
2	1	6	$\Sigma X = 102 \quad \Sigma Y = 98$
3	1	3	$\Sigma X^2 = 706 \quad \Sigma Y^2 = 633$
4	1	1	$\Sigma XY = 524$
5	3	9	$r_{XY} = .14$
6	2	4	
7	2	1	For $n = 21$:
8	4	2	$\Sigma X = 117 \quad \Sigma Y = 113$
9	4	6	$\Sigma X^2 = 931 \quad \Sigma Y^2 = 858$
10	5	8	$\Sigma XY = 749$
11	5	1	$r_{XY} = .45$
12	7	9	
13	7	6	
14	7	4	
15	7	2	
16	8	8	
17	10	9	
18	9	7	
19	9	2	
20	9	1	
21	15	15	

FIGURE 2.6 Hypothetical assessment center data with outlier added.

Now, suppose that there were really 21 individuals in this data base and that the twenty-first person scored extremely high in the assessment center and became a great performer as well (see the last row of Table II.2). The scatterplot would then look like Figure 2.6, and the correlation would jump from $r = .14$ to $r = .45$, a marked increase based on just one extra person! (Of course, outliers can also *reduce* the value of r, depending upon where they appear in the scatterplot. For example, suppose the outlier had been placed so that the Y score was 0 and the X score was very large. Then r would be reduced.)

The above discussion demonstrates how powerful outlying values can be.[5] The question of what to do with them remains unanswered. There are statistical techniques for identifying outliers (e.g., Neter, Wasserman, and Kutner, 1986; Orr, Sackett, and DuBois, 1991), but it is not known which of these techniques is best. Further, are outliers real and to be left in, or error and to be discarded? In the above example, is .14 or .45 a better indication of the predictive capability of the assessment center? (There is no right or wrong answer. The resolution should be informed by good thinking, but the answer is necessarily subjective. In my mind, it's nice to know that life is not predetermined and that statistics can't answer everything!)

By the way, a sensible (and often heard) suggestion is to conduct your analyses both with and without outliers in the data set (cf. Kruskal, 1960, for an early reference). If you don't get the same results, you need to think hard; if you do get the same results, then you can rest easy! For example, look back to the data in Table II.1. It appears that two of the applicants (4 and 8) were substantially better during posttraining performance than the other applicants. It may be that these two data points (as outliers) are responsible for the obtained value of $r_{XY} = .75$. Recomputing r with these two applicants removed still results in a large value of $r = .68$. Now, I don't know if one can rest easy in this case, but we are certainly more confident that our results aren't exclusively due to the outliers.

4. Causation

"Correlation does not imply causation" is a cry heard from every instructor of introductory statistics, so I won't belabor it here. Certainly, a nonzero correlation between daily ice cream consumption and daily water consumption in New York City doesn't imply that one causes the other (how about temperature as a third explanatory variable?). The same is true for any nonzero correlations between satisfaction and performance, between dollars spent on advertising and profit, or many other pairs of organizationally relevant variables.

[5] Early in my career, I was on a research team that analyzed a data base with a sample size of over 500. We computed statistics, interpreted the data, and wrote a beautiful report. Afterward, we discovered one particularly large score (we labeled the person "big z" since we had standardized the data and this z-score was a whopping 7.0!) and subsequently found out that the outlier was due to a miscoding of data in the wrong column of our computer card input (ah, the old days!). Upon reanalysis, most of our interpretations changed (although they were still beautiful!). We should have noticed such an outlier earlier in the process but didn't. Hopefully, you'll know better.

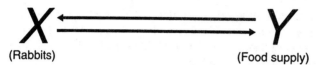

FIGURE 2.7   A dynamic model depicting rabbit population size and food supply.

$$X \longrightarrow Y \quad \text{or} \quad X \sim Y$$

(*X* causes *Y*)   (*X* related to *Y* for some
                                   unanalyzed reason)

FIGURE 2.8   Casual and correlational models for which Pearson *r* is suited.

Here's yet another twist to the correlation or causation notion.[6] Let $X =$ number of rabbits living in a field. Let $Y =$ available amount of grass (for food) in that field. First, as the rabbits multiply, the amount of grass will go down. Fine. Second, as the grass grows, it can support more rabbits and the number of rabbits will increase. Now, the first conclusion said that as X goes up, Y goes down. The second conclusion said that as Y goes up, X goes up also! How can this be (a seeming paradox!)? The answer is in the dynamic nature of the example, where values on one variable affect the other *across time*. Figure 2.7 is a pictorial representation of this example and shows that X affects Y, which in turn updates X, etc. The point here is that a single correlation (r) does not necessarily capture casual, dynamic feedback processes that are time-dependent. The estimator r is more suited to models like those in Figure 2.8.

It is important to realize this *limitation as to when r is an appropriate statistic.*[7] And this is important. For example, consider interactive feedback models between clients and therapists, children and parents, students and teachers, and subordinates and supervisors. Further, models of work motivation (e.g., expectancy theory, goal setting) also incorporate performance feedback loops.

5. Range Restriction and *r*

A property of Pearson product moment correlations is that *correlations are affected (usually reduced) by range restriction*. For example, in selection research, one often computes the correlation between selection test scores (X) and subsequent job performance (Y). If the test is currently in use by the organization, then performance data are available only for individuals who have been selected. Thus, these individuals have test scores that span only the upper end of

[6] I thank Kent Norman for this one.
[7] Some partial statistical solutions to these "bidirectional causal models" can be found in multivariate texts under headings such as "two-stage least squares regression" and "linear structural relations analysis (LISREL)."

the X-score distribution. The variance on X is therefore reduced (i.e., range-restricted). In turn, this tends to reduce the obtained correlation between X and any other variable. Range restriction is so important in practice that an entire chapter in this book is devoted to it (see Chapter V).

. Levels of Analysis and *r*

Remember that correlations between variables (r_{XY}) are computed across n data points (see Equation II.A). The moral of this section is that *the levels of analysis across which correlations are computed can make a very big difference in the resulting value of r*. An example can make this clear.

An example you can take to the bank   Several years back, I consulted with a group of researchers who were investigating the quality of service provided at branches of full-service banks. Specifically, we had two variables of interest: X, the *employee's* perception of the overall quality of service provided, and Y, the *customer's* perception of the overall quality of service. There were 23 branches of a large metropolitan bank in the study. We computed r_{XY} for all employees (and their paired customers) for branch 1 and obtained a value of about $r = 0$. For branch 2 we obtained $r = 0$ as well. For branch 3, we got a slightly negative value; branch 4 revealed a slightly positive r; etc. Essentially, there was no correlation, across subjects, between X and Y for *any* branch. In turn, the average of the 23 correlations[8] was also about 0.

Now, in addition to averaging our 23 results, one of us decided to first combine all the data and compute "one big r" across all subjects in all branches. This correlation was over .60!

So, are employee perceptions of service related to customer perceptions of service or not? The disparity in the above results is related to the units of analysis invoked. For example, at the individual level of analysis within one branch, a typical scatterplot is presented in Figure 2.9. However, the overall analysis included data from 23 branches (i.e., branches became the operational unit). The underlying scatterplot then looked like Figure 2.10 (only 6 branches are portrayed for ease of exposition).

Of course, when the computer looks at these data and computes r, it's essentially seeing 6 big points (Figure 2.11) and not 6 circular scatterplots. Because these "points" have an upward linear trend, the resulting value of r becomes positive and large. In fact, when these data were published in a research journal, the mean values on X and Y were computed for each branch. The 23 pairs of means were used to construct the scatterplot and to compute the correlation across branches. The resulting value of r was .67 (see Schneider, Parkington, and Buxton, 1980, for further details). The explanation for this result was a branch-level explanation. That is, some branches were in decaying urban areas, were overcrowded, and were understaffed. At these branches, both cus-

---

[8] Actually, averaging correlations is tricky and is discussed in Chapter III.

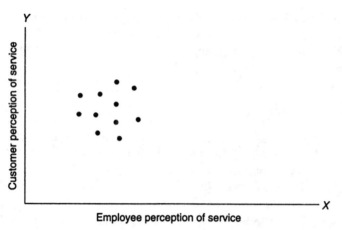

FIGURE 2.9   Typical within-branch scatterplot for customer and employee perceptions of service.

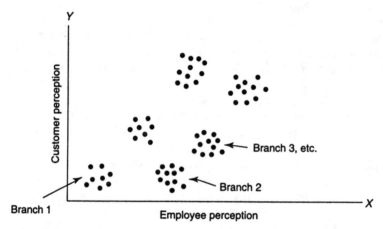

FIGURE 2.10   Scatterplot for customer and employee perceptions across branches.

tomers and employees agreed that service was of poor quality. On the other hand, there were other branches (labeled "country club branches" by the home office) where buildings were newer, customers were more affluent, staffing levels were high, etc. At these branches, which tended to be in the suburbs, everyone agreed that service quality was relatively high.

So, levels of analysis can matter a great deal. In the example above, when the *branch* was the unit, customer and employee perceptions of service were highly related. Within a branch, when *individuals* were the unit of analysis, perceptions of service were not related. By the way, sociologists have paid more attention to this problem than most other researchers and label this issue one of "ecological validity" (cf. Robinson, 1950).

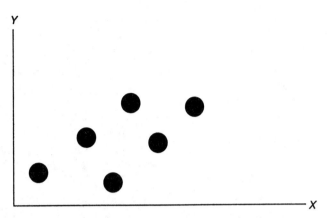

FIGURE 2.11   A scatterplot based on branch means for both X and Y.

Some organizational researchers have recently documented how relationships between variables may change depending upon whether one looks at individuals within an organization or individuals across organizations (e.g., Ostroff, 1992; Ryan, Schmit, and Johnson, 1996). The reader is referred to Ostroff and Harrison (1999) for a thorough review of these issues. Work by Dansereau and colleagues (e.g., Dansereau and Markham, 1987) has tried to analytically address these concerns in personnel management. Overall, it is important to remember that when conducting research in organizations (where individuals, work groups, firms, industries, and nations are all at different levels of analysis), you should be aware of the constant need to specify *your* level of analysis and beware of unnecessarily generalizing your statements to other levels.

Interpreting the Size of r

The underlying question in interpreting the magnitude of a correlation coefficient is, When is r big? The answer is that it depends![9] This is not a facetious answer. *The context in which r is computed matters.* For example, suppose you are in a room with two exit doors (A and B). You are told that when you leave the room, your choice of door will correlate with whether or not your next soda in life will be clear (e.g., 7-Up or ginger ale) or dark (e.g., some type of cola). Then, you are told that this correlation is $r = .01$. My guess is that most of you would not think this is a very big deal or a very big correlation. Now, look at another situation where r is still .01. In this case, you're in the same room (with exits A and B), but you're told that your choice of door is correlated with an increased chance of dying in the next 24 hours (and you're told which door increases that chance). Now, the correlation is still only .01, but my guess is that *it's big enough* (i.e., it's not zero) to affect your behavior, and you'll choose the door with the lower probability for your demise.

[9] This is the correct answer to *all* questions posed of students and professors! The trick is in knowing the response to the follow-up questions: It depends on what?, and then, how?

Again, the perceived "bigness" of r depends on the context. The above correlation of .01 was more useful in one context than in another.

At the other extreme, even correlations of .90 can be considered too small. For example, suppose you take an IQ test. Label your score X. Suppose that you wait a week, take the test again, and label your new score Y. In test theory (see Chapter IV), the correlation between X and Y is called "test-retest reliability." The state of the art in intelligence testing is that reliabilities of existing tests are already in the mid-.90s, so a value of .90 would be no big deal. On the other hand, a personnel manager would be delighted to have a test (X) that predicted future performance (Y) with $r = .90$. In fact, correlations in this predictive situation are typically between .00 and .50. Again, context matters.

Presumably, *any* capability to predict future performance (i.e., any r greater than 0) should be used by personnel managers. However, suppose I now tell you that a selection test, with $r = .30$, tends to exclude blacks (or females) at disproportionately high rates. Or, suppose that the selection test costs $1 million, per applicant, to administer. All of a sudden, $r = .30$ doesn't look as good. See? The context of the situation matters!

Nonetheless, practitioners who obtain correlations of .20 (or whatever) want to verbally describe their correlational results to colleagues, clients, researchers, and anyone else they can get to listen to them. If one obtains $r = .32$ (for example), it's not enough to say that your correlation "is certainly positive" or "is certainly bigger than my previous correlation of .27." The desire is to make more precise statements about the exact magnitude of r. We consider two ways to do this.

7a. Interpreting r Via r^2   The traditional statement in regression texts and journal articles is that $r_{XY} \times 100\%$ *measures the percentage of variance in Y that is associated with variance in X*.[10] This is such a ubiquitous statement that I feel compelled to make the following observations:

i The statement is essentially true.[11]

ii Sometimes people replace the phrase "is associated with" by "is related to." This is fine. Other people, in their zeal to claim strong results, replace the phrase "is associated with" by "is caused by." Our discussion of Property 4 clearly indicates that this is incorrect.

Now, what does it mean when we say that r^2 measures the percentage of variance in Y that is associated with variance in X? Mathematically speaking, this statement is concerned with how well the data fit a sample regression line (see Chapter V). Intuitively, however, just think of a scatterplot with some positive value of r (see Figure 2.12). Notice that there is indeed variation across

---

[10] And vice-versa, since $r_{YX} = r_{XY}$.
[11] That is, the statement is true if you have the entire population of values. In a sample, it's true for sums of squares but not for variances (see Chapter V).

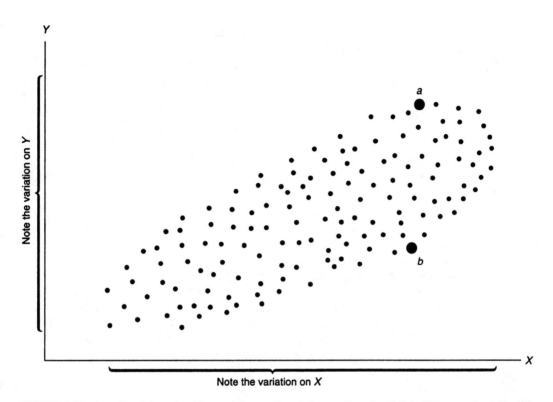

FIGURE 2.12   A scatterplot emphasizing variation on Y, variation on X, and variation of Y-scores for a given X.

the Y-scores (otherwise, the scatterplot would be a straight horizontal line). Similarly, the X-scores vary. Further, as X increases, Y tends to increase. So, part of the reason that Y-scores differ ($r^2 \times 100\%$ of the reason) is related to the differences among the lower and higher X-scores. Of course, unless $r = 1.0$, note that not all differences on Y are related to differences on X. For example, the data points marked a and b in Figure 2.12 have the same X-score, yet very different scores on Y.

It is also important to note that the above mode of interpretation can be "punishing" to the researcher or practitioner, in that r is almost always less than 1.0 and squaring such a number reduces it even further. For example, suppose you're defending a selection test (X) based on the fact that the test (X) and subsequent job performance (Y) correlate with a typical value of $r_{YX} = .30$. Well, this means that $(.30)^2 \times 100\% = 9\%$ of the variation in job performance is associated with differences in test scores. This also implies that 91% of job performance variation is *not* associated with test differences! Part of the problem here came from having to compute r^2 in order to interpret r. We now turn to a way that avoids the use of such a transformation.[12]

7b. Interpreting r Directly   Suppose a selection test (X) correlates with job performance (Y) with $r = .30$. Some individuals claim that *a test with* $r = .30$ *is 30 percent as good as a perfect test*. Note that the value of r is not squared in this interpretation—and the value does not have to be reduced to the $(.30)^2 = .09$ value. One basis for this claim lies in an analytic technique called "utility analysis," which is discussed in Chapter VII. In essence, it can be demonstrated that the utility of a test (usually computed in terms of the dollar value of increased organizational performance) is

$$\text{Utility} = r_{XY} \times s_Y \times \text{other stuff} - \text{cost of testing}$$

where r_{YX} is our old friend, s_Y estimates that standard deviation of value across individual workers (a parameter discussed in greater detail in Chapter VII), and "other stuff" is a factor having to do with the selection ratio used by the organization. The key here is to note that utility is a direct function of r and that the value of r is *not* squared. By "direct function," I mean that a test with $r = .30$ is 30% as good as a perfect test (with $r = 1.0$); it is twice as good (in a utility sense) as a test with $r = .15$; and so on.

OTHER CORRELATION COEFFICIENTS
("YES, VIRGINIA, THERE ARE MANY OTHERS")

There are perhaps as many different types of correlations as there are persons willing to invent them. For example, Kendall (1963) developed a nonparametric index of relationship called "tau," which is suitable when the two variables are ranks (or, even if the data are continuous, one can simply order the values and use the ranks instead of the raw data). Goodman and Kruskal (1954) developed two other measures: "lambda" and "gamma." Lambda is suitable when both variables are categorical (e.g., let X = name of your major in college; Y = area of the country in which you were born). Gamma is suitable when the levels of the categorical variables can be ordered in some way.[13] We will not consider these further in this text. Rather, because of our focus on the Pearson product moment

---

[12] Prentice and Miller (1992) and Abelson (1985) have provided conditions, both theoretical and practical, under which even extremely small values of r^2 can still be deemed impressive. For example, Abelson calculates that a major league ballplayer's skill explains about one-third of 1% of the variance in batting performance (for a single at bat). However, a ballplayer (and, in general, any organizational member) performs on multiple occasions across time. Therefore, the *cumulative* effect of even a small r^2 can be large (e.g., performance taken across an entire baseball season or taken across a series of day-to-day decisions in the workplace).

[13] I've always felt sorry for Kruskal. Certainly, Goodman has the statistic "gamma," a Greek G. So, the other statistic should have been kappa. Why not? I don't know, although there is a fairly standard usage of "kappa" as an index of interrater agreement. Perhaps lambda was chosen because L immediately follows K in the alphabet.

Y (in millions of dollars)

		<1	between 1, 10	>10
X	Male	0	10	0
	Female	5	0	5

FIGURE 2.13 Hypothetical categorical data for volume of insurance sold and gender of the sales agent.

correlation, we consider other (more common) indices of correlation—all of which can be considered special cases of Pearson r and Equation II.A.

> *An interesting aside* I have already noted that Pearson r and all of its special cases are *symmetric* with respect to the treatment of both X and Y. That is, $r_{YX} = r_{XY}$ (check Equation II.A). However, other types of correlations (say, r^*) can be *asymmetric*. In other words, one might be able to predict X from Y (say, r^*_{XY}) with better accuracy than one can predict Y from X (say, r^*_{YX}). In this case, $r^*_{XY} > r^*_{YX}$. Here's a simple example. Suppose the data consist of 20 insurance salespersons (10 males, 10 females). Let $X =$ gender and $Y =$ volume of insurance sold (in millions of dollars). Suppose Y is measured categorically (less than \$1 million, between \$1 and \$10 million, greater than \$10 million) and the resulting data look like Figure 2.13. Note that one can perfectly predict gender from sales volume (if $< \$1$ million, predict female, if between \$1 and \$10 million predict male, if $> \$10$ million predict female). Thus, $r^*_{XY} = 1$. However, if you start from knowledge of a person's gender, you can't perfectly predict their sales volume (e.g., females sell both low and high volumes). So, $r^*_{YX} < 1.0$. Thus, while this example is a bit contrived, it is important to be aware that Pearson correlations are constructed so that the degree of predictability is symmetric.

We now review some special cases of the Pearson r.

pearman's Rho, r_s

Property 3 of the Pearson r noted that the magnitude of r can be greatly affected by outlying values in the data. A straightforward way to bring outliers under control is to use "ranks" rather than raw data (e.g., converting the numbers 1.1, 6, 9, 1005 to the ranks 1, 2, 3, 4 certainly reduces the effect of the 1005 value!).

Also, in some organizational contexts, one may be relatively sure that one person is a better performer than another (or that one organization has a better climate for innovation than another), but precisely *how much* these differences are is unclear. Again, the use of ranks makes sense. In either case, entering ranks into Equation II.A has the effect of simplifying the formula. The result is called "Spearman's rho" (r_s) and is

$$\text{II.B} \qquad\qquad r_s = 1 - \left[\frac{6\Sigma(d^2)}{n(n^2 - 1)} \right]$$

where n is the sample size and d is the difference, for each pair of scores, between the ranking on X and the ranking on Y (see, for example, Table II.3).

Table II.3 displays how Spearman's rho is calculated for the air traffic controller selection data in Table II.1. Note that two scores on Y were tied (i.e., there were two scores of 75.0). If the number of ties is small, one can average the ranks that would have been assigned to these tied values (if the number of ties is large, a correction factor is needed—see Kendall, 1963). Ranking the variables in this manner and computing the squared differences (d's), results in $\Sigma d^2 = 39.5$ and

$$r_s = 1 - \left[\frac{6(39.5)}{13(169 - 1)} \right] = .89$$

Remember that regular old r was .75 for this data and that removing outlying values did not reduce r very much. The fact that r_s is also large confirms the notion that the relationship in these data is not due solely to a few outlying values.

TABLE II.3   CALCULATION OF SPEARMAN CORRELATION FOR THE AIR TRAFFIC CONTROLLER TRAINING DATA IN TABLE II.1

X	Y	Ranked X	Ranked Y	d	d^2
35.0	105.0	6	9	−3	9
45.0	75.0	7	5.5	1.5	2.25
69.0	85.0	10	7	3	9
182.0	208.0	13	12	1	1
48.7	146.1	8	11	−3	9
100.0	100.0	12	10	2	4
25.0	75.0	5	5.5	−0.5	0.25
98.0	300.0	11	13	−2	4
52.0	88.0	9	8	1	1
8.0	16.0	2	2	0	0
22.8	19.2	4	4	0	0
5.9	13.9	1	1	0	0
19.0	17.0	3	3	0	0
					39.5

By the way, it is useful to take a few minutes at this point and commune with Equation II.B. Note that if the rankings on X and Y agree perfectly then all d's will be zero, Σd^2 will be zero, and r_s will be exactly 1.0. So, all's fine in River City! Further, if the rankings on X and Y are in perfectly *opposite* order, then $r_s = -1.0$. (Go on, try, it! Let $X = 1, 2, 3, 4$ and $Y = 4, 3, 2, 1$. Check it out!)

Finally, you may wonder where the 6 came from in Equation II.B. Well, when you use only ranks in the Pearson r equation (Equation II.A), the X data, as ranks, are simply the numbers $1, 2, 3, \ldots, n$. This is also true for the scores on Y. Now, when variances are computed (as in the denominator of Equation II.A), one needs to sum the squares of the scores.[14] And, it is a fact that

$$1^2 + 2^2 + \cdots + n^2 = \frac{n(n+1)(2n+1)}{6}$$

(Go on, try this fact out also!) So, now you know where that 6 comes from.

hi Coefficient

Very often in applied research, variables are scored dichotomously (i.e., as having only two options). For example, test items are usually scored right or wrong. So, correlations between items on a test are usually correlations between dichotomous variables. Other typical dichotomous variables include male versus female, minority versus nonminority, promoted versus not promoted, stayers versus leavers, on time versus tardy, etc. (You should be getting the idea that dichotomous variables can be found everywhere in management and applied psychology!) When two dichotomous variables are considered simultaneously, the data can be cast in a 2×2 contingency table.

For example, two researchers (Bartlett and Goldstein, 1976) were once involved in a court case investigating the use of a telephone reference check as a basis for hiring decisions. These reference checks were scored dichotomously (positive reference or negative reference). In this case, the plaintiffs alleged that blacks received higher rates of negative references than whites. There were 7427 individuals in the data base; of these individuals, 95 received negative reference checks. The data are shown in Figure 2.14. Note that 43 of 4736 whites (0.9%) received negative reference checks, while 52 of 2691 blacks (1.9%) received negative reference checks. The "phi coefficient" (ϕ) is the Pearson correlation between the two dichotomous variables (in this case $X =$ race and $Y =$ reference-check status). To calculate phi, just score the X variable as $X = 1$ if black, 0 if white; score the Y variable as $Y = 1$ if a negative reference was obtained, 0 if a positive reference was obtained. Then, use Equation II.A. Note that, for each person in the data base, all of the scores are nothing but 1s and 0s, but it doesn't matter.[15] One can still compute a correlation between these X- and

---

[14] Remember that s_x^2 can be written as $\dfrac{\Sigma X^2 - (\Sigma X)^2/n}{n-1}$.

[15] In fact, even scoring the variables as 1 or 0 doesn't matter. You could score males $= \sqrt{\pi}$ and females $= -.176$. Since you can get from one scoring system to the other with a linear transformation, the magnitude of the correlation won't change (see Property 2).

Y

	Positive reference	Negative reference	
White	4693	43	4736
X			
Black	2639	52	2691
	7332	95	n = 7427

FIGURE 2.14   Telephone reference-check data (cell values from Bartlett and Goldstein, 1976, p. 2).

Y

a	b
c	d

X (label on left side)

FIGURE 2.15   General form of a 2 × 2 contingency table.

Y-scores using our old friend Equation II.A. *Thus, the phi coefficient is simply a new name for the Pearson r when both variables are dichotomous.*

However, just as in the case of Spearman's rho, the formula for phi is simpler than Equation II.A. In general terms, let the entries in the two-variable table be those in Figure 2.15. Then, r is equivalent to a ϕ-coefficient and the formula simplifies to

II.C
$$\phi = \frac{ad - bc}{\sqrt{(a + b)(c + d)(a + c)(b + d)}}$$

In the court case mentioned above, the ϕ-correlation was therefore

$$\phi = \frac{(4693)(52) - (2639)(43)}{\sqrt{(4736)(2691)(7332)(95)}} = .04$$

and the defendants might have concluded that the correlation between race and promotion was not very big (even though this correlation is statistically significant given the large sample sizes involved).

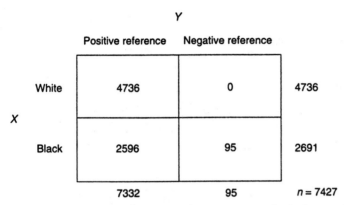

FIGURE 2.16 Maximal (hypothetical) arrangement of telephone reference-check data, with marginals fixed.

However, the plaintiffs knew something critical about phi coefficients: *Phi coefficients usually have maximum values that are much less than 1.0.* For example, consider the 2 × 2 table of data in Figure 2.14. The numbers on the edges of the data table are essentially fixed. (Because these numbers appear on the edges, or margins, they are called "marginals"!) So, 2691 applicants are black, and 4736 are white. That can't be changed within the study. Similarly, 95 negative reference checks were definitely obtained. Thus, the only uncertainty in this table concerns the four values inside the table.[16]

Now, look at the table of data. Given that the marginals are fixed, how can the inside numbers be rearranged to get the biggest correlation between race and the reference-check outcome? This can be done quite easily by arranging the data as shown in Figure 2.16. In other words, assume that *all* negative reference checks were obtained on black applicants. Now, in this case, the value of phi is

$$\text{Maximum } \phi = \phi_{\max} = \frac{(4736)(95) - (2596)(0)}{\sqrt{(4736)(2691)(7332)(95)}} = .15$$

So, even if this selection device were *completely* discriminatory, the correlation would only be .15. Once again, the bottom line of guilt versus innocence (another dichotomous variable!) is a judgment call. On one hand, $\phi = .04$. On the other, it's $(.04/.15) \times 100\% = 27\%$ as large as the maximum.[17]

By the way, $\phi_{\max}$ *can* be 1.0 if the marginals for the rows and the columns are the same. Then, all the data inside the 2 × 2 table can fall on the diagonal. For

[16] Actually, once *one* of these numbers is chosen, the remaining three become determined, given that the marginals are fixed. That's why your introductory statistics book told you there was 1 df in a 2 × 2 contingency table.

[17] There's yet another factor in these data complicating the decision about innocence or guilt, i.e., the values of the percentages involved. Note that the rate of obtaining negative reference checks for whites was 0.9%; for blacks, this rate was 1.9%. Is this a big or a small difference? On one hand, the difference is a "meager" 1.0%; on the other hand, one rate is over 100% as large as the other!

Y

	Positive reference	Negative reference	
White	4736	0	4736
Black	0	2691	2691
	4736	2691	n = 7427

X

FIGURE 2.17   Maximal (hypothetical) arrangement of telephone reference-check data, with marginals in equal proportions.

example, if there were 4736 whites *and* 4736 positive reference checks were obtained (Figure 2.17), then the table would yield $\phi = 1.0$. In practice, though, the row and column marginal distributions are not equal, and values of ϕ will be reduced.

Point-Biserial and Biserial Correlations

The point-biserial correlation (r_{pb}) is suitable for the situation when *one* of the two variables (say, Y) is scored dichotomously. In this case, one scores Y as 0 or 1 and then uses good old r (Equation II.A) to compute the correlation between the X-scores and the Y-scores.

For example, suppose one wanted to see if there was a correlation between an individual's satisfaction with his or her supervisor (X) and turnover (Y). Score turnover as $Y = 0$ if stay and $Y = 1$ if leave. Further, assume that we have a fairly continuous measure of satisfaction (perhaps even the "smiley-face" scale in Figure 2.4). *The Pearson product moment correlation between a continuous variable and a dichotomously scored variable is called a "point-biserial correlation."* Thus, point-biserials are special cases of Pearson r's.

As was the case for the phi coefficient, Equation II.A simplifies a bit in this special case because the scores on Y are either 0 or 1. Suppose there are n data points in all and that n_1 individuals leave and n_2 individuals stay (i.e., $n_1 + n_2 = n$). Then, Equation II.A can be written as

$$\text{II.D} \qquad r_{\text{point-biserial}} = r_{\text{pb}} = \frac{\overline{X}_2 - \overline{X}_1}{s_X} \sqrt{\left(\frac{n_1}{n}\right)\left(\frac{n_2}{n}\right)}$$

where $\overline{X}_1$ and $\overline{X}_2$ are the mean scores on X in the two subgroups and s_X is the standard deviation on X across all n individuals in the study.

By the way, notice that r_{pb} is pretty much based on the comparison between two group means. For example, if $\bar{X}_2 = \bar{X}_1$, then $r_{pb} = 0$. This makes sense. Because one variable (Y) is dichotomous, asking whether Y is related to X is the same as asking whether or not X-scores are different for one group (e.g., stayers) than for the other group (e.g., leavers). In fact, testing the point-biserial for statistical significance (see Chapter III) is numerically equivalent to computing the t-ratio between the means on X.[18] Further, in equal employment opportunity test analyses, it is common to compute and compare mean scores for two groups (e.g., majority v. minority, male v. female). In these situations, the difference in means ($\bar{X}_1 - \bar{X}_2$) is typically standardized by dividing by the average within-group standard deviation. The resulting standardized mean difference is labeled "d." As you might expect, there is a functional relationship between d and r_{pb}. It is $d = r_{pb} / \sqrt{pq\left(1 - r_{pb}^2\right)}$ where $p = n_1/(n_1 + n_2)$ and $q = n_2/(n_1 + n_2)$ (Hunter and Schmidt, 1990).

The use of point-biserials as special cases of the Pearson r is quite straightforward. However, a problem arises if the dichotomous variable is actually a continuous variable that has been scored dichotomously for convenience. For example, I once began a study to predict scores on a 30-item written test used to screen teenagers for driver's licenses. I wanted to correlate the scores on this driver's test (X) with the teenagers' subsequent driving records (Y) (e.g., total dollar damage to their automobiles if they were involved in accidents). However, states do not routinely keep these test scores; rather, they note only whether the individual passes or fails. Thus, my archival data on X was dichotomous, yet it represented a more continuous measure of driver knowledge.

Now, the problem arises that by dichotomizing a continuous variable one naturally loses some information in the data. In fact, suppose a truly continuous variable is artificially dichotomized at the median. It can then be shown that the correlation between this dichotomized variable and any other variable will be reduced to .798 times the underlying true correlation. If the dichotomization takes place at a different point in the distribution (e.g., to pass the driver's test in one state, you might need to be at the 70th percentile; to pass it in a different state, you may only need to be at the 30th percentile), then the reduction in r is even worse (see Cohen, 1983, for an extended discussion of this problem).

One solution to this problem is to compute the "biserial correlation" (r_{bis}). Essentially, *the biserial correlation attempts to estimate the true underlying population correlation between two continuous variables when the sample data for one variable have been artificially dichotomized.* So, in the above example, r_{bis} will provide an estimate of the Pearson correlation between continuous driver's test scores (X) and subsequent driving records (Y), even from data where all that was known about X was pass or fail.

[18] The moral is, beware of unscrupulous people who say, "There was a significant point-biserial r. This fact was *confirmed* by independently comparing the two means on X and obtaining a significant t-ratio." These people have confirmed nothing. They've done the same thing twice!

The derivation of r_{bis} and its properties is complex (cf. Lord and Novick, 1968; Peters and Van Voorhis, 1940), but the resulting estimate can be written as

$$r_{biserial} = r_{bis} = \frac{\overline{X}_2 - \overline{X}_1}{s_X} \frac{p_2 p_1}{\lambda}$$

where p_2 and p_1 are the proportions of cases in the two groups and λ is the height of a standard normal curve at the point where the distribution would be divided into proportions equivalent to p_2 and p_1, respectively.[19] This is a mouthful, and it is more instructive to rewrite the above equation as

II.E
$$r_{bis} = r_{pb}\left(\frac{\sqrt{p_2 p_1}}{\lambda}\right)$$

Now, it can be shown that the ratio $\sqrt{p_2 p_1}/\lambda$ varies from 1.25 (when $p_2 = p_1 = .50$) to about 3.70 (when either proportion is .99). Thus r_{bis} is always *greater* than the corresponding value of the point-biserial. This makes sense, given that we noted that artificial dichotomization implies a loss of information and a reduced value of the point-biserial.

Here are some asides about the point-biserial and biserial correlations.

Aside 1 The equation for the biserial r (Equation II.E) is remarkable in that r_{pb} is always multiplied by a factor greater than 1. Are we getting something for nothing? Not really. First, the computation of a biserial correlation assumes that the variable that was dichotomized is truly normally distributed in the population. If the underlying distribution is not normal, then the biserial r is not a good estimator of the underlying Pearson r. In other words, biserial r is not robust to the normality assumption.[20] Second, the standard error of r_{bis} is always larger than the standard error of the corresponding point-biserial (Pearson) r. This increase in standard error is particularly large when n_2 and n_1 are not equal. Thus, biserial correlations should be used with caution and only when the normality assumption is justified and the sample size is large enough to offset the increased standard error (Guilford and Fruchter, 1978; Lord and Novick, 1968).

Aside 2 We can agree that some variables are dichotomous in nature (e.g., gender, true versus false, hired versus not hired). Hence, the point-biserial correlation is an appropriate correlational index in many cases. Also, it is clear

[19] The formula for the value of λ is beyond the scope of this book. Again, λ is simply the height of the standard normal curve at a particular point. Some extensive tables of normal distributions tend to give, in a separate column, the values of λ associated with each z-score.

[20] In fact, under certain conditions, the value of the biserial r can exceed 1.0. Or, as Kendall and Stuart (1967) say, "In the absence of the normality assumption, we do not know what the biserial ... is estimating in general" (p. 321).

that some data bases have artificial dichotomies (e.g., the above example where only pass or fail rates on drivers' exams were available), in which case the biserial r might be considered. However, there is a substantial middle ground here. For example, consider the variable of turnover. Is this dichotomous or continuous? It's dichotomous if measured as stay or leave. But some researchers (e.g., Kemery, Dunlap, and Griffeth, 1988) imply that the real variable of interest is truly continuous, i.e., intention to quit. Their argument is that the dichotomous measure (leaving or not leaving) is confounded by how long you wait to see if a person leaves (a 5-year wait will obtain larger proportions of leavers than a 1-year wait), prevailing economic conditions in the external marketplace, etc. They advocate the use of biserial corrections when comparing results from turnover studies. (This is not without controversy, however, and will be discussed further in Chapter V.)

Aside 3 Have you thought of this aside yet? Think—we've talked about correcting point-biserials if the dichotomous variable was artificially created, right? Ah—we can also consider correcting phi coefficients if *both* dichotomies were artificially created. Such a correction (or more accurately, the estimate of the true correlation between the underlying, continuous variables) is called a "tetrachoric correlation." The formula for this correlation is very complex and beyond the scope of this chapter. However, just like biserials, tetrachoric r's are greater than their corresponding phi coefficients, they are not robust to nonnormality, have large standard errors, and must be used with extreme caution (see Guilford and Fruchter, 1978, or Lord and Novick, 1968, for details).

PROBLEMS

Suppose you are an executive in charge of hiring for an advertising corporation. A test salesperson stops by your office with a new selection test. This salesperson alleges that the "new and improved" selection test measures "advertising aptitude" and is an excellent predictor of job performance in any advertising corporation. The salesperson has collected data on the test and, luckily for you, is willing to let you analyze the numbers. The salesperson has also measured a variety of other variables on 15 current advertising employees (job incumbents), such that the data base includes

X_1 employee gender (coded male = 0, female = 1)

X_2 peer evaluation of the employee's initial interview (coded good = 1, bad = 0)

X_3 advertising aptitude test score for each employee (maximum score of 25)

Y performance of the employee (supervisor rating with maximum score of 30)

The data are shown in the following table:

Subject	X_1	X_2	X_3	Y
1	Male	Good	24	20
2	Female	Good	18	29
3	Male	Good	21	17
4	Male	Bad	7	8
5	Female	Bad	14	25
6	Male	Good	20	26
7	Male	Bad	8	7
8	Female	Bad	13	12
9	Male	Good	15	18
10	Male	Good	19	22
11	Female	Good	25	23
12	Female	Good	23	27
13	Male	Good	18	10
14	Female	Bad	12	5
15	Female	Bad	17	13

1 Calculate the Pearson correlation (r) between test scores and performance ratings.

2 Note that employee performance is measured on a 30-point scale. Suppose management wants performance scores to range from 0 to 90, so they multiply all existing performance scores by 3.0. What would the correlation (r) be between test scores and this new measure of performance?

3 Interpret the magnitude of the correlation you obtained in Problem 1.

4 Should you use this aptitude test in hiring people for your corporation?

5 Calculate the phi correlation coefficient between gender and peer evaluation.

6 Calculate the value of Spearman's rho between aptitude test scores and performance. When you are done, compare it to the Pearson correlation between these same variables.

7 Calculate the correlation between gender and test score. (*Hint:* It's a point-biserial.)

8 While you're at it, compute the correlation (r) between all pairs of measures in the above data. That is, complete what's called the "correlation matrix" below. [*Hints:* (a) You have already computed some of the correlations—they can be phi's, r's, or point-biserials; (b) you need to complete only the top half or the bottom half of the matrix since $r_{XY} = r_{YX}$.]

	X_1	X_2	X_3	Y
X_1	1.0			
X_2		1.0		
X_3			1.0	
Y				1.0

9 This is not really a problem in which you calculate something, but I thought you might be interested to know that the data in Table II.1 are real. They are not related to the selection of air traffic controllers. Rather, they are taken from a study by Bobko, Karren, and Parkington (1983). In that study, we asked 13 supervisors to estimate the overall worth of a median

(50th percentile) insurance salesperson. We asked them to consider, as a surrogate for overall worth, a salesperson's yearly volume of insurance premiums (in thousands of dollars). We also had each supervisor assist in estimating how much variability there was in worth across different salespersons (this variability is called $\$D_Y$ in the utility literature—see Property 7b in this chapter and Chapter VII for even more detail).

In Table II.1, the column labeled Y is really each supervisor's estimate of median dollar performance (in thousands of dollars); the column labeled X is the estimate of $\$D_Y$. Now, statistical theory states that if overall individual worth is normally distributed (an assumption of utility analysis), then estimates of the median and the standard deviation ($\$D_Y$) should be uncorrelated: i.e., the r between the median and $\$D_Y$ should be 0. So, we computed the Pearson product moment correlation between X and Y. The fact that r was not close to 0 meant something was wrong with the underlying theory, the data collection procedure, or both. In fact, two sets of researchers (Bobko et al., 1983; Burke and Frederick, 1984) have subsequently suggested a modification of the traditional data collection procedure in utility analysis.

REFERENCES

Abelson, R. (1985). A variance explanation paradox: When a little is a lot. *Psychological Bulletin, 97,* 129–133.

Ashford, S., Lee, C., and Bobko, P. (1989). Content, causes, and consequences of job insecurity: A theory-based measure and substantive test. *Academy of Management Journal, 32,* 803–829.

Bartlett, C., and Goldstein, I. (1976). *A validity study of the reference check for support personnel of the National Academy of Sciences.* Training and Educational Research Programs: College Park, MD.

Bobko, P., Karren, R., and Parkington, J. (1983). Estimation of standard deviations in utility analysis: An empirical test. *Journal of Applied Psychology, 68,* 170–176.

Burke, M., and Frederick, J. (1984). Two modified procedures for estimating standard deviations in utility analysis. *Journal of Applied Psychology, 69,* 482–489.

Cohen, J. (1983). The cost of dichotomization. *Applied Psychological Measurement, 7,* 249–253.

Dansereau, F., and Markham, S. (1987). Levels of analysis in personnel and human resources management. In K. Rowland and G. Ferris (Eds.), *Research in personnel and human resources management,* Vol. 5, Greenwich, CT: JAI Press.

Deci, E., Connell, J., and Ryan, R. (1989). Self-determination in a work organization. *Journal of Applied Psychology, 74,* 580–590.

Dunham, R., and Herman, J. (1975). Development of a female faces scale for measuring job satisfaction. *Journal of Applied Psychology, 60,* 629–631.

Farh, J., and Dobbins, G. (1989). Effects of comparative performance information on the accuracy of self-ratings and agreement between self- and supervisor ratings. *Journal of Applied Psychology, 74,* 606–610.

Galton, F. (1888). Co-relations and their measurement, chiefly from anthropometric data. *Proceedings of the Royal Society of London,* Vol. XLV, 135–145.

Goodman, L., and Kruskal, W. (1954). Measures of association for cross-classifications. *Journal of the American Statistical Association, 49,* 732–764.

Guilford, J., and Fruchter, B. (1978). *Fundamental statistics in psychology and education* (6th ed.). New York: McGraw-Hill.

Hull, C. (1928). *Aptitude testing.* Yonkers, NY: World Books.

Hunter, J., and Schmidt, F. (1990). *Methods of meta-analysis: Correcting error and bias in research findings.* Newbury Park, CA: Sage.

Kemery, E., Dunlap, W., and Griffeth, R. (1988). Correction for variance restriction in point-biserial correlations. *Journal of Applied Psychology, 73,* 688–691.

Kendall, M. (1963). *Rank correlation methods* (3rd ed.). London: Griffin.

Kendall, M., and Stuart, A. (1967). *The Advanced Theory of Statistics,* Vol. 1. London: Charles Griffin & Co.

Kruskal, W. (1960). Some remarks on wild observations. *Technometrics, 2,* 1–3.

Kunin, T. (1955). The construction of a new type of attitude measure. *Personnel Psychology, 8,* 65–78.

Lord, F., and Novick, M. (1968). *Statistical theories of mental test scores.* Reading, MA: Addison-Wesley.

May, R., Stewart, W., and Sweo, R. (2000). Environmental scanning behavior in a transitional economy: Evidence from Russia. *Academy of Management Journal, 43,* 403–427.

Miller, D. (1988). Relating Porter's business strategies to environment and structure: Analysis and performance implications. *Academy of Management Journal, 31,* 280–308.

Neter, J., Wasserman, W., and Kutner, R. (1986). *Applied linear statistical models.* Homewood, IL: Irwin.

Orr, J., Sackett, P., and DuBois, C. (1991). Outlier detection and treatment in I/O psychology: A survey of researcher beliefs and an empirical illustration. *Personnel Psychology, 44,* 473–486.

Ostroff, C. (1992). The relationship between satisfaction, attitudes, and performance: An organizational level analysis. *Journal of Applied Psychology, 77,* 963–974.

Ostroff, C., and Harrison, D. (1999). Meta-analysis, level of analysis, and best estimates of population correlations: Cautions for interpreting meta-analytic results in organizational behavior. *Journal of Applied Psychology, 84,* 260–270.

Pelled, L., and Xin, K. (1999). Down and out: An investigation of the relationship between mood and employee withdrawal behavior. *Journal of Management, 25,* 875–895.

Peters, C., and Van Voorhis, W. (1940). *Statistical procedures and their mathematical bases.* New York: McGraw-Hill.

Phillips, A., and Dipboye, R. (1989). Correlational tests of predictions from a process model of the interview. *Journal of Applied Psychology, 74,* 41–52.

Potosky, D., and Bobko, P. (1997). Computer versus paper-and-pencil administration mode and response distortion in noncognitive selection tests. *Journal of Applied Psychology, 82,* 293–299.

Prentice, D., and Miller, D. (1992). When small effects are impressive. *Psychological Bulletin, 112,* 160–164.

Richard, O. (2000). Racial diversity, business strategy, and firm performance: A resource-based view. *Academy of Management Journal, 43,* 164–177.

Robinson, W. (1950). Ecological correlations and the behavior of individuals. *American Sociological Review, 15,* 351–357.

Ryan, A., Schmit, M., and Johnson, R. (1996). Attitudes and effectiveness: Examining relations at an organizational level. *Personnel Psychology, 49,* 853–882.

Schneider, B., Parkington, J., and Buxton, V. (1980). Employee and customer perceptions of service in banks. *Administrative Science Quarterly, 25,* 252–267.

TESTING CORRELATIONS FOR STATISTICAL SIGNIFICANCE

After reading this chapter, you should be able to:

- Identify the statistical techniques appropriate for testing different hypotheses regarding correlations. This includes techniques for dealing with the different types of correlations, as well as situations in which there are two Pearson r's (both independent and dependent cases).

- Suggest examples of studies for which each of the above tests of significance might be appropriate.

- Discuss the influence of sample size on tests of significance for correlations.

- Give several reasons why one might want to test a correlation compared to a nonzero population value.

- Explain why the test that compares a correlation to the value of zero cannot be used when testing a correlation against a nonzero population value.

- Find an average of several correlation coefficients and explain when a weighted average might be used.

- Recognize problems associated with "harvesting" correlations and suggest possible solutions that help to avoid misinterpretations.

In Chapter II, we discussed correlation coefficients and interpretations of their magnitude. In this chapter, we bow to those in the field who live by tests of statistical significance. For example, often it's not enough to collect a sample of data and show there's a positive value of r between a selection test and subsequent job performance, between the use of realistic job previews and subsequent turnover, etc. Rather, one wants some statistical indication that these nonzero sample results will generalize to other groups of individuals (i.e., that the nonnull result is true in the population of interest).[1] This is precisely what statistical significance testing is all about (see the brief review in Chapter I). In fact, testing Pearson product moment correlations for significance is relatively straightforward, although the procedures depend upon the type of hypothesis being tested.

TESTING A SINGLE CORRELATION AGAINST ZERO

The hypothesis H_0: $\rho = 0$, where ρ is the underlying population correlation, is by far the most frequently tested correlational hypothesis. In fact, many researchers run around asking each other, "Was your r significant?" This is researcher shorthand for, "Was your sample value of r significantly different from the hypothesized value of $\rho = 0$?" or "Assuming the population correlation was 0, was your sample value of r so far away from 0 that it was not likely to have occurred by chance?"

Notationally, let ρ be the value of the population correlation, let r be our old friend the sample correlation, and let n be the sample size. Then, it can be shown that the value $r\sqrt{n-2}\,/\sqrt{1-r^2}$ has a t-distribution with $(n-2)$ degrees of freedom. Formally, we have

III.A
$$t_{n-2} \sim \frac{r\sqrt{n-2}}{\sqrt{1-r^2}}$$

Note that the value of r is tested by computing a fairly straightforward (but nonlinear) function of r and comparing the result to well-known critical values of Student's t-distribution.[2] For example, suppose the predictive validity of the Scholastic Aptitude Test (SAT) is being questioned. Assume that a researcher uses a simple random sample of $n = 122$ and obtains a measure of success in college (Y) as well as previous SAT scores (X) for each individual. Suppose the

---

[1] The notion of conducting significance tests on correlations is even given a separate section in equal employment opportunity (EEO) legislation documents. For example, the EEO uniform guidelines state in their technical standards section, "Generally, a selection procedure is considered related to the criterion when the relationship ... [between test scores and performance] ... is statistically significant at the 0.05 level of significance" (U.S. Equal Employment Opportunity Commission et al., 1978, p. 38301). So, the guidelines even state what Type I error rate you should use!

[2] By the way, derivation of the above result assumes bivariate normality for the two variables.

resulting correlation is $r = .27$. Then, Equation III.A gives

$$t_{n-2} = t_{120} \sim \frac{.27\sqrt{120}}{\sqrt{1 - .27^2}} = 3.07$$

The obtained sample value of $t = 3.07$ is larger than the two-sided, $p = .05$ critical t-value of 1.980 (see Appendix, Table A.1). Therefore, this correlation is "significant." More correctly stated, we have rejected the null hypothesis (that the underlying value of ρ is 0) in favor of the alternative hypothesis that ρ is nonzero (but you'll usually just hear the cry, "My r is significant!"). [By the way, the same value of 3.07 is statistically significant at the $p = .01$ level as well. So the researcher's report can use the traditional two-star rating (**) for .01 significance and not just the one-star rating (*) of .05!]

The above is an example that tests the most frequently asked question about a sample r: Is there a statistically significant (from 0) relationship between test scores and future performance scores? In other words, Is the use of a test to select individuals statistically useful? Further, as noted in Chapter II, there is an incredible array of other uses for the correlation coefficient in theory development and application.

Here's another example: Pelled and Xin (1999) predicted, among other things, that an individual's report of positive mood at work (X) would be negatively related to an employee's absence behavior (Y). Thus, these researchers could test H_0: $\rho = 0$ against the alternative H_a: $\rho < 0$. They obtained scores on these two variables for $n = 99$ electronics company employees. Now, *you* take the time to apply Equation III.A. Don't be bashful! Did those researchers get what they wanted? Did they "win"? (Oh, you want the value of r? Details, details. It was $-.36$.)

O.K. You should have concluded (as did Pelled and Xin, 1999) that positive affect was negatively associated with absenteeism. That is, when I used Equation III.A, I obtained $t_{97} = -.36\sqrt{97} / \sqrt{1 - .36^2} = -3.80$, which is certainly greater (in magnitude) than the .05 or .01 critical t-values. Did you get the same answer?

The point to be made so far is that testing correlations (against the value of 0) is very straightforward and has as many applications as the computation of the magnitude of r (see Chapter II). We can gain even further insight into the test procedure by looking at the components and overall format of Equation III.A.

Look at the Test for H_0: $\rho = 0$

1 Note that Equation III.A comes with $(n - 2)$ degrees of freedom. Getting a bit ahead of ourselves (See Chapter VI), one way to think about the term $n - 2$ is to realize that when $r = 0$, the slope of the regression line that best describes or fits the data will also be 0. That is, simple regression will be of the form $Y = b_0 + b_1 X$, where b_0 is the intercept and b_1 is the slope. Because two parameters are being estimated, it is appropriate to think to yourself: "I had n pieces of information in the sample with which to draw inferences from the data; 2 were used up estimating b_0 and b_1; I have $(n - 2)$ pieces of information (degrees of freedom) left."

2 It is very instructive to write Equation III.A as

$$t_{n-2} \sim \frac{r\;\boxed{-0}}{\sqrt{(1 - r^2)/(n - 2)}} = \frac{r_{\text{observed}} - \rho_{\text{null}}}{\sqrt{(1 - r^2)/(n - 2)}}$$

This is just a simple transformation of the original equation. I added the $\boxed{-0}$ to remind you that we are testing r against 0. Now, remember your introductory statistics course (or Chapter I of this book) and the one-sample t-test for a mean, $H_0: \mu = 0$. The t-statistic for that test looked like

$$t = \frac{\bar{X}\;\boxed{-0}}{\sqrt{s^2/n}} \qquad \text{compared to} \qquad t = \frac{r\;\boxed{-0}}{\sqrt{(1 - r^2)/(n - 2)}}$$

This has the same general shape as the test for r. An obvious difference is that r replaces $\bar{X}$! Another difference is that $n - 2$ replaces n. Finally, think of s^2 in the t-test for a mean as the error variance across all scores. The same can be said for $1 - r^2$ in the test for r. That is, the quantity $(1 - r^2) \times 100\%$ indicates variation in Y *not* associated with the variation in X (see Chapter II). The value of $1 - r^2$ is analogous to the percentage of error variance. Thus, the t-test for the significance of a correlation has the same format as the significance test for a sample mean (only the names have been changed to protect the innocent). If you remember this discussion, you won't forget the formula for testing the significance of r.

3 One more thing about Equation III.A should be mentioned. The parameter n is in the right place! It's in the numerator [actually, the denominator of the denominator $(1 - r^2)/(n - 2)$], where it does us the most good. Thus, just like tests for means, tests for correlations become more powerful as n increased. (On the other hand, just like t-tests for means, the value of n is "square-rooted".[3] Thus, it takes approximately a fourfold increase in n to double the sample t-value.)

Of course, the placement of n means that just about any nonzero correlation (no matter how small) can be "significant" *if* the sample size is sufficiently large. For example, suppose a selection test correlates with subsequent job performance with $r = .06$. If this correlation is based on a sample of $n = 1100$, then it's statistically significant ($p = .05$, two-sided test). Would you say that the use of this test for selection was statistically valid? (In fact, if the researcher had only 1000 subjects in the study, the value of r would *not* be significant—check

[3] I know "square-rooted" is not a transitive verb; it's not even a verb! But, I am sure you know what I mean: $\sqrt{n - 2}$ is in the numerator of Equation III.A, not just $n - 2$.

it out!) Was the test worthy of use (in practical, moral, or other terms)? Of course, these are questions considered previously and their answers depend upon the context (again, refer back to the section on interpreting the size of r in Chapter II).

For example, based on some data I once saw, I can remember computing the correlation between cigarette smoking (X) and death rate by lung cancer (Y) to be "only" .06, yet this was significant because the study by the agency from which the data came had 500,000 people! Obviously, this type of result (coupled with the relationship of cigarette smoking to other diseases and malignancies) has caused substantial constraints to be placed on advertising by the tobacco industry.

4 There's another handy fact related to the form of the t-test for r. That is, while an exact expression for the variance of r is complex (see Fisher, 1915; Hotelling, 1953), it is the case that the asymptotic variance for r is $(1 - \rho^2)^2/n$. "Asymptotic" refers to the fact that this expression is approximately true but gets "truer" as n increases. This is a handy expression to remember. For example, suppose I tell you that I have a correlation of .21 and it's based on a sample size of $n = 64$. An estimate of the standard deviation associated with my correlation is

$$\text{SD}(r) \approx \sqrt{\frac{(1 - r^2)^2}{n}} = \sqrt{\frac{(1 - .21^2)^2}{64}} \approx \frac{1}{\sqrt{64}} = \frac{1}{8} = .125$$

Thus, the estimated standard deviation (SD) for the sampling distribution of r in this case is approximately .125. That's a lot of error associated with any point estimate of r — and because r^2 was close to 0, all you had to do to estimate this standard deviation was compute 1 divided by the square root of your sample size!

ESTING A SINGLE CORRELATION VERSUS ANY SPECIFIED VALUE
HE USE OF FISHER'S z)

In the previous section, we tested the null hypothesis H_0: $\rho = 0$. In this section, we consider H_0: $\rho = \rho_0$, where ρ_0 is some specified a priori number (between -1 and $+1$). As noted earlier, many researchers routinely equate the significance of a correlation with whether or not the value of r is different from 0. In some (perhaps many) contexts, this is simply not an interesting operationalization of "significant" and it is imperative to demonstrate that your value of r is much bigger than zero.

I have heard some researchers state, "Just by their placement on the *same* questionnaire, *any* two items will yield a correlation of at least .30." Art Brief (quoted in Webster and Starbuck, 1988) has been a bit more conservative and has suggested that "everything correlates .1 with everything else" (p. 113). Meehl (1990) has charmingly labeled these expected nonzero correlations as the "crud factor." Indeed, within a questionnaire, adjacent items can correlate more highly than remotely placed items (cf. Cascio's 1987 discussion of "proximity bias" in rating scales). Further, the order of attitudinal items can induce spurious correlation (cf. Schuman and Presser, 1981). Thus, when questionnaires are the source of measurement (e.g., questionnaires about attitudes, perceptions, or performance appraisal ratings), a nonzero value of ρ may be more appropriate as a null hypothesis point of comparison.

Another reason to consider tests of hypotheses against nonzero values is provided by folks who use correlations to compute test-retest reliabilities (see Chapter IV). That is, give a test at time 1 and call the result X; then give the same test at time 2 and call the result Y. If the test is measuring a stable trait for individuals across time, r_{XY} should be a relatively large number. For example, state-of-the-art tests of intellectual abilities can yield test-retest reliabilities in the .90s (even across a time span of several years). So, if you develop a test of some particular construct or variable, it's often not enough to demonstrate that the reliability is significantly greater than zero (i.e., getting significance against H_0: $\rho = 0$ is no big deal). Depending upon context, it may be incumbent upon you to show that your measure has reliability greater than .9 (or .8 or whatever). So, your hypotheses might be H_0: $\rho = .9$ versus H_a: $\rho > .9$.

Comparing values of r to other nonzero correlational values is also part of the logic behind "multitrait, multimethod" analyses (Campbell and Fiske, 1959). That is, it is not enough to show that measures of two constructs (say, X and Y) have an r_{XY} greater than zero. It may be the case that X and Y are measured using the same method (e.g., self-report). If so, it is incumbent upon the researcher to demonstrate that r_{XY} is greater than the correlation expected between *any* two scales measured with the same method.

In sum, *you should reflect on what you want as your null hypothesis value* (i.e., your "baseline" correlation) before you conduct any statistical tests of significance.

The Problem, the Solution, and the Test

The problem in testing H_0: $\rho = \rho_0$ is that the t-test of Equation III.A is no longer appropriate. This can be seen by first remembering that r ranges only from -1 to $+1$. Then, note that when H_0: $\rho = 0$ is assumed true, sample values of r are generally close to 0, but some are positive and some are negative. The sampling distribution of r when $\rho = 0$ therefore looks like Figure 3.1. This is a nice, pretty, symmetric distribution and is associated with the t-test in Equation III.A.

However, when H_0: $\rho = \rho_0 \neq 0$ is true, the sampling distribution of r becomes skewed. For example, if $\rho_0 = .7$, the sampling distribution will look like Figure 3.2. This is because every once in a while (by sheer random chance) a sample r is negative (even though $\rho_0 = +.7$). However, there is no value of r large enough to balance out this extremely low value because values of r are constrained to be no greater than $+1.0$. Thus, the distribution is "bunched up" toward the right-hand side (i.e., it's skewed to the left). Thus, any hope of using a pretty, symmetric distribution for hypothesis testing is shattered.

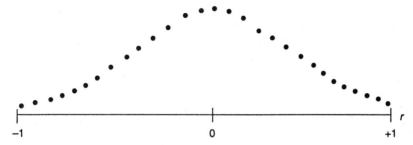

FIGURE 3.1   Shape of sampling distribution of r when population correlation is 0.

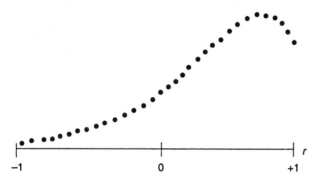

FIGURE 3.2   Shape of sampling distribution of r when population correlation is positive.

Fortunately, R. A. Fisher (*the* Fisher of *the* F-distribution) has already worried about this problem. Actually, he worried about the related problem that the value of ρ and the standard deviation of the sampling distribution of r are dependent. You should remember this from our discussion above about the asymptotic variance of r: the variance of r contains the factor $1 - \rho^2$. Thus, as ρ increases in magnitude, the standard deviation of r goes down. This dependence is a statistical "no-no".[4]

Now, not only did Fisher worry about these problems, he provided a solution! He suggested that researchers work with *transformed values* of r rather than raw values of r. He suggested the following transformation:

III.B
$$\text{Fisher's } z_r = \frac{1}{2}\ln\left(\frac{1 + r}{1 - r}\right)$$

where ln is the natural logarithm function. By the way, for our purposes here, you needn't worry about *where* this transformation came from, although while it

[4] For example, the use of the *t*-distribution in any significance test requires *independence* of the statistic being tested (the numerator) and its associated standard error (the denominator)—see just about any introductory statistics book.

TABLE III.1   SOME VALUES OF FISHER'S z_r AND CORRESPONDING VALUES OF r

r	z_r	r	z_r	r	z_r
.00	.000	.34	.354	.67	.811
.01	.010	.35	.365	.68	.829
.02	.020	.36	.377	.69	.848
.03	.030	.37	.388	.70	.867
.04	.040	.38	.400	.71	.887
.05	.050	.39	.412	.72	.908
.06	.060	.40	.424	.73	.929
.07	.070	.41	.436	.74	.950
.08	.080	.42	.448	.75	.973
.09	.090	.43	.460	.76	.996
.10	.100	.44	.472	.77	1.020
.11	.110	.45	.485	.78	1.045
.12	.121	.46	.497	.79	1.071
.13	.131	.47	.510	.80	1.099
.14	.141	.48	.523	.81	1.127
.15	.151	.49	.536	.82	1.157
.16	.161	.50	.549	.83	1.188
.17	.172	.51	.563	.84	1.221
.18	.182	.52	.576	.85	1.256
.19	.192	.53	.590	.86	1.293
.20	.203	.54	.604	.87	1.333
.21	.213	.55	.619	.88	1.376
.22	.224	.56	.633	.89	1.422
.23	.234	.57	.648	.90	1.472
.24	.245	.58	.662	.91	1.528
.25	.255	.59	.678	.92	1.589
.26	.266	.60	.693	.93	1.658
.27	.277	.61	.709	.94	1.738
.28	.288	.62	.725	.95	1.832
.29	.299	.63	.741	.96	1.946
.30	.310	.64	.758	.97	2.092
.31	.321	.65	.775	.98	2.298
.32	.332	.66	.793	.99	2.647
.33	.343				

looks imposing, it is an "obvious" choice if you follow Fisher's proof. (In fact, remembering your high school trigonometry course, you might note that this transformation is really the inverse hyperbolic tangent of r. Or did you repress this fact?)

Table III.1 contains some values of r and associated values of Fisher's z_r. It's important that you glance at these columns of values. Note that r and z_r are quite similar for low values of r. However, as r gets closer to 1, r and z_r diverge (and z_r becomes greater than 1.0). This all makes sense: remember that the distribution of r was skewed to the left (constrained from above by $+1.0$) when ρ was large and positive. So, Fisher's z_r-transformation takes large values of r and moves them further to the right (even beyond values of 1.0). This means that the bunched-up distribution for r is stretched out to the right when z_r is

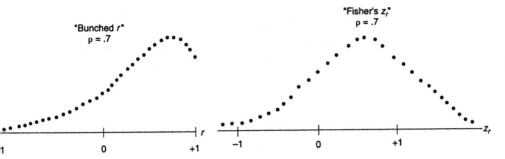

FIGURE 3.3   Comparison of sampling distributions of r and Fisher's z when population correlation is .70.

used (Figure 3.3). Note that the distribution of Fisher's z_r is now prettier (in a symmetry sense). Here are two amazing facts (AFs) about z_r:

AF1 The sampling distribution of Fisher's z_r-statistic is approximately normal (that's why it's labeled z).

AF2 The standard deviation of z_r is approximately

$$\text{III.C} \qquad\qquad \text{SD}(z_r) = \sqrt{\frac{1}{n-3}}$$

Actually, these facts aren't all that amazing—they are a direct result of Fisher's judicious choice of transformation. *And these results make it very easy to test $H_0: \rho = \rho_0$. All you have to do is remember: Don't work with r, work with z_r, and when you work with z_r, you can assume a normal distribution with variance $1/(n-3)$.*

A quick example   Suppose, based on cost considerations, a company will not initiate an assessment center to select their managers unless the correlation between assessment center ratings (X) and subsequent job performance (Y) is significantly greater than .40. Suppose the personnel department then conducts a study on $n = 165$ individuals and obtains $r_{XY} = .54$. Can the personnel group then to go to company headquarters with statistical evidence that the assessment center should be implemented?

In this case, the null hypothesis is $H_0: \rho = .40$ and the alternative hypothesis is $H_a: \rho > .40$. As noted, rather than computing the difference in r's (.54 − .40), we need to first convert *both* values to Fisher's z_r. The value of .54 converts to .604, and the value .40 converts to .424 (see Table III.1). In this case, the standard deviation of z_r is $\sqrt{1/(n-3)} = \sqrt{1/162}$. Thus, we can compute the test statistic as

$$z_{\text{test}} = \frac{z_r - z_\rho}{\sqrt{1/(n-3)}} = \frac{.604 - .424}{\sqrt{1/162}} = 2.29$$

Because z_r is approximately normally distributed (see AF1 above), we can compare the standardized statistic of 2.29 directly to standard normal probability tables. With $p = .05$, the last row of the t-table in the Appendix tells us that the one-sided critical z is 1.645. Thus, the correlation of .54 is significantly greater than .40, and the assessment center can be implemented.

An Important Related Result: Averaging Correlations

Fisher's z-transformations are also particularly useful for averaging different sample values of r. Because of the skewness in their sampling distributions, averaging untransformed values of r can lead to an underestimation of the true average (assuming ρ is greater than zero and, thus, the distribution of r is skewed to the left). Thus, *one should always convert r's to Fisher's z's before averaging* (see Silver and Dunlap, 1987, and Strube, 1988, for the computer simulation verifications of this statement).[5] The average value of z_r can then be "back-converted" in order to estimate the average value of r (i.e., find a value inside Table III.1 that is close to the average z_r you obtained and then find its associated value of r in the margin). An example of this process is given below.

Note that Fisher's z-transformations addressed skewness problems in the distribution of r. If multiple values of r (e.g., r_1, r_2, r_3) are obtained from independent samples of varying size (say, n_1, n_2, n_3), then it is also appropriate to form a weighted average of the r's. This is accomplished by first converting the r's to z's. Further, it is traditional to use weights that are inversely proportional to the variance of each statistic being averaged. Fisher's z_r makes this easy, since each variance is $1/(n_i - 3)$. Thus with three correlations, the average z_r is

$$\bar{z}_r = \frac{(n_1 - 3)\, z_1 + (n_2 - 3)\, z_2 + (n_3 - 3)\, z_3}{(n_1 - 3) + (n_2 - 3) + (n_3 - 3)}$$

This has the effect of giving relatively greater weight to correlations based on larger sample sizes. Again, don't forget to transform r's to z's before averaging![6]

An example   Wilson, Harvey, and Macy (1990) conducted a study of individuals who provided ratings for job analyses (including ratings of time spent

[5] Obviously, a look at Table III.1 indicates that the difference between an average based on r's versus z_r's is minimal if all correlations are small in magnitude. Strube (1988) has also indicated that, as the number of correlations to be averaged increases, the difference in results based on r's versus z_r's decreases. However, it matters in all other cases; hence the suggestion that one always use Fisher's z-transformation.

[6] There are recently developed (and related) methodologies called "validity generalization" and "meta-analysis" that attempt to cumulate results across studies. Both of these techniques depend precisely upon this type of sample-size-weighted averaging. Bobko, Roth, and Potosky (1999) have shown how critical the use of sample weighting can be in meta-analytic procedures. And, Silver and Dunlap (1987) have reaffirmed the importance of averaging z's (not r's).

on each task). In one case, the authors repeated three of the questions to assess whether there was a correlation between what raters said the first time and what they said the second time (see the section on test-retest reliability in Chapter IV). They obtained three correlations (one for each item) as shown in the following table:

Item	r	n	z_r
1	.79	41	1.071
2	.79	34	1.071
3	.44	20	.472

Note that I have added a column based on the Fisher's z-transformed values. For these three items, Wilson et al. (1990, Table 2) report an average correlation of .70. A straightforward average of the three r's yields a value of .67, so the authors didn't do that. However, the average of the z_r-values (in the last column above) yields .8713, which back-converts to a correlation of about .70 (see Table III.1). So, this is what Wilson et al. (probably) did! Finally, notice that each correlation is based on a different sample size. Computing a weighted average yields

$$\frac{38\,(1.071) + 31\,(1.071) + 17\,(.472)}{38 + 31 + 17} = .953$$

which back-converts to a weighted average r estimate of .74. [Note that the choice between .70 and .74, as the average, depends upon whether or not you want to weight the results by their sample sizes. In many instances, but not all, it makes sense to attach more importance to results based on larger samples. See Rosenthal (1978) and Rubin (1982) for excellent summaries of this statistical issue.]

TESTING THE EQUALITY OF TWO INDEPENDENT CORRELATIONS

Often in psychological research, interest is focused on the comparison of two groups or two experimental conditions (e.g., the t-test for two means from independent samples). Given Fisher's z-transformation, we can readily test whether a correlation in one group is equal to a correlation (between the same variables) in another group. For simplicity, we'll denote the correlations from the two groups as ρ_1 and ρ_2. But don't forget that ρ_1 really means "ρ_{XY} for group 1" and ρ_2 really means "ρ_{XY} for group 2."

As an example, Farh and Dobbins (1989) were interested in the correlation between self-ratings of performance (X) and supervisor ratings of performance (Y). They created two experimental conditions. The first condition (group 1) was a control group. Under the second condition (group 2), self-raters were presented with "the same comparative performance information that was available to supervisors'' (p. 606). Farh and Dobbins predicted that r_{XY} would be greater in this "enhanced information group." Thus, their null hypothesis was $H_0: \rho_1 = \rho_2$ and their specific alternative hypothesis was $H_a: \rho_1 < \rho_2$.

O.K. How does one test $H_0: \rho_1 = \rho_2$? The answer involves a straightforward use of Fisher's z_r-transformation. First, just as in the case of the t-test for $H_0: \mu_1 = \mu_2$, interest is really in whether or not the value $\overline{X}_1 - \overline{X}_2$ is close to 0. So, in our current case, the initial step might be to compute the difference between the sample correlations $(r_1 - r_2)$ and see if the value is close to 0.

Can you anticipate why this is not quite right? Good! We must transform the r's to z's and compute $z_1 - z_2$. That's the numerator of our test. The denominator of our test is the standard error of $z_1 - z_2$. This is easily shown to be $\sqrt{1/(n_1 - 3) + 1/(n_2 - 3)}$.[7] Thus, the entire test statistic is

III.D
$$z \sim \frac{z_1 - z_2}{\sqrt{1/(n_1 - 3) + 1/(n_2 - 3)}}$$

Note that z_1 and z_2 are approximately normally distributed. Since any linear combination of normal variables (e.g., $z_1 - z_2$) is normally distributed, this entire test statistic can in turn be compared to a standard normal table of critical values.

In the above example, Farh and Dobbins obtained a correlation between self- and supervisor ratings (for overall performance) of .51 under the enhanced information condition ($r_2 = .51$); their control correlation was .05 ($r_1 = .05$). By the way, the sample size for each of their conditions was about 65 ($n_1 = n_2 = 65$).[8] Applying Equation III.D, they converted the r's to Fisher's z's and obtained a significant difference between their correlations. (Go on, try it! I got a sample z-value of 2.86, which is greater than the $p = .01$ critical value. Do you agree?)

It should be clear that the test for $H_0: \rho_1 = \rho_2$ is particularly useful in the behavioral sciences. It can be applied in any situation where there are two naturally occurring groups (e.g., males and females; blue collar and white collar workers; successful and unsuccessful organizations) or when two groups are experimentally manipulated to be different.

An Important Statistical Aside About Differential Validity

Suppose one tests $H_0: \rho = 0$, with $r = .20$ and $n = 100$. Application of Equation III.A yields a t-statistic of $.20\sqrt{98} / \sqrt{1 - .04} = 2.02$. This is greater than the critical t-value with 98 df ($p = .05$, two sides). So, the r of .20 is

---

[7] Remember that the variance of the difference in two variables, $(X - Y)$, is $\text{var}(X - Y) = \text{var}(X) + \text{var}(Y) - 2\text{cov}(X, Y)$, where cov represents the covariance. Since the two correlations are computed from *independent* samples, the covariance term becomes 0. Thus $\text{var}(z_1 - z_2) = \text{var}(z_1) + \text{var}(z_2)$. Substituting from Equation III.C and then taking the square root yields the denominator in Equation III.D.

[8] Technically, Farh and Dobbins violated the critical assumption of independence (across observations) when they computed their test of significance. That is, each supervisor provided ratings for five subordinates, and so supervisor ratings could have been correlated with each other. However, neither Farh and Dobbins nor the journal noted this, so we won't tell either!

significant.[9] However (there always seems to be a "however"!), suppose one tests H_0: $\rho_1 = \rho_2$ and obtains $r_1 = .40$ and $r_2 = .20$. Note that this example is contrived so that the difference in r's ($.40 - .20 = .20$) is identical to the single $r = .20$ in the first sentence of this paragraph. Further, let's assume that each subgroup correlation is from a sample of size 100 (i.e., $n_1 = n_2 = 100$). Thus, the overall sample size is *double* what it was in the first sentence. Now, application of Equation III.D yields

$$z \sim \frac{.424 - .203}{\sqrt{\frac{1}{97} + \frac{1}{97}}} = 1.54$$

which is *not* statistically significant. The moral is

It is much harder to get a significant difference between two correlations than it is to get one correlation significantly different from zero.

Note that this has nothing to do with the fact that we switched from a t-statistic (for the single-r case) to a Fisher's z-statistic. Indeed, for the two-sample case, the numerator is actually greater than .20 (because of the z-transformation of $.424 - .203$). However, the loss in statistical *power* is due to the larger denominator: the sampling distribution of the difference in r's is much more variable than the distribution of a single r. That is, Equation III.D demonstrates that variances from both samples are added together when the difference in correlations is considered, resulting in a larger standard deviation than you get for either sample alone. (In fact, the denominator is greater in this case by a factor of $\sqrt{2}$.)

This type of problem arises often, particularly in the test fairness literature. In these situations, attention may be focused on the validity of a selection or promotion test [e.g., the correlation between a selection test (X) and job performance (Y)]. The question being asked is whether or not the validity coefficient changes when one looks at different subgroups [e.g., blacks and whites or males and females (cf. Bartlett, Bobko, and Pine, 1977, or Linn, 1978, for a review of this literature)]. And, the underlying issue I'm pointing out here is one of statistical power. For example, Trattner and O'Leary (1980) demonstrated that many validation studies simply do not have adequate sample sizes to detect underlying nonzero correlations. It should be clear from the above that concerns about power become magnified when trying to detect *differences* in two correlations.

An aside to the aside   It gets even worse! Suppose your overall sample size is still 200, as above. However, let $n_1 = 160$ and $n_2 = 40$. This is a typical pattern in test fairness studies, where there are fewer individual workers in one sub-group than in the other subgroup. Now, note that the standard error of $z_1 - z_2$ is $\sqrt{\frac{1}{160} + \frac{1}{40}} = .177$, whereas it was $\sqrt{\frac{1}{100} + \frac{1}{100}} = .141$ in the study

---

[9] The Appendix contains critical values for 60 and 100 df. The critical value for 98 df would be between these two values. Since the sample t-value of 2.02 is greater than either critical value in the table, the result is significant.

with equal samples. In other words, the *smaller* sample size dominates, and increases, the overall error term (also see Hsu, 1993). Thus, even more power is lost when the n_i are not equal.]

TESTING THE EQUALITY OF TWO DEPENDENT CORRELATIONS

So far, we have talked about comparing two *independent* correlations: i.e., correlations obtained from two distinct groups or obtained from two different studies. However, two (or more) correlations can have a built-in dependence if they are computed across the same individuals. For example, within a *single sample*, Fryxell and Gordon (1989) measured (among other things) the following three individual difference variables: Y = satisfaction with a grievance system, X = perceptions of procedural justice, and Z = perceptions of distributive justice. These authors hypothesized that perceptions of both procedural justice (X) and distributive justice (Z) should predict satisfaction with the grievance system. However, they further predicted that procedural justice (X) would be the stronger correlate of satisfaction (Y). They therefore were expecting that in their sample r_{YX} would be greater than r_{YZ}. This motivates the following null hypothesis:

$$H_0: \rho_{YX} = \rho_{YZ} \quad \text{or} \quad H_0: \rho_{YX} - \rho_{YZ} = 0$$

The intuitive way to test this hypothesis would be to obtain r_{YX} and r_{YZ} and then compute $r_{YX} - r_{YZ}$ to see if this value is close to zero. (Or, if you've learned the lesson of the previous section, to first convert these correlations to Fisher's z's and then use a formula similar to Equation III.D.) However, there are some complicating problems here:

1 The two sample correlations are not independent because they are computed on the same sample of subjects.

2 The two sample correlations are not independent because they are computed using a common variable (Y).

3 This double-whammy dependence makes the sampling distribution of $r_{YX} - r_{YZ}$ [or the Fisher's z equivalent ($z_{YX} - z_{YZ}$)] more difficult to derive. For example, as in footnote 7, $\text{var}(r_{YX} - r_{YZ}) = \text{var}(r_{YX}) + \text{var}(r_{YZ}) - 2\text{cov}(r_{YX}, r_{YZ})$. Given the built-in dependence, we can't assume the covariance term is zero (as we did before).

Hotelling (1940) was the first to report a solution to testing the hypothesis $H_0: \rho_{YX} = \rho_{YZ}$ that takes into account all of the dependencies noted above. Williams (1959) then modified the Hotelling test to improve its statistical properties. Thus, the solution to testing $H_0: \rho_{YX} = \rho_{YZ}$ is often referred to as the "Hotelling-Williams test." The test statistic has a Student's t-distribution and is

$$\text{III.E} \quad t_{(n-3)\text{df}} \sim (r_{YX} - r_{YZ})\sqrt{\frac{(n-1)(1+r_{XZ})}{2(n-1)/(n-3)|R| + \bar{r}^2(1-r_{XZ})^3}}$$

where $\bar{r} = (r_{YX} + r_{YZ})/2$ and $|R| = 1 - r_{YX}^2 - r_{YZ}^2 - r_{XZ}^2 + 2r_{YX}r_{YZ}r_{XZ}$.

While this equation looks formidable, it's easy to use if you just persist a bit with the algebra. For example, in their first sample of data, Fryxell and Gordon's (1989) values for r_{YX} and r_{YZ} were .60 and .55, respectively. To use Equation III.E, I also need to tell you that $n = 1518$ and $r_{XZ} = .59$. Then, $r_{YX} - r_{YZ} = .05$, $\bar{r} = .575$, and (after some time on the calculator) $|R| = .3788$. The value of the test statistic in Equation III.E therefore becomes 2.778. Now, the critical t-value with 1515 df and $p = .01$ is approximately 2.58 (see the Appendix). Since the test statistic is greater than the critical value, Fryxell and Gordon can reject H_0: $\rho_{YX} = \rho_{YZ}$ and conclude that procedural justice is a better predictor of satisfaction with a grievance system than distributive justice.[10]

The null hypothesis H_0: $\rho_{YX} = \rho_{YZ}$ and the test procedure implied by Equation III.E have many other uses in the applied literature. A common application is the comparison of a newly developed measure (e.g., X) to an existing, baseline measure (e.g., Z) in the ability to predict a particular outcome (Y). For example, Kulik, Oldham, and Langner (1988) compared the original Job Diagnostic Survey (JDS) of Hackman and Oldham (1975) to a revised version proposed by Idaszak and Drasgow (1987). Both measures were correlated with several outcomes, such as satisfaction, internal motivation, and productivity. Hotelling-Williams tests indicated that the revised scale was a better predictor than the original scale in only 2 of 30 situations [and the conclusion was that substitution of the revised measure "may be premature" (p. 466)]. A second example is provided by Ashford, Lee, and Bobko (1989), who constructed a new measure of job insecurity. Using the Hotelling-Williams test, these authors compared correlations of both their measure (X) and previous measures of job insecurity (Z) with a variety of other outcome and antecedent variables (Y). Ashford et al. repeatedly found greater correlations for their new measure and concluded that the pattern of findings supported adoption of the new measure.

Thoughts and Facts About Equation III.E

1 The form of the t-statistic in Equation III.E should look somewhat familiar. It computes the statistic in question ($r_{YX} - r_{YZ}$) divided by its associated standard error. However, the standard error is a bit complicated and has been algebraically rearranged. As in other equations, part of the numerator $(n - 1)(1 + r_{XZ})$ really comes from being the denominator of the denominator. Notice also that n (actually $n - 1$) is in the usual place: it's in the numerator, but with a square root [the other term involving n's, $(n - 1)/(n - 3)$, is close to the value of 1.0 and is essentially negligible when n is not small].

2 The expression is further complicated by the fact that r_{YX}, r_{YZ}, and r_{XZ} are interrelated (i.e., dependent). The formula actually incorporates the *covariances among these three correlations*. In fact, $|R|$ really stands for the "determinant of the 3 × 3 correlation matrix" (if interested further, see just about any book on matrix algebra). In fact, some statisticians use this determinant as a way of indexing the overall degree of relationship among the variables.

---

[10] Statistically speaking, this statement is true. However, are .60 and .55 really different enough in a practical sense to make such a fuss? That's up to you, the reader!

3 You should know that individuals other than Hotelling and Williams have also suggested ways to test H_0: $\rho_{YX} = \rho_{YZ}$. Neill and Dunn (1975) provided a Monte Carlo investigation of 11 tests of this null hypothesis. They concluded that "for small or moderate samples, Williams' statistic [the one reported here] emerges as the best choice" (p. 531).[11] This choice was based on both the ability to protect the stated alpha level (Type I error) and considerations of power (reduced Type II error).

One other hypothesis test for dependent correlations deserves a passing comment. Statisticians have considered null hypotheses of the form H_0: $\rho_{YX} = \rho_{ZW}$, where X, Y, Z, W are all measured on the same sample. It is hard to imagine many practical uses of this hypothesis (perhaps X and Y measure two traits using a common method, while Z and W measure the same traits using a different, but common method). In fact, a review of the published organizational science literature found very few instances of such a test being performed. Some large sample (asymptotic) statistical procedures for testing this hypothesis have been proposed and Raghunathan, Rosenthal, and Rubin (1996) have empirically shown that a test based on use of Fisher's z tends to have the best properties.

TESTS OF OTHER CORRELATION COEFFICIENTS

Point-Biserial

In Chapter II we noted that when one variable was dichotomous, the formula for the Pearson correlation had a simplified form (see Equation II.D) and the resulting statistic was called a point-biserial correlation (r_{pb}). Testing a point-biserial for significance (against zero) proceeds exactly the same as in Equation III.A. That is, the statistic

$$t \sim \frac{r_{pb}\sqrt{n-2}}{\sqrt{1 - r_{pb}^2}}$$

has a t-distribution with $(n-2)$ degrees of freedom under the null hypothesis of no correlation between the dichotomous and the continuous variables. As suggested in Chapter II, the t-test for point-biserial correlations is equivalent to conducting a t-test on the two means you get by averaging across the continuous variable for each group.

Phi Coefficient

When *both* variables were dichotomous, the Pearson correlation was called a phi coefficient (ϕ). In this case, the data reduce to a 2 × 2 contingency table (see Chapter II) and the test of H_0: "no correlation" proceeds as a chi-square test of

---

[11] By the way, for very large samples, a likelihood ratio test was a small bit better. However, the notion of likelihood testing is beyond the scope of this book, and in fact Neill and Dunn (1975) did not recommend this test because of its intrinsic computational difficulties.

Y

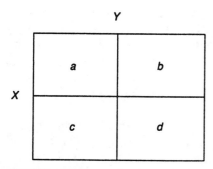

FIGURE 3.4   General form of a 2 × 2 contingency table (originally presented as Fig. 2.15).

Y

	Positive reference	Negative reference	
White	4693	43	4736
Black	2639	52	2691
	7332	95	$n = 7427$

FIGURE 3.5   Specific example of the cross-classification of two dichotomous variables (originally discussed as Fig. 2.14).

independence. For example, Figure 3.4 illustrates the general form of the data in Chapter II, and the specific example presented is shown in Figure 3.5. In this specific case, individuals were being selected for employment based in part upon a telephone reference check. The correlation between race and reference-check status was $\phi = .04$. To test whether this relationship is significantly different from zero, one can test the independence hypothesis using a chi-square test (go back to your introductory statistics text if you have forgotten how to do this—or simply read on!). In fact, there is a very straightforward relationship between the value of ϕ in this 2 × 2 table and the chi-square value (cf. Guilford and Fruchter, 1978, p. 317):

$$\text{Chi-square} = n(\phi^2)$$

The degrees of freedom associated with the chi-square is (rows − 1) × (columns − 1) = (2 − 1) × (2 − 1) = 1. Thus, in the above example,

$$\text{Chi-square} = 7427(.04)^2 = 11.88$$

If you look at your old statistics book, you'll see that the critical value of a chi-square statistic with 1 df and $p = .05$ is 3.841. Thus, the value of $\phi = .04$ is statistically greater than zero (although see Chapter II for a discussion of whether or not this value is practically significant).

Spearman's Rho, r_s

When ranks (rather than raw data) were applied to the formula for the Pearson product moment correlation, the resulting nonparametric correlation was labeled Spearman's r_s (see Chapter II). If n is larger than 10, r_s can be tested for significance (from zero) by adopting Equation III.A (see Kendall, 1948).[12] That is

$$t_{n-2} \sim \frac{r_s\sqrt{n-2}}{\sqrt{1 - r_s^2}}$$

Consider the ranked data presented in Table II.3. In that case, Spearman's r_s was computed to reduce the effect of outliers. A value of $r_s = .89$ was obtained on $n = 13$ observations. Applying Equation III.A will result in a t-statistic of $r_s\sqrt{n-2}/\sqrt{1 - r_s^2} = .89\sqrt{11}/\sqrt{1 - .89^2} = 6.47$. This is substantially greater than the critical t-value with 11 df (whether $p = .05$ *or* .01). Thus, the obtained Spearman's r_s is statistically significant.[13]

SOME COMMENTS ON "HARVESTING" CORRELATIONS

The Problem

I have seen researchers, in search of truth and increased publication records, administer a questionnaire to subjects. The data are coded, entered into a computer, and analyzed. At this point, the first thing these researchers do is obtain the computer's correlation matrix for all variables in the study. This matrix contains each possible bivariate correlation (r) and its associated significance level (tested against the null value of 0). The researcher then takes a pen (usually red) and circles each significant r. Cohen (1990) has referred to this process as "harvesting" correlations. The circled r's are then waved around the researcher's room, and the research team goes about interpreting them (oh, the beauty of behavioral science!).

---

[12] If n is 10 or less, there are special tables of critical values for r_s (see Kendall, 1948, p. 40). Basically, these values are obtained by completely listing the sampling distribution of r_s. It *is* possible to do this. For example, let $n = 7$. Since r_s deals with ranks only, there are just 7! possible orderings of the X's for any given ranking on Y (and, under the null hypothesis, all orderings are equally likely).

[13] Note how this may be cast in a compromising light by unethical folks: the test for r_s and the test for the regular old Pearson r proceed exactly the same. However, in the data in Table II.3, note that r_s is greater than r (i.e., .89 is greater than .75). Thus, in this instance, the t-test for r_s is more likely to be significant than the test for r, since both tests use the same formula and critical value. It would be unscrupulous to conduct both tests and choose the one you wanted! The choice of statistic should be guided by theory and a priori decisions about the quality of the measurement.

Can you see the statistical fallacy here? Right! *If there are a large number of correlations on the computer output, then many of the circled r's are liable to be significant by chance.* More precisely, suppose there are $m = 22$ measures in the study. Then there are $m(m - 1)/2 = 22 \times \frac{21}{2} = 231$ correlations reported in the matrix on the computer output.[14] In turn, at the $p = .05$ level of significance, $231 \times .05 = 11.55 \approx 12$ correlations are expected to be significant *just by chance*. After all, this is what Type I error (and the p-level) is: the probability of falsely rejecting H_0 when H_0 is true. So, you should begin to see the problem. Suppose the above researcher obtains 25 significant correlations (i.e., 25 red circles). Which of the 25 significant r's is truly significant? That is, about 12 r's are significant by chance, so we should discuss only 13 r's. But which ones are they? Unfortunately, there is no absolute answer to this question, but some strategies are suggested below.

First, though, let me try to convince you that this potential issue is quite common. Footnote 1 in Chapter II contained a listing of some typical recent correlational studies. While these particular authors did not harvest correlations, most of these studies did report correlation matrices in their results section. Richard (2000) had a 13×13 matrix, Pelled and Xin (1999) had an 11×11 matrix, May et al. (2000) had a 25×25 matrix, Miller (1988) had a 13×13 matrix, etc. For example, Miller had 4 measures of an organization's environment, 4 measures of structure, and 5 measures of strategic orientation. Some of

---

[14] In fact, the number 22 is no big deal. I've seen this search for significant correlations done with over $m = 100$ measures; i.e., $100 \times \frac{99}{2} = 4950$ correlations!

TABLE III.2   EXEMPLARY CORRELATION MATRIX†, ‡

Variables	1	2	3	4	5	6	7	8	9	10	11	12
Environment												
1. Uncertainty												
2. Unpredictability	76											
3. Dynamism	91	45										
4. Heterogeneity	51	48	43									
Structure												
5. Liaison devices	**05**	**02**	**05**	**06**								
6. Technocratization	**06**	**− 06**	**14**	**15**	24							
7. Delegation	**− 05**	**− 05**	**− 04**	**04**	− 04	22						
8. Formal controls	**− 14**	**− 11**	**− 09**	**13**	20	27	06					
Strategy												
9. Differentiation	**30**	**23**	**27**	**22**	**27**	**26**	**16**	**02**				
10. Cost of innovation	**30**	**12**	**35**	**15**	**18**	**40**	**03**	**08**	47			
11. Cost leadership	**− 13**	**− 16**	**− 08**	**− 07**	**− 20**	**− 09**	**− 11**	**22**	− 25	− 19		
12. Marketing	**22**	**18**	**21**	**12**	**15**	**10**	**− 06**	**11**	18	08	− 29	
13. Breadth	**16**	**14**	**15**	**07**	**31**	**15**	**− 04**	**07**	04	− 04	05	05

† Adapted with permission from Miller (1988).
‡ n = 89 (therefore, correlations greater than .19 are significant at the p = .05 level). Decimals are removed from the correlations for ease of exposition, and between-set correlations are presented in boldface.

his results are displayed in Table III.2. In Miller's case, there were $13 \times \frac{12}{2} = 78$ correlations, of which $78 \times .05 = 3.9 \approx 4$ could be expected to be significant just by chance alone. In Table III.2, any correlations greater than .19 are significant at $p = .05$; in this case, that amounts to 28 significant r's. But which 4 of these are the chance events?

It can get even more interesting. For example, Table III.2 really contains three *sets* of variables. Because of their nature, one would expect to obtain significant correlations within each of these three sets of variables (because they're measuring similar constructs). However, it's the correlations between variables in different sets that are of relatively greater interest (i.e., does an environmental measure significantly correlate with a strategy measure?). In this case, there are $(4 \times 4) + (4 \times 5) + (4 \times 5) = 56$ between-set correlations (boldface in Table III.2). Of these, $56 \times .05 = 2.8 \approx 3$ are expected to be significant just by chance. In fact, of the original 28 significant r's only 13 significant r's are of the between-set variety (and about 3 of these are Type I errors, although no one knows which ones).[15]

Some Solutions

As noted, there's no completely accepted solution to the problem of testing so many correlations, but there are some things a researcher can do (the suggestions are not mutually exclusive):

1 Just be aware of any increase in potential for Type I errors when testing correlations. At least perhaps your conclusions will be appropriately tempered (and you will echo the ubiquitous cry for future research to replicate and cross-validate your findings).

2 Conduct a Bonferroni correction on the alpha level. Basically, Bonferroni proved that if one does k significance tests, each at the p/k level of significance, then the overall Type I error rate for the set of k tests is no greater than p. For example, in an 11×11 matrix (with 55 correlations), conduct significance tests for *each* correlation at the $.05/55 = .0009$ level of significance. If you do this, the overall Type I error rate will be preserved at .05 (i.e., you will make *any* Type I error in only 1 of 20 such studies). Of course this is a very conservative procedure (see any design book for further discussion on protecting experiment-wise error rates). On the other hand, if you get significance with such a procedure, you're really sure of your results!

3 Take Wilson's (1962) hypothesiswise error rate approach. That is, for some correlations in your matrix, your a priori theory might make strong predictions about significant correlations. If so, conduct each test at its own level of $p = .05$ (or .01). After all, why punish yourself for conducting a study with lots of variables and good theoretical specification? (Just make sure you develop your theory *before* looking at your data!) Further, for those correlations where theory

[15] There is no intent here to personally disparage Miller (1988). In fact, he presents a fine study. The example is used just to point out the typicality of the issue in the published literature.

isn't strong (or you're just data-snooping) you can apply a Bonferroni correction on this reduced number of tests.

4 Somehow combine the measures (or correlations) into sets. Then use $p = .05$ for each set of measures. For example, if one had a validity study with 10 predictors and 5 measures of performance, one could conduct 50 tests of significance of empirical validity (see Chapter IV). However, perhaps 4 of the 10 predictors were paper-and-pencil tests of intellectual abilities. Perhaps they can be standardized and combined in some a priori fashion (e.g., unit-weighted). Similarly, it may be that the performance measures really consist of 3 quantity measures and 2 quality measures and can therefore be reduced to 2 performance composites. In this way, the number of measures (and thus, the number of correlations) can be substantially reduced, thereby reducing the potential for Type I errors. Reduction in the number of variables can also be done statistically—by letting the data decide through the use of a multivariate technique such as factor analysis.

The role of good thinking when testing correlations can't be emphasized enough. It should help in determining how to combine measures. Good thinking is also used to interpret the pattern of significance in a correlation matrix. For example, consider Table III.2 again. Notice that the 13 or so significant between-set correlations are not strewn throughout the table willy-nilly. Rather, note that the differentiation variable (9) is significantly correlated with every environmental variable (1 through 4). Interpreting such patterns lends strength to one's conclusions. In fact, in Chapter IV we shall see that the interpretation of *patterns* of correlations is essentially a search for construct validity (Cronbach and Meehl, 1955). The variables are embedded in a nomological net (i.e., a theoretical network), and the actual correlations are perused to see if they make sense, given the theory. If so, the study has provided support for both the measures used and their assumed theoretical relations.

ROBLEMS

Choose $p = .05$ throughout.

1 In Chapter II, we calculated the correlation between selection test scores and performance in a situation where a salesperson claimed that a new test was an excellent predictor of job performance. The correlation was $r = .674$, with $n = 15$.

a Test this correlation to see if it is significantly different from zero.

b Suppose the corporation already has an existing selection test that correlates $\rho = .60$ with job performance. Test to see if the new test (with validity .674) is significantly better than the existing test.

2 In the Chapter II data, it was also found that the point-biserial correlation between gender and selection test score was .088. Test this correlation for significance (against zero).

3 In the Chapter II data, the phi coefficient between gender and peer evaluation was $-.327$. Test this correlation for significance against zero. (To conduct this test, I also need to tell you that the critical value for a chi-square with 1 df, $p = .05$, is 3.841.)

4 Finally, we also computed a Spearman correlation in the Chapter II problem set. It was between test score and performance and was .649. Test this correlation for significance against zero.

5 Suppose the door-to-door salesperson in the problems in Chapter II works for a company that is trying to market the new selection test across all regions of the country. The company has validated the test in four regions with the following results:

North: $r = .58$, $n = 50$
South: $r = .72$, $n = 75$
East: $r = .63$, $n = 60$
West: $r = .81$, $n = 100$

a Calculate the average correlation across the four regions. Use a weighted average.
b Is there a significantly greater correlation in the western region than in the eastern region?

6 A human resource manager in the company suggests that the new selection test may be a better predictor of performance for applicants with previous job experience than it is for applicants with no previous experience. The manager obtains two new samples of data. The value of r_{XY} is .71 in a group of 50 experienced applicants; it's .62 in a different sample of 50 applicants with no previous experience. Is there statistical support for the manager's conjecture?

7 Zaccaro et al. (1991) conducted a study in which they looked at four types of leadership style and four different tasks. The four styles are listed in the accompanying table. The four tasks were a school board simulation (T_1), a manufacturing game (T_2), a discussion of AIDS (T_3), and moon tent production (T_4). Some of the correlations between leadership style tendencies and task performance (taken from their table 1) are shown below:

	T_1	T_2	T_3	T_4
Persuasion	.20*			
Initiating structure	.15	.18		
Consideration	.06	.09	.35*	
Production emphasis	.13	−.03	.14	.16

The sample size was $n = 108$. The asterisks indicate which of the correlations are significantly different from zero at $p = .05$ (you may even want to check this). Zaccaro et al. state that support for their hypotheses of matching leadership style with type of task "would be indicated by a pattern of larger correlations on the diagonal than the off diagonal" (1991, p. 311). While such a pattern is obtained, are the diagonal correlations significantly greater than the off-diagonal correlations? Specifically, see if the correlation of .20 (between persuasion and T_1) is greater than the value of .15 (between initiating structure and T_1). (In order to conduct this test, assume that the correlation between persuasion and initiating structure is .30. Also, when obtaining the critical t-value from the Appendix, feel free to use either 100 or 120 df).

8 In a study testing models of leadership, Field and House (1990) asked 44 managers and 44 subordinates (each subordinate was paired with one manager) to rate attributes about a decision they had both recently faced. Field and House wanted to see if the managers and subordinates agreed in their perceptions, so they computed the correlations between manager ratings (X) and subordinate ratings (Y) for eight different aspects of the decision process. This resulted in eight correlations between Y and X (one for each aspect). The values of the eight correlations were .70, .38, .62, .52, .53, −.13, .44, and .68 (see their table 1). Field and House report an average correlation of .47 (1990, p. 363). This is just a simple average of the eight correlations. Compute the average value of the correlation using Fisher's z-transformation but don't weight by sample size (since the correlations all come from the same sample anyway). (*Hint*: Don't forget to put a minus sign in front of the Fisher's z-value for the −.13 correlation.)

ẾFERENCES

Ashford, S., Lee, C., and Bobko, P. (1989). Content, causes, and consequences of job insecurity: A theory-based measure and substantive test. *Academy of Management Journal*, *32*, 803–829.

Bartlett, C., Bobko, P., and Pine, S. (1977). Single-group validity: Fallacy of the facts? *Journal of Applied Psychology*, *62*, 155–157.

Bobko, P., Roth, P., and Potosky, D. (1999). Derivation and implications of a meta-analytic matrix incorporating cognitive ability, alternative predictors, and job performance. *Personnel Psychology*, *52*, 561–589.

Campbell, D., and Fiske, D. (1959). Convergent and discriminant validity by the multitrait-multimethod matrix. *Psychological Bulletin*, *56*, 81–105.

Cascio, W. (1987). *Applied psychology in personnel management* (3rd ed.). Englewood Cliffs, NJ: Prentice-Hall.

Cohen, J. (1990). Things I have learned (so far). *American Psychologist*, *45*, 1304–1312.

Cronbach, L., and Meehl, P. (1955). Construct validity in psychological tests. *Psychological Bulletin*, *52*, 281–302.

Farh, J., and Dobbins, G. (1989). Effects of comparative performance information on the accuracy of self-ratings and agreement between self- and supervisor ratings. *Journal of Applied Psychology*, *74*, 606–610.

Field, R., and House, R. (1990). A test of the Vroom-Yetton model using manager and subordinate reports. *Journal of Applied Psychology*, *75*, 362–366.

Fisher, R. (1915). Frequency distribution of the values of the correlation coefficient in samples from an indefinitely large population. *Biometrika*, *10*, 507–521.

Fryxell, G., and Gordon, M. (1989). Workplace justice and job satisfaction as predictors of satisfaction with union and management. *Academy of Management Journal*, *32*, 851–866.

Guilford, J., and Fruchter, B. (1978). *Fundamental statistics in psychology and education* (6th ed.). New York: McGraw-Hill.

Hackman, J., and Oldham, G. (1975). Development of the Job Diagnostic Survey. *Journal of Applied Psychology*, *60*, 159–170.

Hotelling, H. (1940). The selection of variates for use in prediction with some comments on the general problem of nuisance parameters. *Annals of Mathematical Statistics*, *11*, 271–283.

Hotelling, H. (1953). New light on the correlation coefficient and its transforms. *Journal of the Royal Statistical Society, Series B*, *15*, 193–225.

Hsu, L. (1993). Using Cohen's tables to determine the maximum power attainable in two-sample tests when one sample is limited in size. *Journal of Applied Psychology*, *78*, 303–305.

Idaszak, J., and Drasgow, F. (1987). A revision of the Job Diagnostic Survey: Elimination of a measurement artifact. *Journal of Applied Psychology*, *72*, 69–74.

Kendall, M. (1948). *Rank correlation methods*. London: Charles Griffin.

Kulik, C., Oldham, G., and Langner, P. (1988). Measurement of job characteristics: Comparison of the original and the revised Job Diagnostic Survey. *Journal of Applied Psychology*, *73*, 462–466.

Linn, R. (1978). Single-group validity, differential validity, and differential prediction. *Journal of Applied Psychology*, *63*, 507–512.

May, R., Stewart, W., and Sweo, R. (2000). Environmental scanning behavior in a transitional economy: Evidence from Russia. *Academy of Management Journal*, *43*, 403–427.

Meehl, P. (1990). Why summaries of research on psychological theories are often uninterpretable. *Psychological Reports*, *66*, 195–244.

Miller, D. (1988). Relating Porter's business strategies to environment and structure: Analysis and performance implications. *Academy of Management Journal, 31*, 280–308.

Neill, J., and Dunn, O. (1975). Equality of dependent correlation coefficients. *Biometrics, 31*, 531–543.

Pelled, L., and Xin, K. (1999). Down and out: An investigation of the relationship between mood and employee withdrawal behavior. *Journal of Management, 25*, 875–895.

Raghunathan, T., Rosenthal, R., and Rubin, D. (1996). Comparing correlated but nonoverlapping correlations. *Psychological Methods, 1*, 178–183.

Richard, O. (2000). Racial diversity, business strategy, and firm performance: A resource-based view. *Academy of Management Journal, 43*, 164–177.

Rosenthal, R. (1978). Combining results of independent studies. *Psychological Bulletin, 85*, 185–193.

Rosenthal, R., and Rubin, D. (1982). Comparing effect sizes of independent studies. *Psychological Bulletin, 92*, 500–504.

Schuman, H., and Presser, S. (1981). *Questions and answers in attitude surveys.* New York: Academic Press.

Silver, N., and Dunlap, W. (1987). Averaging correlation coefficients: Should Fisher's *z* transformation be used? *Journal of Applied Psychology, 72*, 146–148.

Strube, M. (1988). Averaging correlation coefficients: Influence of heterogeneity and set size. *Journal of Applied Psychology, 73*, 559–568.

Trattner, M., and O'Leary, B. (1980). Sample sizes for specified statistical power in testing for differential validity. *Journal of Applied Psychology, 65*, 127–134.

U.S. Equal Employment Opportunity Commission, U.S. Civil Service Commission, U.S. Department of Labor, and U.S. Department of Justice (1978). Uniform guidelines on employee selection procedures. *Federal Register, 43*, 38295–38309.

Webster, J., and Starbuck, W. (1988). Theory building in industrial and organizational psychology. In C. Cooper and I. Robertson (Eds.), *International review of industrial and organizational psychology* (vol. 3), pp. 93–138. New York: John Wiley.

Williams, E. (1959). *Regression analysis.* New York: John Wiley.

Wilson, M., Harvey, R., and Macy, B. (1990). Repeating items to estimate the test-retest reliability of task inventory ratings. *Journal of Applied Psychology, 75*, 158–163.

Wilson, W. (1962). A note on the inconsistency inherent in the necessity to perform multiple comparisons. *Psychological Bulletin, 59*, 296–300.

Zaccaro, S., Foti, R., and Kenny, D. (1991). Self-monitoring and trait-based variance in leadership: An investigation of leader flexibility across multiple group situations. *Journal of Applied Psychology, 76*, 308–315.

IV

APPLICATIONS OF PEARSON CORRELATION TO MEASUREMENT THEORY

After reading this chapter, you should be able to:

- Explain the concept of reliability.
- Discuss and define the different types of reliability and the strengths and/or weaknesses of each.
- Explain the concept of validity.
- Explain why information abut a measure's reliability is not necessarily sufficient information to justify implementation of the measure in practice (i.e., explain why validity information is necessary).
- Discuss the different types of validity and indicate their strengths and/or weaknesses, as well as conditions under which you might use each type.
- Differentiate between concurrent and predictive validity.
- Understand which types of validity can be used to assess the validity of a performance measure.
- State the underlying model for classical test theory.
- Define reliability in terms of classical test theory.
- Define the standard error of measurement.
- Correct a correlation for unreliability in one or both variables.
- Explain why, in selection contexts, you might correct for unreliability in the performance measure (Y) but not for unreliability in the test (X).
- Use the Spearman-Brown formula to see how changes in test length will affect reliability.

Now that we have a pretty good idea what a correlation is and how to test it for significance, I thought it might be worthwhile to talk about a set of handy-dandy applications: the different uses of Pearson r in test theory (or, more generally, the theory of measurement). The intent of the current chapter is to whet your appetite for this application by discussing some famous ideas and equations and the reasoning underlying them. It's important to note that measurement theory (sometimes called "psychometric theory" by psychologists) is a topic in and of its own right, and entire books can be written on this subject. Indeed, many have been written (see Ghiselli, Campbell, and Zedeck, 1981, or Nunnally, 1978, for two excellent texts in this area).

Before we begin, note that some of the correlational examples in the earlier chapters exploited a "selection context"; i.e., a selection test (or predictor X) was used to predict a performance measure (or criterion Y). The position taken in this chapter is that both the predictor and the criterion are measures of behavior and therefore *both* X and Y can be considered "tests." Indeed, notions such as reliability and validity (to be discussed below) apply not only to predictors and performance indices but to *any* measures used in the psychological and organizational sciences.[1]

RELIABILITY

Suppose you have a measure of something [say, a selection test (X) that purportedly measures a particular underlying trait or ability]. The motivating question in test theory is, *How do you know test X is a good test*? As you might expect, there will be several ways to answer this question. In the current section, we consider the answer: A test is good if it is *reliable*.

By "reliability," we initially mean that the measurement shows stability over time.

This sure sounds like a good property of a test. For example, if I'm trying to measure your aptitude for a particular job, I would certainly want my measure to give consistent results regardless of whether I gave you the test on a Tuesday or a Wednesday. This stability of results is similarly desired when your instructor tries to measure your knowledge of statistics at the end of the term.

An aside There is controversy in the literature about when psychological traits are expected to be stable and when they are not (e.g., see Mischel, 1968). For example, construct of cognitive ability are usually assumed to be constant

---

[1] The perspective that test theory applies to both predictor and performance measures is consistent with legal decisions on criterion measurement (see Austin and Villanova, 1992, p. 849, for a summary). Further, the U.S. Equal Employment Opportunity Commission (1978, p. 38296) explicitly states that their guidelines apply to "tests and other selection procedures which are used as a basis for any employment decision." Thus, even on the predictor side, psychometric theory should be applied to such diverse tests as traditional paper-and-pencil measures, computerized assessments, interviews, assessment centers, application blanks, and so on.

over time, but some argue that personality traits and attitudes can truly shift across both time and circumstance. In this chapter, we shall assume that the underlying constructs being measured are relatively unchanged across the time periods involved.

st-Retest Reliability

Now let's get back to the purpose of this chapter: applying Pearson r to measurement theory. Suppose we have a test and want to assess its stability over time, i.e., its reliability. In other words, we are asking, Will persons scoring relatively high today also score high next week? Will persons scoring relatively low today also score low next week? etc. The assessment of reliability is conceptually simple.

Give the test (X) to a sample of individuals at time 1. Wait a bit and then give the test (X) *again* to the same individuals at time 2 (the retest). Correlate X at time 1 with X at time 2. The resulting correlation, denoted by r_{XX}, is labeled the "test-retest reliability."

There are many provisos to the above definition, but first note that this really is a simple application of Pearson r. To the extent that r_{XX} approaches 1.0, the ordering of individuals' scores will be the same across time (and the test is said to be "reliable"); to the extent that r_{XX} gets closer to 0, individuals' scores at one point in time are not related to their scores the next time the test is administered.

A quick example   In Chapter II, I presented an example of the correlation between a selection test (X) and subsequent job performance (Y) for air traffic controllers. To estimate the test-retest reliability, suppose the 13 subjects in Table II.1 retook the selection test (X) a few days after the first occasion of predictor testing. Hypothetical test data for the two occasions are presented in Table IV.1.

To calculate the test-retest reliability (r_{XX}) simply call one column of data X and the other column Y and calculate Pearson r using the formula in Equation II.A. I obtained a value of .784. Did you? (Did you even try it?) Social scientists might talk to each other about this result by saying, "The test-retest reliability was $r_{XX} = .784$." And that's just fine—but don't forget that reliability was computed by simply applying Pearson r to the two sets of test scores. By the way, although both columns of data are hypothetical, note that the second column of data has a higher mean (about 10 points greater) than the initial set of test scores. This was done purposively to reflect the possibility that scores might go up, on average, as a result of some practice effect. However, note that if every score goes up by a constant amount, reliability will be unaffected since Pearson r is invariant to linear scale changes (see Chapter II, property 2).

Other issues   It is appropriate to ask, How long should one wait between time 1 and time 2? The answer, of course, is that it depends on the context and

TABLE IV.1 SIMULATOR TEST DATA OBTAINED
AT TIME 1 AND TIME 2

Applicant†	Test at time 1,† X_1	Retest at time 2, X_2
1	35.0	72.0
2	45.0	24.0
3	69.0	58.0
4	182.0	132.0
5	48.7	85.0
6	100.0	82.0
7	25.0	40.0
8	98.0	129.0
9	52.0	92.0
10	8.0	45.0
11	22.8	11.0
12	5.9	40.0
13	19.0	56.0

†From Table II.1.

purpose of the test! For example, in intelligence testing, IQ is presumed to be a stable aspect of individuals, and long-term placement decisions are often based (in part) on assessments of this type. Indeed, it has been shown that many IQ measures demonstrate reliabilities in the .90s even across multiple-year periods. The need for long-term reliability can be argued in employment testing as well, since one is often trying to select individuals on the basis of their predicted eventual on-the-job performance.

On the other hand, many organizations cannot afford to wait several years to assess reliability before they implement a new selection procedure. Further, the longer the time gap, the more other factors might intervene (e.g., an organization trains those it selects, and not everyone develops at the same pace or has identical early career experiences). Thus, test-retest reliability is often assessed in time spans of days rather than years. In sum, researchers often have to carefully balance multiple needs (specification from theory, short-term utility, long-term utility) when determining time spans in a test-retest design.

Alternate Forms Reliability

Substantially reducing the time span in test-retest reliability results in a different set of problems such as short-term learning and reactions to the test when taking it twice. There is extensive documentation of these effects in the social psychological literature (cf. Orne, 1962, or Fromkin and Streufert's, 1976, review).[2] So,

[2] For example, in tests of cognitive ability, you may remember items you missed on the first administration and perseverate on those particular items the second time around. Or, attitudinal tests might heighten your awareness of issues you don't normally think about, and your responses may then become polarized (more extreme) on the second administration.

researchers invented the notion of alternate forms reliability. Again, Pearson r is the statistic of choice. First, give the test (say, X_1); then, instead of giving the same test again at a later point in time, give an alternate form of the test (say, X_2). The correlation between scores on the two forms is the index of alternate forms reliability.

What's an alternate form? Basically, it is the same kind of test; it just has different particular items.[3] For example, if I want to measure your ability to type, the two alternate forms might consist of two different paragraphs (with the paragraphs being of comparable length and difficulty). In the air traffic controller selection example, alternate forms might consist of two versions of the simulator test: the type of required manipulations might be the same, but particular aircraft on the simulator screen might appear at different times and/or locations. The major point for our purposes though is that Pearson r remains the statistic of choice. For example, if the two columns of data in Table IV.1 were individuals' performance on two alternate forms of the selection test, then the correlation between these values (.784) would be labeled the "alternate forms reliability."

Split-Half Reliability

Informally, I label this type of reliability "lazy person's reliability," and I think you'll see why. Note what a pain it is to compute either of the two types of reliabilities previously mentioned. In both instances, you have to give a test, wait a while, find the same people, and administer a test again (and develop an alternate test in the case of alternate forms reliability). If, like many people, you're impatient and want to get the reliability of your test *now*, some folks have used the following trick. Suppose you give a test with 20 items. To use the Pearson r, you need two sets of scores (our old X and Y) for each person. The trick is to say to yourself, "Gee, I really didn't give one test, I gave two. The first test consisted of the odd-numbered items, and the second test consisted of the even-numbered items. Call the two scores X_{odd} and X_{even} and compute the Pearson correlation between them. *That's* the reliability."

In fact, researchers do this all the time and label the resulting correlation "split-half reliability." Actually, they do more sophisticated things like notice there are *many* ways to split the original test into two halves, and in turn they notice there are many split-half correlations that can be computed.[4] Often, researchers take all of these correlations, average them, and report the average as

[3] Psychometricians have devoted much attention to the precise conditions under which two versions of a test are truly alternate forms for one another. They have identified at least three levels of equivalence of two tests. The most restrictive condition for equivalence is parallelism. By "alternate forms" above, I mean that two tests are parallel. In turn, any two such tests will have the same correlation with a criterion measure (see Allen and Yen, 1979, Lord and Novick, 1968, or Hattrup, Schmitt, and Landis, 1992, for excellent discussions of this topic).

[4] Another twist here is to note that when a test is split in two, each new test obviously has only one-half the number of items as the original test. This will result in a lower correlation than if the two scores had both come from longer tests. Indeed, split-half reliabilities are often adjusted upward to correct for this phenomenon (see discussion of the Spearman-Brown prophecy formula, and Equation IV.I later in this chapter).

the split-half reliability (see Cronbach, 1951, or Kuder and Richardson, 1937, for the original derivations of this thinking).[5]

Now, can you think of a problem that's been introduced here? Exactly! We have lost track of our original definition of reliability as stability over time because no time period is involved between the two scores! Rather, split-half reliability measures whether one part of the test is correlated with the other part: what social scientists label the "internal consistency" of the test. So, if you believe you have a measure of some construct (e.g., spatial ability, Type A behavior tendency, creativity), a split-half reliability close to 1.0 means the items in your test are all measuring some common overall attribute. It says nothing about the measure's stability over time. To the extent that split-half reliability is closer to 0, the items are either unreliable themselves or they are measuring stable but mutually unrelated things.[6]

An aside The switch to a focus on internal consistency leads to yet another application of Pearson r—this time in test *construction*. Suppose you assume that the trait being measured is unidimensional. If you have several items $(i_1, i_2, i_3, \ldots, i_n)$ in your test, then the sum of all the items (or T, for total score) is a good estimate of each person's true score on the trait. Now, if you want the items to be internally consistent, then each item should be positively correlated with the trait. Operationally, this means that each item (i) should positively correlate with the total score (T). And that's what some test developers do: they compute r_{iT} for each item. These correlations are even called "r-i-t's" in the literature. (Some researchers prefer removing item i from the total score before computing such correlations.) If r_{iT} is high, the item is kept; if it's low, the item is tossed. Internal consistency is then guaranteed.

In sum, it is important to remember that split-half reliability is not a substitute for test-retest or alternate forms reliability (cf. American Educational Research Association et al., 1985, p. 21; Campbell, 1990). Thus, you should be very careful when reading research articles or trying to decide which test to adopt. A test that results in the same scores over time may not be internally consistent, or

[5] One of these averaged reliabilities, "Cronbach's alpha," is routinely reported in the literature. Just about any empirical article in management or applied psychology will report an alpha reliability for the dependent and/or independent measures. See Cortina (1993) for a terrific review of the applications and misapplications of Cronbach's alpha. Again, the point of this chapter is that such a coefficient, in its standardized form, is an averaging of correlations. And, see Feldt (1969; 1980) for information about hypothesis tests for Cronbach's alpha.

[6] Technically speaking, a high split-half reliability simply means that items can find other items in the test to which they relate. Thus, there may be several subfactors, or subdimensions, in the test even when this reliability is near 1.0. Researchers often mistakenly assume that a high split-half reliability implies homogeneity; i.e., that the items are all measuring precisely the same thing. As Cortina (1993) has pointed out, internal consistency is necessary for homogeneity, but not sufficient.

vice-versa.[7] This is particularly salient since many application contexts require stability across time, yet it is so much easier (and common) to conduct and report split-half reliability studies. Let the buyer beware!

An interlude   In the beginning of Chapter II, nine articles were mentioned as a casual sample of the ubiquitousness of correlations in management and applied psychological research. While editing the current chapter, I went back to those articles and found that the vast majority provided estimated reliabilities for the measures used. Most articles reported only split-half (Cronbach's alpha) reliabilities. One article (Deci, Connell, and Ryan, 1989), presented both split-half (.70) and test-retest (.80) reliabilities for a measure of supervisory "support for self-determination." The test-retest reliability was computed across a 4-month period.

In the other articles, typical split-half reliabilities were .90 for a measure of positive affect at work (Pelled and Xin, 1999), .92 for interviewer impressions (Phillips and Dipboye, 1989), and values between .83 and .91 for measures of personality and attitudes (Potosky and Bobko, 1997). Interestingly, a few articles claimed that some internal consistency estimates were inadequate. For example, Deci et al. computed a reliability of .51 for a measure of perceived freedom and subsequently dropped that variable from analysis. And, Ashford, Lee, and Bobko (1989) computed a reliability of .44 for someone else's measure of job insecurity. Those authors noted that results surrounding this variable should be interpreted cautiously. Finally, Potosky and Bobko reported a reliability of .11 for a scale measuring random responding. In this instance, the reliability was not questionable—due to the fact that the scale was supposed to be assessing random responding! I think that you, the reader, can see a few things from the above. First, reliabilities measuring stability over time are rare. Second, there seems to be an implicit assumption that split-half reliabilities over .70 or so are minimally acceptable. Indeed, it is typical in the field to cite Nunnally (1978) when invoking such a standard. However, a careful reading of that text (see pages 245–246) indicates that .70 was recommended for early stages of research. For applied, operational settings, Nunnally recommended higher standards.

By the way, Peterson (1994) conducted a meta-analysis of over four thousand values of Cronbach's alpha for measures across a variety of psychology and marketing journals. He found a median reliability of .79. And, on the criterion side of things, a meta-analysis by Viswesvaran, Ones, and Schmidt (1996) reported an average alpha of .86 for supervisory ratings of job performance.

---

[7] A recent instance of this distinction is reported in Campbell and Zook (1990). In their table 2–3, they report the properties of a variety of tests considered for selecting people for military service. Split-half and test-retest reliabilities have differing magnitudes. For example, consider a test where recruits must visually reorient two-dimensional objects (object rotation test). One measure of the internal consistency of this test was .97, yet the test-retest reliability (across a 2-week period) was only .75.

VALIDITY

In the quest to answer the question "What is a good test?" we initially suggested that reliability (conceived as stability over time) was a useful definition. However, suppose I wish to measure a person's aptitude to engage in creative thinking and I tell you that I have a measure of this construct that has a test-retest reliability of $r_{xx} = 1.0$. This sounds pretty good until I tell you that my measure is the last four digits of each person's social security number! That is, people who score high on this "test" today will score high next year; ditto for everyone else. But something's missing. What is it? Exactly! The test is reliable, but it doesn't measure what it purports to measure! So, another property of a good test is labeled "validity":

> **By "validity," we simply mean that a test is measuring the attribute it intends to measure.**

We shall briefly consider four different ways to measure validity: face, content, criterion-related, and construct validity. The latter two typically involve use of Pearson r's and, after all, that's our focus here. Again, if any of this tweaks your interest—and I hope it does—track down the many excellent books on measurement theory. [The "Uniform Guidelines on Employee Selection Procedures" (U.S. Equal Employment Opportunity Commission et al., 1978) also has a very thorough discussion of requirements for conducting content, criterion-related, and construct validation efforts.]

Face Validity

Face validity simply refers to the idea that the test (more generally, the measure) that is used *looks* like the appropriate test. For example, suppose your instructor gave you an exam covering the first three chapters of this book and all items looked like the following: Evaluate $\int_{-\infty}^{\infty} (1/\sqrt{2\pi}) e^{-x^2/2} dx$. Seeing this, you might question the face validity of the exam because this item doesn't necessarily look like it measures your knowledge of statistics.[8] Thus, face validity is simply a subjective judgment that the test accurately reflects the thing you're trying to measure. (Another example? When they first see it, lots of people question the face validity of the Rorschach ink blot test for measuring personality dispositions. Can you think of other tests you've seen where face validity was questionable?)

Content Validity

The idea here is that the content of your measure systematically reflects the construct you're trying to identify. For example, in constructing an end-of-the-semester exam, the instructor might go through the notes from his or her class lectures. This constitutes the universe that's being assessed. In content validity,

---

[8] In case you're interested, this item is related to statistical knowledge, but not at the level of this book. The question asks you to demonstrate that the area under a standard normal curve really is 1.0.

one samples from this universe (i.e., takes certain concepts from each week's lectures) and tries to write items that reflect those samples—thereby helping to ensure that the content of the test reflects the measurement purpose. Thus, content validity is assessed by evaluations of (1) how well the universe of interest has been defined, (2) how systematically one has sampled from that universe, and (3) how accurately the items reflect the sampled domains. Indeed, for almost every test you've ever taken in college, content validity probably formed the basis for the exam. As another example, consider the development of performance appraisal measures. This is often preceded by a very thorough job analysis in which the critically important behaviors, both manifest and cognitive, are heavily sampled and measured.[9] As yet a different example, a thorough job analysis may also precede the content validity based development of a selection test. That is, important tasks for a particular job would be identified, and these tasks would be linked to requisite knowledges, skills, and abilities. In turn, test batteries would be developed which assess these particular constructs. Because content validity typically does not make substantial use of Pearson r's, we will cut short the explanation at this point (again see measurement texts, or selection texts such as Gatewood and Feild, 1998, for more complete details).

Criterion-related Validity

Here's where we get to the Pearson r again! To think about criterion-related validity in the selection test arena, we just need to extend the definition of "validity" from Does a test measure what it's supposed to measure? to Does a test do what it's supposed to do? In selection, the test is supposed to predict performance. So, call the test X and the performance Y. The Pearson r between X and Y is referred to as the test's validity! And, because the performance measure is sometimes called the "criterion," the r is labeled "criterion-related validity." Indeed, such a use of Pearson r is the predominant application in this book. Even in the first example in Chapter II, we considered the correlation between simulator test scores (X) and air traffic controller performance (Y). Because the correlation in this example was $r_{XY} = .75$, most researchers I know would summarize this finding by saying, "The validity of the selection test was .75." By the way, there's a very important caveat here. To say "the validity" can be misleading. For example, the above value of $r_{XY} = .75$ refers to the validity of a measure in a particular context using a particular performance measure. The validity (i.e., value of the correlation) might change substantially if the context (e.g., organization) or performance measure was changed (although the possibility that validities are invariant to some situations is discussed in a later section on validity generalization). The point here is that a test doesn't have

---

[9] If you read recent scientific and legal papers, you'll see that content validity is a strategy that is being increasingly used in the field. However, there is some work indicating that tests developed by item content strategies may be very different than tests developed using criterion-related validity strategies (see Carrier, DaLessio, and Brown, 1990; Ostroff and Schmitt, 1987).

a validity. In fact, the *test* doesn't have validity. Rather, the value of *r* assesses the validity of the *application* of a test to a particular situation.

> ***Is Your Interest Tweaked?*** As noted above, the point of introducing validity in this book is simply to help you understand how Pearson *r* might be used by some folks. If you're interested, feel free to read other works in this area. There are actually written principles for validation efforts (e.g., Society for Industrial and Organizational Psychology, 1987) that present many issues that need to be addressed when conducting a criterion-related validity study (hence computing *r*). For example, the job must be relatively stable; otherwise your prediction of performance (r_{XY}) might be suspect. The performance measure (*Y*) should be relevant and free from contaminating factors.[10] Also, the sample on which *r* is computed should be both (i) representative and (ii) of sufficient size to stabilize estimates of *r*.

The notion of criterion-related validity is often further split into the concepts of predictive and concurrent validity. "Predictive validity" is pretty much what we have been discussing: you give a selection test (*X*), wait a while, collect job performance data (*Y*), and correlate the two sets of scores. However, organizations often feel they cannot wait a while for applicants to be selected, then trained, then placed on the job; i.e., they want to make a selection test decision *now*.[11] Such organizations might take job *incumbents* and measure their performance (*Y*). The incumbents are also asked to take the selection test (*X*) that is being investigated. The correlation between *X* and *Y* is then labeled "concurrent validity"; i.e., both measures are taken at the same time (concurrently). The question then becomes, "Is concurrent validity a good substitute for (estimate of) predictive validity? Some folks suggest these types of validities are not interchangeable. After all, job incumbents may not be very motivated when they take the selection test (*X*) because they already have the job. Also, the distribution of incumbent ability scores may be altered by the fact that low performers have been fired and high performers have been promoted out of the job (see Chapter V on range restriction). Further, all those years of experience may have truly changed the incumbents' abilities and in turn their scores on *X*.[12] You might be interested to know that reviews of the literature indicate that, for tests of cognitive abilities, empirical validities from predictive and concurrent studies seem to be similar (Barrett, Phillips, and Alexander, 1981; Schmitt, Gooding, Noe, and Kirsch, 1984). On the other hand, empirical evidence suggests this distinction may matter for other types of tests such as personality measures (e.g., Schmit and Ryan, 1992).

[10] Otherwise, note that you could artificially increase the validity (r_{XY}) of a test by having both *Y* and *X* be contaminated by the same factor (e.g., both *Y* and *X* are ratings, and both contain gender bias that favors the same group).

[11] This is the same type of motive that led to the use of split-half reliability in place of test-retest reliability.

[12] Of course, if *everyone's* score increased by the *same* amount as a result of training and job experience, then the correlation will remain unaffected (see Property 2 in Chapter II if you don't get this!).

Construct Validity

In a selection context, we assessed the validity of a test by exploiting the purpose of the test: prediction of performance (Y). This trick will work only sometimes. For example, if we want to assess the validity of the performance measure (Y), it is difficult to figure out what to correlate Y with. That is, measures of performance aren't predicting anything. They have use in and of themselves (as criterion measures). Similarly, there are many constructs in the field that are studied pretty much for their scientific merit (e.g., job commitment, job security, satisfaction, anxiety, etc.). We need to have a way of assessing the validity of measures of these variables. The strategy often invoked in these situations is labeled "construct validity."[13]

While the assessment of construct validity can be very detailed (cf. Campbell and Fiske, 1959), let me try a simplified explanation. Suppose you want to assess the construct validity of a measure (Y) of some construct. Based on your theory of that construct, you hypothesize that Y should be positively related to some variables (other Y's or X's), not related to other variables, and possibly even negatively related to yet another group of variables. This hypothesized network of expected relationships is labeled the "nomological net." You conduct the construct validity study by measuring the Y of interest and as many of these other variables as you can get your hands on. *Then, compute the Pearson r's between Y and all these variables and see if the pattern of correlations makes sense (i.e., fits your expectations).* If so, then you're more confident that Y is measuring what it purports to (i.e., it's valid). So, Pearson r can play a crucial role in the assessment of construct, as well as criterion-related, validity. (By the way, note that one never proves construct validity because there are always other variables to look at. But, you can increase the weight of evidence that your measure is valid.)

A quick example   We (Ashford, Lee, and Bobko, 1989) once developed a measure of job insecurity (Y) and wanted to demonstrate its validity. There was no singular purpose in developing such a measure, so a straightforward criterion-related validity strategy could not be invoked. Based on a theory of job insecurity, we suggested that our measure would have particular correlations with other variables; e.g., increases in insecurity should be *positively* associated with anticipated changes in the organization, role ambiguity, somatic complaints, intent to leave, etc. We also suggested that perceptions of job insecurity would be *negatively* related to trust in the organization, organizational commitment, etc. (e.g., the more insecurity, the less trust). Finally, we suggested that our measure of insecurity would correlate with other preexisting measure of insecurity (but not perfectly, because we suggested ours was more complete). Amazingly, all these

---

[13] The variables being assessed are often called "hypothetical constructs." Hence the term "construct" validity. This is a fascinating topic in the philosophy of research methods, and I encourage you to read about it (see classic articles by Cronbach and Meehl, 1995, and MacCorquodale and Meehl, 1948, which started all the discussion; for an excellent, more recent interpretation see Schmitt and Landy, 1993).

correlations turned out to be in the anticipated direction. For example, our insecurity measure correlated .46 with organizational changes, .09 with somatic complaints, .46 with role ambiguity, −.47 with organizational commitment, and −.51 with trust in the organization. Further, our measure correlated .48 and .35 with two existing measures of job insecurity. Again, while we didn't completely prove our measure was valid, we had increased confidence in our measure because it was correlationally "behaving" like one! Isn't the use of correlations fun?

SOME RESULTS IN THE THEORY OF MEASUREMENT

In this section, some very interesting and useful results (and equations) about measurement theory are presented and discussed. As it turns out, they are all quite readily proved. So as not to disrupt the flow of presentations, I have removed the proofs and placed them in the next major section of this chapter. While you definitely want to read the current section, you may be tempted to skip the proofs later on. You certainly may, but first let me say, "Don't be intimidated by them!" The derivations are not necessarily difficult to follow, and my students are often amazed by how readily such famous and useful results can be derived.

Before we get to the results, however, it's important to realize that they are based on "classical test theory." The basic premise of classical test theory is that when you measure someone on a variable, their score (say, X) is made up of two components: the true amount of their ability (or attitude, or performance, etc.), which is sometimes labeled T, and some random error (labeled e). Thus,

IV.A
$$X = T + e$$

Intuitively speaking, the greater the effect of e, the more unreliable X is. Again, the component e is random error—presumably due to lots of factors such as the day the measure was taken, how the person was feeling, the particular items chosen, etc. The component e is assumed to be random and centered at a value of 0. On some days e will be positive; on other days it will be negative. Thus, on average, the factor e won't matter, but it will introduce unwanted variance in test scores from day to day. In turn, by making traditional assumptions of test theory (see next section), it can also be shown that, across individuals,

IV.B
$$\sigma_X^2 = \sigma_T^2 + \sigma_e^2$$

That is, when you measure individuals with test X, people differ on their resulting scores (i.e., σ_X^2 is not zero). Equation IV.B states that these differences are due to two things: (1) the people differ on the trait in question (i.e., σ_T^2 is not zero), and (2) there may be some random error in your measure that causes apparent differences (i.e., σ_e^2 is not zero). In this context, reliability is defined as the proportion of σ_X^2 due to true variance (σ_T^2). Thus,

IV.C
$$\text{Reliability of } X = r_{XX} = \frac{\sigma_T^2}{\sigma_X^2}$$

Note that when there is no random error, $\sigma_e^2 = 0$ and the denominator of Equation IV.C then becomes $\sigma_X^2 = \sigma_T^2 + \sigma_e^2 = \sigma_T^2$. Thus, reliability $= \sigma_T^2/\sigma_X^2$ $= \sigma_T^2/\sigma_T^2 = 1.0$. On the other hand, if σ_e^2 is large, then the denominator of Equation IV.C ($\sigma_X^2 = \sigma_T^2 + \sigma_e^2$) becomes large relative to the numerator, and the reliability is lowered. If the error variance "takes over" completely, then r_{XX} will become 0. With the above as context, we are now ready for some results.

Reliability as a Proportion of Variance

It can be shown that

IV.D
$$\text{Reliability} = r_{XX} = r_{XT}^2$$

This is a fascinating result because, as noted at the beginning of this chapter, reliability is conceptually the correlation between the same test measured on two occasions (hence the symbol r_{XX}). Now, in Chapter II (and we'll come back to this in Chapter VI) we noted that if you squared a correlation, the result indicated the percentage of variance in one variable associated with the variance in another variable. But Equation IV.D points out that the reliability already has a squared interpretation—you needn't square it again! Thus, if the reliability of a measure is $r_{XX} = .70$, then 70% of the variance in test scores (X) is associated with variance in true, underlying scores (T) across individuals.

Standard Error of Measurement

When I talked about the variance of test scores (σ_X^2), I was very careful to note that this is a variance computed *across individuals*. As noted by the model in Equation IV.A, such variance is incurred because of unreliability *and* because people truly differ on the trait in question. In this section, I ask you to switch gears a bit: Suppose you took a test over and over again (i.e., the same person takes the test over and over). Your actual (observed) scores might fluctuate if there was any unreliability in the test. However, by definition, your true score would not change, and thus the variance of your scores across time would be less than the variance of scores across all individuals.

Now, it is traditional to talk about the standard deviation of your scores across time rather than your variance. The hypothetical standard deviation of *your* scores, across test occasions, is labeled the "standard error of measurement" (SEM). It can be shown that

IV.E
$$\text{SEM} = \sigma_X\sqrt{1 - r_{XX}}$$

Notice that this equation starts with the standard deviation of scores across all individuals (σ_X) and reduces this value by the factor $\sqrt{1 - r_{XX}}$. Indeed, as the reliability of the test increases, SEM is reduced. This makes sense: i.e., the more reliable the test, the smaller the standard deviation of your scores across many testing occasions.

An example   In IQ testing, it is typical for reliabilities to be over .90. Let's assume $r_{XX} = .92$. Further, some IQ tests are constructed such that the standard deviation across individuals is 15 points and the mean is 100. Thus, I assume that $\sigma_X = 15$. Application of Equation IV.E is easy and yields SEM = $15\sqrt{1 - .92} = 15\sqrt{.08} = 4.24$. This value (4.24) is the standard deviation attached to your hypothetical distribution of scores and indexes how much difference in IQ you should expect if you took the test on multiple occasions. Indeed, suppose you took the test once and obtained a score of 120. Assuming normal theory, you could add and subtract 1.96 × SEM to obtain a 95% confidence interval for your true IQ.[14] (Try it! I obtained the interval 111.69 to 128.31 for the above example. Do you agree?)

Another example   Sometimes the SEM can be larger than expected. Suppose you work for a corporation where your annual performance appraisal (Y) is presented on a 5-point scale (1 through 5). Suppose individuals receiving 4s and 5s get raises, yet you received only a 3. Is all lost? Perhaps not. Suppose the appraisal process has a reliability of $r_{YY} = .70$. (Note the change here to r_{YY} because we're talking about performance.) Suppose further that the standard deviation of appraisal ratings (across everyone in the company) on this 5-point scale is about $\sigma_Y = 1.0$. Then, SEM = $1.0\sqrt{1 - .70} = 1.0\sqrt{.30} = .548$ and the 95% confidence interval for your true performance would be $3.0 \pm 1.96(.548)$, or the interval 1.93 to 4.07. Note that the confidence interval *does* go over the cutoff point for a raise!

Corrections for Unreliability

Suppose we have two measures (X and Y) and we apply the classical test theory model to each. Thus, we have

$$X = T_X + e_X \quad \text{and} \quad Y = T_Y + e_y$$

For example, in a selection context, the test score is made up of true ability and random error; similarly, the performance measure is composed of a person's true performance plus any random error incurred when measuring job performance.

Now, all through this book, we have been talking about the population correlation between our operational measures Y and X (ρ_{YX}). Notice, though, that this correlation can be "contaminated" since both Y and X might have error in them. Wouldn't it be nice to know the correlation between T_X and T_Y? This would tell us what the correlation would be if we could find a completely reliable measure of both Y and X (i.e., no random error anywhere). Well, it can be shown

---

[14] Just a reminder: the value 1.96 is the critical value from a normal table with a two-sided interval and $p = .05$ (see the last row of Table A.1 in the Appendix).

that

IV.F
$$\rho_{T_X T_Y} = \frac{\rho_{YX}}{\sqrt{\rho_{XX}} \sqrt{\rho_{YY}}}$$

This is a truly amazing equation. Note what the right-hand side of the equation says we should do. Start with the correlation between Y and X. Then divide that correlation by the square root to the reliabilities of both Y and X. The result on the left-hand side is the correlation between true Y and true X scores. You're then estimating the correlation with all unreliability removed. Therefore, Equation IV.F is sometimes labeled the "correction for unreliability" (see Muchinsky, 1996, for a recent review of this correction formula). In sample notation, this correction becomes

IV.G
$$r_{T_X T_Y} = \text{corrected } r = \frac{r_{YX}}{\sqrt{r_{XX}} \sqrt{r_{YY}}}$$

It's also useful to turn Equation IV.G around and solve for r_{YX}:

IV.H
$$r_{YX} = \left(\sqrt{r_{XX}} \sqrt{r_{YY}} \right) \left(r_{T_X T_Y} \right)$$

I think this makes the effect of unreliability pretty clear. That is, suppose T_X and T_Y are substantially correlated. To the extent that you measure X or Y with any unreliability (i.e., r_{XX} or r_{YY} is less than 1.0) your *observed* correlation (r_{YX}) will be smaller in magnitude than the theoretical correlation between the true scores.

An example   George (1990) reported the correlation between negative affect (Y) and prosocial behavior within groups (X) to be $r_{YX} = -.17$ (i.e., negative thoughts lead to less social behavior). She also corrected this coefficient for unreliability by noting that average reliabilities for Y and X were, respectively, $r_{YY} = .87$ and $r_{XX} = .88$. Thus, application of Equation IV.G yields

$$\text{Corrected } r = \frac{-.17}{\sqrt{.88} \sqrt{.87}} = -.194$$

which is consistent (within rounding error) with the value reported by George (1990, p. 113). Thus, the best estimate of the correlation between true negative affect and true prosocial behaviors is about $-.19$.

Hypothesis testing   In the previous chapter, we noted that the null hypothesis $H_0: \rho_{YX} = 0$ could be tested using the sample value of Pearson r and the following t-test (see discussion of Equation III.A):

$$t_{n-2} \sim \frac{r}{\sqrt{(1 - r^2)/(n - 2)}}$$

This t-ratio places r in the numerator and the standard deviation of r in the denominator. It is important to realize that the value of r in this t-ratio should be the original sample value of r *and not the value of r corrected for unreliability*. Thus, in the previous example the value of $-.17$ (and not $-.19$) can be tested for significance. The reason? The t-ratio is derived assuming the sample Pearson r is computed. In turn, the denominator of the t-ratio is the standard deviation of r, i.e., how much variation in r we can expect from sample to sample. By computing corrected r in Equation IV.G we are introducing more sources of variation (i.e., our estimates of reliability can vary from sample to sample, too!). So, the denominator of the t-ratio is not the appropriate standard deviation for testing corrected r. In the literature, it is therefore customary to test the original, uncorrected Pearson r for statistical significance and then report corrected r as the best point estimate of the true relationship between the variables.[15]

Some Validity Implications

Corrections for unreliability are often used by researchers conducting selection test validity studies. As noted above, an index of empirical validity is the correlation between selection test scores (X) and performance (Y), or r_{YX}. To the extent that X or Y is unreliable, the computed validity will be closer to zero than if the true scores had been known. So one might consider correcting validities for unreliability. In validation work, it is customary to correct r_{YX} for unreliability in Y but not for unreliability in X. That is, you are trying to assess the validity of the test you have and not some perfect test (which you don't have anyway). Therefore don't correct for unreliability in the test (X). On the other hand, it can be argued that individuals on the job are doing what they're doing! If you happen to measure their performance unreliably, that's your problem. It's not a reflection of their actual (true) performance, and you ought to correct for this unreliability in Y. Thus, in validation work Equation IV. G reduces to

$$r_{XT_Y} = \text{somewhat corrected } r = \frac{r_{YX}}{\sqrt{r_{YY}}}$$

This is the correction you'll often see reported in test validation research.

There's one more aspect of validity that is based on the equations here. Start with Equation IV.H but ignore any unreliability in Y (i.e., assume $r_{YY} = 1.0$).

[15] Actually, Bobko and Rieck (1980) derived the standard deviation of correlations corrected for unreliability, so the corrected r can be tested directly. However, the derivation is accurate only for large samples, and the appropriate standard deviation is rather complicated (e.g., it depends on how the reliability coefficients were computed). Note that we shall consider corrections for range restriction in the next chapter. In contrast to corrections for unreliability, the appropriate standard deviation for range restriction corrections is straightforward and can be more readily used when testing hypotheses.

Then,

$$r_{YX} = \sqrt{r_{XX}}\,(r_{T_X T_Y})$$

Now, what's the maximum value that $r_{T_X T_Y}$ can have? Right! Since it's a correlation, the maximum value is 1.0. Thus, the maximum value for r_{YX} is $\sqrt{r_{XX}}\,(1.0)$. Or, as is usually written,

$$r_{YX} \leq \sqrt{r_{XX}}$$

Note that the left-hand side is a validity; the right-hand side contains a reliability coefficient. We have therefore demonstrated the following well-known statement:

The validity of a test can be no greater than the square root of its reliability.

This is a fun fact. If you know a test has low reliability, then you know it won't "validate" (i.e., won't correlate highly with any Y-variable). This fact also demonstrates that reliability is necessary, but not sufficient, for validity. That is, even if $r_{XX} = 1.0$, the validity could still take on any value.[16]

Test Length

Suppose I want to measure some individual difference (e.g., your ability to divide four-digit numbers). In general, the more questions I give you, the more reliably I will measure your ability. Think about this intuitively: if the test has only one or two items, you might make a silly mistake on one question and your percentage score would be very low. All else equal, the more items the better. (*Note*: "All else equal" assumes a lot here. I need to assume that I can write more questions that are equally good, that you don't get fatigued answering them, etc.)

Let the number of items on a test be called the "length" of the test, and let's work in multiples of test length (the multiplication factor will be called k). For example, suppose a test has 10 items. If I increase the test length by a factor of $k = 3$, the new test will have $k(10) = 3 \times 10 = 30$ items. Now suppose the original test (with 10 items) has a reliability of r_{XX}. It can be shown that *if the test length is changed by a factor of k, then the reliability of the new test ($r_{\text{new, new}}$) will be*

IV.I
$$r_{\text{new, new}} = \frac{k r_{XX}}{1 + (k - 1) r_{XX}}$$

This equation is often called the "Spearman-Brown prophecy formula" [named after the two people who originally developed it (Brown, 1910; Spearman, 1910)

---

[16] There are many studies in the social sciences that empirically investigate the reliability and validity of particular measures. See either Borman (1978) or Weekley and Gier (1989) for articles looking at empirical upper limits on reliability (versus the theoretical upper limit of 1.0). The latter article uses a unique data base: judgments of Olympic figure skating.

and the fact that it predicts reliability values]. It is a lot of fun to use. For example, go back to the air traffic controller selection test considered at the beginning of the chapter (and in Table IV.1). Our estimate of reliability was $r_{XX} = .784$. Suppose that the test had 30 items and we wanted to increase its reliability by doubling the number of items. In our notation then, $k = 2$. So, Equation IV.I says

$$r_{\text{new,new}} = \frac{2(.784)}{1 + (2 - 1)(.784)} = .879$$

and our estimate of the reliability of the longer test is .879 (again assuming the added items are equally good and test takers don't get bored or fatigued as a result of the increased length).

The beauty of the Spearman-Brown formula (Equation IV.I) is obvious: it allows one to estimate changes in reliability (as a function of changes in test length) without having to conduct a new empirical study! I should also tell you that the formula works for noninteger values of k (e.g., if the test goes from 30 to 45 items, just use $k = 1.5$). It also works for values of k less than 1.0, so you can judge how much loss in reliability would be incurred if you shortened your test. Finally, you can start with the original reliability (r_{XX}) and a desired reliability ($r_{\text{new,new}}$) and solve the equation for k. This of course will tell you how long you need to make your test to get the desired reliability. I told you it was fun!

What the Field's Been Doing Lately

Validity generalization   One well-known topic in validation research concerns the issue of "validity generalization" (cf. Burke, 1984; Callender and Osburn, 1980; Schmidt and Hunter, 1977). The hypothesis of transportability in validity generalization is that a set of correlations (across studies, measurement methods, populations, etc.) are all nonzero and all have the same sign. For example, if I knew a selection test (X) was empirically valid in one organization, then I might potentially defend its use in a different but similar organization by invoking validity generalization.

Now, while it has been documented that test validities (i.e., values of r_{XY}) differ across studies, validity generalization researchers are quick to point out that some of these differences may be more apparent than real. For example, if two organizations measure performance (Y) with differing degrees of unreliability (i.e., values of r_{YY} are different) then, using Equation IV.H, it should be clear that values of r_{XY} will be different even if the true relationships (i.e., $r_{T_X T_Y}$) are the same! So, validity generalization folks first correct their correlations for unreliability and then look for any differences in correlations across the corrected correlations.[17] The cumulation of validities, as well as other effect sizes, across a

---

[17] In this chapter we have considered the effects of unreliability on correlational differences. In the next chapter, the phenomenon of range restriction will be considered as another cause of the apparent differences in r's.

particular research literature has generally been subsumed under the rubric of meta-analysis, which is a bit beyond the scope of this text (see Hunter and Schmidt, 1990, for a good explanation if you are interested). Meta-analysis attempts to correct results in each study not only for unreliability but for a variety of statistical artifacts. The corrected effect sizes are then analyzed for any remaining variation across situations or conditions. Validity generalization and meta-analytic procedures probably provide the most frequent context in which corrections for unreliability are applied in the social sciences. These procedures provide researchers with another very useful set of analytic procedures, but they have not gone uncriticized (see Bobko and Stone-Romero, 1998, or ''validity generalization revisited'' in Chapter V).

Generalizability theory   In thinking about reliability, we started with the classical test theory model of Equation IV.A: $X = T + e$. Recall that we initially defined reliability as stability over time, and we found that a test-retest study allowed us to estimate how much variation in the scores was due to random error (e) across time. Now, go back to the model $X = T + e$ for a moment. In order to describe generalizability theory, you must understand that *there are many potential sources of error in the measurement process*. For example, suppose our measure (X) is a rating of an applicant's interview on the dimension ''has high need for achievement.'' It may be that variation in scores across time is due to (1) the fact that different interviewers (raters) were used on the two occasions, (2) different questions (items) were asked on the two occasions, (3) the two interviews took place for different jobs, etc. Thus, we may wish to take the random measurement component e and break it down into its multiple sources.[18] This extension of classical test theory to account for multiple sources of error has been labeled ''generalizability theory'' (see Cronbach, Gleser, Nanda, and Rajaratnam, 1972, or Shavelson, Webb, and Rowley, 1989, for detailed accounts).

Thus, generalizability theory researchers might systematically vary dimensions (called ''facets'') along which error might occur. Facets might include raters, the type of item (e.g., hands-on demonstration versus a paper-and-pencil test), context of test administration, etc. Based on this systematic variation, one can estimate how much each facet contributes to the overall value of σ_e^2. One of the beauties of generalizability theory is that it can then take this knowledge and combine it with the test length formulas above. That is, generalizability theory [using what are called ''decision'' (or D) studies] can help decide which facets should be increased in length in order to most efficiently increase reliability.[19] For example, such a study might find that simply using two types of items (e.g., observing a simulation *and* an interview) will have a greater increase on reliability than quadrupling the number of raters on either type of test. This combined use of generalizability theory and test length has been productively

---

[18] By the way, we could have mentioned this type of thinking when we introduced alternate forms reliability. In that case, we computed the correlation between a test and its alternate form. We thereby introduced a second reason why r might be less than 1.0; i.e., in addition to random variation over time, the alternate form itself might be a source of differences in scores.

[19] Note the subtle shift here. Depending on the facet, ''length'' may mean the number of items of a particular type, the number of raters, or the number of different types of items.

applied in assessing the reliability and validity of job ratings (Fraser, Cronshaw, and Alexander, 1984; Webb, Shavelson, Shea, and Morello, 1981) and ratings of individual performance (Kraiger and Teachout, 1990).

Item length Equation IV.I clearly indicated that, all else equal, reliability increases as the number of items (test length) increases. There has also been research on the optimal number of responses for each item, or what I'll call "item length." For example, self-reports of attitude are often presented on 5-point scales (go back to the "smiley-face" scale of job satisfaction in Figure 2.3 of Chapter II if you want to see such a scale). Performance appraisal ratings often take the same form. In fact, rating scales with five ordered options are often called "Likert scales," named after the person who first proposed and scientifically investigated them (see Likert, 1932). During the past several decades, it has been suggested that responses to such items would be more reliable if they contained 7, 11, or even 20 or more categories. However, the original work of Likert and computer simulations by Cicchetti, Showalter, and Tyrer (1985) and Jenkins and Taber (1977) clearly indicate that *reliability* plateaus once the number of response options reaches 5 or 7. On the other hand (couldn't you feel that coming?), recent evidence indicates that the *validity* of a measure may depend upon the number of scale points. For example, it has been shown that the capacity to statistically detect interactions in regression analyses (see Chapter IX) depends upon the number of scale points used for the performance measure (Russell and Bobko, 1992; Russell, Pinto, and Bobko, 1991). This research indicates that performance should be measured on a continuum (or near continuum) whenever practically possible. For example, all else equal, using 100-point scales is preferable to using measures which have only a handful of scale points. Indeed, in response to these findings, Aguinis, Bommer, and Pierce (1996) have developed computer software that makes it possible for participants to provide responses that can be scored in a nearly continuous manner. In sum, reliability is unaffected when item length (i.e., the number of scale points) goes beyond 5 or 7, but the validity of explanatory models that use such measures may suffer.

SOME OPTIONAL, BUT EASY, PROOFS

As an optional section, here are some proofs of many of the equations presented in this chapter. As noted earlier, the equations can be derived in a straightforward manner, and following the proofs can be (as they say) quite instructive. The thinking needed to follow them can really help to cement your understanding of how correlations can be put to good use. Before we do this, however, we need to talk a bit about the concept of covariance because our proofs will be much easier if we use covariances in the derivations.

xploiting the Covariance

In a footnote to the formula for Pearson r (see Equation II.A), it was noted that dividing the numerator by the value $n - 1$ resulted in the covariance between X and Y [which we shall denote by cov (X, Y)]. That is,

IV.J
$$\text{cov}(X, Y) = \frac{\Sigma(X - \bar{X})(Y - \bar{Y})}{n - 1}$$

As noted in that footnote, the "covariance" is an index of relationship between X and Y, but it is scale-dependent. That's why the equation for Pearson r had such a complicated denominator—to ensure that r was invariant to scale changes. Further, starting with Equation II.A for Pearson r and dividing through by $n - 1$, it easily follows that

$$r = \frac{\Sigma(X - \bar{X})(Y - \bar{Y})}{\sqrt{\Sigma(X - \bar{X})^2}\sqrt{\Sigma(Y - \bar{Y})^2}}$$

$$= \frac{\dfrac{\Sigma(X - \bar{X})(Y - \bar{Y})}{n - 1}}{\sqrt{\dfrac{\Sigma(X - \bar{X})^2}{n - 1}}\sqrt{\dfrac{\Sigma(Y - \bar{Y})^2}{n - 1}}}$$

and therefore

IV.K
$$r = \frac{\text{cov}(X, Y)}{s_X s_Y}$$

Equation IV.K is a fact that is well known by almost every social scientist who conducts correlational research. It points out that the correlation is the covariance between X and Y, divided by the product of their standard deviations. Rearranging terms in Equation IV.K yields another useful form of this fact:

IV.L
$$\text{cov}(X, Y) = r(s_X s_Y)$$

Now for some fun with the equations. In fact, within a page or so, we will have derived four very useful properties of covariances, which will then be used in the test theory proofs. First, consider the question, What is the covariance between X and X? Well, take Equation IV.J and where you see X, put X; where you see Y, also put X. Thus, $\text{cov}(X, X) = [\Sigma(X - \bar{X})(X - \bar{X})]/(n - 1) = \Sigma(X - \bar{X})^2/(n - 1) = s_x^2$. So, the covariance between X and X is the variance of X!

Second, suppose I have two variables again (say, X and Y) and I know $\text{cov}(X, Y)$. However, suppose I make a linear transformation of one of the variables: i.e., I use $a + bX$ instead of just plain old X.[20] Then, from Equation IV.J,

$$\text{cov}(a + bX, Y) = \frac{\Sigma(a + bX - \overline{a + bX})(Y - \overline{Y})}{n - 1}$$

$$= \frac{\Sigma(a + bX - a - b\overline{X})(Y - \overline{Y})}{n - 1}$$

$$= \frac{\Sigma b(X - \overline{X})(Y - \overline{Y})}{n - 1}$$

$$= \frac{b\Sigma(X - \overline{X})(Y - \overline{Y})}{n - 1} = b\,\text{cov}(X, Y)$$

This is a very useful fact. Note that adding a constant (i.e., a) won't change the covariance, yet multiplying X by a constant (i.e., b) will change the covariance by that factor. (Contrast this with the fact that Pearson r would be unaffected by either a or b.)

We need one more fact, and then we can get on with our proofs. Suppose we now consider linear combinations of variables (i.e., $aX + bY$). This might be useful if X and Y are two items on a test and we want to obtain the total test score by letting $a = b = 1$. Or, perhaps X_1 and X_2 are two selection tests and we want to combine them before making any selection decisions. Almost all of our applications below will be in situations where the weights are 1.0 (e.g., $a = b = 1$). With two variables on each side of the covariance, we ask the question, What is the covariance between $X + Y$ and $Z + W$? Well,

$$\text{cov}(X + Y, Z + W)$$

$$= \frac{\Sigma(X + Y - \overline{X + Y})(Z + W - \overline{Z + W})}{n - 1}$$

$$= \frac{\Sigma\left[(X - \overline{X}) + (Y - \overline{Y})\right]\left[(Z - \overline{Z}) + (W - \overline{W})\right]}{n - 1}$$

$$= \frac{\Sigma(X - \overline{X})(Z - \overline{Z}) + \Sigma(X - \overline{X})(W - \overline{W}) + \Sigma(Y - \overline{Y})(Z - \overline{Z}) + \Sigma(Y - \overline{Y})(W - \overline{W})}{n - 1}$$

$$= \text{cov}(X, Z) + \text{cov}(X, W) + \text{cov}(Y, Z) + \text{cov}(Y, W)$$

---

[20] As noted in Chapter I, a common transformation would be to let $b = 1/s_X$ and $a = -\overline{X}/s_X$. Then $a + bX = (X - \overline{X})/s_X$, which is our old friend the standardized, or z, score.

Phew! Think of this result as cross-multiplying one side of the covariance $(X + Y)$ with the other side $(Z + W)$—then, all of the cross-multiples become covariances.

To repeat, we have four handy-dandy properties (the first being a repeat of Equation IV.L):

Property 1: $\text{cov}(X, Y) = r_{XY}(s_X s_Y)$

Property 2: $\text{cov}(X, X) = s_X^2$

Property 3: $\text{cov}(a + bX, Y) = b\,\text{cov}(X, Y)$

Property 4: $\text{cov}(X + Y, Z + W) = \text{cov}(X, Z) + \text{cov}(X, W)$
$$+ \text{cov}(Y, Z) + \text{cov}(Y, W)$$

ome Classical Test Theory Results

Equation IV.A presented the classical test theory model which says whenever a measure (X) is taken, it is assumed to be composed of a true score (T) plus random error (e). Thus, $X = T + e$. Since the errors $(e\text{'s})$ are random, we assume they are independent of each other and independent of everything else. That is, $\text{cov}(e_i, e_j) = 0$ if $i \neq j$ and $\text{cov}(e_i, T) = 0$. Notice that $\text{cov}(e_i, e_j)$ is *not* 0. Rather, from Property 2 above, this is the variance of the errors (σ_e^2).

Derivation of Equation IV.B   Start with the model $X = T + e$ and compute the variance of X (σ_x^2).

$$\text{var}(X) = \text{var}(T + e) = \text{cov}(T + e, T + e) \quad \text{(by property 2)}$$

$$= \text{cov}(T, T) + \text{cov}(T, e) + \text{cov}(e, T) + \text{cov}(e, e) \quad \text{(by property 4)}$$

Note that the middle two terms are equal to zero, as described in the preceding paragraph. Therefore,

$$\text{var}(X) = \text{cov}(T, T) + \text{cov}(e, e)$$

$$= \text{var}(T) + \text{var}(e)$$

Or, in other words,

$$\sigma_X^2 = \sigma_T^2 + \sigma_e^2$$

We have thus derived Equation IV.B!

Derivation of Equation IV.D Now, consider the correlation between X and T (ρ_{XT}):

$$\rho_{XT} = \frac{\text{cov}(X,T)}{\sigma_X \sigma_T} = \frac{\text{cov}(T+e,T)}{\sigma_X \sigma_T}$$

$$= \frac{\text{cov}(T,T) + \text{cov}(e,T)}{\sigma_X \sigma_T} \quad (\text{by property 4})$$

$$= \frac{\text{cov}(T,T)}{\sigma_X \sigma_T} \quad [\text{since cov}(e,T) = 0]$$

$$= \frac{\sigma_T^2}{\sigma_X \sigma_T} = \frac{\sigma_T}{\sigma_X}$$

Then, squaring both sides of the result yields $\rho_{XT}^2 = \sigma_T^2 / \sigma_X^2 = $ reliability of X (by definition of Equation IV.C). Thus, we have shown that reliability is a squared correlation (ρ_{XT}^2), as in Equation IV.D.

Note that reliability was also conceived as a regular (not squared) correlation of r_{XX}. To see this, think of test X being given twice. The first time we can write $X = T + e$. The second time we can write $X' = T + e'$. Note that there is no $'$ on the T. The true score is assumed to remain the same across all testing occasions (in contrast, random error, hence X, might be different). Now, since we assume σ_e (hence σ_x) doesn't change,

$$\rho_{XX'} = \frac{\text{cov}(X, X')}{\sigma_X \sigma_{X'}} = \frac{\text{cov}(T+e, T+e')}{\sigma_X^2}$$

$$= \frac{\text{cov}(T,T) + \text{cov}(T,e') + \text{cov}(e,T) + \text{cov}(e,e')}{\sigma_X^2}$$

$$= \frac{\text{cov}(T,T)}{\sigma_X^2} \quad (\text{since errors are uncorrelated})$$

$$= \frac{\sigma_T^2}{\sigma_X^2} = \text{reliability}$$

So, the reliability is both ρ_{XX} and ρ_{XT}^2.

Corrections for unreliability In this situation there are two variables (X and Y) and $X = T_X + e_X$; $Y = T_Y + e_y$. Following the logic of Equation IV.G, we want to know the theoretical correlation between the two true scores. So,

$$\rho_{T_X T_Y} = \frac{\text{cov}(T_X, T_Y)}{\sigma_{T_X} \sigma_{T_y}} = \frac{\text{cov}(X - e_x, Y - e_Y)}{\sigma_{T_X} \sigma_{T_Y}}$$

$$= \frac{\text{cov}(X, Y) - \text{cov}(X, e_Y) - \text{cov}(e_X, Y) + \text{cov}(e_X, e_Y)}{\sigma_{T_X} \sigma_{T_Y}}$$

$$= \frac{\text{cov}(X, Y)}{\sigma_{T_X} \sigma_{T_Y}} \quad (\text{since } e\text{'s are uncorrelated})$$

$$= \frac{\rho_{YX} \sigma_X \sigma_Y}{\sigma_{T_X} \sigma_{T_Y}}$$

$$= \frac{\rho_{YX}}{(\sigma_{T_X}/\sigma_X)(\sigma_{T_Y}/\sigma_Y)} = \frac{\rho_{YX}}{\sqrt{\rho_{XX}} \sqrt{\rho_{YY}}}$$

and we have just proved Equation IV.G and the population version of the correction for unreliability.

The Spearman-Brown formula for test length   The formula in Equation IV.I was written generally in order to consider any change in test length. Just to preserve a few steps, we'll prove this equation in the case where test length is doubled (i.e., $k = 2$). The general proof follows the same logic (try it if you wish —it's not hard, just a little more tedious!). Suppose we have a test (X_1) and we double its length by adding another equivalent test (X_2) to it. The new test is therefore represented by $X_1 + X_2$, and its reliability is

$$\rho_{\text{new, new}} = \rho_{X_1 + X_2, X_1' + X_2'} = \frac{\text{cov}(X_1 + X_2, X_1' + X_2')}{\sigma_{X_1 + X_2} \sigma_{X_1' + X_2'}}$$

$$= \frac{\text{cov}(T_1 + T_2 + e_1 + e_2, T_1 + T_2 + e_1' + e_2')}{\sigma_{X_1 + X_2} \sigma_{X_1' + X_2'}}$$

$$= \frac{\text{cov}(T + T + e_1 + e_2, T + T + e_1' + e_2')}{\sigma_{X_1 + X_2}^2}$$

since T and σ_X^2 are unchanged across test occasions. Then, using an extension of the logic in property 4, we can write

$$\rho_{\text{new, new}} = \frac{\text{cov}(T, T) + \text{cov}(T, T) + \text{cov}(T, T) + \text{cov}(T, T) + \text{lots of 0s}}{\sigma_{X_1 + X_2}^2}$$

$$= \frac{4\sigma_T^2}{\sigma_{X_1 + X_2}^2}$$

There are lots of 0s in the above equation because the covariances of the e's with each other are all zero. Also, because $\sigma^2_{X_1 + X_2} = \text{cov}(X_1 + X_2, X_1 + X_2)$, it is easily shown that

$$\sigma^2_{X_1 + X_2} = \sigma^2_{X_1} + \sigma^2_{X_2} + 2\sigma_{X_1}\sigma_{X_2}\rho_{X_1 X_2}$$

Further, since the tests are equivalent, we assume that $\sigma_{X_1} = \sigma_{X_2}$. Thus,

$$\sigma^2_{X_1 + X_2} = 2\sigma^2_X + 2\sigma^2_X \rho_{XX}$$

Substituting this value in the previous equation for $\rho_{\text{new, new}}$ yields

$$\rho_{\text{new, new}} = \frac{4\sigma^2_T}{2\sigma^2_X + 2\sigma^2_X \rho_{XX}} = \frac{4\sigma^2_T}{2\sigma^2_X(1 + \rho_{XX})}$$

$$= \frac{2\sigma^2_T}{\sigma^2_X(1 + \rho_{xx})}$$

$$= \frac{2\rho_{XX}}{1 + \rho_{XX}} \quad \left(\text{because } \frac{\sigma^2_T}{\sigma^2_X} = \rho_{XX}\right)$$

Thus, a specific instance of Equation IV.I has been derived.

Again, I hope these proofs were instructive and I hope you can see that some pretty well-known, famous formulas are not magic. Rather, they are based on a knowledge about covariances and assumptions of classical test theory.

PROBLEMS

1 After reading this chapter, you realize that there is more to a good test than meets the eye. Thus, you ask the test salesperson you met in Chapter II to discuss the reliability of the new selection test.

    a You are in hurry for a new selection test and ask for reliability data within the next few days. What type of reliability are you probably asking for? How might the salesperson quickly conduct a study to obtain this information?

    b You are a patient person and know that your company is not desperate for a new selection test, what types(s) of reliability could you ask for? How might the salesperson conduct a study to obtain this information?

2 You don't have to do any computation in this problem. I just wanted to point out that we also have some validity evidence for the salesperson's new selection test. That is, in the problem set of Chapter II, we computed the correlation between the new selection test (called X_3) and job performance (labeled Y). The value of this correlation was $r_{Y3} = .674$; hence selection folks might claim that the validity of the test is .674. Of course, there was no indication of whether this was a predictive or concurrent validity coefficient. This lack of information is somewhat typical. Also, don't forget that "*the* validity" is a misnomer, since the value of .674 also depends on the choice (and quality) of the performance measure used in the computation.

3 Suppose the reliabilities of the new selection test (X_3) and the performance measure (Y) are .820 and .900, respectively.

   a Correct $r_{XY} = .674$ for unreliability in both measures (i.e., find the correlation between T_X and T_Y).

   b Assume you are doing validation work and are considering adopting the new selection test (X_3). What is the appropriate corrected correlation in this situation?

4 As stated in Problem 3, the reliability of the new selection test is $r_{XX} = .820$. By what factor must the test be increased in order to have a reliability of .90? (To put this in practical terms, suppose the new test as originally proposed had 25 items. How many items in all are therefore required to reach the targeted reliability of .90?)

5 In Chapter III, we presented a correlation matrix adapted from Miller's (1988) study—see Table III.2. One section of that table contained correlations among four measures (variables 5 through 8) of an organization's structure (e.g., use of liaison devices, formal controls, etc.) and is produced below:

	5	6	7	8
5. Liaison devices				
6. Technocratization	.24			
7. Delegation	− .04	.22		
8. Formal controls	.20	.27	.06	

Notice there is no correlation presented between variable 5 and itself. In the sample at hand this would of course be 1.0. However, it is customary to report the variable's reliability in this position of the correlation matrix—assuming reliabilities are available. In fact Miller did report internal consistency reliabilities. Here's what an enhanced correlation matrix might look like (I have followed convention and placed the reliabilities in parentheses):

	5	6	7	8
5. Liaison devices	(.89)			
6. Technocratization	.24	(.60)		
7. Delegation	− .04	.22	(.82)	
8. Formal controls	.20	.27	.06	(.76)

I thought you'd like to know. And, here's a problem just for good measure (pun intended).

   In the above matrix, the correlation between the use of liaison devices and formal controls by organizations is reported to be .20. Correct this correlation for unreliability in both measures.

REFERENCES

Allen, M., and Yen, W. (1979). *Introduction to measurement theory*. Belmont, CA: Wadsworth.

Aguinis, H., Bommer, W., and Pierce, C. (1996). Improving the estimation of moderating effects by using computer-administered questionnaires. *Educational and Psychological Measurement, 56*, 1043–1047.

American Educational Research Association, American Psychological Association, and National Council on Measurement in Education (1985). *Standards for educational and psychological tests*. Washington, DC: American Psychological Association.

Ashford, S., Lee, C., and Bobko, P. (1989). Content, causes, and consequences of job insecurity: A theory-based measure and substantive test. *Academy of Management Journal, 32*, 803–829.

Austin, J., and Villanova, P. (1992). The criterion problem: 1917–1992. *Journal of Applied Psychology, 77*, 836–874.

Barrett, G., Phillips, J., and Alexander, R. (1981). Concurrent and predictive validity designs: A critical reanalysis. *Journal of Applied Psychology, 66*, 1–6.

Bobko, P., and Rieck, A. (1980). Large sample estimators for standard errors of functions of correlation coefficients. *Applied Psychological Measurement, 4*, 385–398.

Bobko, P., and Stone-Romero, E. (1998). Meta-analysis is another useful research tool but it is not a panacea. In J. Ferris (Ed.), *Research in personnel and human resource management*, Vol. 16, pp. 359–397. Greenwich, CT: JAI Press.

Borman, W. (1978). Exploring upper limits of reliability and validity in job performance ratings. *Journal of Applied Psychology, 63*, 135–144.

Brown, W. (1910). Some experimental results in the correlation of mental abilities. *British Journal of Psychology, 3*, 296–322.

Burke, M. (1984). Validity generalization: A review and critique of the correlation model. *Personnel Psychology, 37*, 93–115.

Callender, J., and Osburn, H. (1980). Development and test of a new model for validity generalization. *Journal of Applied Psychology, 65*, 543–558.

Campbell, D., and Fiske, D. (1959). Convergent and discriminant validation by the multitrait-multimethod matrix. *Psychological Bulletin, 56*, 81–105.

Campbell, J. (1990). Modeling the performance prediction problem in industrial and organizational psychology. In M. Dunnette and L. Hough (Eds.), *Handbook of industrial and organizational psychology* (2nd ed.), vol. 1, pp. 687–732. Plato Alto, CA: Consulting Psychologists Press.

Campbell, J., and Zook, L. (1990). *Improving the selection, classification, and utilization of Army enlisted personnel: Final report on Project A*. ARI Research Report 1597. Alexandria, VA: U.S. Army Research Institute.

Carrier, M., DaLessio, A., and Brown, S. (1990). Correspondence between estimates of content and criterion-related validity values. *Personnel Psychology, 43*, 85–100.

Cicchetti, D., Showalter, D., and Tyrer, P. (1985). The effect of number of rating scale categories on levels of interrater reliability: A Monte Carlo investigation. *Applied Psychological Measurement, 9*, 31–36.

Cortina, J. (1993). What is coefficient alpha?: An examination of theory and applications. *Journal of Applied Psychology, 78*, 98–104.

Cronbach, L. (1951). Coefficient alpha and the internal structure of tests. *Psychometrika, 16*, 297–334.

Cronbach, L., Gleser, G., Nanda, H., and Rajaratnam, N. (1972). *The dependability of behavioral measurements: Theory of generalizability for scores and profiles*. New York: John Wiley.

Cronbach, L., and Meehl, P. (1955). Construct validity in psychological tests. *Psychological Bulletin, 52*, 281–302.

Deci, E., Connell, J., and Ryan, R. (1989). Self-determination in a work organization. *Journal of Applied Psychology, 74*, 580–590.

Feldt, L. (1969). A test of the hypothesis that Cronbach's alpha or Kuder-Richardson coefficient twenty is the same for two tests. *Psychometrika, 34,* 363–373.

Feldt, L. (1980). A test of the hypothesis that Cronbach's alpha reliability coefficient is the same for two tests administered to the same sample. *Psychometrika, 45,* 99–105.

Fraser, S., Cronshaw, S., and Alexander, R. (1984). Generalizability analysis of a point method job evaluation instrument: A field study. *Journal of Applied Psychology, 69,* 643–647.

Fromkin, H., and Streufert, S. (1976). Laboratory experimentation. In M. Dunnette (Ed.), *Handbook of industrial and organizational psychology,* pp. 415–465. Chicago: Rand-McNally.

Gatewood, R., and Feild, H. (1998). *Human resource selection* (4th ed.). Fort Worth, TX: Dryden Press.

George, J. (1990). Personality, affect, and behavior in groups. *Journal of Applied Psychology, 75,* 107–116.

Ghishelli, E., Campbell, J., and Zedeck S. (1981). *Measurement theory for the behavioral sciences.* San Francisco: W. H. Freeman.

Hattrup, K., Schmitt, N., and Landis, R. (1992). Equivalence of constructs measured by job specific and commercially available aptitude tests. *Journal of Applied Psychology, 77,* 298–308.

Hunter, J., and Schmidt, F. (1990). *Methods of meta-analysis: Correcting error and bias in research findings.* Thousand Oaks, CA: Sage.

Jenkins, G., and Taber, T. (1977). A Monte Carlo study of factors affecting three indices of composite scale reliability. *Journal of Applied Psychology, 62,* 392–398.

Kraiger, K., and Teachout, M. (1990). Generalizability theory as construct-related evidence of the validity of job performance ratings. *Human Performance, 3,* 19–35.

Kuder, G., and Richardson, M. (1937). The theory of the estimation of test reliability. *Psychometrika, 2,* 151–160.

Likert, R. (1932). A technique for the measurement of attitudes. *Archives of Psychology,* No. 140.

Lord, F., and Novick, M. (1968). *Statistical theories of mental test scores.* Reading, MA: Addison-Wesley.

MacCorquodale, K., and Meehl, P. (1948). On a distinction between hypothetical constructs and intervening variables. *Psychological Review, 55,* 95–107.

Miller, D. (1988). Relating Porter's business strategies to environment and structure: Analysis and performance implications. *Academy of Management Journal, 31,* 280–308.

Mischel, W. (1968). *Personality and assessment.* New York: John Wiley.

Muchinsky, P. (1996). The correction for attenuation. *Educational and Psychological Measurement, 56,* 63–75.

Nunnally, J. (1978). *Psychometric theory* (2nd ed.). New York: McGraw-Hill.

Orne, M. (1962). On the social psychology of the psychology experiment. *American Psychologist, 17,* 776–783.

Ostroff, C., and Schmitt, N. (1987, April). *The relationship between content and criterion-related validity indices: An empirical investigation.* Paper presented at the annual meeting of the Society for Industrial and Organizational Psychology, Atlanta, GA.

Phillips, A., and Dipboye, R. (1989). Correlational tests of predictions from a process model of the interview. *Journal of Applied Psychology, 74,* 41–52.

Russell, C., and Bobko, P. (1992). Moderated regression analysis and Likert scales: Too coarse for comfort. *Journal of Applied Psychology, 77,* 336–342.

Russell, C., Pinto, J., and Bobko, P. (1991). Appropriate moderated regression and inappropriate research strategy: A demonstration of the need to give your respondents space. *Applied Psychological Measurement, 15,* 257–266.

Schmidt, F., and Hunter, J. (1977). Development of a general solution to the problem of validity generalization. *Journal of Applied Psychology, 62,* 529–540.

Schmit, M., and Ryan, A. (1992). Test-taking dispositions: A missing link? *Journal of Applied Psychology, 77,* 629–637.

Schmitt, N., and Landy, F. (1993). The concept of validity. In N. Schmitt, W. Borman, and Associates (Eds.), *Personnel Selection in Organizations,* pp. 275–309. San Francisco: Jossey-Bass.

Schmitt, N., Gooding, R., Noe, R., and Kirsch, M. (1984). Meta-analyses of validity studies published between 1964 and 1982 and the investigation of study characteristics. *Personnel Psychology, 37,* 407–422.

Shavelson, R., Webb, N., and Rowley, G. (1989). Generalizability theory. *American Psychologist, 44,* 922–932.

Society for Industrial and Organizational Psychology. (1987). *Principles for the validation and use of personnel selection procedures* (3rd ed.). College Park, MD: Society for Industrial and Organizational Psychology.

Spearman, C. (1910). Correlation calculated with faulty data. *British Journal of Psychology, 3,* 271–295.

U.S. Equal Employment Opportunity Commission, U.S. Civil Service Commission, U.S. Department of Labor, and U.S. Department of Justice (1978). Uniform guidelines on employee selection procedures. *Federal Register, 43,* 38295–38309.

Viswesvaran, C., Ones, D., and Schmidt, F. (1996). Comparative analysis of the reliability of job performance ratings. *Journal of Applied Psychology, 81,* 557–574.

Webb, N., Shavelson, R., Shea, J., and Morello, E. (1981). Generalizability of general education development ratings of jobs in the United States. *Journal of Applied Psychology, 66,* 186–192.

Weekley, J., and Gier, J. (1989). Ceilings in the reliability and validity of performance ratings: The case of expert raters. *Academy of Management Journal, 32,* 213–222.

V

RANGE RESTRICTION

CHAPTER OBJECTIVES

After reading this chapter, you should be able to:

- Define range restriction and explain its effect on the correlation coefficient.
- Suggest situations where range restriction might occur.
- Explain the difference between direct and indirect range restriction and give examples of both.
- Correct a correlation for direct range restriction.
- List the two assumptions made in correcting for range restriction and know which is more crucial.
- Explain how the issue of range restriction applies to validity generalization and meta-analysis.
- Explain what happens to the standard deviation of a correlation coefficient when that correlation is corrected for direct range restriction.
- Define and give examples of reverse range restriction.

RANGE RESTRICTION ISSUES

Now that we know what a correlation (r) is, how to test it for significance (usually against zero), and some measurement applications, we can turn to a particularly troublesome, yet fun, problem associated with the use of r. In the section on properties of the correlation coefficient in Chapter II, we stated that *correlations are affected* (*usually weakened*) *by range restriction* and noted that this would be discussed in Chapter V. Well, this is Chapter V!

By "range restriction," I initially mean that one of the two variables (say, X or Y) has a certain potential range of values in the population to which one wishes to generalize, yet the study conducted does not have scores that span that entire range. That is, only a portion of the potential range is used (e.g., scores are either all fairly high, all fairly low, or mostly in the middle with few extremes). By "weakened," I mean that the magnitude of r is reduced (although we'll discuss "reverse range restriction" later in this chapter). The effect of range restriction is easily seen by drawing a few pictures.

Suppose, for example, that a certain Professor Resurge is interested in the correlation between a person's level of creativity (Y) and his or her intelligence (X). Suppose, further, that there is a positive correlation, across individuals in the United States, between these two variables as shown in Figure 5.1

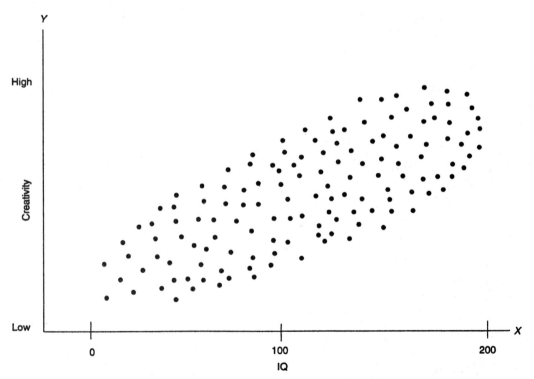

FIGURE 5.1   Hypothetical scatterplot of the relationship between creativity and intelligence.

Now, suppose that Dr. Resurge is a professor at Princesston and that he (his first name is Imusdo) gets a random sample of Princesston students for the study. In order to make this example work, also assume that you can't get into Princesston unless your IQ is greater than 150 or one of your parents donates enough money to name a building after you (just kidding!).

What will Professor Resurge get for a correlational result? Certainly not the pretty scatterplot in Figure 5.1. Rather, the IQ variable (X) has been range-restricted, in the sense that everyone in the professor's sample will have an X-score of at least 150 (i.e., the range has been restricted from below by 150). Thus, Professor Resurge will obtain a correlation only from the extreme right-hand side of the scatterplot (Figure 5.2).

If one isolated this restricted portion of the data, and "blew up" the remaining scatterplot, the picture would then look like Figure 5.3. In this figure, the clear linear relation (in the entire United States) between intelligence and creativity has all but disappeared. That is, the scatterplot in Figure 5.3 looks more like half of a circle than half of a straight line. In fact, if you were to compute the correlation (r) in this range-restricted data, its value would be very close to zero and Professor Resurge would conclude (in his article) that there is no relation between the two investigated variables. He would be correct for range-restricted

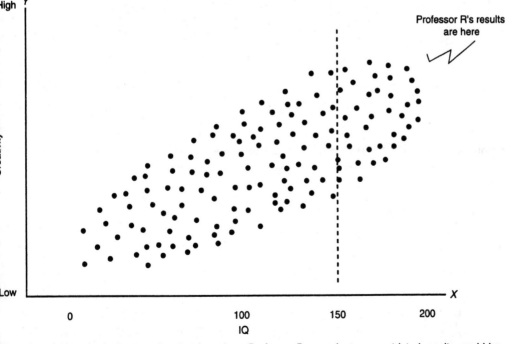

IGURE 5.2 Hypothetical scatterplot showing where Professor Resurge's range-restricted results would be.

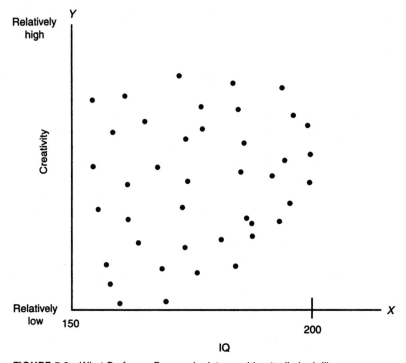

FIGURE 5.3 What Professor Resurge's data would actually look like.

populations like Princesston but mistaken for populations in general. More specifically, this has been a demonstration that

> **Restricting the range of one variable will tend to severely decrease its correlations with other variables.**

Research on the relationship between creativity and intelligence is not a common issue in the fields of human resource management and applied psychology. We now turn to a more typical example. [By the way, there *is* published research on the joint measurement of intelligence (IQ) and creativity. However, the hypothesized relation is one where there is a linear relationship between IQ and creativity for below-average levels of IQ, yet *no* relationship for high levels of IQ. The resultant picture would be Figure 5.4 and has been labeled a "twisted pear" scatterplot by researchers (e.g., Fisher, 1959).]

A More Typical Example

In the mid-1970s, the police department of the city of Philadelphia was sued based on allegations of discriminatory selection and promotion practices. One aspect of the suit was that a test used for admission to the Police Academy was

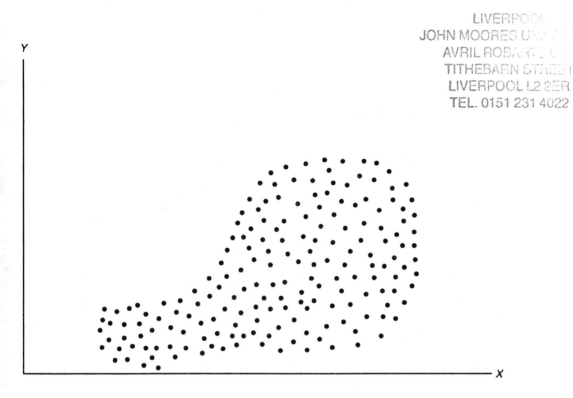

Y

IQ

X

FIGURE 5.4   An example of a twisted pear scatterplot.

biased against black applicants (i.e., black applicants had lower average test scores than white applicants and were therefore less likely to be admitted to the Academy).

In order to defend its use of the test, the city needed to demonstrate that scores on the selection test were valid; i.e., that test scores were significantly correlated with subsequent job performance (see Chapter IV). (*Note*: The test legally needs to correlate with performance only if applicants in protected classes score lower; otherwise it's legal to use any test, such as the seventh digit of a person's social security number, whether related to performance or not!)

So, where does range restriction come into play in this case? Well, I've omitted (until now) one very important detail. That is, the selection test in question had already been in use, and entrance to the Academy was very selective. Only applicants with test scores in the upper 5 percent were admitted. Therefore, while the department would certainly have test scores (X) for all applicants, it could collect performance scores (Y) only for those applicants whom it had admitted (i.e., the top 5% on X). So, the city's researcher who did the validation study could obtain correlational data for a severely restricted group only. Pictorially, assume there was an overall correlation between test scores (X)

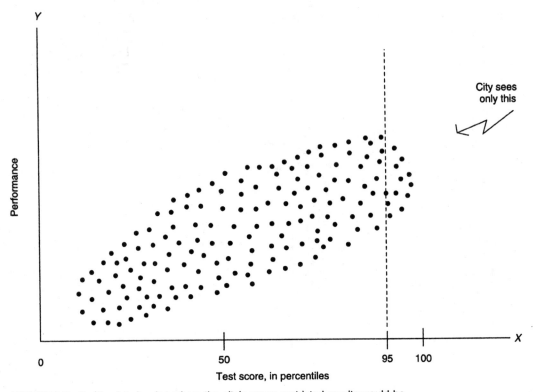

FIGURE 5.5 Scatterplot showing where the city's range-restricted results would be.

and performance (Y). However, the validation researcher would see only the far right-hand side of this picture (Figure 5.5).

In fact, when the city conducted a study, they obtained a small (but statistically significant) correlation of about $r_{XY} = .11$. The plaintiffs immediately attacked this as a *small* correlation. Further, they computed r^2 ($= .0121$) and stated that only 1% of the variance in job performance had anything to do with differences in test scores (if this isn't clear, go back to Chapter II; do not pass "Go" and certainly do not collect $200).

When their turn came, the defense attorneys pleaded "victimization by statistical range restriction." They essentially said, "Your honor, there's probably a large correlation between test scores and performance, but our data are so range-restricted from past usage of the test, that it's a good omen that we even got the positive correlation of .11." (Before you continue reading, pause a moment and think what *you* would do next if you were either a plaintiff or a defendant. O.K. You can continue reading now.) The plaintiffs reiterated their interpretation of r (and r^2) as small values. Further, they even suggested that the city stop using the test and allow all applicants (or a simple random sample of applicants) into the Academy—to indeed see if there was a correlation after the range restriction confound was removed. After all, the plaintiffs argued, the true relation between X and Y might be that shown in Figure 5.6*a* rather than that shown in Figure 5.6*b*.

Well, this suggestion didn't wash with the defendants. In fact, the defense appealed to the judge's sympathy ("Your honor, if you had a young teenage daughter, would you want her to be protected at night by someone at the *2nd* percentile of the selection test just for the sake of increasing the variance on X and proving that low scoring applicants will generally be low performers?"). To further make their point, the defense also used another data base and its associated scatterplot, which didn't appear to be range-restricted (Figure 5.7). In this scatterplot, the correlation across all 888 data points (yes, there *are* 888 of them!) is $r_{YX} = .87$. (See Bobko and Karren, 1979, for further details.) However, if one looks at only the top 5% of scores on X (i.e., the highest 45 scores on X), the correlation drops down to .14. The blown-up, restricted picture (with $r = .14$) and the overall picture (with $r = .87$) were both presented to the judge to demonstrate the extreme effect that range restriction could have. (By the way, the city won its case, but not necessarily on the strength of the above argument—although it couldn't have hurt!)

It should be clear that correlations in human resource management studies are almost always affected by range restriction (usually weakening the magnitude of

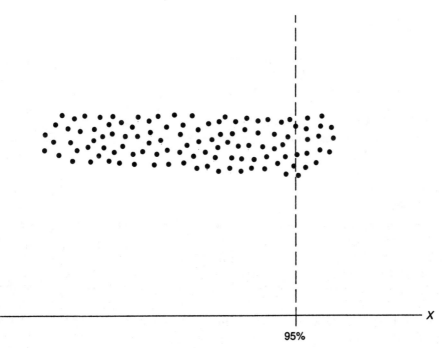

95%

FIGURE 5.6*a*   One possibility for the true relation between X and Y.

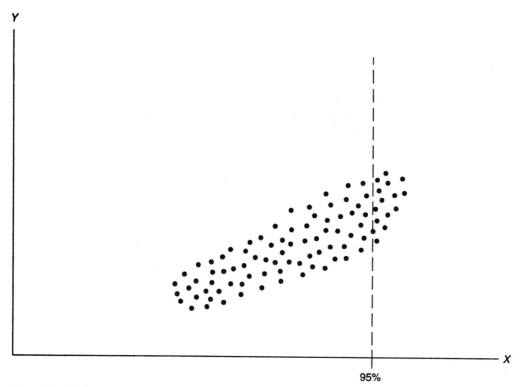

FIGURE 5.6b Another possibility for the true relation between X and Y.

r). After all, most incumbents in organizations are selected on the basis of some type of initial screening (our X). The criterion variable (Y) is often range-restricted, as well. For example, good performers are often promoted (up) from their initial job, while very poor performers are likely to be removed from the organization. This serves to restrict the range from both ends of the performance spectrum. Thus, the magnitude of r can be reduced as a result of range restriction on either variable.

Some Handy Formulas

Think a bit about the scatterplot in Figure 5.7 with 888 data points. Clearly, the implied defense argument was, "We obtained an r of .11 in the range-restricted sample. Surely, if we had had *everyone* on both X and Y, then the obtained correlation would be higher. In fact, a restricted r of .14 in the 45 data points becomes an r of .87 when all 888 data points are considered." It would be nice if, when someone gave us a restricted r, we could estimate what the *unrestricted* r would be in the overall population. In fact, researchers have developed such formulas, and they're not difficult to derive or use.

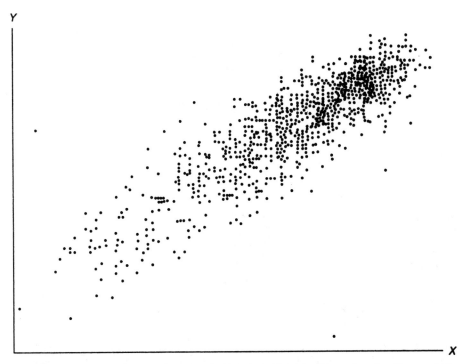

FIGURE 5.7 An exemplary, non-range-restricted scatterplot. (*Reproduced, with permission, from Bobko and Karren, 1979*).

The derived formulas make several assumptions and depend on how the range restriction occurs. First, there can be "direct range restriction" on one of the variables (say, X). That is what happened in both of the above examples and has the effect of directly reducing the variance on the restricted variable (e.g., s_X^2). Second, it is possible that individuals have been selected or restricted on some *third* variable (say, Z) that is related to both X and Y. This will cause "indirect range restriction" in both of the other variables.[1] However, direct range restriction will be the primary focus of this chapter.

Now for some notation. Suppose that we directly restrict the range of X. Then we will have two variances on X:

$s_X^2 = $ the variance of X for the total range

$s_X'^2 = $ the variance of X for the restricted range

In the examples above, then, it is true that $s_X' < s_X$. Also, there will be two correlations, r_{XY} and r_{XY}' for the total and restricted range, respectively.

[1] For example, indirect range restriction can occur in validation studies where the company has already been using a selection test (Z) and is considering replacing it with a new selection test (X). Presumably, Z will be somewhat correlated with both the new test (X) and the criterion (Y) and cause indirect range restriction (on the value of r_{XY}) when a study is done on a sample of current employees.

With some simple assumptions (coming soon!), it can easily be shown that

V.A
$$r'_{XY} = \frac{r_{XY}(s'_X/s_X)}{\sqrt{1 - r^2_{XY} + r^2_{XY}(s'_X/s_X)^2}}$$

Similarly, one can turn Equation V.A "inside out" (i.e., solve for r_{XY}) and obtain

V.B
$$r_{\text{corrected}} = r_c = \frac{r'_{XY}(s_X/s'_X)}{\sqrt{1 - r'^2_{XY} + r'^2_{XY}(s_X/s'_X)^2}}$$

These are *very useful formulas*. For example, take the court case noted above where the obtained correlation was $r'_{XY} = .11$. The police department could certainly compute the variance on X-scores for selected individuals (top 5%) and the variance for all applicants. In fact, the ratio of standard deviations (s_X/s'_X) was about 5:1. Using Equation V.B,

V.B
$$r_{\text{corrected}} = r_c = \frac{.11(5)}{\sqrt{1 - .11^2 + .11^2(25)}} = .48$$

Thus, the defense could argue that .11 was *not* the best estimate of the validity of the selection test. Rather, $r_c = .48$ was a better estimate of the validity because it estimates what the validity would have been had all applicants been hired. This is a substantially greater correlation estimate! (*A notational point*: The resulting correlation in Equation V.B is usually known as the "corrected correlation" and will be denoted throughout this chapter as r_c.)

The reader is also asked to just commune with Equations V.A and V.B for a few minutes. They certainly operate as expected. For example, Equation V.A indicates how much the correlation will be reduced by direct range restriction. The numerator on the right-hand side starts with the correlation for the entire range (r_{XY}). This is multiplied by a "reduction factor" that is related to the 2 standard deviations on X (s'_X/s_X). Clearly, as range restriction becomes more severe (and as s'_X becomes smaller), this ratio gets closer and closer to zero. Note just the opposite in Equation V.B. Here, the restricted correlation (r'_{XY}) is beefed up by the ratio s_X/s'_X. The more the range was restricted, the greater this beefing up ratio will be. Finally, the denominators in both equations are best thought of as factors that make the final result sensible. For example, correlations cannot exceed 1.0, and the denominator of Equation V.B tones down the corrections in the numerator so the upper bound of 1.0 is not surpassed.

Statistical Proof and Assumptions

The statistical proof for the above is very straightforward and will not be presented here. The reader is referred to Ghiselli (1964, pp. 357–369) or Ghiselli, Campbell, and Zedeck (1981, pp. 294–306) for clearly stated derivations. The proofs make two assumptions that require a knowledge of regression (a topic discussed in the next chapter). So, if the assumptions are confusing at this point, just skim over them. You may want to come back to this section after you read Chapter VI—just to see that things aren't all that complex! The two assumptions are

1 Linearity: the slope of the regression is the same in the restricted data as in the total set of scores ($b = b'$).

2 The error variance around the regression lines, in both the restricted and the unrestricted samples, is the same (the old homoscedasticity assumption).[2]

Given the assumptions of linearity and homoscedasticity, the arithmetic of the proof is irrefutable. But there are still some logical questions. How accurate is the estimation? Does the resulting estimate have greater sampling variance than the original, restricted correlation? How robust are Equations V.A and V.B to violations of the assumptions? How do you evaluate whether the resulting estimates are good and/or realistic? More succinctly, is Equation V.B useful or is it simply a "fudge factor" to inappropriately make small correlations look larger?

As you might imagine, lots of researchers have considered these questions, conducted studies, published articles, received tenure, received raises, fed spouses and children, etc., because of these issues. In all the research, one thing is very clear:

1 Sole consideration of a restricted correlation (i.e., r'_{XY}) will provide a very inaccurate estimate of the underlying correlation in the overall population (ρ_{XY}). In general, the use of range restriction correction formulas will provide a better point estimate of the overall ρ_{XY} (cf. Linn, Harnisch, and Dunbar, 1981).

Other related findings are

2 The estimator in Equation V.B has a small negative bias even when all assumptions are met. Thus, even the corrected correlation (r_c) will underestimate the true ρ with a bias of order n^{-1} (so the bigger the sample size, the less this is a problem) (Bobko and Rieck, 1980).

3 The two assumptions for range restriction correction equations were the equality of regression slopes and the homoscedasticity of the residual (error) variances. The correction formula is robust to departures from homoscedasticity. However, violation of the linearity assumption is more crucial, and the corrected correlation may either over- or underestimate the underlying population (ρ), depending upon the form of the nonlinearity (Boldt, 1973; Brewer and Hills, 1969; Greener and Osburn, 1979, 1980).

4 Equations V.A and V.B assume *direct* range restriction on the predictor variable (X). As noted earlier, *indirect* range restriction can occur when selection is based on some third variable (Z) that is related to both X and Y (e.g., Z is

---

[2] The proof proceeds by writing down the two equalities implied by these assumptions, in terms of correlations and standard deviations. Then, one solves for r'_{XY} or r_{XY}. Several pages of algebra later, you get Equations V.A and V.B ("try it, you'll like it"). Again, if you try it and need help, consult Ghiselli et al. (1981, p. 294) or send me a postcard.

the selection test that's currently being used, and you're doing a concurrent validity study for a related test X on those employees already in the organization). Indeed, there are other (different!) correction equations suitable for this indirect restriction situation (see Ghiselli et al., 1981). A question is, What if we truly have indirect range restriction but use the correction for direct range restriction given in Equation V.B? The answer is that the corrected correlation will tend to be too small (see Gross and Fleischman, 1983; Linn et al., 1981).

In summary, the corrected correlations are fairly robust to the assumption of homoscedasticity, while linearity and use of appropriate formulas are more crucial. Note, however, that even corrected correlations often underestimate underlying population correlations. This means that our estimates of ρ will be conservative. This is useful when you're trying to defend these corrections to others—you can generally appeal to the notion that even these (larger) correlations are too small. So, if you get a large value of r_c, you really know you have a big one!

An Extended Break: More Examples

There's more statistical "stuff" we need to talk about, but let's take a break for a moment and think of more examples to show how important the range restriction phenomenon is. Certainly, the above example indicates that the validity of selection devices can be severely attenuated by range restriction effects—and the use of selection tests in organizational settings (public and private) is unquestionably pervasive. Now, try to think of other ways in which range restriction (variance restriction) can occur. I'll list some other situations (four, to be precise) if you promise not to peek before spending time thinking on your own first....

O.K. Did you generate some of these (or even better ones)? *First*, as noted earlier in this chapter, there can be direct range restriction on Y (the dependent variable, say, of job performance) in a validity study. For example, very high performers in a job are promoted; very low performers are fired (or promoted—just kidding, but am I really?). Linn (1983) has also reported this double-whammy range restriction in a validity study for a 2-year college where criterion scores were missing for both low-scoring applicants (rejected by the college) and high-scoring applicants (who went to 4-year colleges).

Second, note that I have primarily focused attention on selection examples where range restriction occurs on a selection test and/or a performance measure (e.g., through turnover or attrition). Schneider (1987) adds yet another dimension to these issues by proposing an "attraction-selection-attrition (ASA) cycle." Based on an interactionist perspective, he notes that organizations are functions of the people they contain. In turn, it should follow that individuals are differentially attracted to careers and organizations, depending upon their interests, values, and personality profiles (see also Chatman, 1989). Schneider proposes that the ASA cycle "produces restriction in range—the range of variance of individual differences in a setting is much less than would be expected by chance" (p. 442). Note that such range restriction is not related solely to performance measures but might also be expected on many of the individual difference measures typically studied by organizational researchers (interests, value structures, commitment, etc.).

Third, note that just about any training program will reduce variance across individuals. Ironically, in the better training programs (e.g., where everyone eventually excels at some particular task), there will be less variance across employees' performance (Y), and correlations between performance and other variables will be very small. A dastardly side to range restriction is when performance variation is reduced as a result of unintended phenomena. For example, informal social norms (through other work group members) may cause high performers to slow down their individual production (a phenomena labeled "group characteristic bias" in the criterion contamination literature). Or when supervisory rating scales are used as a performance measure, the variance of appraisal scores is often restricted because all scores tend to be high.[3]

Fourth, another common problem occurs when one (or both) variables are measured dichotomously (e.g., male versus female, stay versus leave). To see the problem here, you have to remember the following basic probability connection: dichotomous data imply the use of binomial distributions. You then have to remember that the variance of a sample proportion is $p(1 - p)$, where p is the underling population proportion of individuals in one category (e.g., proportion of males, proportion of stayers). In turn, the maximum value of $p(1 - p)$ occurs when $p = .50$.[4] So, if you're correlating scores on some variable (X) with turnover (Y, scored stay $= 1$, leave $= 0$), then Y will have maximal variance when 50% of the workforce leaves within a given period. On the other hand, if turnover rates are very low *or* very high, then the variance of Y can be substantially reduced (e.g., if 10% of the workforce leaves, the variance of Y is .10 $\times$ .90 = .09, compared to a maximum value of .50 $\times$ .50 = .25). When this happens, correlations between turnover and other variables (e.g., actual performance, predictors of turnover) will be reduced in magnitude because of the range restriction effect (cf. Kemery, Dunlap, and Griffeth, 1988).

It is important to remember that this reduction in variance (and consequent reduction in the magnitude of r) might happen *anytime* a dichotomous variable is used (e.g., gender, turnover, item responses coded right or wrong, performance criteria coded acceptable or not acceptable). Further, this is the same set of issues that caused us to talk about maximum values (less than 1.0) for phi coefficients and point-biserial coefficients in Chapter II.

In sum, there are many different situations in management and applied psychology where range restriction might reduce the magnitudes of empirical relationships. You should be on a constant lookout for them.

Validity generalization (and meta-analysis) revisited   As an aside, we noted in Chapter IV that a topic in validation research concerned the notion of

---

[3] Longenecker, Sims, and Gioia (1987) provide a variety of reasons why this typical performance appraisal distribution occurs (e.g., a low rating may be considered more of a reflection on the supervisor than on the poorly performing subordinate).

[4] Try it, you'll see! When $p = .50$, $p(1 - p) = .25$. Any other value of p will give a lower variance.

validity generalization (cf. Burke, 1984; Callender and Osburn, 1980; Schmidt and Hunter, 1977; and many articles on meta-analysis). Remember that one null hypothesis in validity generalization research is that a set of correlations (across studies, variables, populations, etc.) all have the same value. (In this situation, a company could then potentially estimate the validity of a selection test based on other companies' findings.) Now, as was the case when we considered unreliability, if the extent of range restriction differs across these studies, then the empirically obtained values of r will be different even if the underlying population ρ is the same (i.e., studies with more severe range restriction will in general have lower values of r). Thus, it will look like correlations differ across organizational studies even if they truly do not. Advocates of validity generalization note this problem, state that differential range restriction is a "statistical artifact," and indeed correct their empirical correlations (using variants of Equations V.A and V.B) as part of the estimation process. These corrections are not without controversy, however (so what else is new?). For example, in the above turnover example, some researchers (e.g., Kemery et al., 1988) advocate correcting turnover correlations as if they were obtained with 50% turnover (i.e., in Equation V.B, let s_x be $\sqrt{.5(1 - .5)}$ while s'_x is $\sqrt{p(1 - p)}$, where p is the actual turnover rate). Then, the claim is that correlations of variables with turnover will be comparable across studies. However, others (e.g., Williams, 1990) question whether or not differences in turnover can be considered statistical artifacts. That is, are differences in turnover rates really just artifacts or are they reflections of true organizational differences? (Is it live or is it Memorex?) Such questions have also been raised for all types of validity generalization corrections (James, Demaree, Mulaik, and Ladd, 1992). They have not been resolved and are a good example of the fact that statistics is *not* straightforward —and, after all, isn't that what makes this topic fun?

In any case, the effects of range restriction are pervasive. With that in mind, we now turn back to some more juicy little statistical tidbits.

More Statistical Stuff

Hypothesis testing and standard errors   We left off with statistical matters noting that, using the two assumptions of linearity and homoscedasticity, one could derive Equations V.A and V.B with some straightforward algebra. Further, we reviewed some findings on the accuracy of r_c as a point estimate of ρ. However, we still need to know what the standard deviation of r_c is across different random samples. (That is, even if corrected r's are not very biased, we still don't know how variable the estimates are.)

As noted in Chapter III, sampling distribution theory for regular Pearson correlation coefficients says that the standard deviation for r is, approximately (cf. Anderson, 1958, p. 77),

V.C
$$SD(r) \approx \frac{1 - \rho^2}{\sqrt{n}}$$

where ρ is the population correlation and the symbol $\approx$ reminds us that the result is an approximation. The dominant term is in the denominator ($\sqrt{n}$). Thus, with a sample size of $n = 100$, an approximation for the standard deviation associated with any obtained r is

$$\text{SD}(r) \approx \frac{1 - \rho^2}{\sqrt{100}} \approx \frac{1}{\sqrt{100}} = .10$$

(*Note*: If we wanted even more precision, we could replace the assumed value of $\rho = 0$ with the sample value of r.)

Now, when r is corrected for range restriction (i.e., converted to r_c), what happens to its standard error? Do we get something for nothing, in the sense that our correlation value goes up without any change in its standard deviation? As with corrections for unreliability (see Chapter IV), the answer is no. There *is* some statistical balancing of justice. For direct range restriction, it can be shown (see Bobko and Rieck, 1980) that

V.D $$\text{SD}(r_c) = \frac{s_X/s_X'}{\left[1 + r^2\left(s_X^2/s_X'^2 - 1\right)\right]^{3/2}} \text{SD}(r')$$

One check on Equation V.D is obvious: if there is no range restriction, then $s_X/s_X' = 1.0$ and the two standard deviations are identical. More importantly, note that in most range restriction cases s_X/s_X' will be substantially greater than 1.0. As long as r^2 is less than 1.0, the multiplying factor in Equation V.D, $[s_X/s_X'][1 + r^2(s_X^2/s_X'^2 - 1)]^{-3/2}$, will be greater than 1. Thus, $\text{SD}(r_c)$ is greater than $\text{SD}(r')$. So we don't get something for nothing: by applying range restriction corrections, we increase the magnitude of the correlation, but we also increase the associated standard error.

An Aside A heuristic way to test the null hypothesis that H_0: $\rho = 0$ would be to take the ratio $r_c/\text{SD}(r_c)$ and compare it to the appropriate critical value (usually about 2.0). The moral of this aside is that you can't mix apples and oranges. If you test the sample r against 0 in this way, you must use $\text{SD}(r)$; if you test the *corrected* correlation (r_c) against 0, you must use $\text{SD}(r_c)$. Corrected correlations shouldn't be used in traditional hypothesis tests without making appropriate adjustments for all distributional properties.

By the way, because most researchers tend to use uncorrected (restricted) correlations in significance tests, it makes sense to worry about the lack of power when trying to detect underlying nonzero correlations (i.e., since the restricted r is attenuated, it's harder to get significance). Therefore, researchers have addressed the question, Since the restricted correlation is generally small, what minimum sample size (n) does a researcher need to obtain significant results when the population correlation is truly nonzero? The reader is referred to an article by Schmidt, Hunter, and Urry (1976) that considers this question under conditions of direct range restriction. For example, suppose the true underlying validity for a selection test is $\rho = .50$ and one wants to have a power of .90 to detect it (two-tailed test, $p = .05$). Then, a sample size of $n = 38$ is required. However, if the range has been restricted on X by a selection ratio of .30, then a sample size of $n = 125$ is required to maintain that equivalent power. On the other hand, Sackett and Wade (1983) found that required "sample sizes under *indirect range* restriction are substantially smaller" (p. 374) than Schmidt et al.'s findings for direct range restriction. Finally, Alexander, Carson, Alliger, and Barrett (1985) considered even more complicated forms of range restriction. In general, sample size requirements in their situations were greater than under either direct or indirect range restriction scenarios.

A quick example for SD(r_c)   At the beginning of this chapter, a court case was noted where a police academy selection test had an obtained (restricted) validity of $r' = .11$. In this case, there was severe range restriction because only the top 5% of the applicants were selected. In fact, s_X/s_X' was approximately 5.0. As noted earlier, Equation V.B yields

$$r_c = \frac{.11(5)}{\sqrt{1 - .11^2 + .11^2(25)}} = .48$$

So, the magnitude of the estimated correlation went from .11 to .48, an increase of more than a factor of 4! However, Equation V.D indicates that

$$SD(r_c) = \frac{5}{[1 + .11^2(24)]^{3/2}} SD(r')$$
$$= 3.4[SD(r')]$$

So, in this case *the standard deviation goes up but not as fast as the point estimate*. This is a "very happy fact" and is true for all values of r and *any* degree of direct range restriction.

Two Asides

Aside 1   It's obvious that the validation of selection tests (using correlations) is subject to range restriction effects. In selection situations, the selection ratio is often known, yet corrections for range restriction require the value s_X'/s_X (see Equations V.A and V.B). In fact, assuming bivariate normality, one can determine the value of s_X'/s_X just by knowing the selection ratio (cf. Schmidt et al., 1976). The functional relationship is

$$\left(\frac{s_X'}{s_X}\right)^2 = 1 + \left(\frac{c}{SR}\right)[\lambda(c)] - \left[\frac{\lambda(c)}{SR}\right]^2$$

where SR = selection ratio

    c = standardized score corresponding to the selection ratio cutoff point

    $\lambda(c)$ = height of the standardized normal distribution at the value of c

Aside 2   In this chapter, we have indicated how to correct *bivariate* correlations for range restriction. But what does one do in *multiple* regression if more than one of the predictors ($X_i, i = 1, \ldots, p$) suffers range restriction effects? One could correct each bivariate validity (i.e., each $r_{YX_i}, i = 1, \ldots, p$) using Equation V.B. However, this doesn't take into account any natural covariation between the predictors. The answer is to use a "multivariate correction" for range restriction. Such a correction has been developed by Lawley (1943) and is more appropriate than a series of bivariate corrections (see Johnson and Ree, 1994, for a computer program for the multivariate correction). The reader is referred to McHenry, Hough, Toquam, Hanson, and Ashworth (1990) for an excellent use of this multivariate correction. In this case, the U.S. Army was predicting job performance (Y) using four scales derived from the Armed Services Vocational Aptitude Battery (ASVAB). Since all of the subjects were currently in the Army (a concurrent validity study), they had already been selected using ASVAB scores. The extent of the range restriction on the four ASVAB scales was estimated by comparing the selected soldiers' scores to a known national data base for the 1980 youth population.

verse Range Restriction

So far, every case we've considered has involved a reduction in the range of scores such that $s'_X < s_X$. However, it is possible to restrict the range of scores so that the standard deviation in the restricted set is greater than the unrestricted standard deviation. Impossible? Well, consider the scatterplots in Figures 5.8*a* and 5.8*b*. In this example, the scatterplot in Figure 5.8*b* was constructed by "throwing out" all data between X_1 and X_2. So, the potential scores on X have been restricted to include only extreme scores. Since there are no middle scores in Figure 5.8*b*, the variance on X is much larger here. In turn, the correlation in Figure 5.8*b* will be greater than in Figure 5.8*a*.

[*Note*: If it isn't clear that the variances (on X) will be different across the two figures, compute the variance of the following scores—0, 0, 0, 5, 5, 5, 10, 10, 10; then throw out the middle numbers and compute the variance of 0, 0, 0, 10, 10, 10. See, the variance goes up! That's because the middle scores contribute very little to the numerator of the variance [$\Sigma(X - \bar{X})^2$], yet the sample size (and therefore the denominator) is larger in the full data set.]

Now, you might ask, do Equations V.A and V.B work in this reverse range restriction case (i.e., where $s'_X > s_X$)? The answer is

Another nice fact   You bet! As long as the linearity and homoscedasticity assumptions hold, Equation V.B will estimate what the correlation would have been if the middle of the data had not been removed.

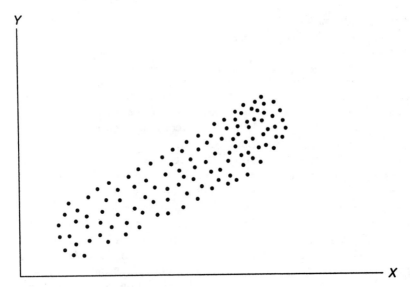

FIGURE 5.8*a* Hypothetical scatterplot.

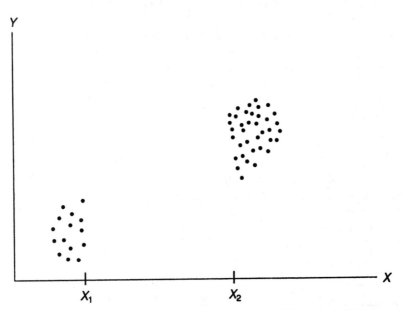

FIGURE 5.8*b* Hypothetical scatterplot with the middle of the data on *X* thrown out.

Of course, in this case the correction formula will actually decrease the obtained (range-restricted) correlation to more correctly reflect the situation in the scatterplot in Figure 5.8 *a* (unrestricted).

By the way, this example is not as strange and unrealistic as you may think. Quite the contrary! To see this, put yourself into an experimental design mode (you do this by counting from one to Zen). For both scatterplots above, let *Y* be the dependent measure in some experiment. Now, look at Figure 5.8 *b* and notice that the missing middle has created two distinct groups on the *X*-variable. If you consider *X* the independent (manipulated variable), then Figure 5.8 *b* is really a depiction of a one-way analysis of variance with two groups (low and high on *X*) and with dependent variable *Y*. For example, the two experimental groups might be no training versus lots of training, and the dependent variable (*Y*) might be subsequent task performance. Now, the experimentalist wants maximal separation between the two groups—that's what manipulation checks check!—so that the resultant means on *Y* will be different, so that significance tests will be significant, and so that everyone can leave the lab on time. But *we* now know that Figure 5.8 *b* creates an *over*estimation of the underlying correlation in Figure 5.8 *a*. So, what one group of researchers is trying to reduce (range restriction effects), the other group is trying to maximize. (Of course, in some experimental conceptualizations, the independent variable is truly categorical and there is no missing middle, but not always!)

ROBLEMS

1 Consider the organization in the problem set for Chapter II. Suppose this organization is currently using a selection test that for these 15 job incumbents correlates .614 with performance. Suppose further that the standard deviation of this currently used test, across these 15 individuals, is $s = 5.407$.

   a Why might the correlation of .614 be subject to range restriction effects?

   b Correct this correlation for range restriction, assuming that the standard deviation of the currently used selection test, across all applicants, is $s = 15$.

2 In the Chapter II data set, the correlation between the proposed new aptitude test (X_3) and performance was $r = .674$.

   a Correct this correlation for *direct* range restriction, assuming that the standard deviation of the proposed new test, across all potential applicants, is $s_{X_3} = 15$. (*Hint:* Don't forget that the standard deviation of X_3 in the sample of 15 employees was 5.444.)

   b Since the restricted correlation used in Problem 2a is based on correlations from a sample of employees who were selected using the current test, is the correction in Problem 2a appropriate? Why or why not?

3 A researcher is interested in the nationwide correlation between a person's gender (*X*) and the degree to which individuals believe that, in order to maximize productivity, organizations need to adopt a great deal of formalization (*Y*). Score *X* as males = 1, female = 0. Assume that the United States is composed of approximately equal numbers of males and females. Also assume that (unknown to the researcher) the correlation between *X* and *Y* in the population is $\rho_{XY} = .40$, such that males tend to endorse the need for greater degrees of formalization. Now, suppose that the researcher gives a survey to 100 adults at a local Boy

Scout meeting and obtains responses from 85 males and 15 females. All else equal, what would you expect the correlation to be between Y and X in this researcher's sample? (*Hint*: It's not .40. Indeed, you should make use of Equation V.A. Note that the population standard deviation on X is $\sqrt{.50 \times .50}$; the standard deviation in the researcher's sample is $\sqrt{.85 \times .15}$.

4 This chapter states that a range-restricted sample correlation typically tends to underestimate the true correlation in the population.

    a Demonstrate this by viewing the 15 subjects in the Chapter II data set as the total population and selecting the lowest 5 performers (i.e., individuals with the lowest 5 scores on Y). For these 5 individuals, compute the correlation between performance (Y) and the proposed new aptitude test (X_3). Compare this value to the value of $r = .674$ obtained across all 15 employees.

    b Take the restricted correlation you obtained in part "a" and correct it for range restriction. (*Hint*: Since the direct range restriction is on the variable Y, you will need to know that $s_Y = 7.891$ and $s'_Y = 2.702$.)

REFERENCES

Alexander, R., Carson, K., Alliger, G., and Barrett, G. (1985). Further consideration of the power to detect non-zero validity coefficients under range restriction. *Journal of Applied Psychology*, *70*, 451–460.

Anderson, T. (1985). *An introduction to multivariate statistical analysis*. New York: John Wiley.

Bobko, P., and Karren, R. (1979). The perception of Pearson product moment correlations from bivariate scatterplots. *Personnel Psychology*, *32*, 313–325.

Bobko, P., and Rieck, A. (1980). Large sample estimators for standard errors of functions of correlation coefficients. *Applied Psychological Measurement*, *4*, 385–398.

Boldt, R. (1973). *Range restriction assumptions assuming quadratic conditional variances*. Research Bulletin 73-59. Princeton, NJ: Educational Testing Service.

Brewer, J., and Hills, J. (1969). Univariate selection: The effects of size of correlation, degree of skew, and degree of range restriction. *Psychometrika*, *34*, 347–361.

Burke, M. (1984). Validity generalization: A review and critique of the correlation model. *Personnel Psychology*, *37*, 93–115.

Callender, J., and Osburn, H. (1980). Development and test of a new model for validity generalization. *Journal of Applied Psychology*, *65*, 543–558.

Chatman, J. (1989). Improving interactional organizational research: A model of person-organization fit. *Academy of Management Review*, *14*, 339–349.

Fisher, J. (1959). The twisted pear and the prediction of behavior. *Journal of Consulting Psychology*, *23*, 400–405.

Ghiselli, E. (1964). *Theory of psychological measurement*. New York: McGraw-Hill.

Ghiselli, E., Campbell, J., and Zedeck, S. (1981). *Measurement theory for the behavioral sciences*. San Francisco: W.H. Freeman.

Greener, J., and Osburn, H. (1979). An empirical study of the accuracy of corrections for restriction in range due to explicit selection. *Applied Psychological Measurement*, *3*, 31–41.

Greener, J., and Osburn, H. (1980). Accuracy of corrections for restriction in range due to explicit selection in heteroscedastistic and non-linear distributions. *Educational and Psychological Measurement*, *40*, 337–345.

Gross, A., and Fleischman, L. (1983). Restriction of range corrections when both distribution and selection assumptions are violated. *Applied Psychological Measurement*, *7*, 227–237.

James, L., Demaree, R., Mulaik, S., and Ladd, R. (1992). Validity generalization in the context of situational models. *Journal of Applied Psychology*, *77*, 3–14.

Johnson, J., and Ree, M. (1994). RANGEJ: A PASCAL program to compute the multivariate correction for restriction of range. *Educational and Psychological Measurement*, *54*, 693–697.

Kemery, E., Dunlap, W., and Griffeth, R. (1988). Correction for variance restriction in point-biserial correlations. *Journal of Applied Psychology*, *73*, 688–691.

Lawley, D. (1943). A note on Karl Pearson's selection formulas. *Royal Society of Edinburgh Proceedings, Section A*, *62*, 28–30.

Linn, R. (1983). Pearson correction formulas: Implications for studies of predictive bias and estimates of educational effects in selected samples. *Journal of Educational Measurement*, *20*, 1–15.

Linn, R., Harnisch, D., and Dunbar, S. (1981). Corrections for range restriction: An empirical investigation of conditions resulting in conservative corrections. *Journal of Applied Psychology*, *66*, 655–663.

Longenecker, C., Sims, H., and Gioia, D. (1987). Behind the mask: The politics of employee appraisal. *Academy of Management Executive*, *1*, 183–193.

McHenry, J., Hough, L., Toquam, J., Hanson, M., and Ashworth, S. (1990). Project A validity results: The relationship between predictor and criterion domains. *Personnel Psychology*, *43*, 335–354.

Sackett, P., and Wade, B. (1983). On the feasibility of criterion-related validity: The effects of range restriction assumptions on needed sample size. *Journal of Applied Psychology*, *68*, 374–381.

Schmidt, F., and Hunter, J. (1977). Development of a general solution to the problem of validity generalization. *Journal of Applied Psychology*, *62*, 529–540.

Schmidt, F., Hunter, J., and Urry, V. (1976). Statistical power in criterion-related validation studies. *Journal of Applied Psychology*, *61*, 473–485.

Schneider, B. (1987). The people make the place. *Personnel Psychology*, *40*, 437–453.

Williams, C. (1990). Deciding when, how, and if to correct turnover correlations. *Journal of Applied Psychology*, *75*, 732–737.

VI

"SIMPLE," TWO-VARIABLE REGRESSION

CHAPTER OBJECTIVES

After reading this chapter, you should be able to:

- Explain and understand how to use an equation for a linear regression.
- Explain the principle behind the "best-fitting" line.
- Understand why regression minimizes the sum of squared error terms rather than simply the sum of the error terms.
- Explain how the slope of the regression line is affected by s_X and s_Y.
- Understand the difference between predicting Y from X and predicting X from Y.
- Suggest the best predicted value for Y, given no information about X.
- Explain the principle behind the index of fit (r^2).
- List and define the assumptions underlying the regression model.
- Understand that testing the regression slope for significance (against zero) is arithmetically and conceptually equivalent to both (i) testing the correlation for significance and (ii) calculating an F ratio for the overall fit of the regression using the traditional analysis of variance.
- Construct and interpret a prediction interval, given an individual's score on X.
- Explain what effect standardization has on a regression.
- Discuss the purpose of residual analysis.
- Discuss, at an intuitive level, the ways in which extreme scores can be categorized (i.e., distance, leverage, and influence).

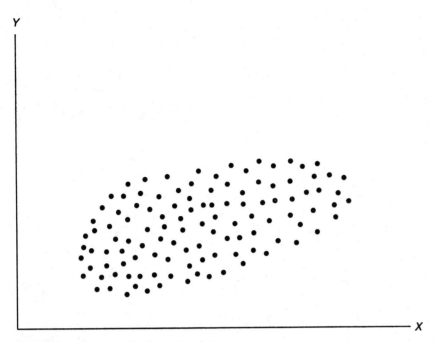

FIGURE 6.1   An example of a scatterplot.

In Chapter II, we made a big fuss about the relationship between two variables. We depicted that relationship with a scatterplot and indexed the magnitude of the relationship using Pearson *r*. Now, I don't know about you, but when I look at a scatterplot like the one in Figure 6.1, I really don't see just the scatterplot. My mind fills in the upward trend using a straight line, and so I tend to see (in my mind's eye) Figure 6.2. This chapter is all about the straight line that seems to fit the data so nicely.[1] As we shall see throughout this and subsequent chapters, the computation of such a line can be used (1) to *describe* the linear relationship for the data at hand, (2) to *predict* values of *Y* given future values on *X*, and (3) to *test* underlying models about the relationship between variables.

HE "BEST"-FITTING REGRESSION LINE

In a sample of data, the linear relation between *X* and *Y* is described by the equation

VI.A $$\hat{Y} = b_0 + b_1 X$$

---

[1] In Chapter II, we noted that Craig Russell thinks of Figure 6.2 as a "hot dog on a stick." So, intuitively, we could refer to this chapter as the "stick chapter." As we'll see in Chapter VII (in the section on regression to the mean), though, we need to be careful: the stick goes through the center of the scatterplot (hot dog), yet the *real* regression line will have a slope that is a bit less than that of the stick.

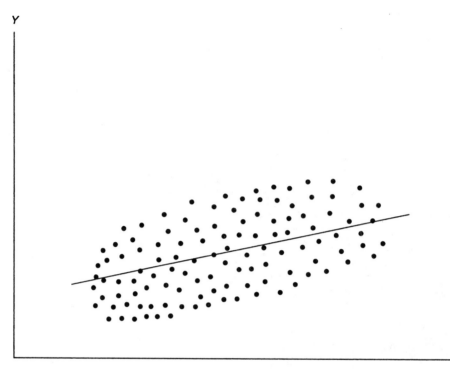

FIGURE 6.2 The scatterplot in Figure 6.1 drawn with a line possibly useful for predicting *Y* from *X*.

In this case, b_0 is the *Y*-intercept and b_1 is the slope of the function. You should also note that I have placed a caret (i.e., a $\hat{}$) over the symbol *Y*. This was done for two reasons. First, the caret notation is a fairly universal symbol meaning "the predicted value" and, as noted, prediction is a major use of regression analysis. Second, it will be crucial (see the next few paragraphs) to distinguish between values of *Y* predicted by the line (which we label $\hat{Y}$) and the actual values of *Y* for the sample data points (which we simply label *Y*).

> ***An aside*** In grade school, you probably learned about straight lines as $y = mx + b$, where *m* was the slope and *b* was the intercept. I suppose there are three reasons that statisticians have changed the symbols: (1) to confuse you, (2) to remind you that notation is arbitrary, and (3) to anticipate that in multiple regression there will be lots of *X*'s and we will index them with subscripts, such as $Y = b_0 + b_1 X_1 + b_2 X_2 +$ etc.

Now, in just looking at a scatterplot, there are many lines that go through the points. Consider Figure 6.3. I think we would all agree that line *a* is not a great choice for the "best-fitting" line. But what about the other lines? They all seem to have their merits (or maybe the best line is somewhere in between them). So, statisticians had to agree upon a definition of what is meant by "best-fitting

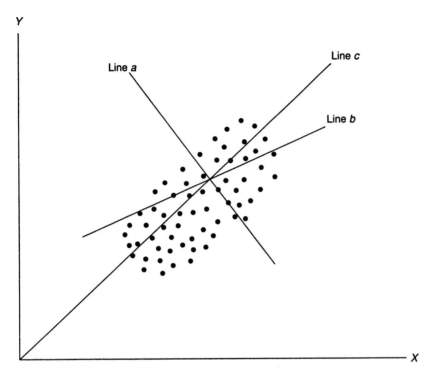

FIGURE 6.3 Scatterplot with alternate prediction lines.

line.'' The first decision was

The best-fitting line is the one that is closest to the data points.

But, what did they mean by "closest"? So, statisticians made a second decision:

A point on the scatterplot, say (X_a, Y_a), is close to the line if the predicted value of Y given X_a (i.e., $\hat{Y}_a = b_0 + b_1 X_a$) is close to the actual value of Y_a. That is, we want the errors $(Y - \hat{Y})$ to be as small as possible.

This is a mouthful, but it is easily understood by looking at the scatterplot in Figure 6.4. In this figure, there are four data points. I've labeled two of them a and c and drawn a potential best-fitting line. If you had the regression line and knew that a person's score on X was X_a, then you would predict a Y score of $\hat{Y}_a = b_0 + b_1 X_a$ (see where the dashed line hits the Y-axis). The difference between this predicted value $(\hat{Y}_a)$ and the actual value (Y_a) is called the "error of prediction." In general then,

$$\text{Error} = Y - \hat{Y}$$

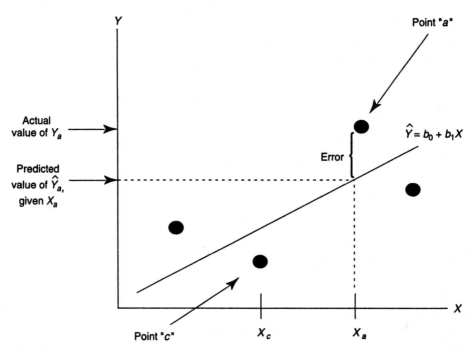

FIGURE 6.4 Simple scatterplot showing the difference between an actual value of Y and its predicted value.

So, "close" means that the errors are small. Further, note that we need to consider the size of the errors across *all* data points. In fact, we might then say, "Add up *all* the errors. The line that makes this sum as small as possible is the best line!" Can you see why people haven't adopted this? Think! O.K., the answer is in point *c* (why else do you think I bothered labeling it?). In the case of point *c*, the regression line prediction $(\hat{Y}_c)$ is *greater* than the actual value of Y_c. Thus, the error $(Y_c - \hat{Y}_c)$ is a negative number. So, if you add up all the errors, there will be both positive and negative numbers in the summation, the sum will be close to zero,[2] and the line might seem to fit the data well even though the magnitudes of the errors are large. To solve this problem, statisticians have decided that you should square the errors before summing them. Squaring certainly gets rid of all the negative signs! Then, the "best" line is the one that results in the smallest sum of squared errors. This criterion, which defines the best line, is called the "least squares criterion," and the resulting line is called the "regression line" (see the next chapter for an explanation of why it's called "regression"). More formally,

> **The least squares regression line $\hat{Y} = b_0 + b_1 X$ is the line that minimizes the sum of the squared errors about the line; i.e., $\Sigma(Y - \hat{Y})^2$ is minimized.**

[2] In fact, you can easily prove that the sum of the errors will always be *exactly* zero.

Here's an interesting question: Is there more than one line that has an equally small sum of squared errors? In the case of least squares regression, it turns out there's a very pleasant answer to this question:

There is always one, and only one, line that minimizes the sum of the squared errors.

The solution to finding the values of b_0 and b_1 that meet the least squares criterion turns out to be a straightforward exercise in calculus.[3] And, the expression for b_1 and b_0 can be put in raw data form as

VI.B
$$b_1 = \frac{\Sigma XY - (\Sigma X)(\Sigma Y)/n}{\Sigma X^2 - (\Sigma X)^2/n}$$

VI.C
$$b_0 = \bar{Y} - b_1\bar{X}$$

These expressions are rather easy to use. Notice that one typically computes b_1 first and then uses that estimate to find b_0. Also, the components in these equations should look familiar. We'll come back to that in a minute. But first, an example.

Example

While I was drafting this chapter, a colleague named Professor Gretzky[4] was in the process of assigning grades to his class of $n = 21$ students. Every semester, this professor told his students that individuals who missed some of his classes were more likely to receive poorer grades on course exams. Despite his constant admonitions, some students missed classes throughout the semester. Table VI.1 contains his entire class data for two variables: $X =$ number of days absent per student, and $Y =$ student's total exam score (maximum of 150). This table also contains the sum of the variables, the sum of their squares, and other summary statistics about the two variables. Application of Equations VI.B and VI.C yields

$$b_1 = \frac{7806 - 71(2444)/21}{469 - (71)^2/21} = -1.996$$

$$b_0 = 2444/21 - (-1.996)(71/21) = 123.13$$

[3] In a nutshell, you want to minimize $\Sigma(Y - \hat{Y})^2$. This is the same as minimizing $\Sigma(Y - b_0 - b_1X)^2$. Take the first derivative of this expression with respect to b_0 and b_1, set the two expressions equal to zero, and solve the resulting two equations for b_0 and b_1. By the way, those two equations are called the "normal equations" in regression analysis. Oh, don't forget (using second derivatives) to show that your solution is a minimum and not a maximum (see your calculus text if you have forgotten about this.)
[4] The professor's name has been changed to an alter ego, but the data are real.

TABLE VI.1 ACTUAL DATA FOR COURSE EXAM TOTAL AND CLASS ABSENCE

Person	No. of absences, X	Course exam total, Y	
1	4	101	
2	0	138	
3	5	118	
4	8	93	
5	0	136	$\Sigma X = 71$ $\Sigma Y = 2444$
6	2	114	$\Sigma X^2 = 469$ $\Sigma Y^2 = 289880$
7	3	93	$\Sigma XY = 7806$
8	0	136	$r_{XY} = -.409$
9	1	136	$s_X^2 = 11.45$ $s_Y^2 = 272.25$
10	4	93	
11	0	102	
12	8	127	
13	5	105	
14	0	148	
15	5	113	
16	5	99	
17	13	113	
18	0	111	
19	3	126	
20	4	121	
21	1	121	

Thus, the least squares regression line that best fits this data is

$$\hat{Y} = 123.13 - 1.996X$$

Both the scatterplot of the data and the graphed regression line appear in Figure 6.5.

The regression line certainly supports Professor Gretzky's statement about being absent! That is, for each additional day that a student is absent (i.e., a unit change in X), this equation predicts that the total score (Y) will go down by 1.996. In round terms, each day's absence is associated with two fewer points on the total score.[5]

SOME THOUGHTS ABOUT REGRESSION LINES

Ah, The Choices We Make

It is important to realize the choices that were made (*for* you) when defining the regression line. Of course, we assumed a linear relationship between X and Y (an assumption we'll remove later). Also, when summing the errors $(Y - \hat{Y})$ across

---

[5] Notice that if you don't miss any classes ($X = 0$), the regression line predicts a score of 123.13. In case you're interested, this value was the cutoff between an A and a B + in Gretzky's class. Cutoffs for adjacent letter grades in this class were separated by about 6 points on the total score (Y). So, all other things equal, someone who missed three classes would be predicted to get an entire letter grade lower than had those classes not been missed.

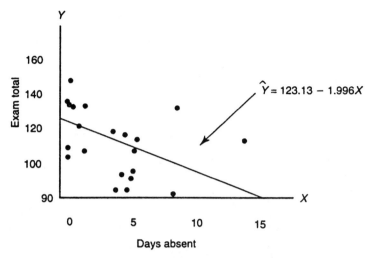

FIGURE 6.5 Regression line for Professor Gretzky's data.

all data points, we took care of the fact that some of these errors were negative by first squaring the errors. Note that this was a conscious choice by statisticians: certainly there are other ways of getting rid of the negative sign.[6] On the surface, it makes more sense to sum the absolute values of the errors ($\Sigma | Y - \hat{Y} |$). Had we minimized the sum of the absolute values of errors, the "best" regression line would be different (i.e., different values for b_0 and b_1)! In my opinion, squares were chosen (rather than absolute values) for a straightforward reason: it is very difficult to prove theorems about functions involving absolute values and relatively easier to prove theorems about squared functions.[7]

Another choice we made concerns the definition of "close," as in "the line should be close to the points." Consider the scatterplot in Figure 6.6. In this figure the error is defined by the vertical distance ($Y_a - \hat{Y}_a$). Making this distance smaller is what we meant by getting the points close to the line.

However, think back to your old trigonometry class. When you wanted to know how close a point was to a line, did you draw a picture like Figure 6.6? Of course not—you did something called "dropping a perpendicular." This meant drawing another line, from the point to the line in question, that formed a right angle to the original line (Figure 6.7). Notice that the distance in Figure 6.7 is different from the value of $Y - \hat{Y}$ = error in Figure 6.6. Again, had we selected dropping the perpendicular to define closeness to the line, and minimized the sum

---

[6] For example, $| Y - \hat{Y} |, (Y - \hat{Y})^4, (Y - \hat{Y})^6$, etc., all result in nonnegative values.

[7] The reason is the discontinuity of the absolute value function. For example, graph $Y = | X |$ for both positive and negative values of X. You'll get a V-shaped picture, with the discontinuity at the bottom of the V, where $X = 0$. This is also why variances are defined by $\Sigma(X - \bar{X})^2/(n - 1)$ and not $\Sigma | X - X |/(n - 1)$. In fact, some statisticians initially conceived of variance, correlations, etc., using absolute values, but the notion was discarded in favor of squares (no pun intended).

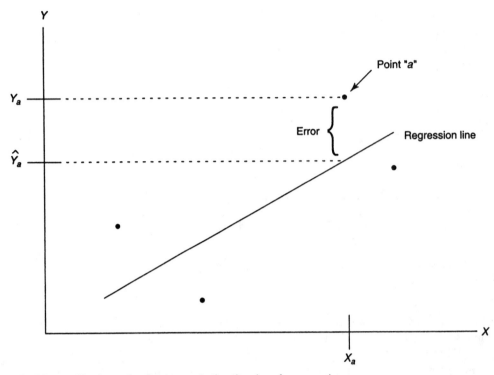

FIGURE 6.6   Simple scatterplot demonstrating the size of a regression error.

of *those* squared distances, we would have obtained yet a different line.[8] So, why do you think the vertical distance $(Y - \hat{Y})$ was adopted as the measure of closeness? Think.... That's right! As noted earlier, a common usage for a regression line is prediction. As such, our errors of prediction are parallel to the vertical Y-axis, and that's where our concerns are.

Here's another extreme point of view. Several pages back we readily dismissed line *a* in Figure 6.3 as a candidate for our regression line. But suppose we redefine "close" by saying that the regression line must *exactly* predict Y. Using this definition, line *a* is actually the best line in Figure 6.3 because it goes exactly through more points (two of them) than any other line drawn. Is this silly? Somewhat, but if you're trying to predict lottery values, isn't it better to be exactly correct once in a while than to be always *almost* correct? (Of course, the flaw here is that we want to predict future events, not just data in the current sample. The other lines probably do have a better chance of being exactly correct in new data.)

---

[8] In fact, a "best" line defined in this fashion has some appealing properties. First, there is no regression to the mean (see Chapter VII) associated with such a line. Second, there would be no difference between the line that predicts Y from X and the line that predicts X from Y (see later in this chapter).

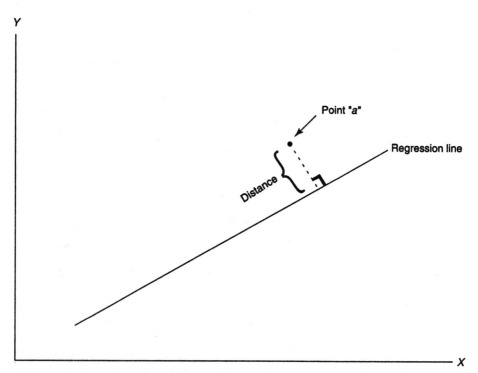

FIGURE 6.7 An alternative way of measuring distance from a point to a regression line.

In sum, there are many choices that can be made in defining the best-fitting line. Most have been made for you, but knowing these choices can help you understand the utility and limitations of regression analysis.

Alternate Formula for b_1

When Equation VI.B was presented, I noted that components of the formula should look familiar. So, go back and take a peek at the equation. Look familiar? Right! The numerator of the equation for b_1 is the same as the numerator for the Pearson correlation coefficient (see Chapter II, Equation II.A). The denominator of the equation for b_1 is similar to the variance of X (except for a division by $n - 1$). By remembering such equations for correlations and variances, it is straightforward algebra to demonstrate an alternate formula for b_1:

VI.D
$$b_1 = \frac{r_{YX} s_Y}{s_X}$$

This is probably the best way to remember the formula for b_1 (the slope). For example, in Figure 6.8 notice that if the scores on the dependent variable (Y) are "stretched out" (i.e., s_Y is large), then the slope of the regression line increases

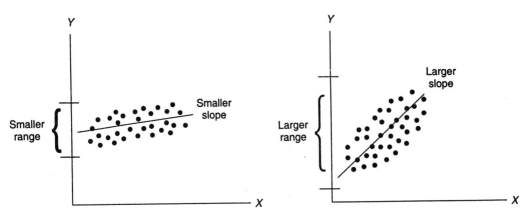

FIGURE 6.8 Two scatterplots demonstrating the relationship between s_Y and the regression slope.

(since s_Y is in the numerator). This makes sense (as does the reverse phenomenon for s_X). Also, note that

The slope, b_1, is related to, but not equal to, the correlation.

When r is positive, so is the slope; when r is 0, the slope is 0; etc. Only when the two standard deviations (s_Y and s_X) are equal will the slope equal the correlation.[9] One time this happens is when the data are standardized (more on standardization later).

There Are Really Two Regression Lines

Earlier in this chapter, it was stated that there was one, and only one, line that best "fit" the data. In fact, this is true if you consider any lines that might predict Y from X. In this case, Equations VI.B and VI.C determine the values of b_0 and b_1 that minimize $\Sigma(Y - \hat{Y})^2$.

However, suppose that one wished to predict X from Y, i.e., form the equation

VI.E $$\hat{X} = b_0^* + b_1^* Y$$

(This makes sense if there isn't any necessary causal priority between the two variables. For example, if Y is job performance and X is job satisfaction, it's

---

[9] A colleague and I once published an article (Bobko and Karren, 1979) demonstrating that even sophisticated psychometricians mistakenly equate slope and correlation. We drew two scatterplots with equal values of r yet different values of b_1. We did this by simply changing the scale (s_Y) on one of our variables. Many respondents mistakenly said the correlation was larger in the scatterplot with the larger slope. Of course, it wasn't. See Chapter IX for further discussion of the distinction between correlational and slope differences.

often just as interesting to predict satisfaction from performance as it is to predict performance from satisfaction.)

In Equation VI.E, the values of b_0^* and b_1^* are chosen such that $\sum(X - \hat{X})^2$ is minimized (the old least squares criterion again). Analogous to the results in Equations VI.C and VI.D, the appropriate solution is

VI.F
$$b_1^* = \frac{r_{YX} s_X}{s_Y}$$

VI.G
$$b_0^* = \bar{X} - b_1^* \bar{Y}$$

For example, in Professor Gretzky's data, the values of b_0^* and b_1^* are 13.15 and $-.084$, respectively. (Try it! See if you agree.) So, you can best predict the number of days a student was absent from his or her total score by the regression

$$\hat{X} = 13.15 - .084Y$$

The point to notice and remember (either through this example, or looking at the equations for $b_0, b_1, b_0^*,$ and b_1^*) is that

The regression line predicting Y from X is not the same line as the regression line predicting X from Y.[10]

To demonstrate this fact, the two regression lines (one predicting X, one predicting Y) from the data in Table VI.1 are shown in Figure 6.9.

If you're still not convinced, consider the case where the data are completely standardized, such that all means are 0 and all standard deviations are 1.0. Then, application of Equations VI.B and VI.C yields

$$\hat{z}_Y = rz_X$$

where z_Y and z_X are the standardized values of Y and X, respectively. Conversely, the least squares solution to predicting X can easily be derived from Equations VI.E through VI.G as

$$\hat{z}_X = rz_Y$$

---

[10] For example, you could solve the equation $\hat{X} = 13.15 - .084Y$ for Y by computing

$$\hat{X} - 13.15 = -.084Y$$
$$Y = (X/-.084) + (13.15/.084)$$
$$= 156.55 - 11.9\hat{X}$$

Note this is not the regression line derived for predicting Y. That was $\hat{Y} = 123.13 - 1.996X$.

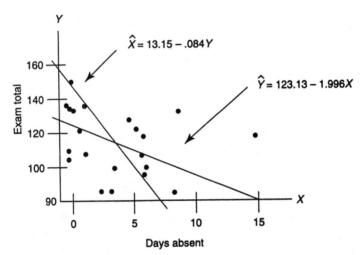

FIGURE 6.9 Professor Gretzky's data with two regression lines plotted (predict Y from X; predict X from Y).

or equivalently

$$z_Y = \frac{1}{r}\hat{z}_X$$

Thus, when z_Y is placed on the left-hand side of the equations, you can see that the two least squares prediction lines are different (one has slope r; the other $1/r$).

Implications for test fairness   Thus, while $r_{YX} = r_{XY}$ (i.e., as we noted in Chapter II, the correlation function is symmetric with respect to Y and X), the regression predicting Y from X is different than the regression predicting X from Y. This is important to remember and does indeed have consequences for our field. For example, one definition of a "fair" test is as follows:

> **Two individuals (e.g., from different EEO groups) who have the same score on a selection test (X) should have the same predicted performance score (Y).**

This famous definition of selection test fairness is attributed to Cleary (1968) and is most definitely based upon the regression predicting Y from X. On the other hand, Cole (1973) and Darlington (1971) argued that a selection procedure is fair if

> **Two individuals (e.g., from different EEO groups) who perform equally on the job should be predicted to have had equal scores on the selection test.**

This definition also seems reasonable and is clearly based on the regression predicting X from Y.

Now, Darlington (1971) demonstrated that these two well-known definitions of test fairness are mutually contradictory. However, should we be surprised by this (not pleasant) finding? No, because the two definitions are based on two different directional predictions and, as noted, the least squares regression solutions are not the same. [See Arvey and Faley (1988), if you're interested in reading a good summary of regression definitions of test fairness.]

GRESSION LINES AND *r*

The regression line was motivated by the desire to find the best-fitting line. The logical question at this point is, *How well did the best line do*? That is, we know there is no better line in the data at hand, but is it really worth it to even bother fitting a line to the scattered array of points? However, as I am often told by literary editors, the above question is incomplete, because editors always add the phrase "compared to what?" So we need a baseline index of fit.

The baseline   Suppose I collect some performance data (Y) for several employees and I share these Y-scores with you. Suppose I then pick an employee at random. I don't tell you whom I picked but ask you to predict his or her performance score. What should you predict? The answer is to compute $\bar{Y}$ (the mean of all the Y-scores) and predict that value for every person I pick. Thus, your baseline prediction equation should be[11]

$$\hat{Y}_{\text{no knowledge about } X} = \bar{Y}$$

This is a completely horizontal prediction line, with a slope of 0, and doesn't depend on X (since you weren't given any data about X: stingy, wasn't I?).

The regression   Now suppose that I really had collected predictor data (X) for each person and shared both X and Y data with you. I will give you values of X and ask you to predict corresponding scores on Y. At this point, you could draw a scatterplot of the data and/or compute the least squares prediction line $\hat{Y} = b_0 + b_1 X$. So, the question is how much better is this regression line than simply predicting $\bar{Y}$ all the time?

The index of fit   Please pay close attention to Figure 6.10. In the absence of information on X, I have plotted the baseline prediction $\hat{Y} = \bar{Y}$. Now consider point *a*. If we use the baseline prediction scheme, we make an error in predicting the value of Y for point *a*. This error (labeled "total error") is the difference

---

[11] In fact, it can be easily shown that $\bar{Y}$ *is* the least squares prediction function in this case. That is, $\Sigma(Y - \bar{Y})^2$ is smaller than any other $\Sigma(Y - \hat{Y})^2$ in the absence of information about X. By the way, this is another reason that statisticians like the mean as a measure of location.

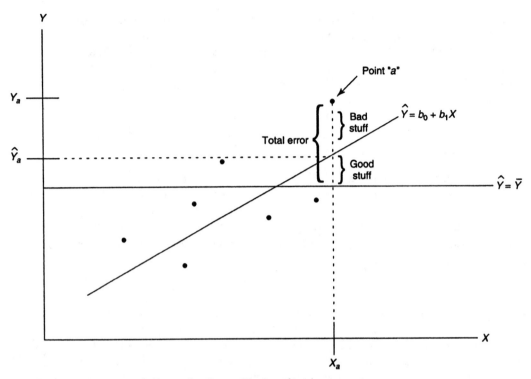

FIGURE 6.10   Scatterplot demonstrating the partitioning of total error.

between the actual Y score (Y) and it's predicted value ($\overline{Y}$). So

$$\text{Total error} = Y - \overline{Y}$$

Notice what happens when you get to use the regression line. If a person scores X_a on the selection test, you predict $\hat{Y}_a = b_0 + b_1 X_a$. Looking at the figure, your prediction ($\hat{Y}_a$) has become closer to the actual value (Y_a) than when you made predictions using just $\overline{Y}$. So, you've improved your predictive capacity (congratulations!). I've labeled this improvement "good stuff." Symbolically,

$$\text{Good stuff} = \text{improvement} = \hat{Y}_a - \overline{Y}$$

On the other hand, your prediction wasn't perfect, even when you used the regression line. There is still some residual error left over, which I've labeled "bad stuff." That is,

$$\text{Bad stuff} = \text{residual error left after regression used} = Y - \hat{Y}$$

(Don't forget that this is the error whose sum of squares is minimized by the regression line!)

Now, from the way I've drawn the figure it should be clear that

$$\text{Total error} = \text{good stuff} + \text{bad stuff}$$

Symbolically,

VI.H $$Y - \bar{Y} = (\hat{Y} - \bar{Y}) + (Y - \hat{Y})$$

(*Note*: The $\hat{Y}$'s "cancel out" on the right-hand side.)

Now, we want an index of how well the regression worked. Clearly, we want the improvement in prediction to be big (i.e., the "good stuff" should be big). This means we want the remaining error ("bad stuff") to be small. So, our index might be the ratio of the relative sizes of these two components. But, one more step is needed before we can go home: remember that, just as in the least squares criterion, we have to concern ourselves with *all* data points and we don't particularly care whether errors are positive or negative. So, we need to compute sums of squares across all data points. And, here comes a *truly amazing fact*:[12]

VI.I $$\Sigma(Y - \bar{Y})^2 = \Sigma(\hat{Y} - \bar{Y})^2 + \Sigma(Y - \hat{Y})^2$$

or $$\begin{array}{ccc} \text{Sum of squares} \\ \text{about means} \end{array} = \begin{array}{c} \text{sum of squared} \\ \text{improvement} \end{array} + \begin{array}{c} \text{sum of squared} \\ \text{error} \end{array}$$

We will also come to write Equation VI.I as

$$\text{SS total} = \text{SS regression} + \text{SS error}$$

or $$\text{SST} = \text{SSR} + \text{SSE}$$

where SS is shorthand for "sum of squares."

> *A Notational Aside* The value of $\Sigma(Y - \hat{Y})^2$ has been labeled "sum of squared error" ("SS error" or SSE for short). The statistics world is divided about fifty-fifty on this terminology. Some folks refer to the residual error $(Y - \hat{Y})$ as "error"; others refer to residual error as the "residual" (e.g., see the section on residual analysis later in this chapter). The folks who prefer the term "residual" note that it is more neutral in connotation than the term "error." I agree, but in this book, I've generally used the term "error" so as to better differentiate between SS regression = SSR and SS error = SSE.

[12] This fact is "truly amazing" because it appears that one can go from Equation VI.H to Equation VI.I simply by squaring each term. It's not quite that easy because when squaring the right-hand side of Equation VI.H, you have cross-products to contend with. The amazing part is that all these cross-products reduce to zero (after a little algebra)!

Now, in thinking about Equation VI.I, it is important to remember a few things. The value $\Sigma(Y - \bar{Y})^2$ indexes how well we do just by predicting the mean. It is our baseline and tells us how much room for improvement we have. The value $\Sigma(Y - \hat{Y})^2$ is *minimized* by the regression line. This is equivalent to saying that our improvement $[\Sigma(\hat{Y} - \bar{Y})^2]$ is *maximized*. Thus, statisticians propose the following index of success of the regression:

$$\text{Index of fit} = \frac{\text{actual improvement}}{\text{total potential improvement}} = \frac{\text{SSR}}{\text{SST}} = \frac{\Sigma(\hat{Y} - \bar{Y})^2}{\Sigma(Y - \bar{Y})^2}$$

I hope this makes sense because we have a really truly amazing fact (RTAF) coming up. (If you're not ready for it, please read the previous few pages again. Thanks.) O.K., the RTAF is

The index of fit, (SS regression)/(SS total), is equal to r^2.

So, we've come full circle back to Chapter II, where we noted that some folks interpret the magnitude of r by first squaring the value of r. That is, r^2 is an index of how much the sum of squared errors can be reduced by using a regression line (relative to the baseline model of always predicting $\bar{Y}$). *In this sense, regression and correlation are highly related.*

A Quick Example

Table VI.2 reproduces Professor Gretzky's data again. This time, several columns have been added so that we can compute the sum of squares needed for Equation VI.I. Note that in general (but not always) the errors after using the regression line are smaller than the baseline errors when $\bar{Y}$ is always predicted. In fact, $\Sigma(Y - \bar{Y})^2 = 5444.96$, while the sum of squared errors after using the regression is reduced to $\Sigma(Y - \hat{Y})^2 = 4533$. Therefore, we have *improved* our predictive capacity by a sum of squares amount of $5444.96 - 4533 = 911.96$. Then, by the really truly amazing fact above,

$$\frac{\text{SSR}}{\text{SST}} = \frac{911.96}{5444.96} = .1675 = r^2$$

Thus, Professor Gretzky can say that 16.75% of the variability in test performance (defined by sums of squares from mean performance) is associated with differences in absence rates. Also, note that the square root of .1675 is .409, which is exactly the magnitude of r reported earlier in Table VI.1!

The Analysis of Variance

The summary results of a regression can be reported in an analysis of variance (ANOVA) format. This is what most computer software packages do. The

TABLE VI.2 REGRESSION ERRORS FOR DATA IN TABLE VI.1

Person	X	Y	$\hat{Y}$	Total error, $Y - \bar{Y}$	Error after regression, $Y - \hat{Y}$
1	4	101	115	− 15.4	− 14.0
2	0	138	123	21.6	15.0
3	5	118	113	1.6	5.0
4	8	93	107	− 23.4	− 14.0
5	0	136	123	19.6	13.0
6	2	114	119	− 2.4	− 5.0
7	3	93	117	− 23.4	− 24.0
8	0	136	123	19.6	13.0
9	1	136	121	19.6	15.0
10	4	93	115	− 23.4	− 22.0
11	0	102	123	− 14.4	− 21.0
12	8	127	107	10.6	20.0
13	5	105	113	− 11.4	− 8.0
14	0	148	123	31.6	25.0
15	5	113	113	− 3.4	0.0
16	5	99	113	− 17.4	− 14.0
17	13	113	97	− 3.4	16.0
18	0	111	123	− 5.4	− 12.0
19	3	126	117	9.6	9.0
20	4	121	115	4.6	6.0
21	1	121	121	4.6	0.0

$\sum(Y - \bar{Y})^2 = 5444.96$ $\sum(Y - \hat{Y})^2 = 4533.00$

ANOVA summary is simply a listing of the results of Equation VI.I. In general, the ANOVA table looks like this:

Source	Sum of squares	df
Regression	$\sum(\hat{Y} - \bar{Y})^2$	1
Error	$\sum(Y - \hat{Y})^2$	$n - 2$
Total	$\sum(Y - \bar{Y})^2$	$n - 1$

So, in the specific case of Professor Gretzky, the computer might spit out something like this:

Source	Sum of squares	df
Regression	911.96	1
Error	4533.00	19
Total	5444.96	20

There is really nothing new in the second column of this ANOVA table. Just always keep in mind that the total sum of squares is the *baseline*, i.e., how well you do if you always predict with $\bar{Y}$. And, the error sum of squares is the quantity that's being minimized by the regression (and the least squares criterion).

(Oh, the third column? We'll come back to the use of these degrees of freedom in the next part of this chapter. For now, note that the degrees of freedom indeed sum to the total degrees of freedom. There's 1 df for regression because we've used one X to predict Y. The $(n - 1)$ total degrees of freedom is our old friend used in the denominator of the formula for variances and/or standard deviations in introductory sadistics books.)

THE UNDERLYING REGRESSION MODEL

It is crucial to realize how far we have gone in this chapter without invoking any underlying distribution theory (e.g., any assumptions about normality or error variances). However, as is usually the case, behavioral scientists wish to test particular hypotheses using sample regressions. To accomplish this, we need to add some assumptions (e.g., normality, independence) so that statisticians can prove their theorems!

A bit of notation   We need to distinguish between population parameters and sample estimates. For population regression weights, boldface capitals are used: e.g., $Y = \mathbf{B}_0 + \mathbf{B}_1 X$. For sample estimates, I will continue to use lowercase letters: e.g., $\hat{Y} = b_0 + b_1 X$.

The Regression Model

So far, we have used equations that assume a linear relation between Y and X (e.g., $Y = \mathbf{B}_0 + \mathbf{B}_1 X$). I suppose if you were a philosophical determinist, such a model would be acceptable. However, most people say, "This model is only an approximation. To make it more realistic *and* more interesting, let's add some random error." Thus, the underlying population model we adopt is

VI.J $$Y = \mathbf{B}_0 + \mathbf{B}_1 X + e$$

where e is a random error component with the following assumed properties:

1 Independence (i.e., the error associated with each data point is independent of every other error value).
2 The population mean of e is 0.
3 For a given value of X, the population variance of e is σ_e^2.
4 For a given value of X, e has a normal distribution.

Now, what do all these assumptions imply? Note that we used the phrase "for a given value of X" a few times. Suppose we consider subjects who all have the same score on X, say X_a. Should all these subjects have exactly the same score on Y (i.e., $Y_a = \mathbf{B}_0 + \mathbf{B}_1 X_a$)? Probably not! (If they did, this would be the deterministic model.)

(If you're not convinced, consider the following example. Let X = SAT math score and Y = grade point average. Does everybody who has an SAT math score of 600 get exactly the same grade point average in college?)

The addition of the e term in Equation VI.J simply means that some individuals will *score higher* on Y than predicted (positive value of e), while other individuals will *score lower* on Y than predicted (negative value of e). However, on average, the Y-score for individuals with X-scores of X_a is exactly $\mathbf{B}_0 + \mathbf{B}_1 X_a$ because the mean of the errors is assumed to be 0.

Here's another way to say the same thing. Let Y/X_a stand for "the Y-score for someone who scores X_a on X" or, as statisticians say, "the score of Y *conditional* on $X = X_a$." If $Y = \mathbf{B}_0 + \mathbf{B}_1 X + e$ and the mean of e is 0 (as assumed), then the mean (expected) Y score, conditional on $X = X_a$ is [13]

$$E\{Y/X_a\} = \mathbf{B}_0 + \mathbf{B}_1 X_a$$

Again, as the X scores get bigger, so do the Y-scores, on average. And this increase is linear! As statisticians say, the value of the conditional means on Y is a linear function of X.

If this has just confused you further, I think a picture will make it clear. In words, the statements are: on average, subjects who have higher scores on X tend to have higher scores on Y (assuming a positive relationship). And, for any particular value of $X = X_a$, there is a mean value of $Y(= \mathbf{B}_0 + \mathbf{B}_1 X_a)$ and a *distribution* of values around that mean value. By assumption, this conditional distribution is a normal distribution, with variance σ_e^2. Figure 6.11 is associated with all these words.

Error Variance

Note that the variance of the errors doesn't depend upon the value of X; e.g., in Figure 6.11, σ_e^2 is the same whether you're at $X = X_a$ or $X = X_b$. This assumption of equal error variance is labeled "homoscedasticity."[14] We'll discuss this assumption later, but it's nice to know another word that has so many syllables! Also, you will often see σ_e^2 written as $\sigma_{Y \cdot X}^2$. This notation is read "the variance of Y, conditional on a particular value of X" and again reaffirms the conditional nature of the variance. Since $\sigma_{Y \cdot X}^2$ is assumed to be the same for *all* values of X (our friend homoscedasticity), this chapter uses σ_e^2 rather than fooling around with any subscripts about X.

[13] Hopefully, the notation $E\{Y/X\}$ is familiar to you. If not, simply realize that $E\{Y/X\}$ is read as "the expected value of Y given a particular value of X." Basically, "expected value" is another way of saying "mean" or "average." So, $E\{Y/X\}$ can be read as the average of the Y-scores associated with a particular X-score. I have used the $E\{\ \}$ notation in this chapter just to show you how statisticians often write regression equations.

[14] The assumption of equal error variances is statistically the *same* assumption as that of equal cell variances in the analysis of variance.

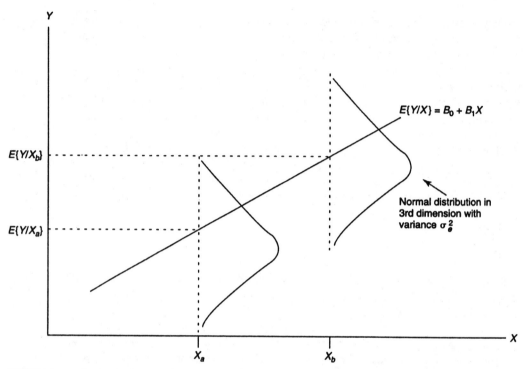

FIGURE 6.11 A three-dimensional model of the underlying assumptions in two-variable regression.

Before considering distribution theory in the next section, it is critical to think even more about σ_e^2. Essentially, σ_e^2 is the *variance* of the *errors* in prediction about the regression line. In the sample, we designated these errors by $Y - \hat{Y}$ and it was the sum of these squared errors $[\Sigma(Y - \hat{Y})^2]$ that was minimized.

Now, here's a fact. The sample estimate of σ_e^2 is

$$\text{VI.K} \quad \hat{\sigma}_e^2 = s_e^2 = \text{variance of sample errors} = \frac{\Sigma(Y - \hat{Y})^2}{n - 2} = \frac{\text{SSE}}{n - 2}$$

The numerator of this fact should be familiar. That is, to compute *any* variance, you substract the mean from each observation, square the difference, and then add the results.[15] In our case, each error is denoted by $Y - \hat{Y}$. However, since the mean of the errors is zero, we don't need to subtract anything further before we square and add the results [i.e., $(Y - \hat{Y}) - 0 = Y - \hat{Y}$].

On the other hand, the denominator of Equation VI.K is a bit of a surprise. In beginning statistics classes, variances are usually formed by dividing by $n - 1$.

[15] For example, the numerator for the sample variance of X is $\Sigma(X - \bar{X})^2$.

However, it is more correct to think of variances as being formed by dividing sums of squares by degrees of freedom. And, as noted in the analysis of variance table in this chapter, the degrees of freedom for error is $n - 2$; hence, Equation VI.K.

We now turn to the properties of b_0, b_1, and s_e^2 necessary to test regression hypotheses.

STRIBUTION THEORY

The following facts are noted (without proof):

1 s_e^2 is an unbiased estimate of σ_e^2; i.e., $E\{s_e^2\} = \sigma_e^2$. (*Note*: The use of $n - 2$ in the denominator of the formula for s_e^2 helps guarantee this result.)

2 b_0 is an unbiased estimate of $\mathbf{B}_0$; b_1 is an unbiased estimate of $\mathbf{B}_1$. In other words, $E\{b_0\} = \mathbf{B}_0$ and $E\{b_1\} = \mathbf{B}_1$.

3 The variance of the sampling distribution of b_1 can be estimated by[16]

VI.L
$$s_{b_1}^2 = \frac{s_e^2}{(n - 1)s_X^2}$$

4 You can test the hypotheses $H_0: \mathbf{B}_1 = 0$ by forming the ratio of $b_1 - 0$ (i.e., how close the sample value of b_1 is to 0) to the standard deviation of b_1 (which you get from Equation VI.L). This ratio has a t-distribution with $(n - 2)$ degrees of freedom. That is,

VI.M
$$t_{n-2} \sim \frac{b_1}{\sqrt{s_e^2/(n - 1)s_X^2}}$$

5 Here's a technical fact that's sort of fun to know. There is a famous theorem in regression analysis (called the "Gauss-Markov theorem") that proves that the estimators b_0 and b_1 are BLUE. This doesn't mean that the estimators are clinically depressed. Rather, BLUE stands for "best linear unbiased estimator."[17]

---

[16] Tests involving the intercept parameter ($\mathbf{B}_0$) are almost never seen in behavioral research. The value of the intercept can be changed by simple mean shifts in the scoring scheme (e.g., $-2, -1, 0, 1, 2$ rather than $1, 2, 3, 4, 5$ for a 5-point scale), and we in the field rarely have agreed upon zero points for our measurement. Nonetheless, for completeness, note that you can estimate the variance of b_0 by

$$s_{b_0}^2 = \frac{s_e^2}{n} + \frac{s_e^2(\overline{X})^2}{n s_X^2}$$

and then conduct a t-test with $(n - 2)$ degrees of freedom for $H_0: \mathbf{B}_0 = 0$ by dividing b_0 by its standard deviation.

[17] Just remember to say, "The estimators are BLUE" and *not* "BLUE estimators." The latter phrase is redundant: "best linear unbiased estimator estimators." It's like saying "the Rio Grande River."

The property of unbiasedness for b_0 and b_1 was noted in fact 2 above. The descriptor "best" here means "minimum variance." For example, for all possible unbiased estimators of $\mathbf{B}_1$ (and there are lots of them), only one estimator (the b_1 we've been using) has the smallest sampling variance (given in Equation VI.L). This is a terrific fact. It means that our estimate of $\mathbf{B}_1$ (i.e., b_1) is the most "accurate" unbiased one available. It also means that when we test $H_0 : \mathbf{B}_1 = 0$, we'll have relatively high power, since the standard deviation of the sampling distribution of b_1 is as small as possible.

An Example

Earlier in this chapter, we considered Professor Gretzky's regression that predicted final exam score (Y) from days absent (X). The data were presented in Table VI.1, and the resulting regression line was

$$\hat{Y} = 123.13 - 1.996X$$

Now, suppose Professor Gretzkey wants to test $H_0 : \mathbf{B}_1 = 0$. Note that this is a useful hypothesis. It's asking whether or not the slope of the regression line is 0. *In other words, should we bother to compute a regression line ($\mathbf{B}_1 \neq 0$) or not ($\mathbf{B}_1 = 0$)?*

The numerator of the t-test for this hypothesis is $-1.996 - 0 = -1.996$. For the denominator, we need the standard deviation of b_1 (obtained from Equation VI.L). From Table VI.1 note that $n = 21$ and $s_X^2 = 11.45$. Further s_e^2 is the variance of the errors discussed in Equation VI.K as

$$s_e^2 = \frac{\text{SSE}}{n - 2}$$

Using ANOVA table for these data (presented earlier), we have

$$s_e^2 = \frac{4532}{(21 - 2)} = 238.58$$

Thus, from Equation VI.L, the sampling variance of b_1 is

$$s_{b_1}^2 = \frac{s_e^2}{(n - 1)s_X^2} = \frac{238.58}{20(11.45)} = 1.042$$

In other words, *the standard deviation of the sampling distribution of b_1* is

$$s_{b_1} = \sqrt{s_{b_1}^2} = \sqrt{1.042} = 1.021$$

The t-ratio is formed as

$$t_{n-2} \sim \frac{-1.996}{1.021} = -1.955$$

The critical t-value with 19 df, two sides, $p = .05$, is 2.093 (see the Appendix, Table A.1). Thus, Professor Gretzky's finding is not statistically significant (although had a one-sided test, $H_0 : \mathbf{B}_1 = 0$ versus $H_a : \mathbf{B}_1 < 0$, been used a priori, significance would be obtained since the critical t-value is then 1.729).

me Thoughts on Distribution Theory Results

First, note that the structure of the equation for the variance of b_1 (Equation VI.L) makes sense. Our old friend n (actually $n - 1$) is once again in the denominator. Thus, as the sample size goes up, the standard deviation of b_1 goes down (by the factor $\sqrt{n}$) and more statistical power (to reject H_0) is obtained. This is what Professor Gretzkey needed above to get statistical significance: a bigger class!

Second, consider the hypothesis that we tested, i.e., $H_0 : \mathbf{B}_1 = 0$. This was tantamount to asking the question, Does it help at all to form a regression line when predicting Y? Of course, you don't need regression analysis to answer this question because you're simply asking, Is there any linear relationship between Y and X? So, we can restate the hypothesis as $H_0 : \rho_{YX} = 0$. (After all, we know from Equation VI.D that $b_1 = rs_Y/s_X$. Thus, the slope is zero if and only if the correlation is 0.) Remember how to test $H_0 : \rho_{YX} = 0$? Exactly! From the t-ratio (see Chapter III)

$$t_{n-2} = \frac{r\sqrt{n-2}}{\sqrt{1-r^2}}$$

A little algebra will demonstrate that this t-ratio is identical to the t-ratio in Equation VI.M. [If you're not convinced, use Professor Gretzky's data. With $r = -.409$ and $n = 21$, you should get, within rounding error, the same (nonsignificant) t-ratio of -1.955 that was obtained when we tested the significance of the value $b_1 = -1.996$.] *In simple (one-predictor) regression, the significance test for $H_0 : \mathbf{B}_1 = 0$ is equivalent to the test for $H_0 : \rho_{YX} = 0$.*

Finally, there is yet another equivalent test of these hypotheses. That is, in your introductory statistics class, an ANOVA table generally had at least two more columns, labeled "mean square" and "F-ratio." The mean square was obtained by dividing a sum of squares by its respective degrees of freedom (as noted earlier, this is how variances are formed). Then, two mean squares were divided to form an F-ratio. Thus, Professor Gretzky's ANOVA computer printout might look like the following table:

Source	Sum of squares	df	Mean square	F-ratio
Regression	911.96	1	911.96	912 / 238 = 3.82
Error	4533.00	19	238.58	
Total	5444.96	20		

The first three columns of this table were displayed earlier in this chapter. The *mean square error* (MSE = 238.58) is our old friend s_e^2! (This is crucial to see. Go back to the definitions of s_e^2 and sum of squared errors if you're not convinced.) The F-ratio (MSR divided by MSE) has 1 df in the numerator and 19 df in the denominator. And, the additional assumptions about error (normality, independence, etc.) allow statisticians to prove that this ratio has an F-distribution.

The F-ratio answers three questions: (1) Was the regression worth it? (2) We tried to fit a line that reduced squared errors better than just predicting $\hat{Y} = \bar{Y}$; was the reduction in sum of squares significant? (3) In Professor Gretzky's case, Is 4533.00 significantly less than 5444.96? These questions, and the associated F-test, are *different ways of asking the same question* contained in the null hypotheses $H_0 : \mathbf{B}_1 = 0$ and $H_0 : \rho_{YX} = 0$. (If you're from Missouri, see for yourself. You just have to remember the old statistics fact that when you square a t-ratio, you get an F-ratio with 1 df in the numerator. Thus, to convert the ANOVA's F-ratio of 3.82 to a t-ratio, take the square root. You get the same value of $t = 1.95$ that we had before!)[18]

An Application of Bivariate Regression

Gordon and Fitzgibbons (1982) investigated the role of seniority in staffing decisions. They noted that "unionists strongly advocate the concept of seniority" (p. 311) in deciding whom to promote from within the workforce. Gordon and Fitzgibbons tested this assumption by constructing a regression line to predict future job performance (Y) from a measure of seniority (X). As a comparison, they also constructed a regression line to predict future job performance (Y) from past job performance (Z).

Here are some relevant statistics. For the measure of future performance (Y, recorded 9 to 12 months after X and Z), $\bar{Y} = 119.5$ and $s_y = 22.1$. For the seniority measure (X, in years), $\bar{X} = 3.94$ and $s_x = 4.30$. The sample size was $n = 162$. OK, can you now estimate the regression equation predicting future performance from seniority? That's right—I still need to provide the correlation between Y and X. It was $r_{yx} = .07$.

The regression using seniority (X) as a sole predictor is $\hat{Y} = b_0 + b_1 X$ where, from Equations VI.D and VI.C,

$$b_1 = r_{YX}\left(\frac{s_Y}{s_X}\right) = \frac{.07(22.1)}{4.3} = .36$$

and

$$b_0 = \bar{Y} - b_1 \bar{X} = 119.5 - .36(3.94) = 118.1$$

Thus, the regression is

$$\text{Future performance} = 118.1 + .36(\text{seniority in years})$$

---

[18] Beware of unscrupulous folks who say, "My correlation was significant. This was supported by a significant test of b_1 and confirmed by a significant F-ratio." Nothing's been independently confirmed or supported. Assuming the t-tests are two-sided tests, it's all mathematically the same thing.

Now, Gordon and Fitzgibbons could have conducted a statistical test to see if $b_1 = .36$ was significantly greater than zero (i.e., test $H_0 : B_1 = 0$). However, they were smart and noted that this test is equivalent to the test of the correlation ($r_{YX} = .07$), which was *not* significant. So, they concluded that seniority does not significantly predict future performance.

I'm sure you can guess what's coming next. The regression predicting future performance from past performance, $\hat{Y} = b_0 + b_1 Z$, *did* have a significant b_1 value (because the correlation between Y and Z, $r_{yz} = .34$, was significant). So, these authors concluded that past performance, and not seniority, had value in staffing decisions.[19]

EDICTION INTERVALS

As noted earlier, one of the primary applications of regression analysis is the prediction of an individual's score on Y (e.g., of future performance). The regression function $\hat{Y}_a = b_0 + b_1 X_a$ provides a *point estimate* of the predicted value of Y for a single individual who scores $X = X_a$. As usual, statisticians get nervous when providing point estimates, and so they qualify their lack of prescience by placing intervals around the single estimate. (This is analogous to the so-called "margin of error" in opinion polls.)[20]

Using regression results given earlier, it can be shown that a 95% prediction interval for $\hat{Y}_a$ (i.e., the predicted value of Y for an individual who scores $X = X_a$) is

$$\text{VI.N} \qquad \hat{Y}_a \pm t_{.975, n-2} \left[s_e \sqrt{1 + \frac{1}{n} + \frac{\left(X_a - \bar{X}\right)^2}{(n-1)s_X^2}} \right]$$

where $t_{.975, n-2}$ is the critical t-value ($p = .05$, two sides) with $n - 2$ degrees of freedom.

me Thoughts About Equation VI.N

The expression in square brackets in Equation VI.N is the standard error of $\hat{Y}_a$. The first component (s_e) is simply the sample estimate of the standard deviation of the errors. However, note that there are more complicated components inside the brackets as well. Intuitively speaking, these other terms arise because, when estimating $\hat{Y}_a$, one first estimates b_0 and b_1—and all of the error associated with

[19] The authors conducted other, more sophisticated, analyses in their study, but the conclusions remained unchanged.

[20] Note that a 95% prediction interval is constructed to have the following property: 95% of the intervals constructed in this manner will contain the true value of the underlying population parameter (in this case, the individual's true value of Y). If you have forgotten about these things, see your introductory statistics book again!

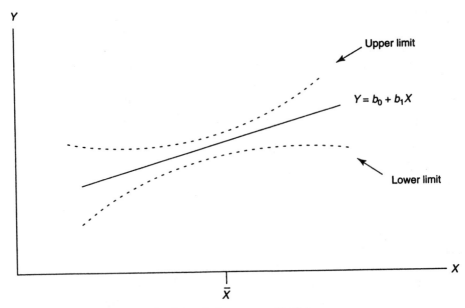

FIGURE 6.12 Typical prediction intervals for a regression line.

those parameter estimates must also be incorporated. (In fact, see Equation VI.L or footnote 16 to get an idea where all these factors come from.)

The term $(X_a - \overline{X})^2$ has an interesting implication. Namely, as X_a gets further from the mean $(\overline{X})$, this term gets larger, the standard error gets larger, and the prediction interval around the value of $\hat{Y}_a$ becomes wider. This means the prediction intervals look like Figure 6.12. In words, this simply says that individuals who score at the extremes on X are predicted with relatively greater error than individuals scoring near the mean.

A Quick Example

Consider Professor Gretzky's data again. Suppose there is a conscientious student (a hypothetical construct?) who normally wouldn't think of missing any classes. However, the student has an opportunity to extend spring break vacation by skipping two classes to get the right travel connections. What's the student's estimated exam score? Should the student go?

In this case, the student will be absent 2 days $(X = 2)$. The predicted total exam score is $\hat{Y} = 123.73 - 1.996X_a = 123.13 - 1.996(2) = 119.31$. For this data, we also know that $s_e = 15.45$, $s_X^2 = 11.45$, $\overline{X} = 3.381$, and $n = 21$. Further, the critical t-value is $t_{.975, 19df} = 2.093$. So, the prediction interval becomes

$$\hat{Y} \pm t_{.975,\,19}\left[15.45\sqrt{1 + \frac{1}{21} + \frac{(2 - 3.381)^2}{20(11.45)}}\,\right]$$

or $119.31 \pm 2.093\ (15.88)$ or 86.07 and 152.55.

By the way, a personal communication from Professor Gretzky indicates that a score of 150 is an A, while a score of 86 is a D. So, this student has quite a predicted range of performance and might have to use other factors to decide (Can missed work be made up? Will the weather be nice? Will parents send sufficient travel money?).

An Aside   Beware of individuals who mistakenly compute prediction intervals as $\hat{Y} \pm t(s_e)$. This is certainly tempting—it's easier. But it's also incorrect because it doesn't account for the variability in estimating b_0 and b_1. In fact, we once published an article (Bobko, Sapinkopf, and Anderson, 1978) where it was reported that over 40% of introductory statistics books in psychology use incorrect prediction interval formulas.

ME REGRESSION LEFTOVERS

ing Beyond the Data

Statistics instructors often say, "Don't use regression lines to predict beyond the range of X scores available in the sample." Certainly Equation VI.N supports this statement, in that prediction gets more variable as you move away from $\overline{X}$. Another basis for the prediction concern is the slope of the regression function. Within the sample data, one finds the best-fitting line. However, there is no guarantee that the regression will continue to be linear *beyond* the sample values of X. Can you think of reasons why? There are lots (e.g., diminishing returns on Y; the scale on Y has a natural limit, such as 100% correct; if X is time, other conditions might intervene at some point such that the entire organization, and all relationships within it, are changed).

ndardization

In the behavioral sciences, most measurement scales have arbitrary means (or zero points). For example, IQ is traditionally centered at 100, yet SAT scores were originally normed to means of 500. Therefore, as noted in Chapter I, some researchers routinely standardize their data (i.e., convert to means of 0 and variances of 1.0) in order to be able to compare results across studies. It is important to note that testing standardized and unstandardized slopes for significance will give *identical* results (i.e., while the value of the slopes are different, their standard deviations change proportionally, and so the *t*-ratio remains unaffected). However, earlier in this chapter, we noted that standardization implies that the *slope* of a regression line becomes the *correlation* (and the standardized intercept is 0). We also stated earlier that b_1 was an unbiased estimator of B_1 (as part of the Gauss-Markov theorem). On the other hand, statisticians know that r is a biased estimate of ρ (cf. Hotelling, 1953). So, there's an inconsistency here. What gives?

The answer is that *standardization of data causes all the nice statistical distribution results in regression to be slightly altered* (cf. Bobko and Schemmer, 1980). For example, as noted, the regression weights (e.g., the slope as the correlation) are no longer exactly unbiased (although the bias, of order $1/n$, is generally ignorable). Intuitively, the reason is that standardization is done by subtracting the *sample* mean and dividing by the *sample* standard deviation. These values can change from sample to sample, and so it's not the same as a fixed linear transformation of the data (which would *not* result in any loss of statistical properties).

The point here is that you don't get something (standardization and comparability across studies) for nothing. As in almost all of statistics, there's a judgement choice involved. In fact, there's one more aspect of standardization and regression. In Chapter V, we noted that correlations are generally attenuated (reduced in magnitude) under range restriction. Therefore, *the standardized slope (a correlation) is also generally reduced by range restriction. This is not the case for unstandardized slope estimates.* To see this, just think about the scatterplot and regression line (i.e., the line of conditional means on Y) in Figure 6.13. As you move the cutoff point further to the right on the X-axis, the value of r for the range-restricted data goes down, but clearly the slope of the line segment regression line remains the same.[21] Again, the decision to standardize has gains *and* costs.

Fixed-*X* Versus Random-*X* Models

You may have run across this distinction in the design of experiments literature as fixed versus random effects. Essentially, the regression model described throughout this chapter fixed a value of X (say, X_a) and then assumed a normal distribution of errors around the mean $B_0 + B_1 X_a$. In theory, the X-values are

---

[21] Something about the slope *does* change with a restricted range on X: since s_x^2 is reduced, the variance of b_1 is increased (look at Equation VI.L again). This makes intuitive sense—with a small range of X values, it's harder to get a handle on the actual slope. Sometimes the slope is much too high; sometimes it's much too low (i.e., b_1 is unbiased but highly variable).

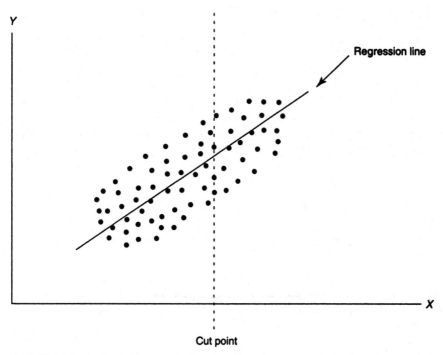

FIGURE 6.13 Scatterplot demonstrating the effect of range restriction in estimates of slopes.

fixed in advance (e.g., letting X be certain levels of a treatment) and all interpretations are made contingent upon these fixed values of X. Now, you and I know that's not the way it often happens in behavioral science. Usually, subjects are chosen at random and you take the values of X (and Y) you get! When making inferences and hypothesis tests, you want to generalize beyond the particular distribution of X-values you obtained (e.g., in Professor Gretzky's data, no subject was absent exactly 6 days, yet this value of X is just as interesting as any other). So, you treat the X-values as scores that *vary* from sample to sample. Such a model is labeled a "random-X" model. Now, a statement that might concern you is that all the results presented so far are true (and easily derived) for the "fixed-X" case. The good news is that, although this is more difficult to prove, all results presented are also true for the random-X case as well (assuming bivariate normality). I thought you'd want to know!

nstrained Regression

As noted earlier, the choice of scale score can be somewhat arbitrary in behavioral science research. Once in a while, though, a true zero point on the

X-and Y-scales can be assumed. For example, a biopsychologist once asked me for statistical advice on an experiment in which he was lobotomizing portions of pigeon brains to see what the pigeons' subsequent behavior (Y) would be. The researcher's independent variable (X) was the proportion of brain tissue left intact. He wanted to conduct a regression predicting Y from X and said, "Clearly, if $X = 0$, then no behavior can occur ($Y = 0$)." Therefore, this researcher wanted to *constrain* the regression line to go through the origin. In other words, the intercept should be 0 and the model to be assumed was $Y = B_1 X + e$. If this example is too bloody for you, here are other examples where constrained regression might be appropriate:

1 $Y =$ number of errors made by a typist; $X =$ number of words typed.

2 $Y =$ dollars earned in the stock market; $X =$ dollars invested in the stock market.

3 $Y =$ number of houses sold by a real estate agent; $X =$ number of houses shown by a real estate agent.[22]

In all of the above cases, the constrained prediction equation might be $\hat{Y} = b_1 X$. Just as in regular old regression, we need to minimize the sum of the squared errors $[\Sigma(Y - \hat{Y})^2]$. However, unlike regular regression, the value of b_1 that satisfies the least squares criterion is now

$$b_1 = \frac{\Sigma XY}{\Sigma X^2}$$

Notice that deviation scores ($X - \bar{X}$ or $Y - \bar{Y}$) are not used. Also, because only one parameter is estimated, only 1 df is used. Therefore, s_e^2 is estimated as $\Sigma(Y - \hat{Y})^2/(n - 1)$.

Finally, if you do conduct constrained regressions, beware of attempts to interpret the value of r^2; it can be outside the range 0 to $+1$. For example suppose the data look like Figure 6.14. As you can see, the constrained regression in this case actually does worse than the baseline prediction $\hat{Y} = \bar{Y}$. (This couldn't happen if you allowed b_0 to vary.)

Residual Analysis

The first half of this chapter developed regression lines to *describe* and *predict* data. We then made a transition to statistical *inference* by making some distributional assumptions about the error term, e (i.e., mean of 0, normality, independence, homoscedasticity). It is becoming common in the literature to check for the validity of these statistical assumptions by plotting the sample values of the errors ($Y - \hat{Y}$) versus sample values of X and visually inspecting

[22] Can you think of better examples? A cursory review of the applied human resource management literature found no examples of constrained regression. If you know of any, feel free to let me know. In any case, the notion of constraining a regression has heuristic value.

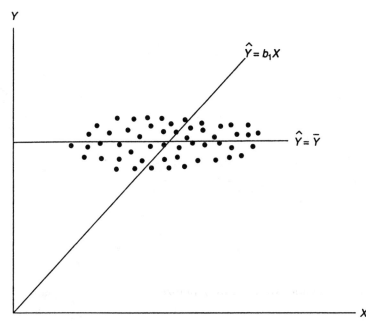

FIGURE 6.14 A scatterplot demonstrating the potential for a poor fit when using a constrained regression.

these plots for abnormal patterns. Since errors are often called ''residuals,'' these procedures are often labeled ''residual analyses.'' Now, if all assumptions about e were fine, then for each value of X you'd expect a normal distribution of errors (residuals), centered at zero, with equal variance regardless of the value of X.

Two hypothetical residual plots are shown in Figures 6.15 and 6.16. In Figure 6.15, things seem to be fine in the sense that, for any given value of X, the mean of the errors is close to zero and the variance (or range) of the errors is constant. However, Figure 6.16 depicts a residual analysis where the homoscedasticity assumption has been violated because the conditional variance becomes greater with increasing values of X.

Another hypothetical residual plot is shown in Figure 6.17. There could be several reasons for the outcome in Figure 6.17. First, it might be that the relationship between Y and X is truly different depending upon whether X is large or not (and, therefore, two regressions lines are needed).[23] Or, if X represents time, then the independence assumption might be violated (i.e., a positive e during one time period may cause a positive e in the subsequent time period).

---

[23] For example, Rothstein (1990) obtained such a result and as a consequence separately analyzed her results for low, medium, and high values of X. In her case, she was predicting performance reliability (Y) from months of job experience (X) and concluded that the relation was different (strongest) during the first year.

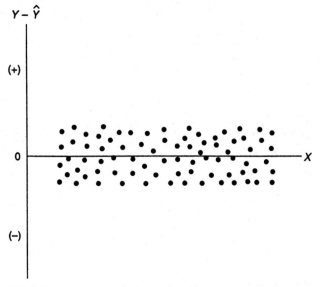

FIGURE 6.15   Hypothetical plot of residuals: 1.

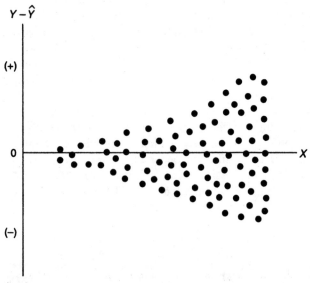

FIGURE 6.16   Hypothetical plot of residuals: 2.

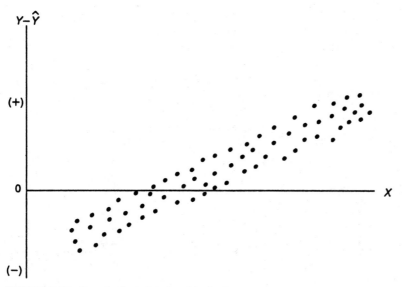

FIGURE 6.17   Hypothetical plot of residuals: 3.

An Aside   An analysis of time series models is beyond the scope of this book. However, there is a statistic, the Durbin-Watson d, that can be used to look for the presence of dependence across residuals. Basically, assume that Y is measured once across each of t time periods (i.e., $X = 1,2....,t$). Let $e_x = (Y - \hat{Y})_X$ be the residual for the Xth time period. The Durbin-Watson statistic is $d = \Sigma_2^t(e_X - e_{X-1})^2/\Sigma_1^t(e_X^2)$. The value of d ranges from 0 to 4. It will tend to be near 2.0 if the residuals are uncorrelated, between 0 and 2 if the residuals are positively related, and between 2 and 4 if the residuals are negatively related.[24]

Of course, if you check for the validity of underlying assumptions using residuals and everything's fine, then you've got it made. However, you should be prepared for answers you didn't want (i.e., violation of assumptions). The question then becomes, What do you do? It is critical to realize that *there are no pat answers to this question*. The answers depend on the severity of the violations and the particulars of your study. In general, here are three rules of thumb regarding the underlying assumptions about error:

1 *Normality.* As in most general linear model applications, the assumption of normality is not too important (i.e., significance tests are robust to violations of normality). Only in extreme cases (e.g., Y is truly dichotomous, therefore the e's

[24] The sampling distribution of d is very complex. If you're interested, see Durbin and Watson (1951) for tables of approximate critical values for d.

are dichotomous), need you worry. (If Y is truly dichotomous, consider techniques outside the scope of this book, such as logistic regression.)

2 *Homoscedesticity.* The assumption of equal error variances is a bit more necessary than normality but often not critical. If you obtain a residual plot like Figure 6.16, you might consider a transformation of the data (see next section) or a regression technique that can incorporate unequal variances (e.g., generalized least squares analysis). In general, unequal error variances will not affect the regression results except to reduce the power of the significance tests.

3 *Independence.* The assumption of independence is absolutely crucial to the validity of inferences in regression. If there is evidence that independence has been violated, the statistical properties of the regression parameters are not those contained in this chapter (e.g., if X is time, a time series analysis should be conducted).

By the way, consider a residual plot of Professor Gretzky's data (in Table VI.2). I get a picture that looks like Figure 6.18. This looks O.K. to me. What do you think?

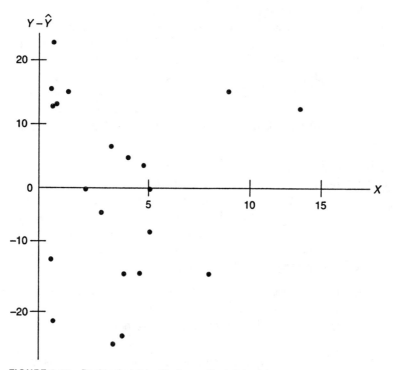

FIGURE 6.18   Residual plot for Professor Gretzky's data.

Outliers revisited   In Chapter II we noted that extremes scores (outliers) can have a substantial effect on the magnitude of correlations. Because regression slopes are determined by correlations and standard deviations (see Equation VI.D), regression parameters can *also* be substantially affected by outliers. In regression, note that a data point (X, Y) can be extreme with respect to the outcome variable (Y), the predictor (X), or both variables. In the statistical literature, data points that are extreme on X are said to have high "leverage," since they have the potential to have a substantial effect on regression weights (indeed, see the discussion of Equation VI.N). Now, I remind you that we also discussed extreme scores in terms of their distance from the regression line (i.e., the sizes of the residuals, $Y - \hat{Y}$). I remind you of this fact because statisticians also talk about data points having high "influence." To have influence, a data point must be both extreme on X (high leverage) *and* lie far from the regression line (high distance).

Consider Figure 6.19. In this example, points a and c are equally extreme with respect to X (high leverage), yet the addition (or subtraction) of point c from the sample would affect the results more dramatically (higher influence) than addition (or subtraction) of point a. Also, point b has a large residual (distance from the regression line), but because it is near the middle of the X-scores, its presence

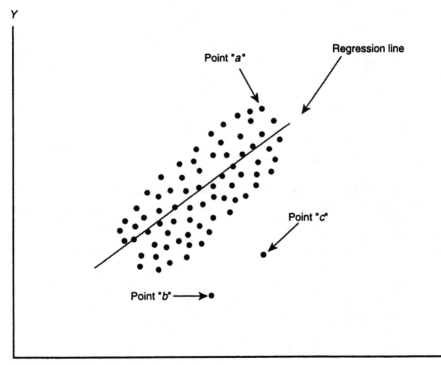

FIGURE 6.19 Scatterplot identifying three points with varying degrees of distance, leverage, and influence.

will not greatly affect the results. It should therefore be clear that a data point has high influence only if it has a large residual and high leverage. Data points with high influence are the types of extreme scores that statisticians tend to worry about.

[By the way, there are various ways to measure distance, leverage, and influence. Indeed, the most common method for measuring influence, Cook's (1979) *D*, is a conceptual product of a distance measure and a leverage measure.[25] For a nice summary and review of all the formulas involved in such indices, see Darlington (1990) or Neter, Wasserman, and Kutner (1989).]

Transformations

Some folks believe that a way to reduce the effects of violations of assumptions (or the effects of outliers) is to perform a "transformation" (usually nonlinear) on the data. For example, suppose the distribution of Y is extremely positively skewed, with most values ranging from 1 to 10, but with a few values around 80 or 90. One way to remove much of the skewness is to take the square root of every value, i.e., compute $Y^* = \sqrt{Y}$. Intuitively, note that computing the square root of small numbers (e.g., 1 or 9) keeps them small (e.g., 1 or 3), but the square root of larger numbers (e.g., 81) really "cuts them down to size" (e.g., 9) while preserving the relative order of each original value. The resulting transformed data are less skewed, and any outliers are relatively less extreme.

In fact, the square root transformation is often suggested as a way to reduce departures from both normality *and* homoscedasticity in regression analyses. For example, reducing skewness presumably helps the normality assumption; and if some errors are really large (see Figure 6.16), the square root transformation should shrink them down as well. More generally, most transformations are of the form $Y^* = Y^a$ (in the square root case, $a = \frac{1}{2}$). The classic reference for the choice of the value of a is Box and Cox (1964).

Should you transform your data if your analyses so indicate? That's the $1 million (and there is no final answer) question! Most practitioners I know go back and forth on this issue, and caution is strongly recommended. Transformations can clearly reduce the impact of outliers and help allay concerns about violating assumptions of normality and homoscedasticity. On the other hand, these two assumptions weren't nearly as crucial as the need for independence. Also, your units of analysis will change when transformations are adopted. If Y is performance (in units of number of widgets sold) and a square root transformation is invoked, the resulting units will be "square root of widgets sold." Is this unit of analysis interpretable? Can it be readily presented to (and accepted by) organizational decision makers? Further, in the sample of data at hand, there is almost always some transformation that will increase predictive power. However,

---

[25] Cook's *D* stands for Cook's distance. As Darlington (1990) notes, Cook's statistic is a measure of influence and the symbol *D* is therefore unfortunate.

whether or not this transformation will be of equal value in a new sample of data is unclear (see Chapter X on validity shrinkage). And in terms of theory development and theory testing, the theory (not the data) should probably drive the use and choice of any transformation. Finally, a statistical note: if you perform a transformation and conduct a least squares regression, the resulting statistical properties (e.g., best, linear, unbiased estimates) are true only on the transformed values. If you "back-transform" the results to the original units, these statistical niceties are lost. Isn't life interesting?

PROBLEMS

In the Chapter II problems, you were introduced to a data set in which a test salesperson was trying to sell a new selection test (X_3) that measured the advertising aptitude of potential employees. The salesperson's data base also include the person's gender (X_1), a peer evaluation of the subject's initial interview (X_2), and a performance measure (Y). Suppose we now enhance this data set to include a measure of the aptitude test that the organization is currently using for selection (say, X_4). Thus, the variables are

X_1: gender (male = 0; female = 1)
X_2: peer evaluation of the employee's interview (good = 1, bad = 0)
X_3: test score on new aptitude test (maximum score of 25)
X_4: test score on currently used aptitude test
Y: performance of the employee (supervisor rating with maximum score of 30)

and the data are shown in the following table:

Subject	X_1	X_2	X_3	X_4	Y
1	Male	Good	24	18	20
2	Female	Good	18	13	29
3	Male	Good	21	17	17
4	Male	Bad	7	13	8
5	Female	Bad	14	28	25
6	Male	Good	20	21	26
7	Male	Bad	8	6	7
8	Female	Bad	13	9	12
9	Male	Good	15	13	18
10	Male	Good	19	15	22
11	Female	Good	25	22	23
12	Female	Good	23	16	27
13	Male	Good	18	13	10
14	Female	Bad	12	14	5
15	Female	Bad	17	12	13

You also computed many of the correlations among these variables in the Chapter II problems. So that you will not have to compute then all over again, here's the entire correlation matrix for this set (with means and standard deviations added).

	X_1	X_2	X_3	X_4	Y
X_1	1				
X_2	$-.327$	1			
X_3	.088	.792	1		
X_4	.171	.261	.486	1	
Y	.206	.621	.674	.614	1
Mean	.467	.600	16.933	15.333	17.467
s	.516	.507	5.444	5.407	7.891

1 Note that the correlation between the new advertising aptitude test (X_3) and job performance (Y) is $r = .674$, with $n = 15$.

  a Calculate the regression equation, predicting performance (Y) from this new aptitude test (X_3).

  b Test the null hypothesis that the slope of this regression line is equal to zero (i.e., that the **B** for X_3 equals zero). Don't forget that you're also simultaneously asking whether or not the use of X_3 significantly improves the prediction of Y over and above just always predicting the mean of Y. Also, note the identical value from this t-test and the test of the correlation between these two variables that we obtained in the Chapter III problems. (*Hint*: To compute your answer, you pretty much have to construct an ANOVA table in order to get the mean squared error. Or, if you're really tricky, you'll remember that $1 - r^2$ is SSE/SST and work backward to get SSE.)

  c Construct and interpret a 95% prediction interval for someone with an aptitude test score, on X_3, of 16. (*Note*: The interval is surprisingly wide.)

2 The correlation between the advertising aptitude test currently in use (X_4) and job performance (Y) is $r = .614$.

  a Calculate the regression equation, predicting performance (Y) from the current aptitude test (X_4).

  b Test the null hypothesis that the slope of this regression line is equal to zero.

  c Construct and interpret a 95% prediction interval for someone with an aptitude test score, on X_4, of 16. (*Hint*: Don't forget the hints in the previous problem!)

3 This chapter noted that regressions predicting Y from X and those predicting X from Y are different.

  a Calculate the regression equation that predicts the new aptitude test scores (X_3) from performance (Y).

  b Test the slope in this regression against the null hypothesis value of 0.

  c In Problem 3b, note that the test of significance for the regression weight when predicting X_3 from Y gives you the same t-value as when testing the regression predicting Y from X_3. However, as noted, the regression lines themselves are different. Demonstrate this fact by plotting the two regressions on the same scatterplot.

4 Plot the residuals for the regressions in Problems 1 and 2. Does it appear that the assumptions of the regression model were met?

5 Calculate the regression equation predicting the currently used aptitude test (X_4) from a person's gender (X_1). When using X_1 as a variable, code males as 0 and females as 1. This is consistent with the manner in which correlations between X_1 and the other variables were computed in the above correlation matrix. (Note that when you are done, the value of the slope will give you the average difference in scores on X_4 between males and females. This is because of the way in which the coding was done and is a handy little fact that we will consider in an upcoming chapter on multiple regression!)

REFERENCES

Arvey, R., and Faley, R. (1988). *Fairness in selecting employees* (2nd ed.). Reading, MA: Addison-Wesley.

Bobko, P., and Karren, R. (1979). The perception of Pearson product moment correlations from scatter plots. *Personnel Psychology, 32*, 313–325.

Bobko, P., Sapinkopf, R., and Anderson, N. (1978). A lack of confidence about formulae for regression confidence intervals. *Teaching of Psychology, 5*, 102–103.

Bobko, P., and Schemmer, M. (1980). A note on standardized regression estimators. *Psychological Bulletin, 88*, 233–236.

Box, G., and Cox, D. (1964). An analysis of transformations. *Journal of the Royal Statistical Society, Series B, 26*, 211–243.

Cleary, T. (1968). Test bias: Prediction of grades of Negro and white students in integrated colleges. *Journal of Educational Measurement, 5*, 115–124.

Cole, N. (1973). Bias in selection. *Journal of Educational Measurement, 10*, 237–255.

Cook, R. (1979). Influential observations in linear regression. *Journal of the American Statistical Association, 74*, 169–174.

Darlington, R. (1971). Another look at "cultural fairness." *Journal of Educational Measurement, 8*, 71–82.

Darlington, R. (1990). *Regression and linear models*. New York: McGraw-Hill.

Durbin, J., and Watson, G. (1951). Testing for serial correlation in least squares regression, II. *Biometrika, 38*, 159–178.

Gordon, M., and Fitzgibbons, W. (1982). Empirical test of the validity of seniority as a factor in staffing decisions. *Journal of Applied Psychology, 67*, 311–319.

Hotelling, H. (1953). New light on the correlation coefficient and its transforms. *Journal of the Royal Statistical Society, Series B, 15*, 193–225.

Neter, J., Wasserman, W., and Kutner, M. (1989). *Applied linear regression models*. Homewood, IL: Irwin.

Rothstein, H. (1990). Interrater reliability of job performance ratings: Growth to asymptote level with increasing opportunity to observe. *Journal of Applied Psychology, 75*, 322–327.

VII

THREE APPLICATIONS OF BIVARIATE REGRESSION: UTILITY ANALYSIS, REGRESSION TO THE MEAN, PARTIAL CORRELATION

CHAPTER OBJECTIVES

After reading this chapter, you should be able to:

- Recognize the form of the equation for utility analysis. That is, you should be able to explain the similarity between regression and utility analysis.
- Understand how changes in r and $\$D_Y$ affect utility.
- Explain the phenomenon of regression to the mean.
- Recognize situations that may be subject to regression to the mean.
- Define partial correlations and know how to calculate them.
- Recognize a spurious correlation and suggest possible examples.
- Explain how a third variable may serve as a mediator between two other variables.
- Define semipartial correlations and know how to calculate them.
- Explain in words the distinction between a semipartial correlation and a partial correlation.

Many researchers who conduct regression analyses tend to use lots of variables (X's) as predictors of the dependent variable (Y). These multiple regression techniques will be the subject of the three subsequent chapters in this book. However, there's still more usefulness (and trouble!) to talk about when considering bivariate (one X and one Y) regression. First, I intend to show you that a topic in personnel selection (utility analysis) and its related fundamental equation are really a straightforward application of bivariate regression. Second, when using the least squares regression line, a funny thing happens along the way—called "regression to the mean"—and we will consider how to account for problems it might cause. Third, we will consider the concept of a "partial correlation," which can be best understood as a correlation between regression residuals. Further, the partial correlation coefficient will help us to interpret the meaning of regression functions in subsequent chapters. (In fact, while I think you should read them, the first two parts of this chapter can be skipped without loss of continuity, but it's absolutely crucial that you know about partial correlation before reading any other chapters in this book.)

ILITY ANALYSIS

Literature in both industrial psychology and human resources management has attempted to answer the question,

> **If one uses a selection test to hire (or promote) individuals, what kind of gains in performance can one expect, compared to hiring (or promoting) people at random?**

Of course, the assumption in this question is that selection test scores (X) are related to job performance (Y) differences, such that individuals scoring higher on the test will tend to perform better on the job (i.e., our old friend Pearson r is being invoked!). In fact, people who ask the above question also request, "Try to put your answer in dollar terms so that we can explain the results to managerial decision makers."

Based on early work by Brogden (1949) and Cronbach and Gleser (1965), it can be shown that the total dollar gain from using a test (X) to select N_s employees is

VII.A
$$\text{Dollar gain} = \frac{N_s r_{YX}(\$D_Y)\lambda}{\text{SR}} - \frac{N_s C}{\text{SR}}$$

where N_s = number of individuals selected

r_{YX} = correlation between test scores (X) and the dollar value of performance (Y)

D_Y = standard deviation across individuals of the dollar value of their job performance[1]

SR = selection ratio (number of individuals selected divided by the number of applicants)

C = cost of testing each individual with test X

λ = height of a standard normal distribution at the selection ratio cutoff point[2]

The point in writing Equation VII.A is not to confuse you or to make you an expert in utility analysis. (If you're interested in this outcome, consider starting with thorough reviews by Boudreau, 1991, or Cascio, 2000.) The point is simply that *Equation VII.A is really a bivariate regression in disguise!*

To see this fact, start with a typical regression prediction equation

$$\hat{Y} = b_0 + b_1 X$$

In the selection/utility scenario above, X will be the selection test. Usually, the variable Y is job performance. In our case, though, Y will be the value of job performance, in dollars.[3] Substituting the least squares solutions for b_0 and b_1 (see Equation VI.C and VI.D), we obtain

$$\hat{Y}_{\text{value}} = b_0 + b_1 X = \left(\bar{Y} - b_1 \bar{X} \right) + \left(r \frac{s_Y}{s_X} \right) X$$

Now, here's a twist that utility analysts place on this regression: they standardize the test scores (X) so that from now on the test scores are labeled Z_x and have mean 0 and variance 1.0. It's O.K. to standardize X since you still preserve the applicants' orderings on the selection test (and that's all you generally need for selection decisions). However, it's important that you don't standardize Y, because that variable is in the units of dollar value and those units are what decision makers often want. Since $\bar{Z} = 0$ and $s_Z = 1$, the above regression equation reduces to

$$\hat{Y}_{\text{value}} = \bar{Y} + \left(s_Y r \right) Z_X$$

[1] Intuitively speaking, the value of D_Y reflects the degree to which employees are worth the same, or worth differing amounts to the organization. To the extent that D_Y is large, then excellent performers are worth much more than average performers. This implies that a focus on selecting the best performers will increase the dollar value of overall performance across job incumbents.

[2] For example, if the selection ration is .10, go to the 90th percentile of the standard normal distribution and find the height of the curve at that point (many introductory statistics books have such tables of values).

[3] Utility analysts assume that job performance and its value are linearly related. Therefore, replacement of performance by its corresponding value won't change things correlationally, because Pearson r is unaffected by linear transformations of the variables (see Chapter II). In the current case, this means that the correlation between the test (X) and job performance is the same as the correlation between the test and the value, in dollars, of job performance. This somewhat tenuous assumption has not been fully explored in the utility analysis literature.

Let's do two more little things. First, the current equation predicts the dollar value of performance for someone who has a standardized score of Z_X on the selection test. However, utility folks are generally interested in the gain in utility *relative* to randomly selecting employees. From our regression chapter, we know that the best predictor of performance in the absence of knowledge about X is to predict $\bar{Y}$. So, we move $\bar{Y}$ to the left-hand side of the equation and get

$$\text{Relative dollar gain in utility} = \hat{Y} - \bar{Y} = (s_Y r) Z_X$$

Second, s_Y is the standard deviation of the dollar value of performance (Y) across individuals. Consistent with utility researchers, we write this as $\$D_Y$ and get

VII.B. $\quad U = \text{dollar gain in utility} = \hat{Y} - \bar{Y} = (\$D_Y) r Z_X$

Now, I'll fill in the remaining details momentarily but I wanted to let you know we have essentially derived the guts of Equation VII.A with our regression in Equation VII.B. In both equations, there are two key components in the determination of utility: r and $\$D_Y$. Note that as r increases, the utility of the selection test increases proportionately (with no need to square r either, as noted in Chapter II). Similarly, as $\$D_Y$ increases, the regression says that utility increases proportionately. This makes sense: if there's lots of variation in the dollar worth of potential performers, then you definitely want to be more accurate in choosing whom to hire; on the other hand, if everyone will perform at the same level ($\$D_y = 0$), then, it doesn't matter whom you pick.[4] Again, don't lose sight of the fact that the dollar gain in utility is readily derived from a regression predicting performance value (Y) from standardized test scores (Z_X).

pleting the Derivation of Equation VII.A

Equation VII.B gives the dollar gain in utility for a particular individual (who scores Z_X on the predictor). The average dollar gain in utility for those selected is therefore

$$\bar{U} = (\$D_Y) r \bar{Z}_X$$

Utility analysts then note that on the average you obtain this gain in dollar performance for *each* person you actually hire. Because we let N_s be the number of employees hired or selected, the total gain is

$$\text{Total gain} = N_s \bar{U} = N_s (\$D_Y) r \bar{Z}_X$$

---

[4] The determination of $\$D_Y$ is one of the most problematic aspects of the utility equation. It's not clear how one estimates the dollar value of individual job performance, let alone the standard deviation of that dollar value (see Bobko, Karren, and Kerkar, 1987, for a review of existing methods and Raju, Burke, and Normand, 1990, for an allegedly alternative approach to the entire issue).

Further, it may be costly to develop and implement a new selection test (e.g., assessment centers require a certain expense for each applicant considered). So, we need to subtract the cost of testing from the total gain. This cost is $N \times C$, where N is the number of individuals (applicants) tested and C is the cost of testing one applicant. Some folks write $N \times C$ as N_sC/SR, where SR is the selection ratio (N_s/N). Thus, the overall gain in dollar utility is

VII.C $$\text{Utility gain} = N_s(\$D_Y)\,r\bar{Z}_X - \text{cost}$$

$$= N_s(\$D_Y)\,r\bar{Z}_X - N_sC/SR$$

We are so close to Equation VII.A that you can sense the tension!

However, we need to add two assumptions at this point: (i) applicants' selection test scores are normally distributed, and (ii) when selecting top-down on the basis of the test scores, everyone you select accepts your offer.[5] *Now* we are ready to compare Equation VII.C to Equation VII.A. Notice that the only difference is that $\bar{Z}_X$ has been replaced by λ/SR. (See above for the definition of λ.) Assuming the two additional assumptions are met, you can do this! By the way, this replacement is an interesting fact to some folks. It says that the average standardized score of those individuals who are selected (i.e., $\bar{Z}_X$) is related to both the height of the normal curve at the cutoff point (λ) and the selection ratio.[6] Once you make this replacement, you obtain Equation VII.A. Hooray!

Thus, as already noted, the "fancy" equation for gain in dollar utility is fundamentally related to a bivariate regression predicting the dollar value of performance (Y) from selection test scores (X). This regression is then modified to fit the particular utility context [e.g., multiply average utility by the number of individuals selected (N_s), subtract cost of testing]. In fact, even "fancier" modifications have been considered from accounting perspectives (cf. Boudreau, 1991). Such modifications include discounting factors (current value of future gains), corporate tax rates, variable costs, the length of time incumbents stay on the job, etc. And recently, Sturman (2000) has demonstrated that making these modifications, and accounting for the issue in footnote 5, can reduce the actual estimated utility by more than 90%! Most interesting, eh?

REGRESSION TO THE MEAN

Suppose you work for an organization that's concerned about some employees who are working at very low levels of performance. So, you pick a particular day, obtain measures of each employee's performance, and identify performers at or below the 10th percentile. You then develop an extensive 6-week retraining program for these employees, put them through your program, and measure their on-the-job performance immediately after the retraining. You find that their training performance has statistically significantly increased. Should you adopt

[5] Murphy (1986) notes that it is unrealistic to expect that all of your top choices will accept your offer of employment. He demonstrates that estimates of selection test utility can be substantially lowered when your top choices reject your offer.

[6] If you know calculus, and you'd like to see a proof of this fact, check out the appendix in Cronbach and Gleser's (1965) book.

the retraining program as a permanent part of your organization's personnel practices? Even if you ignore the cost of such an intervention, the answer to this question is "maybe not," all because of a statistical phenomenon known as regression to the mean.[7] Hopefully, by the end of this section the reason for this reticence will be clear.

Some Equations, Some History

In the regression model $\hat{Y} = b_0 + b_1 X$, the solution for b_1 can be written $b_1 = r s_Y / s_X$ (see Equation VI.D if you have forgotten). Regression to the mean can most readily be seen in the special case where $s_Y = s_X$ (although this is not a necessary condition). Now, *when the standard derivations on Y and X are equal, the slope is the correlation* ($b_1 = r$). Pictorially, imagine having a scatterplot between Y and X in the typical shape of a football (or ellipse, or hot dog). Letting $s_Y = s_X$ is akin to orienting this scatterplot on the 45° line (i.e., the line defined by $Y = X$,[8] as in Figure 7.1).

---

[7] In fact there are many other reasons why the conclusions in the "pre-post design with no control group" may be suspect. These alternative reasons are often labeled "threats to internal validity." For example, the really low performers might have left (voluntarily or involuntarily) the organization during the retraining program. The posttraining scores would go up for this reason alone (the threat to validity here is labeled "differential mortality"). See Cook, Campbell, and Peracchio (1990) for an excellent discussion of threats to validity in experimental designs.

[8] Any other orientation would imply $s_Y \neq s_X$. For example, rotating the scatterplot to the 30° line would, *ceteris paribus*, reduce the variance on Y (try it!).

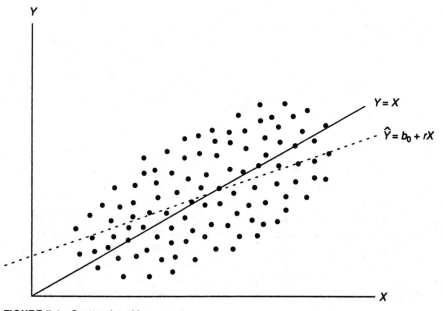

FIGURE 7.1   Scatterplot with $s_X = s_Y$.

Notice that the regression line in Figure 7.1, defined by the least squares criterion, has smaller slope than the $Y = X$ line (unless r_{YX} is a perfect ± 1.0). This was first noticed by Sir Francis Galton (remember him from Chapter II?), who was plotting heights of sons (Y) versus heights of fathers (X). For example, Galton noticed that if he found a tall father (say, $X = 6\frac{1}{2}$ feet), then a regression line would predict that the son would be tall, *but not quite as tall* as the father (i.e., the regression line is lower than the $Y = X$ line for large values of X). Conversely, short fathers would be predicted to have short sons, but not quite as short as the father (i.e., the regression line is higher than the $Y = X$ line for small values of X). Thus, it appeared to Galton that heights of children were regressing toward the mean (not quite as tall if tall fathers, not quite as short if short fathers). This is why regressions are labeled "regressions"!

[By the way, it is true that the least squares prediction line regresses prediction toward mean. However, it is *not* true, as seems to be the case on the surface, that eventually children several generations from now will all be the same, average height. In fact, given the assumptions of regression analysis, future overall distributions of the heights will remain unchanged. That is, while the predicted value (mean of Y conditional on X) is regressed, there's still a distribution of scores around each conditional mean—and the totality of all these distributions will regenerate the original distribution of heights.]

What's Going on Here?

Statistically, the reason for regression to the mean is clear; e.g., when $s_Y = s_X$, the slope is the correlation (r) and r is usually less than 1.0 (and 1.0 would be the slope if you simply used the $\hat{Y} = X$ line). Nonstatistically, you can "see" regression to the mean if you think about taking a test twice (or measuring your job performance on two different days). This is like the test-retest paradigm we considered for reliability in Chapter IV. For lots of extraneous reasons, your score on one day will be a bit different than your score on another day (the weather's nice, the phone interrupted you less often, you weren't feeling well one day, you guessed on a few test items and were luckier one day than on the other, etc.). In other words, the test-retest reliability is less than 1.0, and the scatterplot looks like that in Figure 7.2.

Now, let's pick someone who did extremely well on day 1 (e.g., a person with an X-score of X_a). What's your best prediction of that person's score on day 2? The regression line in Figure 7.2 would say to predict a high score, but not quite as high as on day 1, *and this makes sense*. Most likely, a person with $X = X_a$ is good, and this is one reason for the high score on the day 1 measure. However, if this person guessed on some questions, he or she was generally lucky (given the high score) and on average wouldn't be so lucky next time. Further, given the high score, it's probably the case that most of the other extraneous factors tended to be favorable (feeling good, few interruptions, etc.). On average, these other factors won't be as favorable on day 2, and the score should be predicted to be a bit lower than initial score. Conversely, an individual who scores $X = X_b$ would

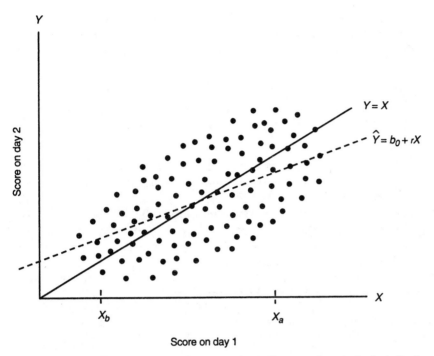

FIGURE 7.2   Scatterplot demonstrating regression to the mean for a test-retest situation.

be expected to score a bit higher on the second day. Clearly, the greater role these extraneous factors play (relative to a person's true ability), the greater the predicted score deviates from the prediction of $Y = X$. In other words, as the role of the extraneous factors increases, the reliability of the measurement process decreases, r decreases, and the predicted future values are greatly affected (more regression to the mean).

Practical Implications

Now go back to the training program example at the beginning of this section. Can you see the regression problem here? Exactly! We picked individuals *because* they performed extremely poorly on a certain measured day. If there is any day-to-day variation in performance (and there usually is!), the next time we measure these individuals we would expect their score to regress to the mean a bit. Thus, even if the retraining program was totally useless, we'd expect an increase in performance due to regression to the mean. In this case, *be careful not to attribute this regression increase to the training program—it's a statistical artifact* arising from the choice of extreme scores.

What can you do about regression to the mean? Obviously, if your retraining sample contains individuals with a complete range of scores, then regression effects will "average out" (some regression *up* to the mean, some *down* to the mean) and you needn't worry. However, if your data collection effort is truly at one extreme or the other, then you should expect a regression effect at the second measurement occasion. Given that you realize the effect is coming,

> **you can statistically control for regression to the mean by predicting the amount of regression you'd expect and comparing your actual increase in performance to the regression expectation (rather than to 0).**

For example, in the retraining program example, measure the performance of a wide range[9] of individuals on two occasions and compute the regression line between the two measurements (see Figure 7.3). For the range on the X that identifies individuals to be retrained (left-hand side of the X-axis in Figure 7.3), you can compute the average difference between the $Y = X$ line and the regression line. This is what you expect the regression effect to be, and you can then compare the actual training performance gain to this expected gain. It's extra effort, but you won't misattribute changes due to regression to the mean to the effectiveness of your training program!

[9] Theoretically you don't need a wide range of performance, but it gives you a better "fix" (less error) on the true underlying regression (if you don't believe this, go back to Equation VI.L).

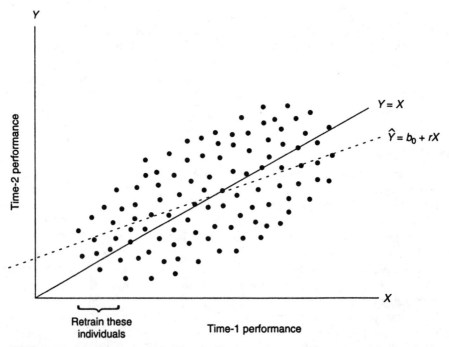

FIGURE 7.3 Scatterrplot demonstrating regression to the mean for a selected group of trainees.

A quick example   The correlation between job performance at two different points in time (i.e., the reliability of job performance—see Chapter IV) has been the subject of several studies. Cascio's (1998, chap. 4) review notes that there is a wide range of test-retest performance reliabilities in the literature. Suppose we have a job of "widget maker," the standard deviation of widgets made (across individuals) is $s_Y = 15$, and the correlation between widgets made during week 1 (X) and week 2 (Y) is $r = .80$. Suppose management notes that three individuals are performing 2 standard deviations below the mean at the end of week 1 (i.e., their X-scores are $Z_X = -2.0$) and makes these individuals take a retraining course over the weekend. Note that, using regression, you would predict their future scores to be $\hat{Y} = .80(Z_X) = .80(-2.0) = -1.6$. So, just as a result of regression to the mean, these employees would be predicted to perform only 1.6 standard deviations below the mean in the second week (compared to 2 standard deviations below the mean in first week). Therefore, there is a statistically expected improvement of .40 standard deviation, or $.40(s_Y) = .40(15) = 6$ widgets, for each of these three employees. Attributing any performance improvement to the weekend training program could only be done to the extent that improvements were *greater* than 6 widgets per individual.

By the way, there are a variety of instances of regression effects "muddying" the results of studies. For example,

1 In 1955, the state of Connecticut had a record number of traffic fatalities on its highways. The governor of that state announced a "crackdown on speeding" to reduce traffic fatalities. Indeed, fatalities went down in 1956, and the governor linked this reduction to his crackdown. However, further analysis of the state's data indicates that it could have been just a regression effect for that pair of years (see Campbell, 1972; Campbell and Ross, 1968).

2 In 1972, Bogatz and Ball found that disadvantaged children who watched *Sesame Street* demonstrated gains in academic skills. However, it has been suggested that statistical regression effects may account for these gains (Neale and Liebert, 1986). In fact, the original Bogatz and Ball (1972) study found that children with the lowest initial scores gained the most—certainly consistent with the regression hypothesis. [Indeed, Jensen (1969) has noted that almost all "enrichment" studies of disadvantaged children need to account for regression effects.]

In sum, regression to the mean lurks in a variety of places. You should expect it whenever any organizational intervention focuses on an extreme-scoring group (e.g., any training intervention tied to remediation). Beware of regression effects! In fact, regression to the mean operates in both directions. If you pick top performers and measure them a second time, their average performance will go down a bit—and not necessarily because they were lazy or got fat heads, but because of regression. This leads to the interesting paradox that if you keep high performers at the same level, you've actually *made progress* relative to the expected regression decline! As I said before, isn't regression fun?

PARTIAL CORRELATION

The notion of partial correlation is a very useful application of (1) Pearson correlation (r) and (2) regression residuals $(Y - \hat{Y})$. In fact, we will see that *a partial correlation is a Pearson correlation between two sets of regression residuals.*

Some Motivations

Here's a well-worn example. Suppose you measure ice cream consumption (Y) in New York City for each day in the year. Suppose you also measure daily water consumption (X) in New York City. Now, the Pearson correlation, across days, between X and Y is probably pretty high. Suppose it's $r_{YX} = .50$. Does this mean that eating ice cream makes people thirsty? Or does it mean that New York City water causes a craving for ice cream? Of course, neither of these explanations is true, and there's something else going on. Can you see it? Right! There's another variable lurking here: daily temperature (Z). As days get hotter (high value of Z), both ice cream *and* water consumption go up; conversely for cooler days. *The partial correlation will answer the question, If I account for the effects of differential temperature (Z), will there be any correlation remaining between Y and X?*

This is accomplished as follows:

1a Compute the regression $\hat{Y}_Z = b_0 + b_1 Z$. (In other words, predict ice cream consumption from daily temperature.)

1b Compute the residual $Y - \hat{Y}_Z$ (i.e., that part of ice cream consumption that's unrelated to daily temperature).

2a Compute another regression $\hat{X}_Z = b_0^* + b_1^*(Z)$ (i.e., predict water consumption from temperature).

2b Compute the residual $X - \hat{X}_Z$ (i.e., that part of water consumption that's unrelated to daily temperature).

Then, *the partial correlation is the Pearson correlation between the two residuals in 1b and 2b. In other words, using linear regression you've "taken out" the effects of the third variable (Z) and correlated whatever was left over. This partial correlation, between Y and X, with Z controlled for, is labeled $r_{YX.Z}$.*

Presumably, when Z is controlled for in this ice cream example (i.e., the partial correlation $r_{YX.Z}$ is computed), the correlation should go way down from the original value of $r_{YX} = .50$. (See the quick example below for some hypothetical results.)

Two Amazing Facts

We'll turn to more practical examples in a moment, but there really are two wonderfully amazing facts (WAFs) about the partial correlation coefficient.

WAF 1   To compute the partial correlation $(r_{YX.Z})$ you needn't go through all the bother of computing the two regressions outlined above and then correlate the residuals. A little bit of algebra will show that this entire process can be reduced to one equation! So, here's an equivalent formula for $r_{YX.Z}$:

VII.D
$$r_{YX.Z} = \frac{r_{YX} - r_{YZ}r_{XZ}}{\sqrt{1 - r_{YZ}^2}\sqrt{1 - r_{XZ}^2}}$$

This really is a useful fact. It is important to remember that Equation VII.D is *identical* to the process outlined above (correlation between regression residuals). Also, it helps to "commune" with Equation VII.D for a minute. Note that most of the statistical information is in the numerator. The sign of this numerator ($-$, 0, or $+$) determines the sign of the partial correlation (the denominator is always positive, except for the extreme case when r_{YZ} or r_{XZ} is exactly ± 1.0). Now, look at the numerator a bit more. Notice that the first factor (r_{YX}) is the original, unadulterated correlation between Y and X. Removing the effects of a third variable (Z) is tantamount to subtracting the product of the two correlations involving Z (r_{YZ} and r_{XZ}). The denominator is pretty much there just for the ride. It helps to think of the denominator as a scaling factor ensuring that the partial correlation, as a correlation (between residuals), never exceeds 1.0 in magnitude.

A quick example   Suppose that in the above example daily temperature (Z) had been correlated with the other two consumption variables as $r_{ZX} = .80$ and $r_{ZY} = .60$. In other words, daily temperature really did correlate with both ice cream and water consumption. Then,

$$r_{YX.Z} = \frac{.50 - (.80)(.60)}{\sqrt{1 - .8^2}\sqrt{1 - .6^2}} = \frac{.02}{.48} = .04$$

and there would be essentially *no* relationship between ice cream and water consumption when daily temperature was controlled for. [10]

Once a partial correlation is computed, researchers want to know, Is it significant? In our example above, this leads to the question, Is the partial correlation .04 significantly different from 0? To answer this question, we have

WAF 2   The sampling distribution of the partial correlation is the same as the sampling distribution of a regular Pearson correlation except that 1 df is lost.

Thus, we can use all the nice statistical tests mentioned in Chapter III. The loss of 1 df means that whatever your sample size, compute your test as if you had

[10] The use of partial correlation is a form of statistical control. If you were an experimentalist you might control for extraneous factors by holding them constant (in our example, this would mean doing the study only on days with a predetermined, fixed temperature). Experimentalists also control for other variables through randomization or including the variable as an experimental factor (see any design book).

one less observation. For example, the t-test for $H_0 : \rho_{yx} = 0$ was given in Equation III.A as

$$t_{n-2} \sim \frac{r\sqrt{n-2}}{\sqrt{1-r^2}}$$

Now, wonderfully amazing fact 2 says that the partial correlation also has a t-distribution under $H_0 : \rho_{YX.Z} = 0$, but you need to remember to reduce n by 1. Thus, for testing $H_0 : \rho_{YX.Z} = 0$, compute

$$t_{n-3} \sim \frac{r_{YX.Z}\sqrt{n-3}}{\sqrt{1-r_{YX.Z}^2}}$$

Or, if Fisher's z were chosen, the appropriate standard deviation would be $\sqrt{1/(n-4)}$ rather than the value of $\sqrt{1/(n-3)}$ given in Equation III.C.

(If the above New York City data were collected for $n = 30$ days, then the t-test statistic would be $.04\sqrt{27} / \sqrt{1 - .04^2}$, while the $p = .05$ critical value would be $t_{27\mathrm{df}} = 2.052$. Then, my computations show that the partial correlation of .04 is not significantly different from 0. Do you agree?)[11]

Further Examples, Spurious Correlations, and Mediators

The above water and ice cream consumption example was of the general form shown in Figure 7.4. That is, the spurious correlation between X and Y was caused by a third factor (Z). Underlying theories in the social sciences are often of this form. For example, suppose there's a substantial positive correlation between the salary a person makes (Y) and that person's gender (X: coded 1 if male, 0 if female). An organization concerned about a positive value of r_{YX} might ask whether this represents bias in salaries or whether there are other factors that spuriously cause the high correlation. Consider the variable job experience (Z). It may be that, for reasons beyond the organization's control, males come to that organization with more experience, and experience is a

---

[11] To me, a more interesting question is, Is .04 significantly less than .50? In other words, I care only if the correlation goes down (significantly) rather than if it goes down all the way to 0. An exact test for this hypothesis of significant change doesn't exist (its distribution is nasty because of the built-in dependence among the correlations). However, Olkin and Finn (1995) have recently presented an asymptotically appropriate procedure for conducting such a test when $n > 200$ (caution is recommended when $60 < n < 200$).

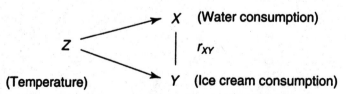

FIGURE 7.4 Model of a spurious correlation between water use and ice cream consumption.

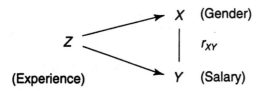

FIGURE 7.5 Possible model indicating the reason for a relationship between gender and salary.

$$X \longrightarrow Z \longrightarrow Y$$

FIGURE 7.6 A mediation model (Z mediates the relationship between X and Y).

compensable factor in the organization's salary scale. Thus, the underlying model might be that in Figure 7.5.

The correlation between gender and salary may be spurious in that differential experience is the common explanatory variable. In such a case, the organization might compute $r_{YX.Z}$ to see if it becomes 0. If so, fine (assuming everything's as stated). If not, perhaps other extraneous variables need to be considered (e.g., differential educational levels), or perhaps the salary structure really is biased. In any case, the partial correlation is a useful tool for analyzing such situations.

Another model that can be considered is of the form shown in Figure 7.6. In a situation such as this, variable Z is said to "mediate" the relationship between X and Y in the sense that X doesn't cause Y directly, just through the mechanism Z.[12] If such a model is true, then we would expect that $r_{YX.Z} = 0$. In other words, if the information due to variable Z is taken out, there should be no relation left between X and Y. If, on the other hand, the partial correlation was not 0, it would mean that there was some aspect of the relationship between Y and X that couldn't be accounted for by Z. So, the model in Figure 7.6 might be modified as in Figure 7.7, where the extra arrow at the top means that X relates to Y *above and beyond* its mediating relationship through Z.

For example, as part of a larger study, Locke, Frederick, Lee, and Bobko (1984) were interested in the individual-level variables of job performance (Y), self-efficacy (X), and level of intended goal (Z). They hypothesized that a person's self-efficacy was related to job performance, but only to the extent that self-efficacy (X) caused a person to accept higher goals (Z) which in turn caused greater performance (Y). That is, they postulated the model in Figure 7.8. As noted, this model implies that $r_{YX.Z} = 0$. In Locke et al.'s study, the correlations were (with $n = 181$)

	X	Z	Y
X	1.00	.54	.61
Z		1.00	.57
Y			1.00

[12] See James and Brett (1984) for a thorough review of the concept of a mediator and tests for mediation hypotheses.

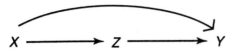

FIGURE 7.7 A modified mediation model (allowing for some direct relationship between X and Y).

(Self-efficacy)   (Goal)   (Job performance)
$$X \longrightarrow Z \longrightarrow Y$$

FIGURE 7.8 The mediating model hypothesized by Locke et al. (1984).

Clearly, X and Y are related ($r_{XY} = .61$). The question is, Does this relationship vanish when Z is accounted for? Using Equation VII.D, the partial correlation is

$$r_{YX.Z} = \frac{.61 - (.54)(.57)}{\sqrt{1 - .54^2}\sqrt{1 - .57^2}} = \frac{.30}{.69} = .44$$

and because this correlation is still substantially greater than 0, the answer was that the relationship does not vanish. That is, self-efficacy clearly influenced job performance *directly* and not just through the mediator of a person's goal level. Locke et al. (1984) modified their model accordingly.

[Sometimes, computing the partial correlation not only brings the value of r close to 0 but actually reverses the sign of the correlation! For example, Bobko and Donnelly (1988) conducted a study on U.S. military jobs where two of the variables were X = minimum aptitude level required to do the job and Y = perceived worth of that job. We assumed that jobs with higher cognitive requirements were probably associated with greater value. However, we found a *negative* correlation between X and Y. After further thought, we realized that some of the jobs in our sample were combat-oriented jobs. The military valued such jobs (given its organizational mission), yet aptitude requirements for some combat jobs were low. So, we used an index of the combat probability of a job (Z) and, sure enough, found that when Z was controlled for, the remaining relationship between X and Y was positive (i.e., $r_{YX.Z}$ was positive).]

So, you can see that the partial correlation is a valuable tool for both (*a*) the statistical control of extraneous variables and (*b*) the testing of certain causal, mediation models. We have two important leftovers to discuss before we begin multiple regression.

Important Leftover 1: Semipartial *r*

The partial correlation above ($r_{YX.Z}$) took a third variable (Z) and removed its effects from both X and Y. In some situations, it makes sense to partial out Z from only *one* of the other variables (say, X but not Y). For example, a group of us (Ashford, Lee, and Bobko, 1989) once developed a measure of perceived job insecurity (X) that predicted, among other things, employees' intentions to quit the organization (Y). Now, someone else's measure of job insecurity (Z) already existed. We wanted to show that our measure (X) was better, i.e., our measure had information in it beyond the preexisting measure. So, we wanted to "take Z out of X" and show that what was left over still had a relationship to Y. (Notice that we're not taking anything away from Y here.)

To do this:

1a Compute the regression $\hat{X}_z = b_0^* + b_1^*(Z)$.
1b Compute the residual $X - \hat{X}_z$ (i.e., that part of X having nothing to do with Z).
2 Correlate Y with the residual $X - \hat{X}_z$.

Since nothing's been taken from Y, the resulting correlation is called a "semi-partial correlation" and is denoted by r_{YX_z}.[13] As in the partial correlation situation, you needn't actually go through the mechanics of computing regression residuals because there is another wonderfully amazing fact. That is, the semipartial r can be computed as

VII.E
$$r_{YX_z} = \frac{r_{YX} - r_{YZ}r_{XZ}}{\sqrt{1 - r_{XZ}^2}}$$

You should immediately note that the equations for partial and semipartial correlations are remarkably similar (compare Equations VII.D and VII.E). In fact, the only difference is one square root factor in the denominator. The numerator's the same—implying that the sign (0, $-$, or $+$) of the partial and semipartial correlations is the same.[14]

Again, the *conceptual* difference is whether or not you want to partial the third variable (Z) from one or both of the other variables. Most often in the behavioral sciences, researchers choose to compute partial correlations. However, as we shall see in the next chapter, the semipartial correlation is also useful for interpretations of multiple regression outcomes.

[By the way, in our job insecurity paper, $r_{YX} = .46$ and $r_{YZ} = .15$. Thus, on the surface, our measure of insecurity (X) predicted intention to quit better than the other measure of insecurity (Z). If I tell you that the two measures of insecurity correlated .35 ($r_{XZ} = .35$), you can compute the semipartial correlation (r_{YX_z}). I obtained $r_{YX_z} = .44$. Do you agree? If so, then it can be noted that our

---

[13] Two things should be noted. A few folks in the field use the label "part correlation" for the concept of semipartial correlation. Also note that using the notation of r_{YX_z} for a semipartial r implies that we could have denoted a partial r as $r_{Y_zX_z}$.

[14] Thus, there's no need for learning new procedures to test the significance of semipartial correlations against zero. In the population, a semipartial correlation is zero *if and only if* the partial correlation is zero. So, to test a semipartial, just compute its related partial correlation and use the previous test statistics in this chapter.

new measure of job insecurity substantially predicts intention to quit above and beyond information in the previous measure.

Important Leftover 2: Multiple Partial *r*

Often, you want to partial many (more than one) variables from a relationship. For example, in the salary (Y) versus gender (X) example above, we partialed out previous experience but we could have also added education level and/or the number of training programs successfully completed to our list of extraneous variables. Although we haven't discussed multiple regression yet, the conceptual operations should be clear. That is,

1a Predict Y from all the extraneous variables (Z_1, Z_2, Z_3, etc.) simultaneously, using a multiple regression.
1b Compute $Y - \hat{Y}$.
2a Predict X from all the Z's
2b Compute $X - \hat{X}$.
3 Correlate the two residuals.

This results in a "multiple partial correlation" with all the properties of the partial correlation discussed above. The only exception to this statement concerns wonderfully amazing fact 2: i.e., if you partial out Z_1, Z_2, ..., Z_p, then p degrees of freedom are lost in the hypothesis test, not just 1. Otherwise, everything's the same (and, yes Virginia, you can have multiple *semi*partial correlations as well).

PROBLEMS

Some notation. Later in this book, we will drop certain subscripts that are unnecessary. I introduce the possibility here because we will have lots of different X's in our data sets. For example, consider the correlation between Y and X_1. Rather than write it as r_{YX_1}, it will be simply denoted r_{y1}. Similarly, the correlation between X_1 and X_3 will be denoted as r_{13}. Further, the partial correlation between Y and X_1, partialing X_2, may be denoted $r_{y1.2}$. In general, since we have only one Y, numerical subscripts will refer to particular X's, and the X doesn't need to go along for the ride!

1 Our data set in Chapter VI included, among other things, gender (X_1), scores on a new advertising aptitude test (X_3), and performance (Y).
  a Compute the partial correlation between performance (Y) and gender (X_1), taking out the effects of ability (X_3) from both variables. [Suppose one assumed that the ability measure pretty much captured what was required on the job. Some folks would suggest that if this partial correlation isn't zero, then the performance rating (Y) might be suspect, in the sense that the ability measure doesn't account for the value of r_{y1} (i.e., unexplained gender differences).] A reminder: $r_{y3} = .674$, $r_{y1} = .206$ and $r_{13} = .088$.
  b Test this partial correlation for statistical significance against the null hypothesis of zero (with $p = .05$).

2 In Problem 1, to see if there were unexplained gender differences in the performance measure, we really only wanted to partial ability from the performance rating (and not necessarily gender). Thus, compute the semipartial correlation between performance (Y) and gender (X_1), partialing ability (X_3) from performance. Note that we don't need to test the result against zero since we have already tested the analogous partial correlation.

3 Using the data set from Chapter VI again, compute the partial correlation between peer evaluation of the candidate's interview (X_2) and performance (Y), taking out the effects of gender (X_1). You should find that the partial correlation actually increases; i.e., $r_{y2.1}$ is greater than r_{y2}. Can you make up some explanation why this might have occurred for these three particular variables?

4 A test salesperson claims that a new advertising aptitude test (X_3) has something unique to offer (by way of predicting performance) over and above the current aptitude selection test (X_4). (By the way, we'll explore the notion of a unique contribution in more detail in the next chapter.) So, we should ask the question, Does X_3 predict Y even after the effects of X_4 have been removed from X_3? State in symbols what correlation is implied by this question and compute the value of the correlation.

FERENCES

Ashford, S., Lee, C., and Bobko, P. (1989). Content, causes, and consequences of job insecurity: A theory-based measure and substantive test. *Academy of Management Journal*, *32*, 803–829.

Bobko, P., and Donnelly, L. (1988). Identifying correlates of job-level, overall worth estimates: Application in a public sector organization. *Human Performance*, *1*, 187–204.

Bobko, P., Karren, R., and Kerkar, S. (1987). Systematic research needs for understanding supervisory-based estimates of SD_y in utility analyses. *Organizational Behavior and Human Decision Processes*, *40*, 69–95.

Bogatz, G., and Ball, S. (1972). *The second year of Sesame Street*: *A continuing evaluation*. Princeton, NJ: Educational Testing Service.

Boudreau, J. (1991). Utility analysis for decisions in human resource management. In M. Dunnette and L. Hough (Eds.), *Handbook of industrial & organizational psychology* (2nd ed.), Vol. 2, pp. 621–745. Palo Alto, CA: Consulting Psychologists Press.

Brogden, H. (1949). When testing pays off. *Personnel Psychology*, *2*, 171–183.

Campbell, D. (1972). Measuring the effects of social innovations by means of time series. In J. Tanur (Ed.), *Statistics*: *A guide to the unknown*, pp. 120–129. San Francisco: Holden-Day.

Campbell, D., and Ross, H. (1968). The Connecticut crackdown on speeding: Time-series data in quasi-experimental analysis. *Law and Society Review*, *3*, 33–53.

Cascio, W. (1998). *Applied psychology in human resource management* (5th ed.). Englewood Cliffs, NJ: Prentice-Hall.

Cascio, W. (2000). *Costing human resources: The financial impact of behavior in organizations* (4th ed.). Cincinnati, OH: Southwestern.

Cook, T., Campbell, D., and Peracchio, L. (1990). Quasi experimention. In M. Dunnette and L. Hough (Eds.), *Handbook of industrial & organizational psychology* (2nd ed.), Vol. 1, pp. 491–576. Palo Alto, CA: Consulting Psychologists Press.

Cronbach, L., and Gleser, G. (1965). *Psychological tests and personnel decisions* (2nd ed.). Urbana, IL: University of Illinois Press.

James, L., and Brett, J. (1984). Mediators, moderators, and tests for mediation. *Journal of Applied Psychology, 69,* 307–321.

Jensen, A. (1969). Environment, heredity, and intelligence. *Harvard Educational Review, 39,* 1–123.

Locke, E., Frederick, E., Lee, C., and Bobko, P. (1984). The effect of self-efficacy, goals, and task strategies on task performance. *Journal of Applied Psychology, 69,* 241–251.

Murphy, K. (1986). When your top choice turns you down: Effect of rejected offers on the utility of selection tests. *Psychological Bulletin, 99,* 133–138.

Neale, J., and Liebert, R. (1986). *Science and behavior: An introduction to methods of research* (3rd ed.). Englewood Cliffs, NJ: Prentice-Hall.

Olkin, I., and Finn, J. (1995). Correlations redux. *Psychological Bulletin, 118,* 155–164.

Raju, N., Burke, M., and Normand, J. (1990). A new approach for utility analysis. *Journal of Applied Psychology, 75,* 3–12.

Sturman, M. (2000). Implications of utility analysis adjustments for estimates of human resource intervention value. *Journal of Management, 26,* 281–299.

VIII

MULTIPLE (MOSTLY TRIVARIATE) REGRESSION

CHAPTER OBJECTIVES

After reading this chapter you should be able to:

- Understand the similarities between the models for bivariate and multiple regression (and, in particular, understand that bivariate and trivariate regression are special cases of multiple regression).
- Suggest situations appropriate for the use of multiple regression.
- State and explain the underlying distributional assumptions about the error term associated with multiple regression.
- Recognize the problems associated with interpreting the magnitude of regression weights.
- Explain the similarity between partial and semipartial correlations and regression weights.
- Interpret the meaning of the squared multiple correlation (R^2).
- In trivariate regression, understand the difficulty inherent in deciding how much of R^2 comes from X_1 and how much comes from X_2.
- Conduct a statistical test of significance for the overall value of R^2.
- Test the statistical significance of regression weights.
- Explain how multicollinearity of predictors can affect the outcomes of a regression analysis.

The preceding two chapters of this book were concerned with linear relationships between *two* variables, Y and X. Often, the variable to be predicted (Y) is called the "outcome variable" or the "dependent variable." Not surprisingly, the variable used to predict Y (i.e., the X variable) is called the "predictor variable" (amazing, eh?) or the "independent variable." This chapter introduces the possibility that there are *many* X's (i.e., lots of predictors, or independent variables). After all, life would be pretty boring if our behavior could be predicted (or determined or modeled) by only one variable. The working assumption of multiple regression is that many predictors (X's) will be more accurate in predicting Y than any single X.

In general, then, we will have p predictors, $X_1, X_2, \ldots, X_p$. The underlying regression model will be

$$Y = \mathbf{B}_0 + \mathbf{B}_1 X_1 + \mathbf{B}_2 X_2 + \cdots + \mathbf{B}_p X_p + e$$

Thus, Y is assumed to be a linear combination of many X's, plus random error.

However, we will first spend considerable time on the situation with two predictors and one Y ("trivariate," or three-variable, regression). Many of the lessons of multiple regression can be demonstrated more clearly in the situation where $p = 2$. Later in this chapter, we will return to the more general case of p predictors.

TRIVARIATE REGRESSION

Three Examples

Example 1 Uses of multiple regression, even in the special case where $p = 2$, can be found just about everywhere in the social science literature. Remember Professor Gretzky from Chapter VI? In his data, exam scores (Y) were predicted from class absences (X_1). There are certainly other variables he might have used to help predict these scores. Can you generate a list? Mine includes number of hours each student studies (X_2), attitude toward class content (X_3), student's age (X_4), number of previous courses taken in the content area (X_5), grades from previous courses (X_6), etc.[1] Indeed, Tables VIII.1 and VIII.2 (to be discussed later) contain data and summary statistics for the number of hours each student studied (X_2).

Example 2 The United States Army's Project A is acknowledged to be the single largest selection and classification study ever conducted (8 years, tens of thousands of soldiers, and tens of millions of dollars were involved; see Campbell and Zook, 1990, for a summary). Among other things, Project A demonstrated that the degree of "effort and leadership" a soldier demonstrated on the job (Y) could be significantly predicted from the Army's current selection test of

---

[1] Notice that we did not consider X_7 = number of courtesy hockey tickets given to Professor Gretzky.

TABLE VIII.1   DATA FOR COURSE EXAM TOTAL, NUMBER OF ABSENCES, AND HOURS STUDIED PER WEEK

Person	Exam total, Y	Absences, X_1	Hours studied, X_2
1	101	4	8
2	138	0	11
3	118	5	11
4	93	8	9
5	136	0	14
6	114	2	12
7	93	3	6
8	136	0	11
9	136	1	14
10	93	4	12
11	102	0	11
12	127	8	7
13	105	5	12
14	148	0	15
15	113	5	7
16	99	5	5
17	113	13	8
18	111	0	9
19	126	3	12
20	121	4	12
21	121	1	11

TABLE VIII.2   SUMMARY STATISTICS FOR DATA IN TABLE VIII.1

$n = 21$

$\bar{Y} = 116.38$	$\bar{X}_1 = 3.381$	$\bar{X}_2 = 10.33$
$s_Y = 16.50$	$s_1 = 3.38$	$s_2 = 2.73$

$r_{Y1} = -.409$

$r_{Y2} = .586*$

$r_{12} = -.519*$

*Statistically significant, $p = .05$, two-sided test.

cognitive ability (X_1).[2] An interesting question was whether or not additional predictors (e.g., X_2 = a personality inventory) could increase the predictability of Y. Indeed, a multiple regression was conducted, and it was demonstrated that a combination of X_1 and X_2 predicted soldier performance better than either X alone.

Example 3   The first two examples asked the same basic question, Can two predictors do better than one? Multiple regression can also be used to statistically control for the effects of other variables. For example, Romzek (1989) wanted to

[2] The existing selection measure is known as the Armed Services Vocational Aptitude Battery (ASVAB).

show that a person's organizational involvement (X_1) could predict his or her *career* satisfaction 2 years later (Y). However, Romzek wanted to control for *job* satisfaction (X_2) because job satisfaction was assumed to be a related, but separate (from career satisfaction), construct. So, she "ran" a multiple regression and found that X_1 (organizational involvement) helped predict Y even though X_2 was in the equation.[3]

The Underlying Model and the Prediction Equation

In bivariate regression, the underlying model (see Equation VI.J) was

$$Y = \mathbf{B}_0 + \mathbf{B}_1 X + e$$

The extension to trivariate regression is straightforward; i.e., Y is presumed to be a linear combination of X_1 *and* X_2 and error. Thus, the model is

VIII.A $$Y = \mathbf{B}_0 + \mathbf{B}_1 X_1 + \mathbf{B}_2 X_2 + e$$

where, for purposes of hypothesis testing, e has essentially the same properties as in bivariate regression. That is, the e's are normally distributed with mean equal to 0 and variance σ_e^2 (which, for given values of X_1 and X_2, is constant), and the e's are independent of one another.

In the bivariate case, it was easy to draw a picture of what was going on: there were two variables (Y and X), and the regression was a straight line through the scatterplot. Now, when two X's are used ($p = 2$), there are three variables and every point in the data set has *three* associated values (Y, X_1, and X_2). Thus, the scatterplot in this case is three-dimensional (Figure 8.1). For example, person A in this figure is a certain amount to the right on X_2, a certain amount out on X_1, and a certain amount up on Y.

When we collect sample data and attempt to estimate the model in Equation VIII.A, we will use the following prediction equation:

VIII.B $$\hat{Y} = b_0 + b_1 X_1 + b_2 X_2$$

where the b_i are sample estimates of the population $\mathbf{B}_i$. Now, think back to high school geometry again: the equation $\hat{Y} = b_0 + b_1 X_1$ defines a straight line through two dimensions; the equation $\hat{Y} = b_0 + b_1 X_1 + b_2 X_2$ defines a two-dimensional plane in the three-dimensional Figure 8.1. Thus, the geometric role of multiple regression (where $p = 2$) will be to orient a plane (flat surface) so that it best describes (gets close to) the points in three-dimensional space, as shown in

---

[3] Think back to Chapter VII. Romzek could have just as easily computed the partial correlation ($r_{Y1.2}$) to test her hypothesis. In fact, regression and partial correlation are quite related—see ensuing discussion of Equation VIII.C.

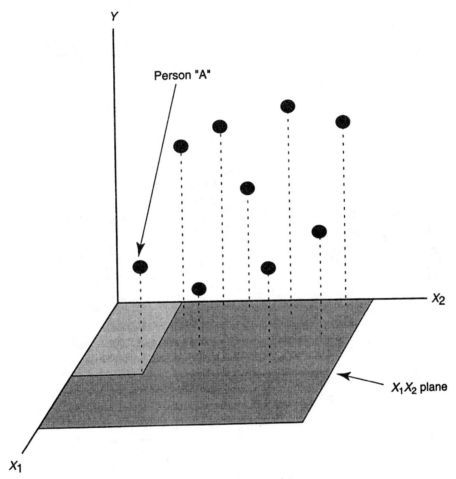

FIGURE 8.1 An example of a three-dimensional scatterplot.

Figure 8.2. The error associated with each data point is the vertical distance from the point to the plane.

As in bivariate regression, error $(Y - \hat{Y})$ is defined as the distance between a person's actual score on Y and the person's predicted score ($\hat{Y} = b_0 + b_1 X_1 + b_2 X_2$). Also, as before, we square each of the errors, add the squared errors together, and minimize the sum. That is, $\Sigma(Y - \hat{Y})^2$ is minimized. And, once again, it turns out that there is one and only one solution (for b_0, b_1, and b_2) that minimizes the sum of the squared errors! While the derivation of the b_i is somewhat complex,[4] the values for b_0, b_1, and b_2 can be written quite simply in

---

[4] It's really not too hard. To minimize $\Sigma(Y - \hat{Y})^2$, rewrite it as $\Sigma[Y - (b_0 + b_1 X_1 + b_2 X_2)]^2$, differentiate with respect to b_0, b_1, and b_2, set each equation equal to 0, and solve the system of three equations. By the way, these are called "normal equations."

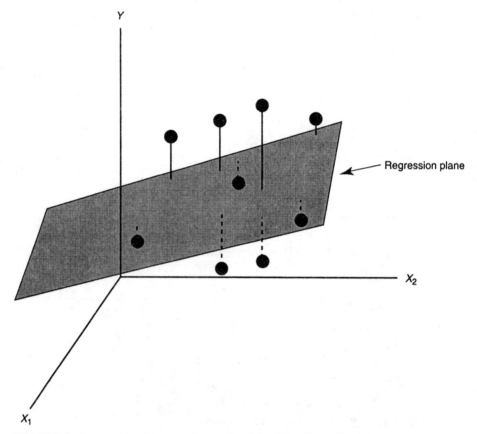

FIGURE 8.2 An example of a regression surface (plane) in a three-dimensional scatterplot.

terms of correlations and standard deviations (where r_{12} stands for the correlation between X_1 and X_2, s_1 is the symbol for the standard deviation of X_1, etc.) as

VIII.C
$$b_1 = \left(\frac{r_{Y1} - r_{Y2}r_{12}}{1 - r_{12}^2} \right) \left(\frac{s_Y}{s_1} \right)$$

VIII.D
$$b_2 = \left(\frac{r_{Y2} - r_{Y1}r_{12}}{1 - r_{12}^2} \right) \left(\frac{s_Y}{s_2} \right)$$

VIII.E
$$b_0 = \bar{Y} - b_1 \bar{X}_1 - b_2 \bar{X}_2$$

Interpreting b_1 and b_2

It is worthwhile to reflect on the equations for b_1 and b_2. There are three things I want to point out. *First*, note that the equations for b_1 and b_2 have two factors that are multiplied. The first factor is composed of correlations; the second is composed of standard deviations. Thus, if the data are standardized, the second component (e.g., s_Y/s_1 for determining b_1) doesn't affect the regression weight. On the other hand, if the data are not standardized, *the magnitudes of the weights (e.g., the sizes of b_1 and b_2) depend upon the scales being used.* For example, in the previous example, Professor Gretzky measured absence (X_1) as number of *classes* missed. Suppose each of his classes lasted 2 hours and he had measured absence (X_1) as number of *hours* of class missed. Then, all scores on X_1 would double, s_1 would double, *and b_1 would be halved,* even though the information in the data was essentially unchanged. *For this reason (and others to be discussed below) it can be quite dangerous to try to interpret the magnitudes of regression weights.*[5]

Second, consider the correlational factor in Equation VIII.C. It is $(r_{Y1} - r_{Y2}r_{12})/(1 - r_{12}^2)$. Does any of this look familiar? Think! That's right, the numerator of this factor is the same numerator as in the partial correlation $(r_{Y1.2})$ or the semipartial correlation (r_{Y1_2}). (See Chapter VII if you have forgotten. In fact, don't just "see" it; you probably want to reread it!) Also, remember that the information in the equations for partial and semipartial r's was in the numerator; i.e., the value of $r_{Y1} - r_{Y2}r_{12}$ determined the sign of the partial r. Therefore, if $r_{Y1.2}$ is 0, then b_1 is 0; if $r_{Y1.2}$ is positive, so is b_1. This should give you some key to understanding regression weights. In fact,

> b_1 **provides an answer to the following question: Suppose I already have X_2 in my prediction equation. Given that X_2 is in the equation, is it worthwhile to assign some weight to X_1? In other words, does X_1 help predict Y over and above X_2? The answer is that if b_1 is significantly different than 0, then X_1 helps predict Y over and above the use of just X_2.**

Of course, these ways of thinking about regression weights are true whether one considers b_1 or b_2. That is, if b_2 is nonzero, it indicates that X_2 deserves some weight (in predicting Y), given that X_1 is already being used in the equation. In fact, to reaffirm these interpretations, some researchers use the phrase "partial regression weights" for the b's in order to indicate that the b_i are formed by partialing information from the other predictor(s).

The *third* comment about b_1 and b_2 is related to the second. In the prediction equation $\hat{Y} = b_0 + b_1 X_1 + b_2 X_2$, note that a unit change in X_1 is predicted to make a b_1 change in Y (i.e., increase a person's score on X_1 by 1.0; then, $\hat{Y}$ changes by $b_1 \times 1.0$). In fact, it is more correct to say that

> **A unit change in X_1 is predicted to make a b_1 change in Y, assuming X_2 is held constant.**

[5] However, the statistical significance of the regression weight will not change (see later section, Hypothesis Testing).

This reflects the fact that b_1 is computed as a partial weight, partialing the X_2 variable out (i.e., holding X_2 constant).[6]

An Example

Consider the example from Chapter VI, where Professor Gretzky predicted course exam total (Y) from each student's number of class absences (X_1). Suppose one of our additional predictors, the number of hours studied per week (X_2), is also used. The original data $(Y$ and $X_1)$ appeared in Table VI.1. The augmented data (with X_2 added) appeared in Table VIII.1.

Table VIII.2, presented on page 179, contains the means, standard deviations, and correlations for the three variables. Please go back and peruse Table VIII.2 for a few minutes. Note that the correlations "look reasonable." The correlation between exam scores and absences is the same as before $(r_{Y1} = -.409)$. The fact that r_{12} is negative $(-.519)$ also makes sense: individuals who miss more classes tend to study less. Finally, by itself, number of hours spent studying is positively related to exam score $(r_{Y2} = .586)$.

Using the data in Table VIII.2 and Equations VIII.C through VIII.E is easy:

$$b_1 = \left[\frac{-.409 - .586(-.519)}{1 - (-.519)^2}\right]\left(\frac{16.50}{3.38}\right) = -.703$$

$$b_2 = \left[\frac{.586 - (-.409)(-.519)}{1 - (-.519)^2}\right]\left(\frac{16.50}{2.73}\right) = 3.095$$

$$b_0 = 116.38 - (-.703)(3.381) - (3.095)(10.33) = 86.78$$

Thus, the least squares prediction equation (or, best-fitting plane in three-dimensional space) is

$$\hat{Y} = 86.78 - .703X_1 + 3.095X_2$$

The weight $b_1 = -.703$ can be interpreted as follows: a unit change in X_1 (i.e., one more missed class) is associated with a predicted *decrease* of .7 points on the exam, assuming the number of hours studied per week (X_2) doesn't change. Similarly, each extra hour studied *increases* the predicted exam score by 3 points (assuming no other classes are missed). Oh, and don't forget! Just as in bivariate regression, no other prediction equation gets as close to the data [in terms of minimizing $\Sigma(Y - \hat{Y})^2$].

[6] While the statement in boldface is true, it sometimes makes regression interpretations difficult. For example, in practice X_1 and X_2 are often correlated (i.e., $r_{12} \neq 0$). So, changing X_1 without changing X_2 is sometimes impossible, yet this is the way one must interpret b_1 and b_2.

⟨e Analysis of Variance

Computer software packages typically report regression results in the following analysis of variance (ANOVA) format:

Source	Sum of squares	df	Mean square
Regression	$\Sigma(\hat{Y} - \bar{Y})^2$	2	$\Sigma(\hat{Y} - \bar{Y})^2 / 2$
Error	$\Sigma(Y - \hat{Y})^2$	$n - 2 - 1$	$s_e^2 = \Sigma(Y - \hat{Y})^2 / (n - 2 - 1)$
Total	$\Sigma(Y - \bar{Y})^2$	$n - 1$	

This table is almost identical to the ANOVA table for bivariate regression in Chapter VI. That is, one starts with the premise that in the absence of information about X_1 and X_2, one predicts Y using the equation $\hat{Y} = \bar{Y}$. Thus, the total sum of squared errors is $\Sigma(Y - \bar{Y})^2$. Using a regression reduces the sum of squared errors to $\Sigma(Y - \hat{Y})^2$. After all, this value is what is minimized in choosing b_0, b_1, and b_2. The difference between the total and error sum of squares is the improvement due to regression. Also, mean square error (s_e^2) estimates the assumed-to-be-constant error variance (σ_e^2). The *only* new aspect of the above table is that the sum of squares regression is now associated with 2 df because there are now two predictors in the regression equation.[7]

By the way, you should check it out for practice, but here's what I get for the ANOVA of the Professor Gretzky data set:

Source	Sum of squares	df	Mean square
Regression	1953.3	2	976.6
Error	3491.7	18	194.0
Total	5445.0	20	

⟨ultiple R^2

In bivariate regression, we asked the question, how much did we increase the predictability of Y by using a regression? We proposed an index of fit as:

$$\text{Index of fit} = \frac{\text{actual improvement}}{\text{total potential improvement}} = \frac{\text{SSR}}{\text{SST}}$$

There was an associated amazing fact: the index of fit equaled r^2.

---

[7] Since total degrees of freedom must be $n - 1$, this means there are also fewer degrees of freedom for estimating the error variance (i.e., degrees of freedom error is now $n - 2 - 1 = n - 3$, not $n - 2$).

Now, for multiple regression, the same index of fit makes sense, i.e., SSR/SST. After all, this ratio is still an index of how much we've reduced the error sum of squares relative to $\Sigma(Y - \bar{Y})^2$. In our multiple regression with $p = 2$,

> **The ratio SSR / SST is labeled the "squared multiple correlation" and is denoted in the sample by $R_{Y.12}^2$.**

The symbol $R_{Y.12}^2$ indicates that we are predicting Y from a linear combination of X_1 and X_2. Also, note that $R_{Y.12}^2$ is a more general case of the Pearson correlation. That is, in the bivariate case, $R_{Y.1}^2 = r_{Y1}^2$.

Interpreting the Magnitude of $R_{Y.12}^2$

Our index of fit is

$$\frac{\text{SSR}}{\text{SST}} = R_{Y.12}^2$$

As with Pearson correlations, most researchers go around saying things like "My R^2 is .70. Therefore X_1 and X_2 account for 70% of the variance in Y. Equivalently, the predictors fail to account for 30% of the variance." Such statements are, for our purposes, just fine. In fact, I'm sure you'll hear these statements and/or make them yourselves on many occasions.

> *An aside*   I just want to point out that, technically speaking, interpretations of multiple squared correlations as percentages of variance are not quite correct. Because sum of squares regression (SSR) and error (SSE) must sum to sum of squares total (SST), we can rewrite $R_{Y.12}^2$ as
>
> VIII.F $$R_{Y.12}^2 = \frac{\text{SSR}}{\text{SST}} = \frac{\text{SST} - \text{SSE}}{\text{SST}} = 1 - \frac{\text{SSE}}{\text{SST}}$$
>
> Now, if you take a look at the right-hand side of Equation VIII.F, you'll see that $R_{Y.12}^2$ has to do with proportions of sums of squares accounted (or not accounted) for. That is, this right-hand side has SSE and SST components, not variance components. Furthermore, to convert sums of squares to variances, one needs to divide them by degrees of freedom. Looking at the ANOVA table, note that df error is $n - 3$, while df total is $n - 1$. So, we cannot just divide the numerator and denominator of the last term in Equation VIII.F by the same value to convert to variances. Again, technically speaking, $R_{Y.12}^2$ is an index related to sums of squares, not variances. However, in most practical applications, n is large enough so that the proportional difference between $n - 3$ and $n - 1$ is negligible. I just thought you'd want to know. Besides, I think it helps reinforce an understanding of $R_{Y.12}^2$.

"Unpacking" the Value of $R^2_{Y.12}$

In trivariate regression, we used X_1 *and* X_2 to predict Y and obtained an index of fit of $R^2_{Y.12}$. Had we used only one variable to predict Y (say, X_1), our index of fit would have been r^2_{Y1}. Presumably, using two predictors provides a better fit to the data than using one predictor.[8]

The underlying question in this section is, *How much of* $R^2_{Y.12}$ is due to the use of X_1, *and how much* is due to the use of X_2? It would be just ducky if we could answer, "To get $R^2_{Y.12}$, just add the value of r^2_{Y1} and r^2_{Y2}." Unfortunately, this is true only when $r_{12} = 0$. Generally speaking, we can't simply add r^2_{Y1} and r^2_{Y2}: there may be some overlap between X_1 and X_2 (i.e., $r_{12} \neq 0$), and by simply adding r^2_{Y1} and r^2_{Y2} we're adding the same thing (the overlap) twice.

So, what is the correct answer? Well, *one* answer is

VIII.G $$R^2_{Y.12} = r^2_{Y1} + r^2_{Y2_1}$$

That is, on the right-hand side of Equation VIII.G, we can start with r^2_{Y1}, but then we can add only the squared *semipartial* correlation ($r^2_{Y2_1}$). Note that this makes sense because the semipartial correlation tries to predict Y from that part of X_2 that has nothing to do with X_1 [and the information from X_1 has already been accounted for in the first term (r^2_{Y1})]. (See Chapter VII if you have forgotten about semipartial correlations.)

For example, in Professor Gretzky's data (see ANOVA results above and Table VIII.2), $R^2_{Y.12} = \text{SSR}/\text{SST} = 1953.3/5445.0 = .359$, and Equation VIII.G results in

$$R^2_{Y.12} = .359 = r^2_{Y1} + r^2_{Y2_1}$$

$$= .167 + .192$$

Thus, it's tempting to walk around saying, "I've explained about 36% of the variance in Y with my regression. About 17% of that total is due to X_1; the remaining 19% is due to X_2."

However (yet another "however"), there's *another* way to unpack the value of $R^2_{Y.12}$. It is

VIII.H $$R^2_{Y.12} = r^2_{Y2} + r^2_{Y1_2}$$

This equation also makes sense. It says to first start with X_2's contribution (r^2_{Y2}) and then add the squared semipartial correlation with X_2 taken out X_1. Again, for Professor Gretzky's data, this yields

$$R^2_{Y.12} = .359 = r^2_{Y2} + r^2_{Y1_2}$$

$$= .343 + .016$$

---

[8] In fact, in the original sample, $R^2_{Y.12}$ can't be less than r^2_{Y1}. After all, the weights b_i are chosen to minimize SSE and, if X_2 is useless, then b_2 will be assigned a value of 0.

A person using Equation VIII.H might therefore come to a different conclusion than was made in the previous paragraph: about 2% of the explained variance is due to X_1; the remaining 34% is due to X_2.

Can you see the problem here? We have two mathematically correct ways of unpacking $R^2_{Y.12}$, so

There's no single unambiguous way to answer our original question regarding how much of $R^2_{Y.12}$ is due to X_1 and how much is due to X_2.[9]

It should be fairly obvious that the problem here is a choice between starting with X_1 and then adding X_2 (Equation VIII.G) or starting with X_2 and then adding X_1 (Equation VIII.H). The way statisticians remove the ambiguity is to *change the original question slightly to, How much unique explanatory variance is attributable to each of the predictors?* In this case, unique variance for a particular X is obtained only after all other X-values are used first. For example, in our two-predictor case, the unique variance for X_1 assumes that X_2 has already been used (i.e., Equation VIII.H).

You should now see precisely what "unique variance" is in trivariate regression. Think! That's right, it is the squared semipartial correlation! So, for Professor Gretzky's data, the unique variance for X_1 is $r^2_{Y1_2} = .016$; the unique variance attributed to X_2 is .192. Further, note that the sum of these two values is less than the overall value of $R^2_{Y.12} = .359$. That's because there's some overlap between X_1 and X_2 ($r_{12} = -.519$) which contributes to the overall $R^2_{Y.12}$ but makes no contribution to the uniqueness question. We will return to this notion of uniqueness, as it will be *the* way to interpret tests of significance of the regression weights (i.e., $H_0: \mathbf{B}_i = 0$).

It is also possible to geometrically portray these issues using a Venn diagram. For example, Figure 8.3 contains three circles that represent the variables Y, X_1, and X_2, respectively. Metaphorically, the more any two circles overlap, the higher the correlation between the two variables. Figure 8.3 portrays a situation where Y, X_1, and X_2 are all somewhat correlated (i.e., all circles partially overlap each other).

Since $R^2_{Y.12}$ represents how well we predict Y from X_1 *and* X_2, the value of $R^2_{Y.12}$ in Figure 8.3 is represented by the totality of all three shaded areas (labeled a, b, and c). Note, however, that while X_1 correlates $a + c$ with Y, the unique contribution of X_1 in predicting Y is just the shaded area a. Similarly, the unique contribution of X_2 is indicated by the shaded area b. It's the shaded area c that is causing the problem.[10]

---

[9] This is a version of Murphy's law: "A man with one watch knows what time it is. A man with two watches is never sure" (Bloch, 1978, p. 79).

[10] Note that if $r_{12} = 0$, then the circles for X_1 and X_2 don't overlap and there will be no area labeled c. We are then back at the simple case where $R^2_{Y.12}$ is $r^2_{Y1} + r^2_{Y2}$. By the way, some people really like using Venn diagrams when thinking about regressions. On the other hand, there is no simple way to distinguish negative correlations from positive correlations in a pictorially correct yet meaningful way. If you come up with one, please let me know!

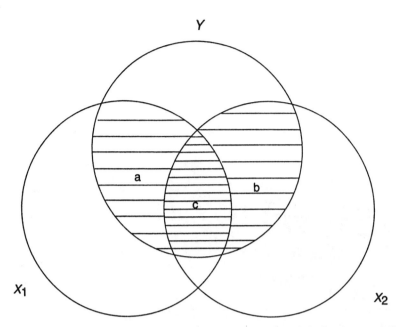

FIGURE 8.3 A Venn diagram depicting some overlap (heuristically, the correlation) among the variables Y, X_1, and X_2.

Aside: Why Always Square the Multiple Correlation?

When there was one Y and one X, we had good old Pearson r as our measure of relationship. It ranged from -1.0 to $+1.0$. Have you noticed that with two X's we use $R^2_{Y.12}$ and not $R_{Y.12}$ as the measure of choice? Thus, the multivariate measure of relationship is nonnegative and ranges from 0 to $+1.0$. This choice is made for two reasons. First, when computing our error components (e.g., SSE), we didn't care whether errors $(Y - \hat{Y})$ were positive or negative, and so we squared them. Second, *it would make no sense to attach a sign to the value of* $R^2_{Y.12}$. To visually understand this, remember that trivariate regression fits a plane to a three-dimensional scatterplot. It is quite easy to orient a hypothetical plane (regression surface) such that as X_2 goes up, Y goes up, yet as X_1 goes up, Y goes down. Figure 8.4 is my attempt at illustrating such a plane. The sign of $R^2_{Y.12}$ has no meaning in this case. The relationship between Y and the predictors seems to be positive if X_2 is considered, yet negative when X_1 is considered. So, indexing fit by use of R^2 rather than R avoids this confusion. Just more food for thought.

ΨPOTHESIS TESTING

ιe Squared Multiple Correlation

The first question usually asked in a results section of an empirical article is, Did anything useful happen when we conducted the regression? Our index of the

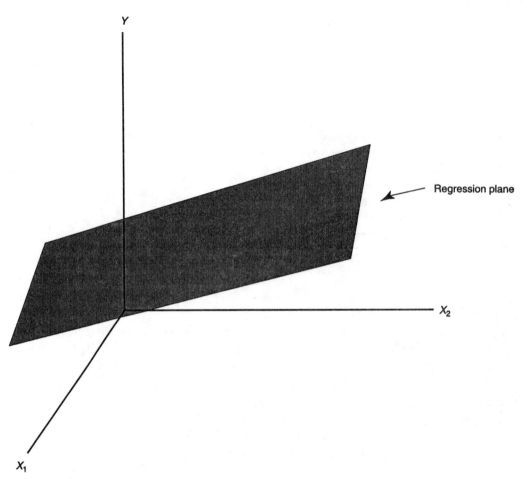

FIGURE 8.4 A regression plane where the sign of R is ambiguous.

overall utility of the regression was $R^2_{Y.12}$. If this index was 0, then the regression did not help in reducing the sum of squared errors relative to the baseline value of $\Sigma(Y - \bar{Y})^2$. For notational purposes, let $\mathbf{R}^2_{Y.12}$ be the squared multiple correlation in the population. Then, the null hypothesis to be tested is

$$H_0 : \mathbf{R}^2_{Y.12} = 0$$

Statisticians have derived a very straightforward test of this hypothesis based upon the analysis of variance of the sample data.[11] The result is that

---

[11] This test, and the ones for the b_i in the next section, all assume that the distributional properties of the errors (e.g., normality, homoscedasticity) are met.

Under the null hypothesis of zero multiple correlation, the ratio MSR / MSE has an *F*-distribution with 2 df in the numerator and $(n - 2 - 1)$ degrees of freedom in the denominator.

That is, if $\mathbf{R}^2_{Y.12}$ is truly 0, then the sample ratio MSR/MSE is expected to have a value of about 1.0 (the expected value of F under H_0). To the extent that the population multiple correlation is greater than zero, the F-ratio will be substantially greater than 1.0. Thus, the significance test is implicitly one-sided; the alternative hypothesis is $H_a : \mathbf{R}^2_{Y.12} > 0$.

Gretzky's data again   Earlier in this chapter, we noted that Professor Gretzky obtained a sample $R^2_{Y.12}$ value of .359 based on $n = 21$ subjects. Look back at the analysis of variance table and you'll see

$$\frac{\text{Mean square regression}}{\text{Mean square error}} = \frac{976.6}{194.0} = 5.03$$

Now, the numerator degrees of freedom is $p = 2$ and the denominator degrees of freedom is $n - 2 - 1 = 18$. And for $p = .05$, the critical F-value is $F_{.05, 2, 18} = 3.55$ (see the Appendix, Table A.2). Since Professor Gretzky's sample F of 5.03 is larger than 3.55, he can reject the null hypothesis that $\mathbf{R}^2_{Y.12} = 0$. If he ever writes his results in journal article format, there would be a statement such as, "Course grade can be significantly predicted from a linear combination of class absence and hours studied" or "The value of $R^2_{Y.12} = .359$ is statistically significant."

A handy formula   To use the above test for $H_0 : \mathbf{R}^2_{Y.12} = 0$, one needs the results of an analysis of variance to obtain mean square regression and mean square error. However, remember that $R^2 = \text{SSR}/\text{SST}$ and that $1 - R^2 = \text{SSE}/\text{SST}$. Also, the F-ratio above can be written as

$$F = \frac{\text{MSR}}{\text{MSE}} = \frac{\text{SSR}/2}{\text{SSE}/(n - 2 - 1)}$$

Now, divide the numerator and the denominator by SST to obtain

$$F = \frac{\dfrac{(\text{SSR}/\text{SST})}{2}}{\dfrac{\text{SSE}/\text{SST}}{n - 2 - 1}} = \frac{\dfrac{R^2}{2}}{\dfrac{1 - R^2}{n - 2 - 1}}$$

Therefore, we have derived the following:

VIII.I
$$F = \frac{(n - 2 - 1) R^2}{(1 - R^2)(2)}$$

So, you don't need the analysis of variance table to compute the sample F-ratio; you just need R^2 and n. Try it for Gretzky's data! Letting $R^2 = .359$ and $n = 21$ in Equation VIII.I should result in the same sample F-value of 5.03 as before. Please note that Equation VIII.I is really handy. Research reports generally give only the sample size and the value of R^2 and not the complete analysis of variance table. You will find that you will use Equation VIII.I often.

The Regression Weights, B$_i$

The significance test of the multiple R^2 told you whether anything was going on in the regression equation (i.e., whether or not it was statistically useful to use the set of X's to predict Y). The next logical question is, Of all the X's used in the equation, were some more useful than others?—or, Is it possible that some of the X's were doing all the work and other X's weren't doing anything? Indeed, perhaps these other X's just happened to be in the same regression with some terrific predictors that made the overall R^2 significant.

The tests usually conducted at this point in the analysis are of the form

$$H_0: \mathbf{B}_i = 0 \quad \text{versus} \quad H_a: \mathbf{B}_i \neq 0$$

That is, if $\mathbf{B}_i$ is truly 0, then X_i has no weight in the regression prediction equation and that predictor ought not to be used.[12]

Before describing the statistical test procedure, it is very important to understand the exact interpretation of $H_0: \mathbf{B}_i = 0$. For example, consider the predictor (X_1). *First,* we noted that the sign of the estimator b_1 (i.e., whether it was negative, 0, or positive) was completely determined by the factor $r_{Y1} - r_{Y2}r_{12}$ (see Equation VIII.C). *Second,* in unpacking the value of $R_{Y.12}^2$ we noted that the unique contribution of X_1 was related to the semipartial correlation (r_{Y1_2}). The sign of this semipartial correlation was completely determined by the same factor ($r_{Y1} - r_{Y2}r_{12}$) (see Equation VII.E). Therefore, by linking these two facts, it should be clear that X_1 will receive nonzero weight in the regression equation only if it contributes to the prediction of Y over and above the use of X_2. In general, then,

The test of $H_0: \mathbf{B}_i = 0$ asks whether or not X_i contributes to the prediction of Y over and above all other predictor variables in the equation. (Of course, in trivariate regression, there's only one other predictor.)

[12] While one usually tries to reject null hypotheses, the possibility that a particular null hypothesis is true (i.e., $\mathbf{B}_i = 0$) can also be an interesting theoretical proposition. For example, in trying to predict an individual's task performance (Y), some goal-setting researchers use the predictors of initial ability (X_1) and the level of goal a person is striving for on the particular task (X_2). Theory postulates that a person's initial ability (X_1) certainly affects the goal they set (X_2), which in turn affects how well they perform (Y). However, theory also says that all you need to predict performance (Y) is the person's goal (X_2) and that knowing initial ability (X_1) doesn't help the prediction (because it's effect is already inside X_2). Thus, it would be hypothesized that $\mathbf{B}_1 = 0$ when predicting Y from X_1 and X_2 (see Locke, Frederick, Lee, and Bobko, 1984, for an example).

Another helpful (and equivalent) way of making this statement is to say that the test of $H_0 \colon B_i = 0$ asks whether or not X_i would have contributed to the regression equation if X_i was the last variable to be considered. This is equivalent to

The test of $H_0 \colon B_i = 0$ asks whether the squared multiple correlation would significantly increase if X_i was added to the regression equation after all other variables had already been entered.

The actual mechanics of the test for b_i are straightforward and similar to the test for the slope in a bivariate regression (see Chapter VI, Equation VI.M). That is, under the null hypothesis, the ratio

VIII.J
$$\text{Sample } t_{n-2-1} = \frac{b_i \boxed{-0}}{\text{SD}(b_i)}$$

has a Student's t-distribution with $(n - 2 - 1)$ degrees of freedom (i.e., the degrees of freedom associated with the error sum of squares). Now all I have to give you is an expression for the standard deviation of a regression weight, $\text{SD}(b_i)$. In trivariate regression, this standard deviation can be stated as

VIII.K
$$\text{SD}(b_i) = \sqrt{\frac{\text{mean square error}}{ns_i^2 (1 - r_{12}^2)}}$$

Before we use this standard deviation, take a peek at some of its factors. The numerator of Equation VIII.K is the mean square error in the sample (i.e., s_e^2). So, to the extent that our regression error variance is small, the standard deviation of a regression weight will also be relatively small. Further, note the ubiquitous n in the denominator. This factor is where is ought to be because when the t-ratio in Equation VIII.J is formed, an increase in n will increase the overall t-ratio (by the usual factor of $\sqrt{n}$).

Notice that the sample variance of X_i (s_i^2) also affects the value of $\text{SD}(b_i)$. Because Equation VIII.K has a square root sign in it, the standard deviation of b_i [$\text{SD}(b_i)$] is inversely proportional to the standard deviation of X_i (s_i). This is related to an earlier statement made in this chapter: we noted that changing the scale of a variable (e.g., going from number of classes missed to number of class hours missed) would change the magnitude of a regression weight. However, the fact that s_i appears in Equation VIII.K means that

If the scale is changed, the value of $\text{SD}(b_i)$ will change in the same proportion as the value of b_i. Thus, the t-ratio, and resulting test of significance, is *not* affected by a change in scaling.

Finally, the term $1 - r_{12}^2$ in the expression for $\text{SD}(b_i)$ is so interesting that it will be considered in a special section later in this and other chapters (see the section on collinearity below).

Two Examples

Professor Gretzky's data again The prediction equation for the data in Table VIII.1 has already been derived as

$$\hat{Y} = b_0 + b_1 X_1 + b_2 X_2 = 86.78 - .703(X_1) + 3.095(X_2)$$

or

$$\text{Predicted grade} = 86.78 - .703 \,(\text{absence}) + 3.095(\text{hours studied})$$

To compute the test of $H_0: \mathbf{B}_2 = 0$, note that $b_2 = 3.095$. Further, the analysis of variance showed that the mean squared error was 194.0, and Table VIII.2 gives $n = 21$, $s_2 = 2.73$, and $r_{12} = -.519$. Thus, from Equation VIII.K,

$$\text{SD}(b_2) = \sqrt{\frac{194.0}{21(2.73)^2(1 - .519^2)}} = 1.302$$

and, from Equation VIII.J, the sample t-ratio is

$$\text{Sample } t = \frac{3.095}{1.302} = 2.38$$

At $p = .05$, the two-sided critical t-value with 18 df is $t_{.05, 18} = 2.101$ (see the Appendix, Table A.1). Therefore, the sample t-value of 2.38 is greater than the critical value, and Professor Gretzky can state that (1) the sample value of b_2 is significant (i.e., different than 0) and/or (2) the variable of hours studied per week (X_2) significantly adds to the prediction of course grade over and above the other predictor (X_1 = number of absences for each student).

Now it's your turn. Check out the regression weight for the absence predictor (X_1). Is $b_1 = -.703$ significantly different than zero? [I obtained $\text{SD}(b_1) = 1.052$ and a sample $t = -.668$, which is smaller than the magnitude of the critical value 2.101. Therefore $H_0: \mathbf{B}_1 = 0$ is not rejected. Do you agree?]

A study about IPOs Welbourne and Andrews (1996) studied the performance of companies that went through the process of initial public offerings (IPO). The study looked at both short-term performance (e.g., stock-based valuations at IPO) and longer-term performance (e.g., survival of the company five years later). Let's consider the dependent variable of stock valuation (Y, an index of perceived potential based upon stock price and book value). Two predictors of this valuation outcome were considered in the initial model: X_1, the degree to which each company claimed to value employees as an explicit asset; X_2, the use of rewards based on organizational performance. The variable X_1 included assessments of each company's mission statement, minimal use of part-time employees, mention of an employee training program, etc. The variable X_2 assessed the degree of stock options and profit sharing available to employees.

Thus, Welbourne and Andrews estimated the regression $\hat{Y} = b_0 + b_1 X_1 + b_2 X_2$ across $n = 136$ organizations undergoing an IPO. These authors wanted to assess the unique contribution of each predictor (i.e., look at $H_0: \mathbf{B}_i = 0$). They reported that $b_0 = 71.66$, $b_1 = 2.03$ and $b_2 = -4.53$. Let's look at b_2 for a moment. Can we reject $H_0: \mathbf{B}_2 = 0$? Those authors do report that $s_2 = 1.17$ and $r_{12} = .21$. And, I need to tell you that from the statistics they provided, I calculated MSE $= 574.10$. Application of Equation VIII.K yields

$$\text{SD}(b_2) = \sqrt{\frac{\text{MSE}}{ns_2^2(1 - r_{12}^2)}} = \sqrt{\frac{574.10}{136(1.17)^2(1 - .21^2)}} = 1.80$$

and the sample t is

$$\text{Sample } t = \frac{-4.53}{1.80} = -2.52$$

At $p = .05$, two sides, the critical t (with $136 - 3 = 133$ df) is approximately 1.96. Therefore, they can claim (as they did!) that invoking organization-based rewards significantly (and uniquely) predicted early IPO performance.

The negative value for b_2 is interesting. As Welbourne and Andrews suggest, investors will "react negatively" (p. 906) to firms that use compensation in the form of stock options and profit sharing. Indeed, these authors also found that their results held even when they separated management rewards from employee rewards. On the surface, this may appear to be a bit counterintuitive. On the other hand (there's that phrase, again!), when the criterion shifted to survival five years later (a longer focused criterion, indeed), the use of organizationally based rewards significantly, and *positively*, predicted survival. In case you're interested, the degree to which companies explicitly valued human assets, X_1, did not predict IPO stock price but did predict survival.

By the way, the fact that the predictor X_2 behaved differently for short-term and long-term criteria is substantively fascinating. Psychometrically, it also harks back to what was said in Chapter IV—where it was noted that the phrase "the validity of a measure" (in this case X_2) does not have much meaning. As we noted there, validity is a function of the *application* of a measure (in this case short- or long-term performance).

Collinearity

In multiple regression, it should be obvious that the degree to which the predictors (X_i) are related to the outcome measure (Y) substantially influences the results (higher r's between Y and the X_i meaning better predictability). *However, the degree to which the predictors are correlated among themselves can also substantially affect regression results.* The interrelationships among predictors is often labeled "predictor multicollinearity."

In trivariate regression, there are two predictors and the degree of collinearity in the predictors is indexed by the value of r_{12}. All other things equal, it is often better to have $r_{12} = 0$. For example, when $r_{12} = 0$, it was noted that $R^2_{Y.12}$ could be decomposed as $r^2_{Y1} + r^2_{Y2}$ and the contribution of each variable to the prediction equation could be unambiguously assessed.

Another way to see the effects of collinearity is to look back at Equation VIII.K. Note that as r_{12} increases, the value $1 - r^2_{12}$ decreases and the standard deviation of a regression weight gets larger. This makes sense if you think about it. Intuitively speaking, if the two X's measure similar things, then it hardly matters whether you give weight (i.e., the b's) to X_1 or X_2. From one sample to another sample, the regression gives weight, willy-nilly, to one X or the other (depending on sample idiosyncracies), so the sampling variance of any b_i (across samples) is large, even though the overall value of $R^2_{Y.12}$ is fairly stable. In turn, this means that it is hard to reject $H_0: \mathbf{B}_i = 0$ because $SD(b_i)$ is so large. (Again, this harkens back to the interpretation of $H_0: \mathbf{B}_i = 0$. If the two X's have a high degree of overlap, then the X's have little unique contribution.)

In fact, it is sometimes the case in applied research that the overall $R^2_{Y.12}$ is statistically significant yet neither b_i is! This is usually because the collinearity in the data (r_{12}) is large. What to do? I'd suggest three things. First, simply remember this section of the book and realize such possibilities can occur and the reason for them. Second, increase your sample size. All else equal, an increase in n will increase your statistical power [remember, n is in the denominator of $SD(b_i)$]. Third, somehow reduce your collinearity. For example, you may drop one of the variables from the regression equation. Or, rather than throw away variables or data, perhaps combine (in an a priori way) the two related predictor variables. Or, consider why the collinearity exists. If there's common method variance, use different methods for the two variables if possible.

MULTIPLE REGRESSION IN GENERAL

Regression *Is* Popular

I want to reemphasize that the use of multiple regression can be found in almost all issues of any empirical social science journal. Just to give you an idea of regression's widespread use, here is a sampling of articles that crossed my desk while I was outlining and revising this chapter.

1 Neuman and Wright (1999) wanted to see if they could predict the *group* level performance of teams of human resource representatives. Predictors included team-level cognitive ability and personality (in both cases, constructs were indexed by the lowest scoring member of each team).

2 Gregersen and Black (1992) computed regressions that predicted organizational commitment from a variety of personal, job, and nonjob factors. Actually, they conducted two regressions: one predicting commitment to the employee's parent company and one predicting commitment to the company's foreign operation. The authors wanted to compare and contrast variables that affected these two types of commitment.

3 Evans and Carrere (1991) predicted stress levels of bus drivers at work using individual difference variables (age, smoking behavior, marital status, perceived job control) and the level of traffic congestion encountered.

4 Dulebohn and Ferris (1999) predicted employee evaluation of the fairness of the performance evaluation process from the types of influence tactics used by the employees. Additional predictors included performance ratings, as well as perceptions of decision control and opportunity for a formal voice.

5 Provan and Skinner (1989) predicted how often dealers of farm equipment would engage in opportunistic behavior with their suppliers (based on measures involving alternative suppliers and the formalization of the relationship).

6 Frederickson and Iaquinto (1989) predicted changes in an organization's strategy from changes in organizational size and continuity of the executive team.

7 Conlon and Sullivan (1999) predicted how long it took to resolve a corporate dispute from characteristics of the dispute, including plaintiff type (individual or organization), the number of issues in dispute, and the number of lawyers involved on each side.

Again, these are but a sample of the many content domains in which multiple regression can be applied. Have gun, will travel; have regression, will predict!

With our extended discussion of trivariate regression in hand, it's really a straightforward leap to generic multiple regression. Many facets are identical and will be briefly presented in the remainder of this chapter in what is tantamount to a review of previous material. Then, two chapters will be devoted to the question, What havoc we wrought by so many X's? and to some specialized regression topics.

This Is Really a Review

The model and prediction equation   In multiple regression, the underlying model is

$$Y = \mathbf{B}_0 + \mathbf{B}_1 X_1 + \mathbf{B}_2 X_2 + \cdots + \mathbf{B}_p X_p + e$$

where e has the same assumed properties as in bivariate and trivariate regression. The only thing new is the existence of p predictors rather than just 1 or 2. The underlying model is estimated in the sample by

$$\hat{Y} = b_0 + b_1 X_1 + b_2 X_2 + \cdots + b_p X_p$$

where, as before, the b_i are chosen so that $\Sigma(Y - \hat{Y})^2$ is minimized (the old least squares criterion again).

By the way, in trivariate regression, we fit a two-dimensional plane to a three-dimensional scatterplot. With p predictors in the regression, the new twist is that we're fitting a p-dimensional hyperplane to a $(p + 1)$-dimensional scatterplot! The formulas for the weights (the b_i) are not as simple to write down as they were when we had only two X's (see Equations VIII.C and VIII.D). But, I promise you that one *can* derive them and, with a bit of calculus and matrix algebra, it's even a straightforward thing to accomplish. However, for our purposes, we can assume that computer software packages will do the correct job for us in estimating the sample regression weights.

Once derived, each sample regression weight (b_i) indicates the predicted change in Y per a 1-unit change in the corresponding X_i, assuming the other X's are held constant. This interpretation is unchanged from the case with just two predictors. And the analysis of variance is shown in the following table:

Source	Sum of squares	df	Mean square
Regression	$\Sigma(\hat{Y} - \bar{Y})^2$	p	SSR$/p$
Error	$\Sigma(Y - \hat{Y})^2$	$n - p - 1$	SSE$/(n - p - 1) = s_e^2$
Total	$\Sigma(Y - \bar{Y})^2$	$n - 1$	SST$/(n - 1) = s_Y^2$

That is, with the exception of using p predictors rather than 2 predictors, the analysis of variance table is unchanged. Also as before, the index of fit for the entire regression is the ratio of the regression sum of squares to the total sum of squares. Thus, the general form of the squared multiple correlation is denoted and defined as

$$R^2_{Y.12\ldots p} = \frac{\text{SSR}}{\text{SST}}$$

Hypothesis testing To test the null hypothesis $H_0: \mathbf{R}^2_{Y.12\ldots p} = 0$, the ratio MSR/MSE has an F-distribution—just as in trivariate regression. However, in this more general case, the F-statistic is associated with p and $(n - p - 1)$ degrees of freedom in the numerator and denominator, respectively. Thus, the generalized form of Equation VIII.I becomes

$$F = \frac{(n - p - 1)R^2}{(1 - R^2)(p)}$$

Further, as before, the test of the hypothesis $H_0: \mathbf{B}_i = 0$ asks whether or not variable X_i has any unique contribution to predicting Y above and beyond the use of all other X's (i.e., as if X_i were the *last* variable to be considered). However, there is an interesting change here: the more general expression for the standard deviation of the sampling distribution of b_i is now

VIII.L
$$SD(b_i) = \sqrt{\frac{\text{mean square error}}{n \, s_i^2 \left(1 - R^2_{i.\text{all other } X\text{'s}}\right)}}$$

where $\left(R^2_{i.\text{all other } X\text{'s}}\right)$ symbolizes the squared multiple correlation when one predicts the particular X_i in question from the remaining $(p - 1)X$'s. Indeed, this R^2 is the way regression indexes the degree of multicollinearity in the predictors.

By the way, there's one other small change in the t-test for $H_0: \mathbf{B}_i = 0$. The value for degrees of freedom is now $n - p - 1$. Note that this value arises from the more general degrees of freedom associated with mean square error—and mean square error definitely plays a role in the determination of $SD(b_i)$. Thus, under the null hypothesis that $\mathbf{B}_i = 0$,

$$\text{Sample } t_{n-p-1} = \frac{b_i}{SD(b_i)}$$

has a Student's t-distribution with $(n - p - 1)$ degrees of freedom.

Note that the multicollinearity problem is potentially worse here. That is, with two predictors, the collinearity index in the expression for $SD(b_i)$ was r_{12}^2 (see Equation VIII.K). In multiple regression (hence in Equation VIII.L), the index of collinearity is the degree to which X_i can be predicted from the remaining X's (all $p - 1$ of them). It may be that some strange linear combination of the other X's can predict a particular X_i (perhaps a combination not easily seen from inspection of the simple correlations among the X's). Thus, there's lots of potential for multicollinearity here, which in turn increases the standard deviations of b_i (see equation). As a result, statistical power may be reduced when trying to test each individual regression weight. We will return to the issue of multicollinearity in the next chapter.

Two Asides About Tests of $B_i = 0$

Aside 1 Some researchers state that the test of $H_0: \mathbf{B}_i = 0$ should be conditional on the test for $H_0: R^2_{Y.12\ldots p} = 0$. That is, they claim that regression weights shouldn't be tested for significance unless the entire regression is significant (i.e., R^2 is significantly greater than 0). After all, why interpret individual variables if the entire equation doesn't reduce the sum of squared errors over and above the baseline value of $\Sigma(Y - \bar{Y})^2$? The other (related) reason not to look at the b's unless R^2 is significant has to do with "data snooping." That is, as in the discussion about testing or "harvesting" many correlations (see Chapter III), 5% of the tests of $H_0: \mathbf{B}_i = 0$ will be significant just by chance (if an alpha level of .05 is used). So, if there are many X's in the regression, then some b's will be significant by chance. Requiring a significant R^2 helps to control for some of this capitalization on chance.

On the other hand, some researchers feel that the requirement of a significant R^2 before looking at the b's must be used flexibly. For example, imagine that you have a terrific predictor (X_1) of Y, based on a strong theoretical rationale and/or previous empirical results. However, when you conduct your study, you also "throw in" lots of other X's that seem on the surface to be interesting predictors to study. Suppose the other X's turn out to have very small correlations with Y. At this point, the effect of X_1 in the overall regression will be "swamped" by the other, nonuseful X's, and the value of R^2 might not be significant.[13] So, some researchers go ahead and test the value of b_1 anyway since there were a priori reasons to consider this test of significance. (Again, see the Chapter III discussion of using hypothesiswise error rates rather than a single overall error rate).

Aside 2 Suppose your study initially uses 17 X's in a regression analysis. Based on tests of the b_i, you decide that two of the X's do not have significant regression weights, so you remove them from your analysis. Be aware that "rerunning" the regression analyses with the remaining 15 X's may completely change the values of the b's. That is, regression is designed to find weights that minimize the residual sum of squares (i.e., maximize R^2) in the sample at hand. If the dropped X's were in any way correlated with the remaining X's, then the values of the remaining 15 b's are likely to change. So, what many researchers do is conduct statistical tests of the b's on the full model (all X's used). Then, when results are reported, a final model is also estimated. This consists of the re-estimated regression using only those X's remaining after significance tests were conducted. Of course, there's no guarantee that the remaining X's will still have significant regression weights when this final model is estimated! Indeed, one could remove nonsignificant X's from the "final" model, though I wouldn't recommend such an iterative procedure. It smacks of infinite regress, and no one really knows what the error rate is with such a data-driven way of removing X's in this layered approach. Isn't regression fun?[14]

---

[13] To see the potential for a lack of significance, look at the formula for the F-ratio that tests R^2 against the null value of 0. Adding additional X's will *not* lower the value of R^2 in the sample. However, additional degrees of freedom will be used up. In particular, the denominator of the F-ratio is directly proportional to the number of predictors used (p). So, adding useless X's could decrease the sample F-ratio and reduce the chance of getting a significant R^2.

[14] Although beyond the scope of this book, note that values of b_i can change for an even more complex reason: measurement error. However, this problem is usually ignored by researchers in management and psychology (see Becker and Huselid, 1992, or Busemeyer and Jones, 1983, for exceptions). Suppose the X's are measured with some unreliability (see Chapter IV). Then, it can be shown that the error terms in regression are no longer uncorrelated with the predictors, and the b_i will be *biased* estimates of $\mathbf{B}_i$ (cf. Maddala, 1988). In a bivariate regression where X is measured unreliably, b will underestimate $\mathbf{B}$, but in multiple regression the size and direction of the bias depends upon *many* factors. You might think that you could correct all correlations by using the bivariate formulas in Chapter IV. However, it is statistically not right to simply apply these corrections to all pairs of variables in a multivariate correlation matrix. Although beyond the scope of this text, Bock and Petersen (1975) provide a multivariate correction for unreliability that involves solutions to a two matrix eigenvalue problem.

TABLE VIII.4 BIVARIATE CORRELATIONS FROM THE PROVAN AND SKINNER (1989) STUDY†,‡

	Y	X_1	X_2	X_3	X_4
Y (opportunism)					
X_1 (service dependence)	−.31				
X_2 (number of suppliers)	.13	−.13			
X_3 (quality of alternatives)	.21	−.31	.17		
X_4 (formalization of control)	.08	.02	−.03	−.08	
X_5 (centralization of control)	.25	−.17	−.04	.26	−.04

†n = 226. Correlations greater than .12 in magnitude are statistically significant (two-sides, $p < .05$).
‡Adapted with permission from Provan and Skinner (1989).

Example of Multiple Regression

As noted earlier in this section, Provan and Skinner (1989) conducted a regression study looking at how farm and power equipment dealers ($n = 226$) interacted with their primary suppliers. The dependent variable (Y) was "opportunistic behavior by dealers in relations with their primary supplier" (p. 205). The independent variables (the X's) included both (i) measures of how dependent the dealer was on the supplier and (ii) measures of the amount of control suppliers had over dealer decisions. There were three measures (X_1, X_2, X_3) of dealer dependence and two measures (X_4, X_5) of supplier control. The matrix of correlations among the variables is presented in Table VIII.4

Note that the correlations in Table VIII.4 make sense. For example, the first column of correlations give all the regular old r's between Y and each of the X's (these correlations are often called the "bivariate validities of the X's"). Note that the more dependent the dealer is on the supplier (X_1), the less the dealer engages in opportunism ($r_{y1} = -.31$). On the other hand, the existence of other suppliers and a higher quality of these alternatives lead to greater opportunism.[15] Finally, the more control by suppliers, the more opportunism by dealers (positive r's of .08 and .25). Provan and Skinner had even hypothesized this latter finding, suggesting that as dealers "have their freedom constrained, they are likely to resist... and improve their condition... [in] the form of opportunistic behavior" (p. 205).

The remaining correlations in Table VIII.4 provide all of the interrelationships among the predictors. By the way, note that the three measures of dependence correlate higher, on average, among themselves than they do with the other two measures of control. Consistent with the thinking and discussion of Chapter IV, Provan and Skinner (1989) could have identified this pattern of correlations as further construct validity for their two types of predictors. On the other hand, the correlation between the two measures of control is close to zero ($r_{45} = -.04$). So, there would be no empirical justification for combining X_4 and X_5 into a single index of control.

[15] A sad, but true, commentary on human nature!

I mention these issues here to underscore the importance of looking at simple statistics (e.g., means, variances, r's) when doing multivariate analyses. Knowledge of your variables can aid the interpretation of complex analyses. Looking at simple statistics first can also help ensure that your variables are "behaving" the way you expect them to. Every once in a while, this inspection may indicate that the data have been miscoded, there is no variance on a particular variable, scores are outside their presumed range, or variables have been scored in the direction opposite from what you assumed. The temptation in multivariate analyses is to look only at the last page of output (e.g., the regression solution), but don't forget that simple checks often help in finding errors as well as assisting in interpretations.

Speaking of the last page of output (!), Provan and Skinner (p. 208) reported the following regression result after standardizing all their variables:[16]

$$\hat{Y} = -.25X_1 + .10X_2 + .08X_3 + .11X_4 + .19X_5$$

The analysis of variance for their data is shown in the following table:

Source	Sum of squares	df	Mean square
Regression	36	5	7.20
Error	189	220	.86
Total	225	225	

This results in

$$R^2_{Y.12\ldots5} = \frac{\text{SSR}}{\text{SST}} = \frac{36}{225} = .16$$

So, overall, the authors can state that they have explained 16% of the variation in dealer's opportunistic behavior by a linear combination of five predictors. Is this statistically significant? You bet! (Otherwise, do you think they would have published the article?) To demonstrate this significance, remember that the sample F-ratio for testing hypotheses regarding multiple correlations was formed by taking a ratio of mean squares. Thus,

$$\text{Sample } F\text{-ratio} = \frac{\text{MSR}}{\text{MSE}} = \frac{7.20}{.86} = 8.37$$

This ratio has 5 numerator and 220 denominator degrees of freedom. With $p = .05$, Table A.2 in the Appendix indicates that the critical value is between 2.21 and 2.29. Since the sample F-ratio of 8.37 is greater than the critical F, we can reject $H_0: \mathbf{R}^2_{Y.12\ldots5} = 0$.

[16] Besides all standard deviations being 1.0, standardization also implies that all means are equal to zero. That's why b_0 is zero in their regression (take a peek at Equation VIII.E to see why).

Now let's take a look at the five sample regression weights (the b_i). I haven't told you precisely *how* to get them, other than the fact that computer software packages will spew them out at you (if you put in the data and punch the right buttons!). However, it is important that you keep in mind what these regression weights do:

> **Because they are least squares weights, the values $-.25, .10, .08, .11,$ and $.19$ (b_1 through b_5) minimize the sum of the squared errors $[\sum(Y - \hat{Y})^2]$. No other set of five weights can do as well in this data!**

O.K. We know that the overall regression significantly predicts Y, with $R^2_{Y.12\ldots5} = .16$. The next issue concerns which, if any, of the b_i's are significantly different than zero. For example, consider the variable X_1 = service dependence. We know that this variable is significantly related, by itself, to Y ($r_{Y1} = -.31$). However, the test of $H_0: B_1 = 0$ asks the question, Does X_1 significantly contribute to the prediction of Y over and above the other four X's (i.e., as if it were the last predictor to be used)?

From Equation VIII.L, the standard deviation of b_1 is

$$SD(b_1) = \sqrt{\frac{MSE}{ns_1^2(1 - R^2_{1.2345})}}$$

To compute this value, note that we would obtain $MSE = .86$ from the ANOVA table, that $n = 226$, and that $s_1 = 1$ (because all variables were standardized). The value of $R^2_{1.2\ldots5}$ is a bit trickier. Indeed, you need to instruct the computer to conduct another regression, this time with X_1 as the dependent variable and with X_2, X_3, X_4, and X_5 as the four predictors. My computations show that $R^2_{1.2\ldots5} = .10$. Therefore,

$$SD(b_1) = \sqrt{\frac{.86}{226(1 - .10)}} = .065$$

and the sample t-ratio is

$$\text{Sample } t = \frac{b_1}{SD(b_1)} = \frac{-.25}{.065} = -3.85$$

Because the magnitude of this sample t-ratio (3.85) is greater than the critical t-value (approximately 1.97 with 220 df, $p = .05$, two sides), Provan and Skinner could claim that b_1 was statistically different than zero. In fact they *did* claim this! By the way, the t-tests of the regression weights for all predictors listed in Table VIII.4 were significant, except for X_3. Thus, four of five predictors had unique contributions to the prediction of dealer opportunism, and the authors could claim support for their theory and hypotheses.

I hope the above example has helped. Multiple regression can indeed be considered a straightforward extension of bivariate and trivariate regression. I will next turn to the use of statistically creative types of predictors, which will provide additional flexibility to multiple regression analyses. On the other hand, the introduction of many predictors (X's) can also lead to a variety of new problems. These problems and issues are also considered in the next two chapters.

PROBLEMS

The first several problems for this chapter are based on the full data set given in the problems section of Chapter VI. In that data base, there was a measure of performance (Y) and four potential independent variables/predictors: employee gender (X_1), peer evaluation of the employee (X_2), test score on the proposed new selection test (X_3), and test score on the currently used selection test (X_4). Means, standard deviations, and correlations for these data were also provided at the end of Chapter VI.

1 Conduct the multiple regression predicting performance (Y) from the currently used test (X_4) and the proposed new test (X_3).

   a Compute the regression equation. (*Hint*: This is a trivariate regression, so you can use the formulas for the b's found early in this chapter.)

   b Compute the value of $R^2_{Y.34}$ and then test it for statistical significance against 0 with $p = .05$. (*Hint*: To compute the value of R^2, you could compute the three sums of squares in the analysis of variance. This would be the direct way of getting R^2. Or, you could take a peek at Equation VIII.G or VIII.H and compute R^2 as a combination of squared correlations and squared semipartial correlations.)

   c Conduct the tests of significance for the two regression weights for X_3 and X_4. Use $p = .05$. Interpret the results. (To make your computational life easier, I'll tell you that SSR is 489.65 and SSE is 382.08. You're welcome!)

   d What is the value of the unique contribution of each of these tests to predicting Y? (*Hint*: Here you'll definitely have to look at Equations VIII.G and VIII.H.)

2 The test salesperson notes that gender (X_1) is somewhat correlated with the performance measure ($r = .206$). (Since males are coded 0 and females are coded 1, the positive correlation means that females have higher performance scores, on average, than males.) The salesperson suggests that the proposed new test (X_3) will predict Y even after the effects of gender have been taken out of the performance measure; i.e., X_3 will have a significant weight in predicting Y even when X_1 is in the equation. (Again, to make life easier, I'll tell you that SSR = 415.02 and SSE = 456.72 in the regression predicting Y from both X_1 and X_3.)

   a Compute the regression weights for the model that predicts Y from X_1 and X_3.

   b Compute the value of $R^2_{Y.13}$ and test it for significance ($p = .05$).

   c Test the individual regression weights for statistical significance. In particular, is the salesperson's claim upheld?

   d Compute the value of the unique contribution to R^2 for each of the two X's in the regression.

3 Now let's try a regression with more than two X's: e.g., predict Y from a linear combination of both selection tests and gender (X_3, X_4, and X_1). Note that I haven't provided formulas for getting the values of the b_i when the number of predictors is greater than two. This is because these formulas get rather cumbersome and are not particularly instructive. Generally, one would use a computer software package to generate the results. So that's what was done here. The results with my package looked like those in the following table:

N:15	MULTIPLE R: .756		SQUARED MULTIPLE R: .572
VARIABLE	COEFFICIENT	STD ERROR	T
CONSTANT	-3.320	5.630	-.590
X1	1.549	3.060	.506
X3	.712	.327	2.176
X4	.522	.333	1.567
	ANALYSIS OF VARIANCE		
SOURCE	SUM OF SQUARES	DF	MEAN SQUARE
REGRESSION	498.351	3	166.117
ERROR	373.383	11	33.944

Note that the package has given you the four regression weights (e.g., $b_0 = -3.320$, $b_1 = 1.549$). The sums of squares are computed as well. Just add them up to get a sum of squares total. The column labeled "STD ERROR" (shorthand for "standard error") is also handy-dandy. This column provides the standard deviations of the regression weights [i.e., the values SD(b_i) given by Equation VIII.L].

a State the regression equation for predicting Y from X_1, X_3, and X_4. (This is not a difficult question. One of the problems in life will be for you to decide on your own when decisions and questions are difficult and when they are straightforward.)

b Compute $R^2_{Y.134}$ and test it for significance against zero.

c Test the weights of the three predictors for statistical significance using $p = .05$ (again, this is not difficult given the computer output). Interpret your findings.

d Here's an extra-credit question: What's the value of the unique contribution of gender (X_1) to the prediction of Y in this equation? (*Hint*: In Problem 1, you computed R^2 using X_3 and X_4. In the current problem, you have computed R^2 using all three predictors.)

e Another related "extra-credit" question might be whether or not this unique contribution of gender is statistically significant (i.e., significantly greater than zero). Using what you remember about tests of regression weights, and the computer software package information above, answer this question.

4 This question is intended to get you thinking in multiple regression ways. To do this, I simply chose two issues of the *Journal of Applied Psychology* somewhat at random. I will give you a study and you are to generate the kinds of predictors (X's) that you might have used. If you want to see what really happened, the journal articles are easily accessible (see references).

a Matthews, Jones, and Chamberlain (1992, p. 407) wanted to predict how well job incumbents at a post office could code mail for subsequent computerized coding. "Using a series of coding rules and memorized codes, the operator keys the appropriate code for each letter, which results in series of phosphor dots' [sic] being printed on the envelope. The dots form a binary code that can be decoded by sorting machines." These authors wanted to consider both personality and cognitive ability measures as predictors of success on this task. What kinds of X's would you have chosen in these two categories?

b Seibert, Crant, and Kraimer (1999) wanted to show that differences in proactive personality (demonstrating initiative and perseverance) explained variation in career success. However, using multiple regression, they first wanted to control for other possible relevant variables that had been found to be predictive of career success. What kinds of X's might you have chosen to study as such "controls"?

REFERENCES

Becker, B., and Huselid, M. (1992). Direct estimates of SD_y and the implications for utility analysis. *Journal of Applied Psychology, 77,* 227–233.

Bloch, A. (1978). *Murphy's law and other reasons why things go wrong.* Los Angeles: Price/Stern/Sloan.

Bock, D., and Petersen, A. (1975). A multivariate correction for attenuation. *Biometrika, 62,* 673–678.

Busemeyer, J., and Jones, L. (1983). Analysis of multiplicative combination rules when the causal variables are measured with error. *Psychological Bulletin, 93,* 549–562.

Campbell, J., and Zook, L. (1990, March). *Improving the selection, classification, and utilization of Army enlisted personnel: Final report on Project A,* Army Research Institute Report 1597, Alexandria, VA.

Conlon, D., and Sullivan, D. (1999). Examining the actions of organizations in conflict: Evidence from the Delaware Court of Chancery. *Academy of Management Journal, 42,* 319–329.

Dulebohn, J., and Ferris, G. (1999). The role of influence tactics in perceptions of performance evaluations' fairness. *Academy of Management Journal, 42,* 288–303.

Evans, G., and Carrere, S. (1991). Traffic congestion, perceived control, and psycho-physiological stress among urban bus drivers. *Journal of Applied Psychology, 76,* 658–663.

Frederickson, J., and Iaquinto, A. (1989). Inertia and creeping rationality in strategic decision processes. *Academy of Management Journal, 32,* 516–542.

Gregersen, H., and Black, J. (1992). Antecedents to commitment to a parent company and a foreign operation. *Academy of Management Journal, 35,* 65–90.

Locke, E., Frederick, E., Lee, C., and Bobko, P. (1984). The effect of self-efficacy, goals, and task strategies on task performance. *Journal of Applied Psychology, 69,* 241–251.

Maddala, G. (1988). *Introduction to econometrics.* New York: Macmillan.

Matthews, G., Jones, D., and Chamberlain, A. (1992). Predictors of individual differences in mail-coding skills and their variation with ability level. *Journal of Applied Psychology, 77,* 406–418.

Neuman, G., and Wright, J. (1999). Team effectiveness: Beyond skills and cognitive ability. *Journal of Applied Psychology, 84,* 376–389.

Provan, K., and Skinner, S. (1989). Interorganizational dependence and control as predictors of opportunism in dealer-supplier relations. *Academy of Management Journal, 32,* 202–212.

Romzek, B. (1989). Personal consequences of employee commitment. *Academy of Management Journal, 32,* 649–661.

Seibert, S., Crant, M., and Kraimer, M. (1999). Proactive personality and career success. *Journal of Applied Psychology, 84,* 416–427.

Welbourne, T., and Andrews, A. (1996). Predicting the performance of initial public offerings: Should human resource management be in the equation? *Academy of Management Journal, 39,* 891–919.

EXPANDING THE REGRESSION REPERTOIRE: POLYNOMIAL AND INTERACTION TERMS

CHAPTER OBJECTIVES

After reading this chapter, you should be able to:

- Understand why (or how) there are some nonlinear relationships between X and Y that can be analyzed using a general "linear" model.
- Define polynomial regression and suggest situations appropriate for its use.
- Explain why the linear term (e.g., X) typically remains in an analysis when using polynomial regression.
- Explain what an interaction is and suggest situations in which it would be appropriate to use an interactive regression.
- Understand why the statistical power for detecting interactions can be lower than one might have hoped for.
- Explain how changes in coding affect regressions containing interaction terms.

As in the previous chapter, we are still going to consider the multiple regression model

IX.A $$Y = \mathbf{B}_0 + \mathbf{B}_1 X_1 + \mathbf{B}_2 X_2 + \cdots + \mathbf{B}_p X_p + e$$

However, our focus in this chapter will be on the question, How can we algebraically modify the X's to fit our theoretical requirements? For example, we will soon discuss (among other possibilities) the idea of replacing X_2 by X_1^2. Then, the underlying regression model becomes

IX.B $$Y = \mathbf{B}_0 + \mathbf{B}_1 X + \mathbf{B}_2 X^2 + e$$

Such a model will be handy-dandy if we believe that Y and X are related in nonlinear ways. Specifically, Equation IX.B suggests that Y is related to the square of X as well as to X itself.

Before we begin, a comment is in order about what we mean by "linear models." Note that we will be able to analyze some relationships between Y and X that appear to be "nonlinear." For example, we can use the above trick of including X^2 as a predictor in the regression. On the other hand, statisticians still label the model in Equation IX.B a "general *linear* model." What they mean is that Y is assumed to be a linear combination of the predictors, plus error. That is,

$$Y = \mathbf{B}_0 + \mathbf{B}_1 \times \text{predictor} \#1 + \mathbf{B}_2 \times \text{predictor} \#2 + \cdots + e$$

In other words, it doesn't matter what the predictor looks like. It can be $X, X^2, \sqrt{X}$, or $\sin X$, as long as Y is a constant ($\mathbf{B}$-weight) times a predictor plus another constant ($\mathbf{B}$-weight) times another predictor, etc. Thus,

$$Y = \mathbf{B}_0 + \mathbf{B}_1 X + \mathbf{B}_2 \sin X + e$$

is a legitimate linear model (it might even be useful if you thought there was a particular repeating pattern in the relation between Y and X as the X-scores increase). On the other hand, the model

$$Y = \mathbf{B}_0 + \mathbf{B}_1 X_1 + X_2^{\mathbf{B}_2} + e$$

is *not* a legitimate linear model because the predictors are not linearly combined (i.e., not multiplied by weights and then summed); rather, the beta weight ($\mathbf{B}_2$) is in the exponent of X_2. The results in this book apply only to linear models.[1]

---

[1] While the model $Y = X^{\mathbf{B}} + e$ is not a linear model, regression folks often use a trick. They use the sample equation $Y = X^{\mathbf{B}}$, take logarithms of both sides, and obtain $\log Y = b \log X$. A linear regression is then run using $\log Y$ and $\log X$ as the two variables. Unfortunately, because logarithms are not linear transformations, the estimate of b obtained by this trick does not provide the best linear unbiased estimate of $\mathbf{B}$ in the original nonlinear model.

There are many ways of using nonlinear terms (e.g., X^2) in a general linear model frame. We now consider two well-known possibilities: polynomial regression and interactive regression.

POLYNOMIAL REGRESSION

If you think back to your algebra courses, you'll remember that polynomials are creatures of the form $a + bx + cx^2 + dx^3 + \cdots$. "Polynomial regression," therefore, simply means that terms like X^2, X^3, etc., are considered predictors in the general linear model.

Now, *why would you want to put a predictor such as X^2 in your regression?* I can think of a variety of reasons (in addition to just trying to make life complicated!). Figure 9.1 depicts two such situations.

As a faculty member, I have seen situation A first-hand. That is, to perform well on an exam, you need to be attentive, awake, and have a certain level of concern or anxiety (X). However, neither extreme on X is functional. Being overly anxious causes students to "freeze" on their exams ("Dr. Bobko, I knew the material, but I just freaked on the final!"); students who take the exam half-asleep (low on X) don't do well, either.

Situation B in Figure 9.1 is a well-documented finding in the behavioral aesthetics literature (cf. Berlyne, 1974). For example, individuals typically prefer both music and artwork to be at *moderate* levels of complexity. Repetitive art or music is not enjoyable; neither are works that are so complex that they seem like complete chaos.

Now, how would data from either situation be analyzed? As noted in Chapter II, the correlation measures linearity of relationships. In either situation above, the implied relation is positive for low values of X, zero for intermediate values

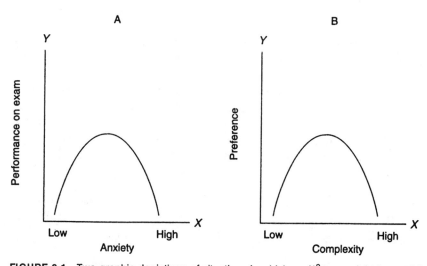

FIGURE 9.1 Two graphic depictions of situations in which an X^2-term might be useful.

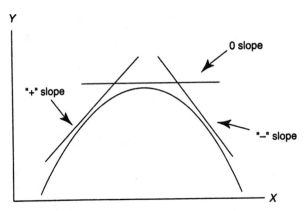

FIGURE 9.2 Another look at why Pearson *r* doesn't readily detect parabolic relations.

of X, and negative for large values of X (Figure 9.2). Thus, on average, $r = 0$. If we estimated the regression $\hat{Y} = b_0 + b_1 X$ on this data, we would also get $b_1 = 0$ (remember how r and b_1 were related). So, it should be obvious at this point what to do. Note that both parabolas in Figure 9.1 have general equations of the form $Y = a + bX + cX^2$. Therefore, we should consider the model

$$Y = \mathbf{B_0} + \mathbf{B_1} X + \mathbf{B_2} X^2 + e$$

and thus conduct the sample regression analysis using

$$\hat{Y} = b_0 + b_1 X + b_2 X^2$$

Note that all you tell the computer is that you have two predictors—and that's all! You needn't tell it that one predictor is the square of the other (I promise not to tell, either). Then, if you truly believe in the depictions of situations A and B, you are asserting that the X^2-term is adding valuable information over and above just using X in the model. And this additional, unique contribution of X^2 is precisely captured by testing H_0: $\mathbf{B_2} = 0$ (see Chapter VIII again for the interpretation of regression weights). In fact, the "upside-down" nature of the parabolas implies that the coefficient on the X_2-term will be negative.[2] Thus, our alternative hypothesis in this case could be the one-sided H_a: $\mathbf{B_2} < 0$.

[2] To see the effect of changing signs on the coefficient for X^2, consider the equation $Y = 1 + 2X + 2X^2$. Graph this function for values of $X = -2, -1, 0, 1,$ and 2. You'll see a nice parabola that is U-shaped. Then, reverse the sign on the squared term and graph the equation $Y = 1 + 2X - 2X^2$ using the same values for X. You'll again get a pretty parabola, but this time it will have an upside down U-shape.

Example (and Some Additional Ideas)

Before beginning, an important point is in order. In applied social science research, complete parabolic relationships (such as situation A or B in Figure 9.1) are rare. Rather, presumed relations are often of the variety illustrated in Figure 9.3. For example, situation C is a depiction of the so-called diminishing returns function. Situation D might occur when there is some escalation effect (e.g., individuals better on X are really better on Y; as training programs improve, job incumbents really learn a lot; as time demands increase, stress really increases; etc.). Now, the trick in analyzing situations C and D is to realize that they could be modeled as incomplete portrayals of parabolas. For example, model C in Figure 9.4 could be thought of as a portion of model A in Figure 9.1. Thus, a regression of the form $\hat{Y} = b_0 + b_1 X + b_2 X^2$ might still be used to analyze the "partial" model in situation C.[3]

Now we're ready to consider an example. To do so, return to the data in Chapter II, Table II.1. In that data set, the performance (Y) of air traffic controllers was being predicted from a selection test (X). Suppose the organization using such a test wants to look at the potential for nonlinear relationships in the data. Specifically, it may be that there is some minimum standard of required ability (X) in order to become an air traffic controller. However, beyond a certain point on X, additional ability is not necessarily required to be a good controller (e.g., beyond certain values of ability, other factors such as a person's motivation may become more important). Thus, the hypothesized relation between Y and X

---

[3] Similarly, situation D is really half of a "right-side-up" parabola (i.e., a parabola with a positive coefficient on the X^2-term). Also, another regression trick is to add a variable computed as $\sqrt{X}$ or log X. This has the same general form as model C. If you don't believe it, try plotting values of the equations $Y = \sqrt{X}$ and $Y = \log X$.

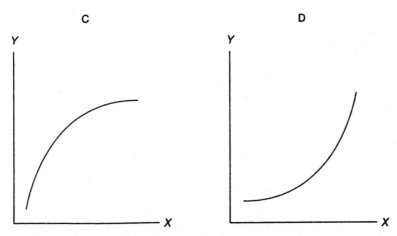

FIGURE 9.3 Two typical curvilinear relations.

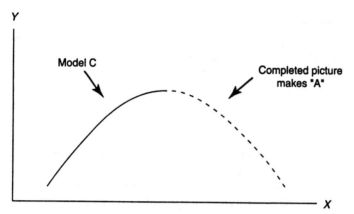

FIGURE 9.4 Using a parabola to model the relation in Fig. 9.3, part C.

might be of the diminishing returns form (Figure 9.5). If so, one appropriate sample regression equation might be

$$\hat{Y} = b_0 + b_1 X + b_2 X^2$$

and the organization would look for a significant, and negative, value for b_2. If $H_0: \mathbf{B}_2 = 0$ was rejected, one could then say that a parabolic curve component added significantly to the prediction of Y above and beyond just X itself.

The data for this example have been reproduced in Table IX.1. Note that an extra column of data has been added, i.e., values for X^2. Thus, there are now two predictors of Y.

The correlation matrix and other statistics for these three variables are presented in Table IX.2. Again, when computing these correlations, simply treat all columns as being derived from different variables: for the purpose of computing r's, it doesn't matter that one column of numbers contains the squares of the other data column.[4]

Notice that $r_{YX} = .749$. This is precisely what we obtained in Chapter II: the test X is already an excellent linear predictor of air traffic controller performance. To derive the enhanced regression equation, simply use the formulas for trivariate regression given in Chapter VIII for the equation $\hat{Y} = b_0 + b_1 X_1 + b_2 X_2$. All you have to remember is that X_1 is now X, and X_2 is now X^2. For example, Equation VIII.D stated that

$$b_2 = \left(\frac{r_{Y2} - r_{Y1} r_{12}}{1 - r_{12}^2} \right) \left(\frac{s_Y}{s_2} \right)$$

[4] However, this does create a problem regarding collinearity, which we will address in the next section of this chapter.

FIGURE 9.5 Hypothesized relationship between selection test scores and controller performance.

TABLE IX.1 SIMULATOR TEST DATA, SQUARED TEST DATA, AND PERFORMANCE DATA FOR 13 HYPOTHETICAL APPLICANTS FOR AIR TRAFFIC CONTROL TRAINING

Applicant	Test, X	Test Squared, X^2	Performance, Y
1	35.0	1,225.0	105.0
2	45.0	2,025.0	75.0
3	69.0	4,761.0	85.0
4	182.0	33,124.0	208.0
5	48.7	2,371.7	146.1
6	100.0	10,000.0	100.0
7	25.0	625.0	75.0
8	98.0	9,604.0	300.0
9	52.0	2,704.0	88.0
10	8.0	64.0	16.0
11	22.8	519.8	19.2
12	5.9	34.8	13.9
13	19.0	361.0	17.0

TABLE IX.2 MEANS, STANDARD DEVIATIONS, AND CORRELATIONS FOR THE HYPOTHETICAL DATA IN TABLE IX.1

	Y	$X_1 (= X)$	$X_2 (= X^2)$
Y	1.00	.749	.623
X_1		1.000	.951
X_2			1.000

$$\bar{Y} = 96.015 \qquad s_Y = 83.223$$
$$\bar{X} = 54.646 \qquad s_X = 48.818$$
$$\overline{X^2} = 5186.103 \qquad s_{X^2} = 9045.229$$

In our example, r_{Y2} is the correlation between Y and X^2 (i.e., it's .623). Completing the equation for b_2 yields

$$b_2 = \left[\frac{.623 - (.749)(.951)}{1 - .951^2} \right] \left(\frac{83.223}{9045.229} \right) = -.009$$

The negative sign on b_2 is consistent with our expectations of an upside-down parabola. The remaining regression weights can be readily computed using other, similar equations from the previous chapter (please try it!). The result is

$$\hat{Y} = -11.563 + 2.777X - .009X^2$$

Also, as in the previous chapter, one could derive an analysis of variance for these data and then estimate things like $SD(b_i)$, multiple R^2, etc. To avoid aggravation, let me just tell you that I "cheated" by putting these data through a computer regression program. It turns out that $R^2_{Y.12} = .642$ and that $SD(b_2) = .006$. Now, notice that when we used only X to predict Y, we explained $(.749)^2 \times 100\% = 56.1\%$ of the variation in controller performance. By adding the X^2-term, we increased R^2 to .642 and explained an additional $(64.2 - 56.1) \times 100\% = 8.1\%$ of the performance variation. Is this a statistically significant increase? To test this, simply look at H_0: $\mathbf{B}_2 = 0$. That is, don't forget what we said in Chapter VIII: the test for b_2 tells us if X^2 has any unique contribution to the prediction of Y over and above all other predictors (i.e., X alone). The t-statistic for testing H_0: $\mathbf{B}_2 = 0$ is

$$\text{Sample } t = \frac{b_2}{SD(b_2)} = \frac{-.009}{.006} = -1.5$$

For the critical t-value, we have $n - p - 1 = 13 - 2 - 1 = 10$ df. The critical t, with $p = .05$ and a one-sided test, is 1.812 (see the Appendix, Table A.1), so H_0: $\mathbf{B}_2 = 0$ is not rejected. Clearly, with 13 subjects we have little power to detect an increment in R^2. In Figure 9.6, I have displayed a scatterplot of the data and plotted the nonlinear regression function. It's clear that the sample size in this fictitious example is too small to make any definitive conclusions. However, had the regression weight (b_2) remained nonsignificant with a larger data set, the organization could have concluded that Y and X are only linearly related and that they should focus recruiting attention on getting the best (highest on X) applicants they could. In contrast, if the nonlinear regression in Figure 9.6 was true, it might be recommended that the organization search for any individuals with X-scores greater than, say, 90. After this point, there doesn't seem to be much differentiation on predicted performance.[5]

---

[5] By the way, there *are* characteristics of controllers where hypotheses are of this nonlinear nature. For example, controllers need to be decisive. However, after a point, individuals can be too decisive; i.e., they react without getting appropriate information to make an accurate decision. Just how much decisiveness is maximal is open to debate.

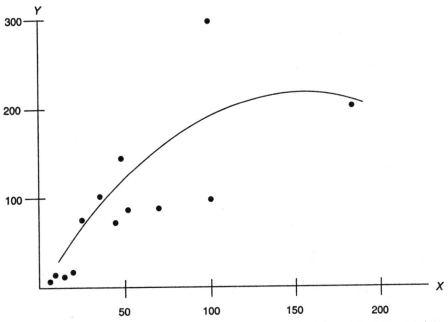

FIGURE 9.6 A scatterplot of the air traffic controller data in Chapter II, Table II.1 (with a quadratic regression plotted).

Polynomials and Power

It is important to notice that when placing polynomial factors in a regression, we always used models of the form $\hat{Y} = b_0 + b_1 X + b_2 X^2$ and did *not* use $\hat{Y} = b_0 + b_1 X^2$. That is, we always left the linear term (X) in the model, even in the presence of X^2. This was done for a variety of related statistical and philosophical reasons, most notably parsimony and our old friend collinearity.

Regarding parsimony, journal editors, philosophers of science, professors, etc., generally acknowledge that a model that uses just X or sums of X's is "simpler" than models using X^2 or other more complicated terms.[6] So, if a simpler model explains just as much variance as a more complex model (e.g., the b-weight for the X^2-term is not significant), then the simpler model is preferred. Thus, *the burden of proof is on the (relatively) more complicated terms.* For example, if you entertain the notion of introducing X^2 (or X^3, etc.) terms in a regression, they must have unique predictive power over and above the use of X alone.

Regarding collinearity, did you notice the large correlation between X and X^2 in the air traffic controller data (it was .951)? What's happening here is that X

---

[6] In fact, many social scientists have concluded that just *adding* variables is often as good as, or better than, more complicated combinations of the variables (e.g., Dawes and Corrigan, 1974; Wainer, 1976). We will return to this notion when we discuss shrinkage in the next chapter.

and X^2 are carrying a great deal of similar information.[7] Since our primary focus is on the unique explanatory power of X^2, all effects due to X alone need to be partialed out first. Can you see the problem here? Exactly! As we noted in Chapter VIII, when the degree of collinearity increases, it becomes progressively more difficult to reject H_0: $\mathbf{B}_2 = 0$. [If you have forgotten this, go back to the discussion of collinearity and $SD(b_i)$ in Chapter VIII.] Thus, it has historically been very difficult to detect curvilinear models in the social sciences. (Indeed, in addition to a small sample size, this is another reason why the X^2-term in the controller data was not statistically significant.) We will return to these issues in the second half of this chapter after we consider other ways of complicating the regression.

Two Additional Comments and Examples

Researchers really do look at polynomial terms For example, Morrison and Brantner (1992) predicted how well a person had learned a job (Y) from the amount of time (X), in months, the person had been on the job. Just as in the air traffic controller example, they hypothesized a diminishing returns effect for the number of months on the job. Indeed, they obtained a regression weight for X^2 that was significantly less than zero.

Along with the explicit role of theory in suggesting the use of polynomial regression, researchers have also used X^2-terms to analyze differences in correlations across studies. For example, Matthews, Jones, and Chamberlain (1992) conducted two validity studies correlating a selection test (X) with performance of mailroom clerks (Y). The two studies were really the same study done at two different locations (say, sites A and B), and the authors obtained a different value of r across the two sites. While there was considerable overlap of abilities (on X) across sites A and B, Matthews et al. also noticed *mean* differences on X across these two sites. In trying to explain the differences in values of r_{YX}, Matthews et al. wanted to rule out the following possibility. Similar to the logic in Figure 9.2, and consistent with the mean differences across sites, the relationship between Y and X might have been as shown in Figure 9.7. If so, can you see that the value of r_{YX} for site A could be larger than r_{YX} for site B? Good. Now, what's the solution? Right again! Simply include an X^2-term in the regressions. If such a term is significant, then this type of nonlinear relationship might be an explanation for the differing values of r. In fact, Matthews et al. did this, found no significant curvilinear trends in either sample, and therefore ruled out any such trend as an explanation for their effect.[8]

Researchers even consider terms like X^3 Functions of the form $b_0 + b_1 X + b_2 X^2$ are called "polynomials of order 2" or "quadratic functions." They

---

[7] If you don't believe it, let X take on the values 1, 2, 3, 4, 5. The X^2-values are then 1, 4, 9, 16, and 25. Make a scatterplot of these X-versus-X^2 values. You'll see that a straight line captures a lot of the relationship in the data (i.e., Pearson r is large).

[8] Of course, don't forget our discussion of the reduced power in detecting significant contributions by X^2. *This* may be the reason Matthews et al. didn't find a curvilinear trend.

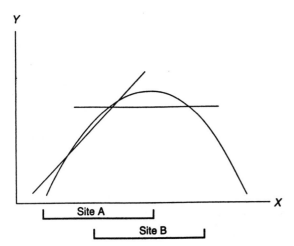

FIGURE 9.7 A portrayal of the nonlinearity that Matthews et al. (1992) were looking for.

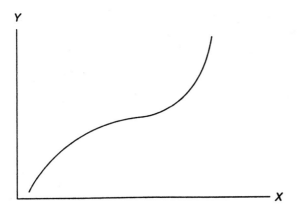

FIGURE 9.8 An example of a cubic function.

are characterized by *one* turn in the curve; hence they have the form of a right-side-up or upside-down parabola. Polynomials of order 3 (e.g., $b_0 + b_1 X + b_2 X^2 + b_3 X^3$) are characterized by *two* turns in the curve. Such a possible "cubic" function is depicted in Figure 9.8. That is, looking at the curve from left to right, the curve starts with a high positive slope, turns down a bit (lower slope), and then turns back up (ending in a higher slope again).

In the utility analysis literature (remember Chapter VII?) two independent sets of researchers found that utility functions have the S-shape characteristic shown in Figure 9.8 (cf. Pritchard, Jones, Roth, Stuebing, and Ekeberg, 1988; Sadacca, Campbell, DiFazio, Schultz, and White, 1990).[9] That is, for intermediate levels of individual performance, an individual's level of performance (X) is approximately linearly related to the perceived value of that performance to the organiza-

[9] It looks like it takes lots of industrial psychologists to publish a paper on utility functions!

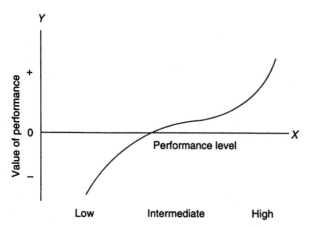

FIGURE 9.9 The usual cubic relation found between performance level (X) and the value of performance (Y).

tion (Y). However, for really low performance (X), the value of that performance drops precipitously (indeed it could even have a negative value); similarly, high performance on X is perceived to have an extremely positive value (Y) to the organization. The resulting function is shown in Figure 9.9. Indeed, Sadacca et al. (1990) found statistical evidence for terms of $X, X^2,$ *and* X^3 in their analyses. In their military study, they used such a cubic regression to project utility values for which they had little empirical data.

INTERACTION TERMS

We started this chapter by noting that regression analyses could be made more flexible by adding predictors to the equation that were nonlinear functions of the original X's. For the remainder of this chapter, we consider probably the most common of all nonlinear terms used in the social sciences: the *product* of two predictors (e.g., the term X_1 times X_2). Before formally beginning, note that product terms provide classical models in applied psychology and human resource management; e.g., a common model is performance = ability × motivation[10]; in behavioral learning theory, response strength is drive *times* habit strength (Hull, 1943); in work motivation, the force required to produce effort is a product of three variables: instrumentality, expectancy, and valence (Vroom, 1964). Indeed, as we shall see, adding product terms to regressions produces some pretty wondrous examples that increase the flexibility of our social science models.

---

[10] In other words, a person can have all the ability in the universe. But if his or her motivation is zero, then predicted performance is still zero. The product term says this is equally true if motivation is high but ability is completely zero.

The Interactive Model

Suppose we had started with one criterion measure (Y) and two predictors $(X_1$ and $X_2)$. We can add a third predictor by creating a third variable which is the product of the first two X's $(X_3 = X_1 X_2)$. The regression model is then

IX.C1 $\qquad Y = \mathbf{B}_0 + \mathbf{B}_1 X_1 + \mathbf{B}_2 X_2 + \mathbf{B}_3 X_1 X_2 + e$

As with the squared terms in the previous section, you needn't tell the computer where X_3 comes from. However, by using this cross-product term, we can now rewrite Equation IX.C1 to illuminate what wonderful things we have just done. Equation IX.C1 can be configured as

IX.C2 $\qquad Y = (\mathbf{B}_0 + \mathbf{B}_2 X_2) + (\mathbf{B}_1 + \mathbf{B}_3 X_2) X_1 + e$

or

IX.C3 $\qquad Y = \mathbf{Q}_0 + \mathbf{Q}_1 X_1 + e$

where $\mathbf{Q}_0 = \mathbf{B}_0 + \mathbf{B}_2 X_2$ and $\mathbf{Q}_1 = \mathbf{B}_1 + \mathbf{B}_3 X_2$.

Notice that in Equation IX.C3, the regression is written so that Y is a linear function of X_1, plus error. However, since $\mathbf{Q}_0 = \mathbf{B}_0 + \mathbf{B}_2 X_2$ and $\mathbf{Q}_1 = \mathbf{B}_1 + \mathbf{B}_3 X_2$, the parameters $\mathbf{Q}_0$ and $\mathbf{Q}_1$ both depend on what X_2 is! Thus, when the cross-product or interaction term is added,

Y is linearly related to X_1, but the linear relation changes as a function of X_2 (because both Q_0 and Q_2 are conditional on X_2).

This analysis is symmetric with respect to X_1 and X_2. That is, Equation IX.C1 can also be reconfigured such that Y is a linear function of X_2 and that function depends on X_1 (try it!). In Equations IX.C2 and IX.C3, the variable X_2 is said to "moderate" the relation between Y and X_1 (Zedeck, 1971). The choice of labeling X_1 or X_2 as the moderator usually depends on the context of the study.

Interpreting B₃: An Extended Example

An ensuing section of this book will present a sampling of the many interactive models you'll see in management and applied psychology. Before we get there, though, take another look at Equations IX.C1 and IX.C2. We added the interaction term $X_3 = X_1 X_2$. What does the test of H_0: $\mathbf{B}_3 = 0$ tell us? Notice that $\mathbf{B}_3$ appears inside the second set of parentheses in Equation IX.C2. That is, the slope that relates Y to X_1 is $\mathbf{B}_1 + \mathbf{B}_3 X_2$. If $\mathbf{B}_3 = 0$, then the slope of X_1 is simply $\mathbf{B}_1$. Thus, if $\mathbf{B}_3 = 0$, then the slope of the relationship between Y and X_1 is constant. On the other hand, if $\mathbf{B}_3 \neq 0$, then the slope of the relation between Y and X_1

depends upon the particular value of X_2. Here's an example of how this operates in practice.

An extended example   Suppose you're a real estate appraiser for a statewide company and want to be "scientific" in the way you value of house.[11] You realize that the selling price of a house (Y) definitely depends upon its size, or square footage (X_1). You are also a devotee of the maxim that location is critical to determining house value. Luckily for you, the state has just completed a study that places each community on a 5-point quality-of-life scale (X_2). The scale ranges from 1 (not a terrific location, near smog areas, overcrowded schools, etc.) to 5 (allegedly the best location, great schools, many parks, etc.). Now, if you believe in regression, you might believe that price (Y) is related to a linear combination of both size (X_1) and location (X_2). If you also believe in interactive regression, you might further say that *the relation between price and size depends on location*. For example, I can imagine that in relatively low-quality neighborhoods, houses cost about $40 per square foot. However, in "ritzier" neighborhoods, the cost might be $70 per square foot. Thus, the regression relating house size (X_1) to price (Y) might have greater slope for the highest rated neighborhoods.

It's very important to notice that we're not just saying that you pay an additional fixed amount for houses in better areas. If *that* were the case, then the regressions between Y and X_1 might look like Figure 9.10. Notice that the regression lines are parallel in Figure 9.10. For any given value of X_1 (i.e., any house size), there's a constant price difference between houses in ritzy and in low-quality neighborhoods. In other words, the slope is the same for both types of neighborhoods. In terms of Equation IX.C, these parallel lines mean that $B_3 = 0$ since the slope does not depend on X_2.

On the other hand, suppose prices per square foot really are different across the neighborhoods. For example, suppose an extra few hundred square feet in a ritzy neighborhood home *really* shoots the house price up relative to extra space in a low-quality location home. Then the regression function might look like Figure 9.11. In this case, the regression weight for X_1 depends upon X_2, and this can be accomplished in the regression model only by letting $B_3 \neq 0$ in Equation IX.C.

O.K. Now for some data. Tables IX.3 and IX.4 contain fictitious data for house prices (Y, in thousands of dollars), house size (X_1, in hundreds of square feet), and quality of location (X_2, using the above 5-point scale). For this data set, assume the real estate appraiser has chosen four homes each from low-quality ($X_2 = 1$), moderate-quality ($X_2 = 3$), and high-quality ($X_2 = 5$) areas. A column of product term values ($X_3 = X_1 X_2$) has also been added (why else would the example be in this chapter?).

If you were to make a scatterplot of the data, using just Y and X_1, it would look like Figure 9.12. Thus, this figure shows a relationship between Y and X_1

---

[11] Actually, appraisers use many more variables than the following example.

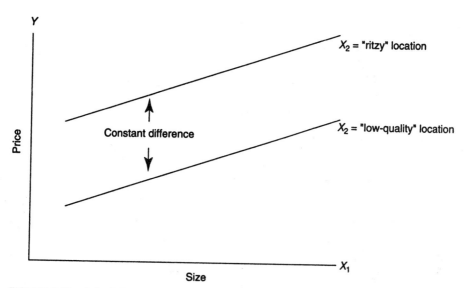

FIGURE 9.10   A depiction of no interaction between house size (X_1) and location (X_2).

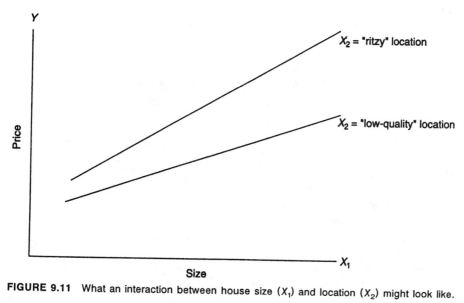

FIGURE 9.11   What an interaction between house size (X_1) and location (X_2) might look like.

TABLE IX.3 HYPOTHETICAL DATA ON 12 HOUSES FOR HOUSE PRICE, HOUSE SIZE, AND QUALITY RATING OF LOCATION

House	Price Y, thousand $	Size X_1, hundred sq ft	Quality rating, X_2	$X_1 \times X_2$, X_3
1	265	30	5	150
2	179	27	3	81
3	57	11	1	11
4	155	15	5	75
5	101	12	3	36
6	121	25	1	25
7	257	28	5	140
8	135	19	3	57
9	85	16	1	16
10	190	21	5	105
11	148	23	3	69
12	101	22	1	22

TABLE IX.4 SUMMARY STATISTICS FOR HYPOTHETICAL HOUSE PRICE DATA IN TABLE IX.3

	Price Y, thousand $	Size X_1, hundred sq ft	Quality rating, X_2	$X_1 \times X_2$, X_3
Mean	149.50	20.75	3.00	65.58
SD	64.59	6.27	1.71	47.18

Correlations:

	Y	X_1	X_2	X_1X_2
Y	1.000	.782	.830	.982
X_1		1.000	.340	.675
X_2			1.000	.895
X_1X_2				1.000

(indeed r_{Y1} is .782 in Table IX.4). However, the relationship can be further illuminated and unpacked by placing information about X_2 on the scatterplot. This is accomplished in Figure 9.13 by using dots, stars, and circles to represent low-, intermediate-, and high-quality location data points, respectively. Then, the complete picture is Figure 9.13.[12]

To conduct the interactive regression, simply place the data from Table IX.3 into a regression analysis with three predictors. Again, you needn't tell the

[12] The scatterplot and implied regression lines in Figure 9.13 are somewhat deceiving. There really *are* three different slopes across the three types of locations—as will be statistically seen in the next several paragraphs. Indeed, some people look at this figure and see three different slopes. Others, however, see three parallel lines. That's why it is always nice to have both (1) a picture of the data *and* (2) statistical results.

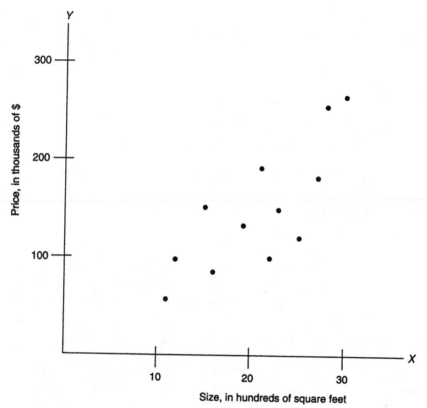

FIGURE 9.12 The scatterplot between house price (Y) and house size (X_1) taken from Table IX.3.

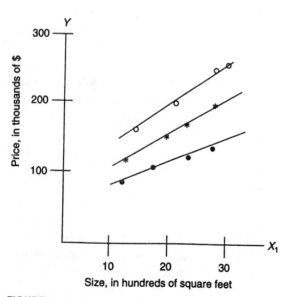

FIGURE 9.13 The scatterplot between house price (Y) and house size (X_1) with house location information (X_2) added.

machine that X_3 is the product of X_1 and X_2. When I did this with a computer software package, the machine spit out the following sample output:

$$\hat{Y} = 13.89 + 2.90X_1 + 4.87X_2 + .93X_3$$

or, equivalently,

$$\hat{Y} = 13.89 + 2.90X_1 + 4.87X_2 + .93X_1X_2$$

The machine also told me that the weights for both X_1 and $X_3 (= X_1X_2)$ are statistically significant (from zero) at $p = .01$ [e.g., the SD(b_3) was .202, and the t-ratio .93/.202 was significant]. The analysis of variance is

Source	Sum of Squares	df
Regression	45,525.48	3
Error	357.52	8
Total	45,883.00	11

Thus, $R^2_{Y.123}$ is a whopping $45,525/45,883 = .992$. It's also instructive to take a more detailed look at the regression equation.

For low-quality locations, remember that $X_2 = 1$. Therefore, take the empirical results above, actually replace X_2 with the value of 1, and then combine terms.

$$\hat{Y}_{low} = 13.89 + 2.90X_1 + 4.87(1) + .93X_1(1)$$

$$= 18.76 + 3.83X_1$$

This is one of the lines graphed in Figure 9.13. Since Y is in thousands of dollars and X_1 is in hundreds of square feet, the interpretation of the weight 3.83 is that in low-quality locations each additional square foot costs about $38.

For high-quality locations (i.e., $X_2 = 5$), the corresponding equation is

$$\hat{Y}_{high} = 13.89 + 2.90X_1 + 4.87(5) + .93X_1(5)$$

$$= 38.24 + 7.55X_1$$

Thus, for homes in high-quality locations, each additional square foot costs about $76. (Try it for moderate-quality locations, i.e., $X_2 = 3$. I get prices to be about $57 per square foot. Do you agree?) Again, these differential relationships (across location, as a function of X_2) could easily be modeled because we added the interaction term X_1X_2.

Applied Literature Is Chock Full of Interactions

The title of this section says it all: many models in management and psychology assume that the nature of the relationship between two variables (Y and X_1) depends on a third variable (X_2). Here are some recent examples.

In a study briefly mentioned in Chapter II, Richard (2000) was interested in the relation between racial diversity and firm performance. Although there was no overall linear relationship between these two variables, Richard found that business strategy interacted with racial diversity. In particular, diversity was positively related to firm performance for organizations categorized as having a growth strategy.

Lee, Ashford, and Bobko (1990) found that increasing amounts of Type A behavior (X_1) were related to increased work performance (Y), but only when the work situation was stable enough so that the person had control over his or her environment (X_2). (Otherwise, the Type A folks tended to spend most of their time trying to regain control rather than working on their job task.) In a related study, Fox, Dwyer, and Ganster (1993) found that the relationship between workload (X_1) and job satisfaction (Y) also depended upon employee's perceptions of the amount of control they had (X_2).

Chen and MacMillan (1992) found a relationship between an organization's delay in responding to an event (Y) and the organizations's dependence on competitors (X_1). Using an interaction term, they found that this relationship changed as a function of the "irreversibility" of the potential response (X_2).

Gelfand and Realo (1999) were interested in studying the relationship between accountability (having to explain and justify one's behavior) and several criterion measures in an intergroup negotiation scenario (e.g., willingness to make a concession, impressions of the opponent, etc.). These authors hypothesized, and found support for, the fact that an individual's collectivistic tendency interacted with accountability. For example, collectivism was positively related to an intention to make concessions when accountability was high; but the relationship was negative when accountability was low.

Finally, a fairly common use of interactive models appears in the equal employment opportunity, or test fairness, literature. Suppose Y is a performance measure, X_1 is a selection test, and X_2 is scored dichotomously and distinguishes between males and females. Using the model of Equation IX.C, tests of $\mathbf{B}_1$ and $\mathbf{B}_2$ will indicate whether the selection test and/or a person's gender are uniquely related to performance. The test of $\mathbf{B}_3$ will indicate whether or not the relation between the selection test and job performance is the same for men as for women.

A related aside In the test fairness literature, the significance test of H_0: $\mathbf{B}_3 = 0$ is often called a test for "differential prediction" (Bobko and Bartlett, 1978; Boehm, 1977). This is an appropriate label, since $\mathbf{B}_3 \neq 0$ implies that slopes of regressions between Y and X_1 depend on values of X_2 (e.g., gender). To confuse things, note that slopes can differ for a variety of reasons. Remember simple regression in Chapter VI? For a regression line between Y

and X_1, Equation VI.D stated that $b_1 = r_{Y1} (s_Y/s_1)$. So, if the above regression slopes (i.e., b_1) differ for males and females, it may be that the correlations (validities) of the test with performance differ. Or, it may be that the ratio of s_Y/s_1 is different for male and female subgroups. Thus, different slopes (i.e., an interaction) are often associated with differential correlations, but *not necessarily*. Here's another instance in statistics where it's helpful to look at simple subgroup statistics as well as the fancier overall regression results typically found on the last page of computer output. [By the way, the distinction between (and confusion over) different slopes versus different correlations has been noted in the literature (e.g., Arnold, 1982; Champoux and Peters, 1987). For example, Arnold (1982) has suggested labeling slope differences as "form" differences; differences in correlations are labeled differences in "degree."][13]

Another related aside   Suppose one considers the noninteractive model $Y = B_0 + B_1 X_1 + B_2 X_2 + e$. The test of $H_0: B_2 = 0$ in this regression is equivalent to a famous definition of test fairness proposed by Cleary (1968) and adopted by the EEOC Uniform Guidelines (1978). In this definition, a selection test is "Cleary-fair" if b_2 is not significantly different from zero. In other words, a selection test that is Cleary-fair neither overpredicts nor underpredicts subgroup performance. To understand this statement, consider what it means to reject $H_0: B_2 = 0$. If H_0 is rejected, then X_2 still has unique predictive capacity beyond the use of X_1 alone. This is equivalent to saying that in using the test (X_1) to predict job performance (Y), the residuals can still be predicted by a person's gender (X_2). Thus, if the null hypothesis is rejected, the selection test systematically overpredicts performance in one gender group and underpredicts performance in the other group.

My Goodness, What Have We Done?

It should be apparent that regressions can be made wonderfully flexible by using interaction terms as predictors. However (how many of these "howevers" are there in this book?), the use of interaction (cross-product) terms also leads to two major concerns when the technique is applied: concerns about statistical power and about coding.

Power   With the use of Equations IX.C1 through IX.C3, the interpretation of a significant interaction was that the relationship between Y and X_1 depended on the variable X_2. In this context, it has already been noted that applied researchers often label the variable X_2 a "moderator" (Zedeck, 1971). Thus, one can say that X_2 moderates the relationship between Y and X_1. Unfortunately, it has been very difficult to demonstrate the existence of moderator effects in the social

---

[13] While selection researchers have historically been interested in correlational (degree) differences, the slope can be vital, too. For example, in the utility analysis function in Chapter VII, Equation VII.A, dollar gain was determined in part by r_{XY} times $\$D_y$. This product is the *slope* of the utility function (there's no s_x because it was set equal to 1).

sciences. In other words, the statistical power to detect interactions (i.e., the probability of correctly rejecting $H_0: \mathbf{B}_3 = 0$) is notoriously low (Blood and Mullett, 1977; Bobko, 1986; Cronbach, 1987; Zedeck, 1971).

The reason for this relatively low power is straightforward: when the term $X_1 X_2$ is added to the equation, the "simpler" X_1 and X_2 terms remain in the equation. These simpler terms should remain in for reasons of parsimony discussed earlier in this chapter (when we talked about adding X^2-terms). That is, the burden of proof is on the $X_1 X_2$ term to demonstrate that it predicts Y over and above a linear combination of X_1 and X_2. But, by keeping X_1, X_2, and $X_1 X_2$ in the same regression, we have markedly increased chances for collinearity problems. After all, X_1 and $X_1 X_2$ are probably highly correlated—both variables have X_1 in common! (For example, note that X_1 and $X_1 X_2$ are probably highly correlated .675 in our hypothetical house data.) Now, think back to our discussion about $\text{SD}(b_i)$ in Chapter VIII. As the correlation between predictors increases, $\text{SD}(b_i)$ increases, and it becomes less likely that $H_0: \mathbf{B}_i = 0$ will be rejected.[14]

So, when using interactive (or polynomial) terms in your regression, be aware that you need either large effects or large sample sizes to help achieve statistical significance. Further, Aguinis and Stone-Romero (1997) considered the issue of statistical power when one of the X's is dichotomous (e.g., a two-group moderator). They confirmed that sample size and effect size influenced power. They also demonstrated that power decreases both in the presence of range restriction and as the proportion of individuals in the two subgroups deviates from .50.

By the way, several researchers (Blood and Mullett, 1977; Morris, Sherman, and Mansfield, 1986) have suggested potential solutions to the above regression problem, i.e., solutions that allegedly increase the power to achieve significant interactive effects. Unfortunately, these suggestions are flawed (Cronbach, 1987; Wise, Peters, and O'Connor, 1984). So, the need for larger effects and/or larger sample sizes still holds—unless *you* solve the problem directly and get famous!

Here is one more, relatively complex, set of thoughts about interaction and power. Lubinski and Humphreys (1990) and Cortina (1993) have both suggested that any models using interactions in regression analyses should also include relevant quadratic terms. (After all, a quadratic term such as X^2 is really an interaction between X and itself, because $X \times X = X^2$!) These articles focused on Type I error, i.e., erroneously concluding that an interaction exists. On the other hand (you saw that coming, right?) Ganzach (1998) focused on Type II error, i.e., the value $(1 - \text{power})$. He showed that under certain conditions, using quadratic terms decreased power to detect interactions and, under other conditions, *not* using quadratic terms also decreased power to detect interactions. Complex, eh?

[14] It gets potentially worse! In footnote 14 of Chapter VIII, we noted that measurement error in the X's can cause bias in the regression weights. Evans (1985) used a computer simulation to demonstrate that measurement error in the X's will also reduce the effect of moderators in interactive regressions. Although beyond the scope of this text, Jaccard and Wan (1995) have proposed a method for estimating regression interaction effects in the presence of unreliability using structural equation modeling.

Coding In psychological measurement, the scoring of scale values is often arbitrary. For example, do you score a 5-point scale 1 through 5, or -2 through $+2$? Do you measure IQ on a scale with a mean of 50 and a standard deviation of 10 (as is typically done in education) or with a mean of 100 and a standard deviation of 15 (as is often done in psychology)? Way back in Chapter II, we noted that correlations are invariant to linear transformations of scale. For example, the correlation between Y and X is the same as the correlation between Y and $a + bX$ (assuming $b \neq 0$). Furthermore, we noted in Chapter VI that tests of significance for b-weights are invariant to linear shifts in scale (e.g., standardization of the data). In contrast,

When an interaction (or polynomial) term is added to a regression analysis, tests of main effects for X_1 and X_2 (i.e., of b_1 and b_2) are *not* necessarily invariant to scale changes in the variables (Gocka, 1974; Southwood, 1978). In particular, the significance of regression weights for the main effects can be changed just by shifting the means of a predictor (i.e., by adding points to or subtracting points from each score).

To demonstrate this fact, consider an example similar to one presented by Bobko (1990). Suppose researcher A conducts an interactive regression and obtains

$$\hat{Y} = 10 + 3X_1 + 6X_2 + 2X_1X_2$$

Suppose that X_1 was measured on a 5-point scale scored as $-2, -1, 0, 1, 2$ (see Chapter II, Figure 2.4, for an example of this scale.) Also, suppose that researcher B used the *same* data base, except that X_1 was scored 1, 2, 3, 4, 5 (as in Figure 2.3). Call this "new" measure X_1^*. Then, it is easy to see that you get from X_1^* to X_1 by the simple linear transformation of subtracting 3 from each value: i.e., $X_1 = X_1^* - 3$. Substituting $X_1^* - 3$ for X_1 in the above regression will tell you what researcher B will find.

$$\hat{Y} = 10 + 3(X_1^* - 3) + 6X_2 + 2(X_1^* - 3)X_2$$
$$= 10 + 3X_1^* - 9 + 6X_2 + 2X_1^*X_2 - 6X_2$$
$$= 1.0 + 3X_1^* + 2X_1^*X_2$$

Note that for researcher B the variable X_2 receives no weight, whereas researcher A might have concluded that X_2 had a significant effect!

This has been a dramatic but simple illustration of the fact that the magnitude and/or sign of the weights for X_1 and X_2 can be changed at will by simple linear changes in the coding schemes.[15] On the other hand, it can be proved that

[15] Life is quite ironic here. Note that we changed the coding scheme on X_1, yet it is the weight for X_2 that gets altered. No one said life, or regression analysis, was ever completely fair!

the significance test of the weight for the interaction term (b_3) *is* invariant to linear transformations of X_1 and X_2. Thus, if you want to know if the $X_1 X_2$ term adds unique predictive variance, you're O.K. However, don't try to interpret the values of b_1 and b_2 in such an equation. If you must test weights for X_1 and X_2, as well as $X_1 X_2$, you should adopt a "layered" approach.

First, you consider the model $\hat{Y} = b_0 + b_1 X_1 + b_2 X_2$. Tests for these weights will be invariant to scale shifts because there is no interaction term present.

Second, you add the term $X_1 X_2$, resulting in the extended model of $\hat{Y} = b_0 + b_1 X_1 + b_2 X_2 + b_3 X_1 X_2$. At this point, you conduct a test only for b_3 because the tests for b_1 and b_2 are scale-dependent. (You can also look at the overall $R^2_{Y.123}$—that's invariant to coding as well.) And don't forget—the test of b_3 is subject to the reductions in power noted earlier!

An aside: centering the data   To reduce collinearity problems, some individuals prefer to use centered, or even standardized, data. By "centered," I mean simply subtracting the sample mean from each score so that a variable is represented by $X - \bar{X}$ and not just X. When $X - \bar{X}$ is used in polynomial or interactive regression, it often reduces the collinearity among predictors. For example, let $X = 1, 2, 3, 4$, and 5. Then, as we noted at the beginning of this chapter, the (linear) correlation between X and X^2 is substantial. Centering the data results in $(X - \bar{X})$ scores of $-2, -1, 0, 1$, and 2. In this extreme example, the correlation between $X - \bar{X}$ and $(X - \bar{X})^2$ will then be 0 (because the centered data include negative numbers and both sides of the parabola are equally represented—graph the data and see). Similar reductions in collinearity will often occur when variables are centered in interactive models. However, about the only gain from centering is that the new b's will be estimated with less variance (e.g., r^2_{12} is reduced in Equation VIII.K). Since centered data are obtained from a linear transformation of the original data, tests of significance that have been noted in this book will be unaffected by such centering, and any concerns about power will remain unchanged.

VE "LEFTOVERS" ABOUT INTERACTIONS

es, Interactions Can Contain More Than Two X's

The use of interaction components generalizes beyond two predictors in a straightforward way. For example, with X_1, X_2, and X_3, it is possible to have the term $X_1 X_2 X_3$. Basically, this term implies that the interactive relation between Y and two X's (say, X_1 and X_2) changes yet again as a function of another variable (say, X_3). That is, X_1 and X_2 interact, but the nature of the interaction shifts as a function of X_3. Confusing, huh? Further, if $X_1 X_2 X_3$ is in the regression, then previous appeals to parsimony imply that the simpler interaction terms $X_1 X_2$, $X_1 X_3$, and $X_2 X_3$ should also be in the regression model. So, the regression would look like $\hat{Y} = b_0 + b_1 X_1 + b_2 X_2 + b_3 X_3 + b_4 X_1 X_2 + b_5 X_1 X_3 + b_6 X_2 X_3 + b_7 X_1 X_2 X_3$. All these extra terms increase the magnitude of the collinearity problem even further, so it's really hard to get significant

$X_1 X_2 X_3$ interactions (and it is not recommended that you even try unless a theory strongly dictates this type of model). Further, linear transformations have the same effect as before: only the test of the most complex term in the particular equation at hand (i.e., b_7) is unaffected by scale changes. Thus, as above, one would adopt a layered regression approach. To test the weights of the X's, just use X_1, X_2, and X_3 in a regression. To test the simple interactions, add all of the cross-products involving pairs of predictors (i.e., $X_1 X_2$, $X_1 X_3$, and $X_2 X_3$). Make sure to look at *their* weights only at this stage, not those of X_1, X_2, or X_3 again. Don't forget that at this stage the weight for $X_1 X_2$ is assessing the unique contribution of this interactive term over and above the X's themselves and the two other interaction terms. Finally, you should add in $X_1 X_2 X_3$ and test only its weight (see Evans, 1991).

If you want to see an example of a three-way interaction, check out research by Govindarajan and Fisher (1990). They predicted a business unit's performance (Y) from the degree of managerial control (X_1), the type of strategy employed (X_2), and the degree of resource sharing with other units (X_3). They hypothesized and found evidence for an interaction term of $X_1 X_2 X_3$ (although they also reported significance tests for the simpler terms in this same overall regression—but we won't tell!)[16]

Measurement Suggestions

It's already been noted that the power to detect significant interactive effects can be quite low and that attempts to *statistically* increase the power of such regressions have proven unsuccessful. Rather than a statistical approach, it is possible to take a *measurement* approach which may increase chances of detecting interaction effects.

First, in footnote 14 it was noted that measurement error in the X's can reduce the effects of moderators. So, use predictors that are as reliable as possible.

Second, consider the model in Equation IX.C1 again. Suppose Y, X_1, and X_2 are all measured on 5-point rating scales (e.g., scored 1 through 5). Note that the existence of an interaction term implies that the third variable ($X_3 = X_1 X_2$) has a range of scores from 1 ($= 1 \times 1$) to 25 ($= 5 \times 5$). Thus, the X_3 variable on the right side of Equation IX.C1 is finer-grained (with more data points) then Y (with only five possibilities). In turn, Russell, Pinto, and Bobko (1991) hypothesized that an interactive regression analysis might be too "sophisticated" for the number of scale points used on the dependent variable (Y). We suggested that measurement of Y should have many scale points (i.e., essentially measure Y as a continuous variable) if the regression analysis could hope to capture the sophistication of the interactive function. Indeed, Russell and Bobko (1992) empirically verified this hypothesis by showing that the increase in R^2 associated with an interaction term was almost 90% greater when Y was measured continuously.

[16] And, if you want to see a *six*-way interaction, check out an article by Hitt and Barr (1989) on managerial selection!

While further research is needed (a common cry among academicians!), I suggest that if you conduct an interactive regression and are concerned about low power, try to have a dependent measure with as many scale points as possible in addition to using reliable predictors and a large sample size.

The Chow Test

As will be seen below, the Chow test (Chow, 1960) is really an extension of interactive regression (why else would it be mentioned here?). The test assumes that one has two regression equations, computed from two independent samples, and that each equation has the same variables. If these assumptions are met, one might be interested in testing whether or not the patterns of b-weights are the same across both regressions.

For example, Gomez-Mejia, Tosi, and Hinkin (1987) developed regression equations predicting executive compensation in both owner-controlled and management-controlled corporations. The hypothesis was that the two regressions would have different patterns of regression weights.[17] Essentially, the Chow test combines the data from both samples into one big data set. An extra predictor is then created (say, X^*) that is coded 1 if the data point comes from one sample and 0 if the data point comes from the other sample. This extra predictor (called an "indicator" variable—see Chapter X) is then multiplied by every predictor in the study, thereby creating lots of additional interaction terms. If the set of interaction terms significantly increases the multiple R^2 over and above the original predictors, then the weights of the original X's depend on the value of X^*. In turn, the two sample regressions have been demonstrated to be different. That is, when $X^* = 1$, the linear regression between Y and the original X's is different than the regression when $X^* = 0$ (again, the weights depend on the value of X^*). The purpose of mentioning the Chow test here is to make you aware of how interaction terms provide even greater flexibility to regression analyses. If you like the test and ever need to conduct one, Johnston (1972, pp. 199–207) provides an explicit set of formulas.

Moderators and Mediators

The introduction of an interaction term (e.g., $X_1 X_2$) in a regression allowed us to start with a linear relation between Y and X_1, and consider the possibility that the relation changes as a function of X_2. As noted previously, X_2 is sometimes called a "moderator" of the relationship between Y and X_1. (Again, whether you call X_1 or X_2 the moderator depends on the context.) In any event, the point of this leftover is to try and increase the likelihood that you don't confuse moderators (in this chapter) with "mediators" (see Chapter VII). Mediators are typically embedded in fairly strict causal models, such as $X_1 \rightarrow X_2 \rightarrow Y$. In such

---

[17] For another example, see Skinner, Donnelly, and Ivancevich's (1987) use of a Chow test in a study on power dependence relations.

a model, the *mediator* X_2 explains (sometimes completely; sometimes partially) why X_1 is related to Y. As a mediator, X_2 is "in the middle" of the relationship between X_1 and Y. However, if X_2 was a *moderator*, it might precede or simultaneously coexist with Y. And, the moderator's role is different. For example, the use of a cross-product term (X_1X_2) often means that some pattern of scores on X_1 and X_2 (e.g., X_1 high and X_2 low) is associated with the highest scores on Y. By not confusing moderators and mediators you will make many statistics instructors happier.

Experimental Design

(*Note*: This "leftover" is intended only for those of you who have taken a course in the design of experiments where data were analyzed using an analysis of variance. Otherwise, please wait until Chapter X, where these issues will be discussed in a bit more detail.)

In a typical two-factor analysis of variance design, you had two independent variables (A and B) and an outcome variable (Y). The ANOVA split total sums of squares (SS) into SSA, SSB, SSE, and something called the interaction term, SSA $\times$ B. *The interaction in ANOVA means the same thing as the interaction in regression*; i.e., if the statistical test (an F-ratio) for $A \times B$ is significant, then the effect of factor A (on Y) depends upon which level of factor B you consider. Indeed, you were probably taught to graph cell means for factor A as a function of levels of factor B. An interaction was indicated by the graphs being nonparallel. This is the same thing as the difference between Figures 9.10 and 9.11 earlier in this chapter. When there was an interaction between house price and location (i.e., $b_3 \neq 0$), the regression lines for different values of location had differing slopes (i.e., the lines were not parallel). Further, an interactive relationship was made possible in regression by introduction of the cross-product term (X_1X_2). This is why interaction in analysis of variance is also symbolized by a product term (e.g., $A \times B$).

By the way, should you ever take a course on general linear models, you will find that the similarity between regression and ANOVA is not just coincidental. In fact, *ANOVA is a special case of multiple regression*. For example, in the two-factor design above, one simply replaces X_1, X_2, and Y by factor A, factor B, and the outcome variable, respectively. There are a few tricks in doing this replacement, but they are straightforward.[18] Books by Pedhazur (1982) and Cohen and Cohen (1983) provide excellent, detailed expositions of this relationship. Indeed, some of these tricks will be briefly highlighted at the end of the next chapter.

While interactions make regressions very flexible, we have also seen that they bring along some statistical problems (e.g., loss of power, coding interpretations). Since ANOVAs are special cases of regressions, do the same problems arise? You betcha! For example, Wahlsten (1991) noted that in some situations the power to detect interactions in an ANOVA was about the same as the power to

---

[18] For example, if factor A has three levels (or categories), you need two X's in a regression to model that factor; i.e., let $X_1 = 1$ if level 1, 0 otherwise; let $X_2 = 1$ if level 2, 0 otherwise.

detect main effects. On the other hand, in other straightforward 2 × 2 designs, he concluded, "when 2 factors are multiplicative, the sample size require to detect the presence of nonadditivity is 7 to 9 times as large as that needed to detect main effects with the same degree of power" (p. 587). As another problem that extends to ANOVA, we noted earlier that the burden of proof was on the interaction term; i.e., the term $X_1 X_2$ must demonstrate significance over and above the main effects (X_1 and X_2). Within the experimental design literature, this burden of proof has been contested; i.e., in interpreting interactions, researchers disagree on whether one should look at cell means before or after the main effects have been partialed out (Meyer, 1991; Rosnow and Rosenthal, 1989, 1991). Again, interactions are fun, both in their flexibility and their capacity to generate difficulties in interpretation.

PROBLEMS

Throughout this book, you have been working with a data set in which a test salesperson is trying to sell a new selection test (X_3) that measures the advertising aptitude of potential employees. This data set also includes a variety of other variables (see the description below). Let's also add a second performance measure to the data set. Suppose that after a few years on the job, employees are being evaluated for their management potential (i.e., they have just been assessed on their capacity to be promoted to managerial ranks). Label this measure of management potential Y_2. Thus, the variables are

X_1: gender (male = 0; female = 1)

X_2: peer evaluation of the employee's interview (good = 1; bad = 0)

X_3: test score on new aptitude test

X_4: test score on currently used aptitude test

Y_1: performance of the employee (supervisor rating with maximum score of 30)

Y_2: managerial potential score obtained after 2 years of employment (maximum score of 50)

and the data are listed in the following table:

Subject	X_1	X_2	X_3	X_4	Y_1	Y_2
1	Male	Good	24	18	20	31
2	Female	Good	18	13	29	46
3	Male	Good	21	17	17	25
4	Male	Bad	7	13	8	10
5	Female	Bad	14	28	25	40
6	Male	Good	20	21	26	42
7	Male	Bad	8	6	7	8
8	Female	Bad	13	9	12	16
9	Male	Good	15	13	18	28
10	Male	Good	19	15	22	34
11	Female	Good	25	22	23	35
12	Female	Good	23	16	27	45
13	Male	Good	18	13	10	12
14	Female	Bad	12	14	5	8
15	Female	Bad	17	12	13	17

To save time and energy on your part, the correlation matrix for this enhanced data set (including means and standard deviations) is also presented:

	X_1	X_2	X_3	X_4	Y_1	Y_2
X_1	1					
X_2	−.327	1				
X_3	.088	.792	1			
X_4	.171	.261	.486	1		
Y_1	.206	.621	.674	.614	1	
Y_2	.218	.610	.659	.626	.996	1
Mean	.467	.600	16.933	15.333	17.467	26.467
s	.516	.507	5.444	5.407	7.891	13.799

Use $p = .05$ throughout the problems.

1 In Chapter VI, it was found that the regression predicting performance (Y_1) from the currently used aptitude test (X_4) was statistically significant. After reading this chapter, you wonder if perhaps there is a point at which predicted performance should level off even though scores on the aptitude tests are extremely high.

   a Calculate the appropriate polynomial regression. [*Hint*: This means using both X_4 and $(X_4)^2$ in the regression. One would need to make sure to create another column of numbers, generated by squaring the X_4 values. So that you can use the equations for the *b*-weights from previous chapters, let me tell you that the mean of the $(X_4)^2$ scores is 262.4 and that their standard deviation is 188.319. Also, these squared scores have a Pearson r of .977 with X_4 and a Pearson r of .566 with Y_1. This should make your computational life much easier!]

   b Test whether or not $(X_4)^2$ has a unique predictive capacity in the above regression (i.e., see if R^2 significantly increased as a result of using a quadratic term). [*Hint*: To help here, let me tell you that the standard deviation of the *b*-weight for $(X_4)^2$ is .044. Isn't it nice of me to tell you this?]

2 The individuals conducting the management assessment project are interested in discovering the extent to which previous performance (Y_1) predicts management potential several years later (Y_2). They are also interested in looking for nonlinear relationships in the data. [*Hint*: Notice that one of the performance measures (Y_1) and its square will now take on the role of predictors.]

   a Calculate the regression predicting Y_2 from a linear combination of Y_1 and $(Y_1)^2$. [Again, let me try to simplify the hand calculations here. Let me tell you that the mean of the $(Y_1)^2$ scores is 363.20 and the standard deviation is 272.111. Further, these squared scores correlate .984 with Y_1 and correlate .989 with the Y_2 measure.]

   b Test the regression weight for $(Y_1)^2$ for significance (against the value of zero). To make life easier for you, I will tell you that the standard deviation for this regression weight is .006. Interpret your findings. [*Hint*: Don't also lose sight of the fact that the simple correlation between Y_2 and Y_1 is .996 (see the above matrix of correlations), which is statistically significant. Thus, we already know there is a significant linear component to the prediction of Y_2.]

3 The folks who developed the management assessment program are also interested in whether or not previous performance (Y_1) interacts with gender (X_1) in its prediction of Y_2.

   a State the regression model that you would use to consider this question and the implied null hypothesis to be tested.

b Assuming you did part a correctly (and I suppose even if you didn't!), let me tell you what the computer output might provide for such a regression. The predictors will be X_1, Y_1, and the product $X_1 \times Y_1$. The criterion measure is Y_2. Here are the regression weights and their respective standard deviations:

Variable	Coefficient	SD
Constant	−4.889	1.303
X_1	1.926	1.841
Y_1	1.790	.075
$X_1 \times Y_1$	−.090	.098

Now, write down the sample regression equation and test to see if the interaction term was significant. Briefly interpret this finding.

4 As noted above, we found that scores on the currently used aptitude test (X_4) significantly predicted job performance ratings (Y_1). Suppose the test salesperson wants to demonstrate that the current test is questionable because it predicts job performance differently for men and for women.

a State the underlying regression model that the test salesperson should be using and the null hypothesis that should be tested.

b Test the interaction for statistical significance. (*Hint*: To do this, you'll need the regression output results.) Using the same format as in the previous question, the results are as follows:

Variable	Coefficient	SD
Constant	−2.539	8.582
X_1	11.135	11.259
X_4	1.279	.569
$X_1 \times X_4$	−.631	.707

5 Consider the regression results for Problem 4, where the sample regression was $\hat{Y} = -2.539 + 11.135X_1 + 1.279X_4 - .631X_1X_4$. Notice that in this data set, X_1 was scored 0 if male and 1 if female. Suppose a different researcher had the same data but chose to score gender in the opposite direction. Call this new variable X_1^* (i.e., 1 if male and 0 if female). Thus, there has been a linear transformation of the gender variable. Can you see what it is? Good, it's $X_1^* = 1 - X_1$. Now for the question.

a What would this second researcher's regression weights be if the same interactive model was used? (*Hint*: To do this, just follow what we did in the text. That is, note that we can solve for X_1 and get $X_1 = 1 - X_1^*$. Then replace X_1 by this value in the regression results.)

b Which weight(s) is(are) affected by this simple change in coding scheme? (Note that if a weight is affected in this interactive regression, its statistical significance might also change.)

REFERENCES

Aguinis, H., and Stone-Romero, E. (1997). Methodological artifacts in moderated multiple regression and their effects on statistical power. *Journal of Applied Psychology, 82,* 192–206.

Arnold, H. (1982). Moderator variables: A clarification of conceptual, analytical, and psychometric issues. *Organizational Behavior and Human Performance, 29,* 143–174.

Berlyne, D. (1974). *Studies in the new experimental aesthetics.* New York: Wiley.

Blood, M., and Mullett, G. (1977). *Where have all the moderators gone?: The perils of Type II error.* Technical Report 1, College of Industrial Management, Georgia Institute of Technology, Atlanta.

Bobko, P. (1986). A solution to some dilemmas when testing hypotheses about ordinal interactions. *Journal of Applied Psychology, 71,* 323–326.

Bobko, P. (1990). Multivariate correlational data analysis. In M. Dunnette and L. Hough (Eds.), *Handbook of Industrial & Organizational Psychology* (2nd ed.), Vol. 1, pp. 637–686. Palo Alto, CA: Consulting Psychologists Press.

Bobko, P., and Bartlett, C. J. (1978). Subgroup validities: Differential definitions and differential predictions. *Journal of Applied Psychology, 63,* 12–14.

Boehm, V. (1977). Differential prediction: A methodological artifact: *Journal of Applied Psychology, 62,* 146–154.

Champoux, J., and Peters, W. (1987). Form, effect size, and power in moderated regression analysis. *Journal of Occupational Psychology, 60,* 243–255.

Chen, M., and MacMillan, I. (1992). Nonresponse and delayed response to competitive moves: The roles of competitor dependence and action irreversibility. *Academy of Management Journal, 35,* 539–570.

Chow, G. (1960). Test of equality between sets of coefficients in two linear regressions. *Econometrica, 28,* 591–604.

Cleary, T. (1968). Test bias: Prediction of grades of negro and white students in integrated colleges. *Journal of Educational Measurement, 5,* 115–124.

Cohen, J., and Cohen, P. (1983). *Applied multiple regression/correlation analysis for the behavioral sciences* (2nd ed.). Hillsdale, NJ: Lawrence Erlbaum.

Cortina, J. (1993). Interaction, nonlinearity, and multicollinearity: Implications for multiple regression. *Journal of Management, 19,* 915–922.

Cronbach, L. (1987). Statistical tests for moderator variables: Flaws in analyses recently proposed. *Psychological Bulletin, 102,* 414–417.

Dawes, R., and Corrigan, B. (1974). Linear models in decision making. *Psychological Bulletin, 81,* 95–106.

Equal Employment Opportunity Commission, Civil Service Commission, Department of Labor, and Department of Justice. (1978). Adoption by four agencies of uniform guidelines on employee selection procedures. *Federal Register, 43,* 38290–38315.

Evans, M. (1985). A Monte Carlo study of the effects of correlated method variance in moderated multiple regression analysis. *Organizational Behavior and Human Decision Processes, 36,* 305–323.

Evans, M. (1991). The problem of analyzing multiplicative composites. *American Psychologist, 46,* 6–15.

Fox, M., Dwyer, D., and Ganster, D. (1993). Effects of stressful job demands and control on physiological and attitudinal outcomes in a hospital setting. *Academy of Management Journal, 36,* 289–318.

Ganzach, Y. (1998). Nonlinearity, multicollinearity and the probability of Type II error in detecting interaction. *Journal of Management, 24,* 615–622.

Gelfand, M., and Realo, A. (1999). Individualism–collectivism and accountability in intergroup negotiations. *Journal of Applied Psychology, 84,* 721–736.

Gocka, E. (1974). Coding for correlation and regression. *Educational and Psychological Measurement, 34,* 771–783.

Gomez-Mejia, L., Tosi, H., and Hinkin, T. (1987). Managerial control, performance, and executive compensation. *Academy of Management Journal, 30,* 51–70.

Govindarajan, V., and Fisher, J. (1990). Strategy, control systems, and resource sharing: Effects on business-unit performance. *Academy of Management Journal, 33,* 259–285.

Hitt, M., and Barr, S. (1989). Managerial selection decision models: Examination of configural cue processing. *Journal of Applied Psychology, 74,* 53–61.

Hull, C. (1943). *Principles of behavior.* New York: Appleton.

Jaccard, J., and Wan, C. (1995). Measurement error in the analysis of interaction effects between continuous predictors using multiple regression: Multiple indicator and structural equation approaches. *Psychological Bulletin, 117,* 348–357.

Johnston, J. (1972). *Econometric methods* (2nd ed.). New York: McGraw-Hill.

Lee, C., Ashford, S., and Bobko, P. (1990). The interactive effects of Type A personality and perceived control on worker performance, job satisfaction and somatic complaints. *Academy of Management Journal, 33,* 870–881.

Lubinski, D., and Humphreys, L. (1990). Assessing spurious "moderator effects": Illustrated substantively with the hypothesized ("synergistic") relation between spatial and mathematical ability. *Psychological Bulletin, 107,* 385–393.

Matthews, G., Jones, D., and Chamberlain, A. (1992). Predictors of individual differences in mail-coding skills and their variation with ability level. *Journal of Applied Psychology, 77,* 406–418.

Meyer, D. (1991). Misinterpretation of interaction effects: A reply to Rosnow and Rosenthal. *Psychological Bulletin, 110,* 571–573.

Morris, J., Sherman, J., and Mansfield, E. (1986). Failure to detect moderating effects with ordinary least squares moderated multiple regression: Some reasons and a remedy. *Psychological Bulletin, 99,* 282–288.

Morrison, R., and Brantner, T. (1992). What enhances or inhibits learning a new job? A basic career issue. *Journal of Applied Psychology, 77,* 926–940.

Pedhazur, E. (1982). *Multiple regression in behavioral research* (2nd ed.). New York: Holt, Rinehart, & Winston.

Pritchard, R., Jones, S., Roth, P., Stuebing, K., and Ekeberg, S. (1988). Effects of group feedback, goal setting, and incentives on organizational productivity. *Journal of Applied Psychology, 73,* 337–358.

Richard, O. (2000). Racial diversity, business strategy, and firm performance: A resource-based view. *Academy of Management Journal, 43,* 164–177.

Rosnow, R., and Rosenthal, R. (1989). Definition and interpretation of interaction effects. *Psychological Bulletin, 105,* 143–146.

Rosnow, R., and Rosenthal, R. (1991). If you're looking at the cell means, you're not looking at only the interaction (unless all main effects are zero). *Psychological Bulletin, 110,* 574–576.

Russell, C., and Bobko, P. (1992). Moderated regression analysis and Likert scales: Too coarse for comfort. *Journal of Applied Psychology, 77,* 336–342.

Russell, C., Pinto, J., and Bobko, P. (1991). Appropriate moderated regression and inappropriate research strategy: A demonstration of the need to give your respondents space. *Applied Psychological Measurement, 15,* 257–266.

Sadacca, R., Campbell, J., DiFazio, A., Schultz, S., and White, L. (1990). Scaling performance utility to enhance selection/classification decisions. *Personnel Psychology, 43,* 367–378.

Skinner, S., Donnelly, J., and Ivancevich, J. (1987). Effects of transactional form on environmental linkages and power-dependence relations. *Academy of Management Journal, 30,* 577–588.

Southwood, K. (1978). Substantive theory and statistical interaction: Five models. *American Journal of Sociology, 83,* 1154–1203.

Vroom, V. (1964). *Work and motivation.* New York: Wiley.

Wahlsten, D. (1991). Sample size to detect a planned contrast and a one degree-of-freedom interaction effect. *Psychological Bulletin, 110,* 587–595.

Wainer, H. (1976). Estimating coefficients in linear models: It don't make no nevermind. *Psychological Bulletin, 83,* 213–217.

Wise, S., Peters, L., and O'Connor, E. (1984). Identifying moderator variables using multiple regression: A reply to Darrow and Kahl. *Journal of Management, 10,* 227–236.

Zedeck, S. (1971). Problems with the use of "moderator" variables. *Psychological Bulletin, 76,* 295–310.

X

MORE ABOUT REGRESSION, AND BEYOND

CHAPTER OBJECTIVES

After reading this chapter, you should be able to:

- Understand that regression maximizes R^2 and that the value of R^2 in the original sample is probably too large.
- Understand the difference between Wherry-type shrinkage and Lord-Nicholson-type shrinkage.
- Explain how sample size and the number of predictors effect shrinkage.
- Intuitively explain what ridge regression is and how the properties of ridge weights differ from the b's in least squares regression.
- List possible ways researchers can weight X's in prediction equations and be able to indicate some of the strengths and/or weaknesses of each.
- Understand how suppressor variables work.
- Explain the use of indicator variables and give examples of some indicators in content domains of interest to you.
- Explain how analysis of variance (in experimental design) can be construed as a special case of regression.

In this chapter, I intend to introduce some pretty "meaty" topics that are associated with the use of regression. If this book is your first introduction to regression and correlation, you may want to read this chapter simply with an eye to getting an overview of the kinds of topics that will be considered in future courses in this area. On the other hand, if some of the earlier chapters have been refreshers and/or new ways of thinking about old knowledge for you, the topics herein should motivate you to engage in even more sophisticated thinking about the use and application of regression.

There are a variety of topics in this chapter. We consider the notion of validity shrinkage and the potential bias in the value of the sample squared multiple correlation (R^2). This leads to some thoughts on sample size requirements in regression. I then introduce a rather esoteric topic, ridge regression, which leads to a more encompassing discussion about weighting schemes. Topics on residuals and suppressors are also considered. We then discuss the notion of indicator variables, which leads in turn to a consideration of the overlap between regression and the analysis of variance. At that point, I hope your appreciation for general linear models will have increased and your appetite whetted to seek out additional courses and books on multivariate techniques that go beyond regression.

VALIDITY SHRINKAGE

As we shall see, the title of this section could also have been "You Don't Get Something for Nothing!" The focus of attention here is on the value (i.e., magnitude) of the squared multiple correlation ($R^2_{Y.12\ldots p}$). For simplicity, let's just call it R^2, but don't forget that it's based on a regression using p predictors.

In regression, what criterion did we choose to find the best line, plane, or hyperplane? Right! The least squares criterion! This criterion *minimized* the sum of squared errors in the sample at hand relative to the total sum of squares. Because $R^2 = \text{SSR}/\text{SST} = 1 - \text{SSE}/\text{SST}$, this means that

> **Regression weights were chosen such that R^2 was *maximized* in the sample at hand.**

That is, there is no other set of weights ($b_0, b_1, \ldots, b_p$) that will result in an R^2 quite as large in that particular sample of data.

The mixed blessing here is that regression uses *all* of the sample information to choose the b_i, hence maximize R^2. This sample information includes means, standard deviations, and all of the intercorrelations among the X_i. Indeed, the regression *should* use this information, as well as the sample intercorrelations among the X's and Y. However, relative to the unknown population, this information is not perfect. For example, suppose the regression has five predictors ($p = 5$) and we pick on X_5 for a minute. Note that the correlation between X_5 and Y (r_{Y5}) will vary from sample to sample because of good old sampling error. *So, if in your sample r_{Y5} is a bit higher than it should be, the regression will use this idiosyncracy to minimize SSE and maximize R^2.*[1]

Again, use of the sample idiosyncracies will maximize R^2 in the sample at hand. But when this regression is applied to new data, it won't do as well as you think because the new data won't have the same idiosyncracies as the sample in which the regression was developed.

This is very important stuff! Don't forget that one of the major reasons for using regression analyses is *prediction*. You conduct a study, collect data, and develop an equation predicting Y (e.g., predicting job performance). You then want to know how well that equation will do in the future with new subjects. The point here is:

In terms of R^2, the regression won't do as well (in new samples) as it did in the original sample. That is, the sample value of R^2 is generally too high (it's biased), and it needs to be reduced down a bit. The expected amount of reduction is called "shrinkage."

How much to reduce or shrink R^2 will be addressed in a minute. First, however, let's consider another way of seeing why sample values of R^2 are generally too large. For simplicity, let's start with Y and one X. Suppose there's no correlation between Y and $X(\rho_{YX} = 0)$. Now, take a sample of size 2 ($n = 2$) and draw a scatterplot. Since there's no correlation between X and Y, I closed my eyes and threw two darts, at random, at the scatterplot. Figure 10.1 shows where they landed. Now, if I ran a regression on this sample of data, I would get $R^2_{Y.1} = 1.00$ because you can always perfectly fit a line to two points (Figure 10.2).

---

[1] For example, if r_{Y5} is greater than ρ_{Y5}, the regression might give undue weight to X_5. Or, if r_{Y5} turned out be negative (even though ρ_{Y5} was positive), the regression might mistakenly make b_5 negative.

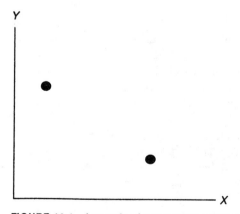

FIGURE 10.1   A sample of two random points from a population with zero correlation.

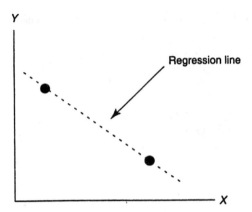

FIGURE 10.2   Sample-based regression line for two random points ($p = 1$, $n = 2$).

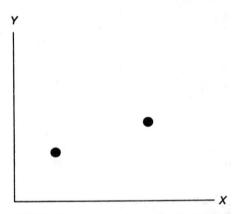

FIGURE 10.3   A second sample of two random points from a population with zero correlation.

However, if I took *another* two points from the population where $\rho_{YX} = 0$, these two random darts might end up as in Figure 10.3. In this case, the regression line from my original "study" won't fit this new data quite as well (in fact, Figure 10.4 shows that the line fits horribly!). It's clear that the original sample value of $R_{Y.1}^2 = 1.0$ overestimates how well I will do in predicting Y from X. Thus, the estimate of R^2 as 1.0 should be reduced. It is important to notice a property of my contrived example: I had one predictor ($p = 1$) and a sample size of only 2 ($n = 2$).

Clearly, as the sample size increases relative to the number of predictors, there will be less of a problem. For example, as n is increased in Figures 10.1 through 10.4 (where $\rho_{YX} = 0$), the scatterplot will become more like a circle and the regression line will tend toward zero slope in most samples. However, it's not just n that matters. If you let p increase as well, things get worse again. Indeed, if you let p be exactly 1 less than n ($p = n - 1$), you'll *always* get $R^2 = 1.0$ in

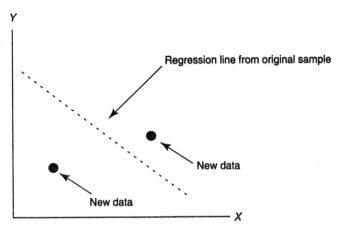

Y

Regression line from original sample

New data

New data

X

FIGURE 10.4   Fitting the original sample regression in Figure 10.2 to new data.

the original sample. For example, you can always perfectly fit three data points with two X's (i.e., you can always fit a two-dimensional plane to three data points). As we will see next, the degree to which R^2 should be reduced depends upon both n and p.

Shrinkage Formulas

Wherry shrinkage   As it turns out, there are two ways of thinking (worrying?) about validity shrinkage: (1) Wherry-type shrinkage and (2) Lord-Nicholson-type shrinkage (to be discussed in the next section). Wherry (1931) was interested in estimating the true value of $\mathbf{R}^2_{Y.12\ldots p}$; that is, the value of $\mathbf{R}^2$ in the population, using population $\mathbf{B}$-weights. This estimate might be useful if a researcher wants to estimate the theoretical degree of relationship between Y and a set of X's. As noted above, it should be clear that the sample R^2 will generally overestimate true $\mathbf{R}^2$. Since the sample size is less than the population size, the sample idiosyncracies will get relatively too much attention when computing the b's, and in turn, sample R^2 will tend to overestimate the population $\mathbf{R}^2$. Given a sample R^2, Wherry's (1931) estimate of the population value is

$$(\text{X.A}) \qquad \hat{\mathbf{R}}^2_{\text{pop}} = 1 - \left(\frac{n-1}{n-p-1}\right)(1-R^2)$$

where R^2 is the squared multiple correlation derived from the sample of size n.

Notice a few things about Equation X.A. First, it really does shrink R^2. For example, in Professor Gretzky's data in Chapter VIII, $R^2 = .354$, $p = 2$, and $n = 21$. Application of Wherry's shrinkage formula yields

$$\hat{\mathbf{R}}^2_{\text{pop}} = 1 - \left(\frac{20}{18}\right)(1-.359) = .288$$

So, the best estimate of the underlying squared population correlation (predicting test grades from hours studied and absences) is really only .288, not .359.

A second thing to notice about Equation X.A is how it's constructed. One starts with the proportion of variation not accounted for $(1 - R^2)$ and increases it by a factor of $(n - 1)/(n - p - 1)$. This increase in unexplained variation is then subtracted from 1.0 to obtain $\hat{R}^2_{pop}$. If you read Wherry's proof, you'll see that it's not a coincidence that the factor $(n - 1)/(n - p - 1)$ is the ratio of df total to df error! In fact, notice that the factor $(n - 1)/(n - p - 1)$ is the only factor by which R^2 is reduced. Without this factor, $\hat{R}^2_{pop}$ would be equal to R^2. Now, take a closer look at his factor. If you ignore the 1's, then the factor becomes

$$\frac{n}{n - p} \quad \text{which is equivalent to} \quad \frac{1}{1 - (p/n)}$$

Thus, the ratio p/n is the critical (and only) factor in determining the degree of Wherry shrinkage in R^2. As suggested by Figures 10.1 through 10.4, shrinkage depends on both the sample size *and* the number of predictors. The greater the sample size relative to p, the less the shrinkage.

Lord-Nicholson shrinkage Lord-Nicholson-type shrinkage addresses the question of how well a *sample* regression (using sample b's) will predict scores, on average, within new samples (i.e., how well the sample equation predicts future individual cases). Notice that this is different than Wherry shrinkage, which considers how well the *population* equation (using theoretical **B**'s) does in the population (i.e., an estimate of the true $\mathbf{R}^2$). Thus, a researcher developing a sample regression for *predictive* purposes would probably choose a Lord-Nicholson type of shrinkage estimator.

The equation for Lord-Nicholson shrinkage is more complicated than that for Wherry shrinkage. Indeed, there are actually two sets of formulas, depending upon whether the X's are considered to be fixed or random.[2] Also, the reason I have called this type of shrinkage "Lord-Nicholson" is that both Lord (1950) and Nicholson (1960) were the first to independently derive such shrinkage formulas. However, because of the very complicated nature of the problem, their solutions are only approximations.[3] It turns out that Browne (1975) has developed even better equations. In the case of fixed X's, Browne's estimate of the shrunken R^2 is (see Cattin, 1980):

X.B
$$R^2_{shrunk} = \frac{(n - 1)\rho^4 + \rho^2}{(n - p)\rho^2 + p}$$

[2] See Chapter VI for a brief reminder about the difference between fixed- and random-X models.
[3] In fact, all estimates of shrunken R^2 (both Wherry and Lord-Nicholson type) are approximations to exact solutions. Wherry's estimate has bias of order n^{-1} (Montgomery and Morrison, 1973), implying that it becomes more accurate as n increases. Browne (1975) improved on the estimators of Lord and Nicholson, reducing bias to the second or third decimal place. Indeed, many other researchers have offered and/or studied differing forms of Equation X.B (e.g., Rozeboom, 1978; Schmitt, Coyle, and Rauschenberger, 1977). See Cattin (1980) or Raju, Bilgic, Edwards, and Fleer (1997) for thorough reviews of these issues.

where p and n are as before and ρ^2 is Wherry's estimator as defined above in Equation X.A.[4]

As an example, consider Professor Gretzky's data again. If he were interested in knowing how well his *sample* regression would predict future individuals, he would compute

$$R^2_{\text{shrunk}} = \frac{(21 - 1)(.288)^2 + .288}{(21 - 2)(.288) + 2} = \frac{1.947}{7.472} = .261$$

That is, while Gretzky's original R^2 was .359 (i.e., 36% of variance explained) and the best guess of the *population* $\mathbf{R}^2$ is .29, he should expect to explain only about 26% of test score performance if he applies his sample equation to the prediction of future data.

ome Comments About Shrinkage

Shrinkage can be dramatic   Notice that Lord-Nicholson-type shrinkage reduces R^2 to a greater extent (i.e., is more "punishing") than does Wherry shrinkage. Since prediction is often the reason for using regression in applied settings, you should routinely report Lord-Nicholson estimates of how well your equation will do, along with the original sample value of R^2. Computer software packages often report shrunken R^2 in their regression output, typically under the heading "adjusted R^2." Unfortunately, they almost always report Wherry shrinkage which, as we have seen, doesn't shrink R^2 enough if the focus is on future prediction.[5]

It should now be clear why this chapter began with the alternate title, "You Don't Get Something for Nothing." Regression analysis exploits sample characteristics to maximize R^2, yet that very criterion for solving regression problems inflates (creates a positive bias in) the sample R^2. In many cases, application of either Equation X.A or X.B can result in a dramatic reduction in the estimated percentage of variance explained. Table X.1 presents values of Lord-Nicholson shrinkage (R^2_{shrunk}) given differing values of n, p, and the original sample-based R^2. For example, suppose a researcher uses a form of expectancy theory to predict the performance of 100 workers ($n = 100$) from a set of 10 predictors ($p = 10$) and obtains $R^2_{Y.12\ldots10} = .20$. I chose $R^2 = .20$ because it is greater than the typical validity for expectancy theory (Pinder, 1984). Note that Table X.1 (or Equation X.B) indicates that such an equation would explain only 7% of the variation in other samples of workers. Indeed, if we had used 20 predictors

---

[4] Make sure that you read Equation X.B carefully! The last term in the denominator is different; it's p, not ρ. In fact, Lautenschlager (1990) has pointed out that several statistics texts fail to make this distinction, and this distinction *matters*.

[5] Adjusted, or shrunken, R^2 also comes under the heading "cross-validation." That is, it answers the question, How well will your equation validate when it's used (crossed) on a new set of data?

TABLE X.1   VALUES OF LORD-NICHOLSON-TYPE SHRUNKEN R^2 GIVEN SOME VALUES OF n, p, AND SAMPLE R^2

Sample R^2		Shrunken R^2†	
		$n = 100$	$n = 200$
.20	$p = 10$	.07	.13
	$p = 20$	—	.07
	$p = 40$	—	—
.40	$p = 10$	.28	.34
	$p = 20$	.16	.28
	$p = 40$	—	.16
.80	$p = 10$	.76	.78
	$p = 20$	.70	.76
	$p = 40$	.56	.71

†The value of shrunken R^2 is computed using Equation X.B.
Source: This table and the explanatory example in the text are taken from Bobko (1990, pp. 642–643). Reproduced by special permission of the Publisher, Consulting Psychologists Press, Inc., Palo Alto, CA 94303 from *Handbook of Industrial & Organizational Psychology*, Second Edition, Volume 1 by Marvin D. Dunnette and Leaetta M. Hough, Editors. Copyright 1990 by Consulting Psychologists Press, Inc. All rights reserved. Further reproduction is prohibited without the Publisher's written consent.

(i.e., $n = 100$, $p = 20$, $R^2 = .20$), R^2_{shrunk} could not be estimated because the Wherry estimate is already less than zero! The appropriate shrinkage formula should be applied, and results reported. Not to do so can be deceptive.

Read research carefully   Consider Dulebohn and Ferris' (1999) study predicting perceptions of the fairness of performance evaluations (Y) from several predictors and their interactions (overall, $p = 14$). The R^2 is .82 and $n = 128$. Application of Equation X.A results in a Wherry estimate of .80. Application of Equation X.B shows that the predictive efficiency of their interactive regression function in future data would be $R^2_{shrunk} = .78$. All in all, there is not much shrinkage here, and Dulebohn and Ferris' results appear to be stable. On the other hand, Evans and Carrere (1991) predicted bus driver stress from a combination of six control variables (age, caffeine consumption, etc.) and level of traffic congestion. In predicting a nonadrenaline stress indicator, they report an $R^2 = .16$ with $p = 7$ and $n = 60$. No shrunken R^2 is reported. Applying Equations X.A and X.B yields $\hat{R}^2_{pop} = .047$ and $R^2_{shrunk} = .025$, respectively. Thus, while these authors note that the level of traffic congestion variable had a significant regression weight, it is also true that less than 3% of the variance in future stress will be predicted by their overall model. The practical significance of this finding is subjective and up to you, the reader! The point here is that shrunken/adjusted R^2 should be reported so that accurate and informed decisions can be made. (If you do see adjusted R^2 reported, note that it will almost always be Wherry's population estimate and not the cross-validity estimate.)

Clinical shrinkage   It should be clear from the above that simply adding more predictors to the regression will not always increase R^2 to the extent that you think. That's because with n fixed, any increases in p will engender greater shrinkage. I want to point that there's an analogous finding in the clinical psychology literature. Bartlett and Green (1966) had counseling psychologists predict student grade point averages (Y) after being given information on 4 ($p = 4$) valid predictors (X's). Predictions were also made by giving counselors the *same* 4 predictors plus an additional 18 predictors which were also judged to be related to grade point average (total $p = 22$). It was demonstrated that prediction was *better* when the counselors had only 4 pieces of information. The moral is that when thinking in terms of shrinkage, more is not always better—or at least it will not always result in the improvement you think it will.[6]

SAMPLE SIZE

The previous discussion on validity shrinkage also has implications for sample size. First, it should be clear that as n increases, there is less shrinkage (as always, bigger n's are preferred in any study, all else equal). In some methodology and statistics texts, rules of thumb are often presented in answer to the question, Just how large should my sample size be? For example, Thorndike (1978) gives an "informal guide" (p. 184) of 10 subjects per predictor and suggests adding another 50 subjects when p is small.

Now, we have already seen that the bigger the n, the better, in the sense that the standard deviations of the b_i are reduced by increasing n (see the discussion of Equation VIII.K). On the other hand, the value of $SD(b_i)$ also depended on the collinearity of the predictors, so any simple rule for required sample sizes can't possibly suffice. A glance at Table X.1 also reveals that sample size requirements are complex issues. In this table, note that the magnitude of shrinkage is a function of the value of R^2 as well as the p/n ratio. Shrinkage is less severe when R^2 is large—even for identical p/n ratios. Determination of n is therefore a function of statistical power (through reduced standard deviations), the number of predictors, their collinearity, the underlying magnitude of R^2, requirements for practical significance, etc. The user of regression should consider all these factors and not accept simple rules of thumb for arriving at sample size.[7]

---

[6] Indeed, Wherry also proposed using shrinkage as a way of deciding which predictors (items) to include in an equation. That is, add items one at a time and, at each stage, compute both R^2 and $\hat{R}^2_{pop}$. The values of sample R^2 will never go down as items are added. But, sooner or later, the corresponding values of $\hat{R}^2_{pop}$ will not only level off, they will *drop*. At that point, stop adding X's to your equation.

[7] To indicate the arbitrary nature of simple rules, I offer the following hypothesis: had we all been three-toed sloths, our rules for n would be in multiples of 6, rather than 10!

RIDGE REGRESSION

It has been repeatedly noted throughout this book that collinearity among the predictors (X's) can make it difficult to get stable estimates of the $\mathbf{B}_i$. That is, SD(b_i) is large when collinearity is high. In the 1970s, an alternative to least squares regression labeled "ridge regression" was developed and extensively studied (Dempster, Schatzoff, and Wermuth, 1977; Guilkey and Murphy, 1975; Hoerl and Kennard, 1970). I mention ridge regression here because it quite nicely brings together discussions about collinearity in regression, statistical bias, and validity shrinkage.

Indeed, ridge estimation was developed in direct response to concerns about collinearity. While technically complex, ridge regression proceeds by adding a constant (k) to the variance of each predictor. Now, think back to the Chapter II discussion of a correlation coefficient. The discussion of the formula for Pearson r (i.e., the discussion of Equation II.A and footnote 2) indicated that the correlation between any two X's (say, X_1 and X_2) could be written as

$$r_{12} = \frac{\text{cov}(X_1, X_2)}{\sqrt{s_1^2}\sqrt{s_2^2}}$$

So, adding the value k to each variance (s_1^2 and s_2^2) increases the denominator and in turn reduces the value of r_{12} (i.e., reduces the collinearity). The choice of k is somewhere between science and art form (Guilkey and Murphy, 1975).[8]

Now, when we used least squares regression, we ended up with a prediction equation that looked like

$$\hat{Y} = b_0 + b_1 X_1 + b_2 X_2 + \cdots + b_p X_p$$

When ridge regression is conducted, this "arbitrary" value of k changes the regression weights because all the correlations among the X's are changed (i.e., these correlations are generally lowered). Call the new (ridge) regression

$$\hat{Y} = b_0^* + b_1^* X_1 + b_2^* X_2 + \cdots + b_p^* X_p$$

Now, the interesting fact is that the SD(b_i^*) are indeed less than the corresponding SD(b_i). However, as usual, you don't get something for nothing. It turns out that while the standard deviations of the b^*'s are lower, the addition of k makes the b^*'s become biased. So the tradeoff is, In the presence of collinearity, how much bias are you willing to put up with in order to keep the standard deviations down?

[8] Looking ahead to Figure 10.5, the ambiguity in the choice of k reflects the trade-off between (1) increased bias and (2) reduced sampling variance of the regression weights.

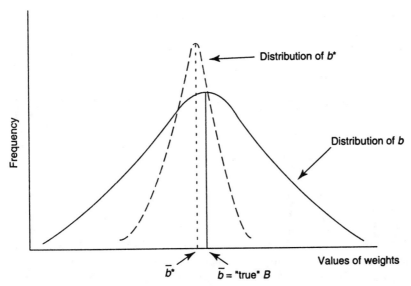

FIGURE 10.5 Sampling distributions of ordinary least squares regression weights (*b*) and ridge regression weights (*b**). (Adapted from Bobko, 1990, p. 644. Reproduced by special permission of the Publisher, Consulting Psychologists Press, Inc., Palo Alto, CA 94303 from *Handbook of Industrial & Organizational Psychology*, Second Edition, Volume 1 by Marvin D. Dunnette and Leaetta M. Hough, Editors. Copyright 1990 by Consulting Psychologists Press, Inc. All rights reserved. Further reproduction is prohibited without the Publisher's written consent.

Figure 10.5 portrays the issue. In this figure, note that the sampling distribution of the least squares weight (*b*) is exactly centered at the true value of **B**, but the variance of *b* (from sample to sample) is large.

On the other hand, the *variance* of *b** is much smaller (i.e., doesn't change much from one sample to another), but on *average* the actual value of *b** is a bit smaller than it should be (i.e., *b** is biased, and its mean is smaller than the true value of **B**). To repeat a statement from previous chapters, regression is fun; we once again see that statistics requires value judgements. If you're willing to trade some bias for reduced variance, consider ridge regression; otherwise, use least squares regression and live with the collinearity problems.

Before you get excited about ridge regression as a solution to collinearity, be aware that no one knows how to do hypothesis testing with this technique (Price, 1977).[9] So, stick with the techniques in the earlier chapters if you're like many of us who want to make statistical inferences. On the other hand, if your interest is pure prediction, the increased stability of the *b**'s may better predict future behavior than the less stable (but unbiased) least squares *b*'s. Indeed, it has been shown that ridge regression is subject to much less validity shrinkage than least

[9] Price (1977) provides a nice, readable review of the ridge regression technique. If interested, see other good reviews by Darlington (1978) and Rozeboom (1979).

squares regression (Dempster et al., 1977; Faden and Bobko, 1982; Gunst and Mason, 1977).

OTHER WEIGHTING SCHEMES

Mentioning ridge regression was akin to opening Pandora's box regarding the weights for the X's in prediction. That is, our prediction function has been a linear combination of X's:

$$\hat{Y} = b_0 + b_1 X_1 + \cdots + b_p X_p$$

And, throughout this book, we have focused (like almost all social scientists) on the way to find the b_i such that the sum of squared errors is minimized or, equivalently, $R^2_{Y.12\ldots p}$ is maximized. As we have seen, the solution (least squares regression) is both a powerful and flexible technique which has many advantages. On the other hand, some of the disadvantages have included large standard deviations of the b_i (when the X's were interrelated) and a positive bias in the sample R^2 (requiring the need to shrink or cross-validate the magnitude of R^2).

Aside from ridge regression, researchers have offered other ways of weighting the X's, often with an eye toward simplification and as a way of avoiding (or reducing) the need to shrink the results (or cross-validate them in a new sample of data). For example, some researchers have proposed simply "unit-weighting" the X's, i.e., using 1.0 for all the weights (e.g., Einhorn and Hogarth, 1975). In order to make sure each predictor has an equal contribution, the predictors are first standardized (turned into z-scores—see Chapter I). The resulting prediction function is then

$$\hat{Y}_{\text{unit}} = 1.0z_1 + 1.0z_2 + \cdots + 1.0z_p$$

There's lots of intuitive appeal to this method of combining predictors. First, we do it all the time (think about how many tests you've taken where your total score was simply the sum of how well you did across the items—i.e., the number correct). Second, there's no need to shrink the resulting correlation between Y and the sum of the z's because you didn't use any sample properties to determine the weights (i.e., the use of $b_i = 1.0$ for all X's was determined a priori). Third, it's a technique that is both simple to use and easy to explain to others.

On the other hand, some would argue that unit weighting doesn't use all the information at hand (i.e., the data may clearly indicate that some predictors deserve more weight than others). This leads to other suggestions for weights. The technique of "validity-weighting" creates differential weights (r_{yi}) by computing the correlation between Y and each X_i. These correlations (validities) become the weights, and the prediction function is

$$\hat{Y}_{\text{validity}} = r_{Y1}z_1 + r_{Y2}z_2 + \cdots + r_{Yp}z_p$$

It should be obvious that this technique was motivated by the need to incorporate sample information in the prediction (i.e., use of r_{Yi}). However, in contrast to least squares regression, this technique does not take into account the interrelationships of the X's.[10]

Yet another way to obtain weights is to ask subject matter experts for their judgments.[11] See Cook and Steward (1975) for a listing of ways this might be done (e.g., "There are 7 predictors in the study. Allocate 100 points, as weights, across these 7 X's.") Presumably, each judge uses knowledge about job performance, the predictors, and their relationships to estimate the weights.

w Did We Do?

We now have a variety of weighting schemes for prediction:

1 Unit-weighting
2 Validity-weighting
3 Subject matter judgments
4 Least squares regression
5 Ridge regression

A natural question is, Which of these techniques is most accurate in terms of prediction? Note that, in the sample at hand, least squares regression *must* be the most accurate: the weights are derived to maximize $R^2_{Y.12...p}$. That is, $b_0 + b_1 X_1 + \cdots + b_p X_p$ predicts Y better than any other combination of X's. But, thinking about shrinkage, we know that the sample regression won't do as well in future samples as it did in the original sample. On the other hand, there is no shrinkage in unit-weighting. That is, unit weights don't use sample idiosyncrasies and will, on average, therefore predict Y just as well regardless of which random sample of data is chosen. So, we know that least squares weights start out the best and that all the other techniques don't do as well (in the original sample). The key question is therefore, In new samples of data, will least squares prediction shrink just a bit and remain best, or when shrunk, will R^2 cross below the predictive capacity of other techniques?

In the 1970s, empirical research compared the first four techniques listed above (Claudy, 1972; Dawes and Corrigan, 1974; Dorans and Drasgow, 1978; Einhorn and Hogarth, 1975; Schmidt, 1971). The findings are clear: human-generated weights are not as good as statistically generated ones. *And, unit weights often do almost as well as least squares regression weights and sometimes do better* (again, in terms of predictive accuracy for new data). This is particularly

---

[10] Of course, neither does unit-weighting. Therefore, in both unit-weighting and validity-weighting, if there are a lot of X's of one type (e.g., overlapping tests of verbal skill) and only a few X's of another type (e.g., overlapping tests of math skill), then the prediction will by definition be most affected by the larger predictor set.

[11] Subject matter experts are often called "SMEs." Who are SMEs? Presumably individuals who are most familiar with the context of the organization in which the study occurs (e.g., incumbents, supervisors). Unfortunately, SMEs often become any warm bodies willing to fill out your questionnaire!

true if sample sizes are only small or moderate, since SD(b_i) in least squares regression can be large when n is small. Indeed, Wainer (1976) summed up this research in his eloquent title: "Estimating Coefficients in Linear Models: It Don't Make No Nevermind." Further, the above section on ridge regression led to similar findings: ridge weights generally did as well or better on cross-validation than least squares weights.

In sum, it appears that if prediction is the sole criterion for combining X's, then the simplest technique of all (unit weights) seems to be among the best. On the other hand, if theory building and hypothesis testing are of interest, and you have an adequately sized sample, least squares regression will provide you with increased amounts of inferential information.

RESIDUAL ANALYSIS

Someone's got to be the shortest person in a particular group. Well, here's the shortest *section* in the book. In Chapter VI, we discussed visually checking the regression data for violation of underlying assumptions. This was done by inspecting the errors $(Y - \hat{Y})$ plotted against corresponding values of X. This residual analysis still makes sense in multiple regression. That is, each observation still has an associated actual Y-value and a predicted value $(\hat{Y})$. The difference from Chapter VI is that $\hat{Y}$ is now computed as a linear combination of many X's, but there's still just one value of $Y - \hat{Y}$ for each data point. A major practical difference in residual analysis for multiple regression is that one has *several* residual plots to inspect. That is, one has a plot of each X_i against the corresponding $Y - \hat{Y}$. Wasn't that easy?

SUPPRESSOR VARIABLES

Occasionally in regression, the sign of a regression weight (b_i) is inconsistent with its simple correlation with Y. For example, suppose that the correlation between Y and X_2 is exactly 0 (r_{Y2}). Then, you would expect that $b_2 = 0$. However, as demonstrated below, this may not always be the case. In fact, depending on other variables in the regression, b_2 could be zero, positive, or negative!

A real example   A company called Aerospace Sciences (1991) reported a validation study in which researchers used a computerized selection test (X_1) to predict the training performance (Y) of air traffic controllers.[12] Because the selection test was a computerized simulation, these researchers also gave subjects a questionnaire assessing their previous computer experience (X_2). In the study, $n = 358$, and the resulting correlation matrix was

---

[12] Indeed, this type of research motivated the examples used in Chapters II and IX.

	Y	X_1	X_2
Performance (Y)	1.00		
Test (X_1)	.43	1.00	
Computer experience (X_2)	−.06	.25	1.00

Note that the selection test did indeed predict performance ($r_{Y1} = .43$). This is a significant correlation and suggests that the organization had room for optimism about the selection test. Note also that there is essentially *no* direct relationship between earlier computer experience and performance ($r_{Y2} = −.06$, not significant). Thus, if we conducted the regression $\hat{Y} = b_0 + b_1 X_1 + b_2 X_2$, we might expect that b_2 would be zero (or at least not significantly different from zero).

However (there's that word again!), if you assume all data are standardized, application of Equations VIII.C and VIII.D results in

$$\hat{Y} = .475X_1 − .179X_2$$

Further, application of Equation VIII.K yields SD(b_2) = .0484. Thus, the null hypothesis H_0: $B_2 = 0$ is rejected. (Try it. My *t*-ratio, with 355 df, was $−.179/.0484 = −3.70$. Do you agree?) Therefore, the *b*-weight for X_2 is *significantly* less than zero, even though this variable did not correlate very much with Y.[13]

The explanation here is somewhat straightforward. Think about the computerized selection test. It may indeed be measuring some aspects of the applicant's true ability. However, since it was a computerized simulation, some applicants might have done better because they had lots of previous experience with computers and computer games. In contrast, applicants with little previous computer experience may have had to spend more time adjusting to the mechanics of the test—thereby lowering their selection test scores. Figure 10.6 presents a picture of this possibility.

Now, can you see why X_2 enters this regression even though it doesn't correlate with Y? Good! That is, X_2's function in life is not its direct prediction of Y. Rather, X_2's function is to remove the "noise" from X_1. That's why X_2 entered the regression with a significant *negative* weight—the computer experience variable (X_2) helps subtract unwanted variance from X_1 (i.e., helps remove the box on the right-hand side of Figure 10.6). The resulting difference ($.475X_1 − .179X_2$) is an even stronger predictor of Y than X_1 alone.

So, it is indeed true that the signs of regression weights can be in unexpected directions. *When a variable's regression weight is different in nature* ($−, 0, or +$) *than its simple correlation with Y, individuals have labeled that measure a* "*suppressor variable,*" Obviously, the simple correlation and weight can differ

---

[13] Please note that even if r_{Y2} had been exactly zero, the same thing would have occurred, i.e., b_2 would have been significantly less than zero!

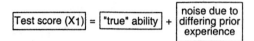

FIGURE 10.6   Possible explanation for a suppressor effect when using a computerized predictor test.

in many ways. If you're interested, see Conger (1974) or Cohen and Cohen (1983) for two taxonomies of types of suppressors. The important point for us, though, is to remember that such "inconsistent" weights can arise.

It is also instructive to statistically understand *why* suppressors arise. Note that had only X_2 been used to predict Y, the simple correlation and simple regression weight would produce similar results. However, in multiple regression the weight b_2 *is calculated in the presence of* X_1. Once again, our friend collinearity has an effect here. Consider the numerator of the formula for b_2 (see Equation VIII.D). It contains the factor $r_{Y2} - r_{Y1}r_{12}$. So, even if r_{Y2} is exactly zero, the weight b_2 will not be zero as long as X_2 is correlated with X_1 (and, of course, X_1 correlates with Y). *More generally, in the presence of lots of X's,* all of the intercorrelations among them come into play in determining the b_i. Thus, it is quite possible to create the appearance of a suppressor variable when many collinear X's are used in regression. So, suppressors can be very difficult, if not impossible, to interpret.[14]

In fact, it is pretty much standard operating procedure that when suppressors arise most researchers dismiss the finding as a statistical artifact unless there is very strong theoretical explanation for the result. This happens for three reasons. First, as noted above, when many intercorrelated predictors are used, it is very difficult to begin to explain the suppressor in terms of all the possible relationships to the other X's. Second (and this reason is related to the first reason), in the presence of collinearity among X's, we noted in Chapter VIII that the standard deviations of the b_i become large (see the discussion of Equation VIII.K). Thus, most researchers just chalk up the unexpected signs of b-weights to sampling error (i.e., in a new sample, the highly variable b-weight might change sign yet again). Third, policy and/or philosophical concerns arise when trying to apply suppressors—particularly in selection arenas. Consider the air traffic controller selection test example presented at the beginning of this section. Suppose we actually used the regression result of $\hat{Y} = .475X_1 - .179X_2$. Note that this result made conceptual sense because the negative weight for X_2 (previous computer experience) helped make X_1 a better predictor of Y. But operational use of the multiple regression implies that, all else equal, an applicant who has relatively *more* computer experience will have a *lower* predicted performance score and will be less likely to be selected! At an intuitive level, this

---

[14] For example, suppose you have 17 predictors; $r_{Y,15} < 0$, yet $b_{15} > 0$. It's nearly impossible to unpack how the interrelationships among the other 16 X's and X_{15} "caused" the inconsistency.

seems to be a potentially flawed selection system, and many researchers would not adopt such a procedure in practice.[15]

IICATOR VARIABLES

In many instances in social science research, variables can be categorical in nature. We have already routinely encountered categorical variables throughout this text: for example, when one of the variables was a person's gender (two categories: 1 for males, 0 for females, or vice-versa). *In this text, we will define "indicator variables" as a set of 0 versus 1 measures that determine which category a particular data point belongs to.* With such a scoring scheme, we can still apply all the regression and correlation formulas listed herein. For example, in Chapter II we already used dichotomous variables in the formulas for Pearson r (and noted that the field sometimes renamed the resulting measures "phi's" or "point-biserials"). Also, in the end-of-chapter problems, gender (coded 0 or 1) was routinely placed in regression analyses. Then, in Chapter VII we considered the partial correlation between gender and salary, controlling for previous experience. Finally, in Chapter IX we noted that coding for gender or minority status was routinely done in applications of test fairness models.

The point I want to make is that indicator variables can be extremely useful and can make multiple regression even *more* flexible. For example, suppose a researcher is interested in seeing if salaries (Y) for a particular job are greater for males than females. So, code X_1 as 1 if male, code X_1 as 0 if female, and correlate Y with X_1. However, as in Chapter VII, the researcher might argue that such a correlation is misleading (i.e., it may be that males in the study have, on average, higher levels of education, greater performance, more previous years of experience on the job, etc.). Therefore, salary differences are not necessarily bias but might be due to differences in compensable factors. Suppose the researcher thinks of 12 such explanatory variables (call them $X_2, \ldots, X_{13}$). It is then common to estimate the regression

$$\hat{Y} = b_0 + b_1 X_1 + b_2 X_2 + \cdots + b_{13} X_{13}$$

and test the hypothesis H_0: $\mathbf{B}_1 = 0$. Remember the interpretation of this test? Right! The null hypothesis will be rejected only if X_1 (gender) is related to salary *over and above* these other explanatory variables. Indeed, if b_1 is significant, the organization should be concerned about potential bias in their salaries (because

[15] If you're the researcher in this case, what might you do next? I suppose you could ignore the suppressor and just use X_1. However, since X_1 and X_2 are positively related, individuals who have more experience will do better on the selection test. If computer experience is related to socioeconomic status, and in turn minority status, then use of X_1 alone has potential for substantial adverse impact. An alternative approach to the whole problem might be to redesign the selection test (X_1). For example, let everyone practice (and become familiar with the computer) as long as they want before actually taking the measure of X_1. Indeed, this is what Aerospace Science attempted to do. However, it's not clear whether or not this is practical or how long you'd have to wait. Can you think of other ideas?

salaries can't be completely explained by the other factors). Further, if b_1 is significant, interpretation of its magnitude is straightforward. That is, since females are coded 0, the weight b_1 will have no effect on $\hat{Y}$ for females. However, for males, $\hat{Y}$ will be increased by an amount equal to $b_1(X_1) = b_1(1) = b_1$. Therefore, b_1 is the average difference in male and female salaries after the other X's are controlled for (i.e., the mean salary bias).

Multiple Categories

All of the examples of indicators in this book used dichotomous (two-category) scoring. The possibilities here are numerous: male or female, union or nonunion, an item being right or wrong, a score being above or below the median, etc. However, regression can become even more flexible by incorporating variables with many categories. For example, suppose that Professor Gretzky (remember him?) also wants to add student's major as a predictor of course grade (Y) beyond absence (X_1) and hours studied (X_2). For simplicity, assume all students are either management, marketing, finance, or accounting majors. Then, you will need *three* indicator variables as follows:

$X_3 = 1$ if management major; 0 otherwise
$X_4 = 1$ if marketing major; 0 otherwise
$X_5 = 1$ if finance major; 0 otherwise

These three indicator variables completely determine which of four majors a student has chosen. For example, suppose I tell you a particular student scores $X_3 = 0$, $X_4 = 1$, $X_5 = 0$. What's his or her major? Right, marketing! What would an accounting student's scores on these indicators be? Right, $X_3 = X_4 = X_5 = 0$.

[*Note*: Notice that you don't need a fourth indicator variable to determine four categories. If you have k categories, you always need $(k - 1)$ indicators. If you made the mistake of adding X_6 (i.e., 1 if accounting, 0 otherwise) above, what would happen? Well, since X_3, X_4, X_5 completely determine membership in the four categories, X_6 can be perfectly predicted by the other three X's, and the regression would not run at all. For example, check out the formula for $SD(b_i)$ in Equation VIII.L. In this case, the value of $R^2_{i.\text{all other } X's}$ will be 1.0 and you'll end up dividing by zero! The computer software package will print an error message at this point.]

To repeat, it's taken three indicator variables to characterize the four-category student major variable. *To test the hypothesis that student major significantly predicts course grade (Y), we need to look at the set of three indicator variables and ask if this set significantly increases R^2.* In other words, compute both $R^2_{Y.12}$ and $R^2_{Y.12345}$ *and ask if* $R^2_{\text{diff}} = R^2_{Y.12345} - R^2_{Y.12}$ is significantly greater than zero. In Chapter VIII we stated that $H_0: \mathbf{R}^2 = 0$ could be tested by

$$F = \frac{(n - p - 1)R^2}{(1 - R^2)(p)}$$

or, equivalently,

X.C
$$F = \frac{R^2/p}{(1 - R^2)/(n - p - 1)}$$

where F had p and $(n - p - 1)$ degrees of freedom.

The test for R^2_{diff} looks very similar. First, the denominator of Equation X.C $[(1 - R^2)/(n - p - 1)]$ doesn't change. It has to do with overall error. So, let it be, calculating R^2 with *all* variables and letting p be the total number of variables. Second, the numerator (R^2/p) shifts slightly. Since we are interested in testing R^2_{diff}, replace R^2 in the numerator by R^2_{diff}. Also, the value of p in the numerator of Equation X.C was originally the number of variables used in computing overall R^2. Because we are now interested in R^2_{diff}, the value for p in the numerator is replaced by the number of variables unique to R^2_{diff}, i.e., p_{diff}. (In our case, $p_{\text{diff}} = k - 1 = 3$ since $(k - 1)$ indicator variables are needed to document k categories.) So, the test for R^2_{diff} becomes

X.D
$$F = \frac{R^2_{\text{diff}}/p_{\text{diff}}}{(1 - R^2)/(n - p - 1)}$$

where F has p_{diff} degrees of freedom in the numerator and $(n - p - 1)$ degrees of freedom in the denominator.

An example The data in Table VIII.1 have been augmented in Table X.2 to include the students' majors using these indicators. Take a look at this table and make sure you understand just how the indicators were constructed. Do you understand, for example, that there are five management majors and nine accounting majors? Good! Note that the data for X_3, X_4, and X_5 are all ones and zeros. That's O.K. In fact, just as when we created interaction terms (see previous chapter), the machine doesn't care *where* the X's come from.

When I pushed the regression button on my computer, the result was

$$\hat{Y} = 86.261 - .643X_1 + 3.027X_2 + 1.033X_3 + 1.908X_4 + 2.799X_5$$

and $R^2_{Y.12345} = .362$. Other than the constant term, the *only* b-weight even approaching statistical significance is $b_2 = 3.027$. This is consistent with our earlier analysis of these data (i.e., hours studied seemed to matter). Also, in Chapter VIII we found $R^2_{Y.12} = .359$. Therefore R^2_{diff} is a very small $.362 - .359 = .003$.

To statistically test this difference, apply Equation X.D. This yields a sample statistic of

$$F = \frac{.003/(4 - 1)}{(1 - .362)/(21 - 5 - 1)} = .024$$

TABLE X.2 DATA FOR COURSE EXAM TOTAL, NUMBER OF ABSENCES, HOURS STUDIED PER WEEK, AND INDICATORS FOR STUDENT MAJOR

Student	Exam total, Y	Absences, X_1	Hours studied, X_2	Major		
				X_3	X_4	X_5
1	101	4	8	1	0	0
2	138	0	11	1	0	0
3	118	5	11	1	0	0
4	93	8	9	1	0	0
5	136	0	14	1	0	0
6	114	2	12	0	1	0
7	93	3	6	0	1	0
8	136	0	11	0	1	0
9	136	1	14	0	1	0
10	93	4	12	0	0	0
11	102	0	11	0	0	0
12	127	8	7	0	0	0
13	105	5	12	0	0	0
14	148	0	15	0	0	0
15	113	5	7	0	0	0
16	99	5	5	0	0	0
17	113	13	8	0	0	0
18	111	0	9	0	0	0
19	126	3	12	0	0	1
20	121	4	12	0	0	1
21	121	1	11	0	0	1

where F has 3 and 15 df. Since the $p = .05$ critical value is 3.29 (see the Appendix, Table A.2), the difference in R^2 due to the set of indicators is not significant. That is, there are no overall significant mean differences in course grades across student majors after accounting for the other predictors.[16]

Indicators are used   It should be apparent that the capacity to incorporate categorical variables in regression, using indicators, makes multiple regression analysis very flexible. I have seen indicators used for gender, racial grouping, type of training, type of performance feedback, type of job, corporate strategy, and so on. For examples within strategic management see either Aulakh, Kotabe, and Teegen (1999) or Johnson, Sambharya, and Bobko (1989). The former study controlled for country (two indicators for the three countries of Brazil, Chile, and Mexico) as well as industry type (three indicators for four industries). The latter

[16] The test in Equation X.D indicates whether the set of indicator variables significantly increases R^2. That's because the variable student major is represented by the entire set of indicators. One *could* look at the individual *b*-weights. In fact, notice that I randomly chose management, marketing, and finance majors to be represented by 1s in the coding of X_3, X_4, and X_5. Thus, accounting majors received all 0's in the system. It turns out (see Cohen and Cohen, 1983, for a nice explanation) that the interpretation of the *b*-weights is always relative to accounting majors: i.e., $b_3 = 1.033$ means that management majors score, on average, 1.033 points higher than accounting majors (not a significant difference).

study grouped airlines into four overall strategic orientations using three indicators. In both cases, the indicators helped predict firm-level outcome variables. I encourage you to consider indicator variables whenever you want to incorporate categorical variables as predictors in a regression.

ANALYSIS OF VARIANCE

Now that we've discussed regression and the use of indicator variables, it's just a very short step to analyzing experimental data using the analysis of variance. First of all, as we shall see below *ANOVA is just a special case of regression.* Indeed, note that we reported regression results using ANOVA tables (e.g., sums of squares total, regression, and error)!

Now let's think about regression and a traditional one-way ANOVA. In regression, we had a bunch of X's and were trying to predict Y. In a one-way ANOVA, we have a dependent (or outcome) variable (Y), and a single factor, with multiple levels. The interest is in knowing whether $\bar{Y}$ differs across the multiple levels of the factors. This is the same as asking, Can values of Y be at all predicted from knowing which level of the factor a person is in? Thus, we want to predict Y from knowledge of factor levels (i.e., the factor level is like an X). Since the factor is by definition categorical in nature, then all we need to do is create indicator variables (e.g., if there are three levels, create two indicators). Then, conduct a regression predicting Y from these indicators.

The resulting regression (and its analysis of variance) will be identical to a traditional one-way ANOVA.

For example, suppose we have a one-way ANOVA in which the outcome variable (Y) is job performance and the single factor is type of training. Suppose this factor has three levels: no training, classroom training, experimental training. The format or design for this situation is depicted in Figure 10.7.

In this case, $n = 12$, the number of categories (k) is 3, and the Y_i represent each person's score on the dependent variable. The traditional analysis of variance would produce:

Source	Sum of squares	df
Factor *A*	SS factor *A*	$k - 1 = 2$
Error	SSE	$n - k - 1 = 8$
Total	SST	$n - 1 = 10$

To convert this problem to a regression, note again that the independent variable (type of training) is categorical. Thus, one could create indicator

FACTOR A (type of training)		
None	Classroom	Experiential
Y_1	Y_5	Y_9
Y_2	Y_6	Y_{10}
Y_3	Y_7	Y_{11}
Y_4	Y_8	Y_{12}

FIGURE 10.7   Depiction of a one-way analysis of variance (cell size of 4).

variables as follows: $X_1 = 1$ if classroom training, 0 otherwise: $X_2 = 1$ if experiential training, 0 otherwise. For example, person 11's data would be $Y = Y_{11}$, $X_1 = 0$, $X_2 = 1$. Now you try. What would person 2's data look like? Good, it's $Y = Y_2$, $X_1 = 0$, $X_2 = 0$. At this point, one conducts the regression

$$\hat{Y} = b_0 + b_1 X_1 + b_2 X_2$$

Paralleling the previous discussion in Chapter VIII, the regression ANOVA table would then be

Source	Sum of squares	df
Regression	SSR	$p = 2$
Error	SSE	$n - p - 1 = 8$
Total	SST	$n - 1 = 10$

The point is that

The two ANOVA tables (for the traditional experimental design and the regression) would be identical!

For example, SSR = SS factor A across the two tables. Also, note that all degrees of freedom are identical across the tables. Indeed, this is why you were taught to let factor A have $(k - 1)$ degrees of freedom—because that's how many regression indicator variables you need to characterize that factor!

At this point, I hope I've "tweaked" your interest about the relation between experimental design and regression. This book is on regression and correlation, not on the design of experiments, but I did want to point out that most of the lessons learned herein apply to experimental design as well.[17] If you want to know more, I refer you to several excellent discussions of how to code experimental data to fit regression (e.g., Cohen, 1968; Cohen and Cohen, 1983;

---

[17] Indeed, take a peek again at the end of Chapter V. There we noticed that even range restriction (or its opposite, range enhancement) operated in design considerations!

Pedhazur, 1977; 1982). However, I can't resist two further comments on the relation between regression and design: one about incorporating additional factors and the other about cell sizes.

dding Other Factors

It's not difficult to extend the above example to two-way designs (and beyond). For example, suppose there was another factor in the experiment, say, the gender of the employee (factor B). Then, the design might look like Figure 10.8.

In Figure 10.8, there are three levels of factor A ($k = 3$) and two levels of factor B ($j = 2$). A traditional ANOVA table would decompose the sum of squares as:

Source	Sum of squares	df
Factor A	SS factor A	$k - 1 = 2$
Factor B	SS factor B	$j - 1 = 1$
Interaction ($A \times B$)	SS $A \times B$	$(k - 1) \times (j - 1) = 2$
Error	SSE	6
Total	SST	$n - 1 = 11$

Now, what would the regression analysis look like? Notice that we already concocted two indicator variables (X_1 and X_2) for factor A. For factor B, we need to add only one more indicator, X_3 (e.g., females coded 1, males coded 0). Again, note that the number of indicators corresponds *exactly* to the degrees of freedom for factors A and B in the ANOVA (i.e., they're conceptually the same phenomena). Further, think how regression incorporated interaction. When there were two predictors, we simply multiplied the variables to create a new interaction term (see Chapter IX). In the situation in Figure 10.8, we have two categorical factors, so we have to *conceptually multiply the two factors*. Since there are two indicators for factor A and one for factor B, we need to create two interaction variables: $X_4 = X_1 \times X_3$ and $X_5 = X_2 \times X_3$. Thus, to re-create the ANOVA table, one would have to conduct a regression predicting Y from X_1, X_2, X_3, X_4, and X_5.[18] This is why there are 2 df for the interaction sum of squares. And, as previously noted in Chapter IX, this is also the reason why design books label interactions as products (i.e., $A \times B$): because they are!

ell Size (and Collinearity)

Note that when we tried to interpret R^2 in multiple regression, we made a big deal about the fact that it was difficult to apportion the overall R^2 to particular X's (see the discussion in Chapter VIII). Remember why this was the case?

---

[18] For example, take person 11 again. Note that the person is male. His scores would be $Y = Y_{11}$, $X_1 = 0$, and $X_2 = 1$ as before. Also, $X_3 = 0$, $X_4 = 0 \times 0 = 0$, and $X_5 = 1 \times 0 = 0$. Now you try it for person 2. I get $Y = Y_2$, $X_1 = 0$, $X_2 = 0$, $X_3 = 0$, $X_4 = 0 \times 0 = 0$, $X_5 = 0 \times 0 = 0$. Do you agree?

		FACTOR A (type of training)		
		None	Classroom	Experiential
FACTOR B	Female	Y_1	Y_5	Y_9
(gender)		Y_2	Y_6	Y_{10}
	Male	Y_3	Y_7	Y_{11}
		Y_4	Y_8	Y_{12}

FIGURE 10.8 Depiction of a two-way analysis of variance with cell sizes of 2.

Right! When the X's were correlated, it was very difficult to decide which particular X should get the credit for the value of R^2.

I wanted to point out that traditional analysis of variance uses a neat trick to avoid this problem. Indeed, notice that there was never any question in your design courses as to how much of the total sum of squares should be allocated to each of the factors. How does ANOVA do this? *The answer is quite simple: make sure you have equal numbers of data points in each combination of factors (i.e., each cell).*

To see why this is the case, look back at Figure 10.8. In this figure, each combination of factors has exactly two individuals (i.e., all cell sizes are 2). Now, suppose I tell you that I have picked a person at random from the overall data set of $n = 12$ and suppose I tell you that this person is female (i.e., I tell you something about factor B). Does this tell you anything about which level of factor A the person is in? No, because for all females, there's still an equal chance (one-third) that she is in a particular training type. Thus, *factors A and B are uncorrelated, and sums of squares can be unambiguously assigned to each factor.*[19]

To make the point more strongly, what would happen if we added six more females to the experiential training condition? In this case, there would now be cell sizes of 2 in five of the conditions, and one cell size of 8. Now go back to the earlier question. If I tell you that the randomly drawn person was female (information about factor B), this should give you some probabilistic information about factor A (i.e., the person most likely belongs to the experiential condition). Thus, when cell sizes are unequal, factors A and B are correlated and life isn't as pretty. Now do you see why it was suggested that you put equal numbers of data points in each cell? Pretty neat trick, huh?

CODA

I hope that over the course of these chapters you have been excited by how interesting correlation and regression analysis can be. Multiple regression is a particularly flexible technique. In addition to its direct relationship to experimen-

---

[19] By the way, this is true for the main effects, A and B only. The interaction term is a different story. However, ANOVA solves that just like we did in interactive regression. That is, put the main effects in the model first. Then, the sum of squares due to $A \times B$ is what's left *only* after A and B have their chance.

tal design, it can be made even more flexible by the use of indicator variables, polynomial terms, and interactions among predictors. Indeed, the topics covered in this chapter are just an introduction to the more global domain of multivariate techniques. Here are some brief summaries of the next layer of problems that have been addressed by statisticians.

Suppose there are many Y's   In multiple regression, we have considered many X's but only one Y. However, there are occasions when multiple outcome measures might be considered (e.g., when multiple performance measures are available).[20] So, what do you do? You could conduct a regression for each Y, but this process would be subject to increased overall Type I error rates. Or, you could combine the Y's (via a priori weights, subject matter expert judgments, or simple addition). Or, you could let the machine combine the Y's, just as regression combines the X's, based on statistical properties of the data. This latter technique is called "canonical correlation analysis."

Suppose there's a single Y but it's categorical in nature   Note that we handled categorical X's through the use of indicator variables. The same thing can be done if Y is categorical.[21] To the extent that Y had more than two categories, this implies that there would be multiple indicators of Y. Thus, one would have to conduct a "canonical correlation analysis" where the Y's were indicators. Since this is tantamount to predicting (from the X's) which category on Y the person is in, such a technique is often called "multiple group discriminant analysis." If there are only two categories and consequently only one indicator variable on Y, the technique reduces back to a regular old multiple regression (with Y being 0 or 1). In this case, the technique is labeled "two-group discriminant analysis." Such a situation is commonplace in social science research. For example, the turnover literature is chock full of articles (some referenced in Chapter V) that report attempts to predict the outcome variable of stayers versus leavers from a variety of X's (employee satisfaction, geographical preferences, availability of alternative jobs, etc.). Finally note that even though the dependent variable (Y) might truly be dichotomous (e.g., 0 versus 1), the use of a regression with continuous X's will create a continuum of predicted values $(\hat{Y})$ in the sample. Thus, $\hat{Y}$ might be $-.35$ or $.76$ or 1.2, even though the true Y can be only 0 or 1. In order to restrict $\hat{Y}$ to be in the range 0 to 1, some statisticians replace the linear model introduced in Chapter VI with a "logistic

---

[20] For example, Cascio (1998, p. 42) provides an entire table of performance dimensions such as quantity of output, quality of output, leadership potential, teamwork, absences, and so on.

[21] For example, you might be trying to predict which of several career paths individuals choose after college. Or, a management researcher might try to predict which of several strategic orientations a corporation chooses to adopt. Can you think of categorical dependent variables in *your* areas of interest?

regression function'' (cf. Maddala, 1988, for a review of this technique). Such an analysis more naturally reflects the probability model implied by dichotomous dependent variables. Ganzach, Saporta, and Weber (2000) provide a nice illustration of the pros and cons of logistic regression versus the least squares regression analyses presented in this book.[22]

Suppose there are no Y's (or no X's, but not both!)   It is often the case that you have a bunch of variables and just want to know how they're related to each other rather than their relationship to some outside criterion. This situation most typically happens in measurement studies where the variables are test items and you want to know how the items interrelate. In this situation, the questions are often focused on how the test items are structured, how they group together, how many subdimensions there are in the test, etc. Techniques to answer such questions include ''factor analysis,'' ''cluster analysis,'' and ''multidimensional scaling analysis.'' You can also cluster or factor multiple measures of performance, different types of organizations, individuals, etc.

Suppose causality is involved   As noted throughout this book, our interest in regression was in the prediction of Y from a set of X's. Sometimes the X's themselves can have a prespecified temporal sequence. If so, techniques will be concerned with causal modeling. (Very simple causal models were introduced in Chapter VII, in particular Figures 7.6 through 7.8. Don't be lazy, go back and take a peek!) A relatively old technique in this arena is labeled ''path analysis.'' However, if you believe that your variables are measured with some unreliability, you have multiple measures of each variable (i.e., the variables factor together into constructs), or causality may be reciprocal, then relatively newer techniques are needed, such as ''two-stage least squares regression'' or ''linear structural relations (LISREL) analysis.''

All these techniques are fascinating and have the potential to help us triangulate our understanding of human behavior. To cover them all would take many books. Indeed, many books and articles have been written about these methods, and I hope this particular text has motivated you to want to learn and understand even more about the fun of thinking about statistics.[23] Happy reading!

PROBLEMS

1 In Problem 1 in Chapter VIII, the multiple regression equation that predicted performance from the currently used aptitude test (X_4) and the new test (X_3) was $\hat{Y} = -2.993 + .713X_3 + .547X_4$ with a value of $R^2_{Y.34} = .562$ (based on $n = 15$).

---

[22] See Huselid and Day (1991) for another statement that traditional regression models might be statistically inappropriate when the dependent variable is dichotomous. In fact, empirical work by these authors suggests that some findings in the turnover literature are a function of misapplications of linear regression models.

[23] If you like the style of this book, consider Bobko (1990) as an intuitively based source on multivariate techniques. In increasing order of difficulty, other books I have personally found useful are Dillon and Goldstein (1984), Morrison (1976), and Anderson (1958). These are but a few of the many books and articles worth perusing.

   a Compute Wherry's estimate of the population $\mathbf{R}^2$.

   b Compute the Lord-Nicholson estimate of R^2 in future samples.

2 In Problem 2 in Chapter IX, the quadratic regression equation predicting supervisory potential (Y_2) from previous performance (Y_1) and its square was $Y_2 = -.669 + 1.257Y_1 + .014Y_1^2$, with a multiple R^2 of .994 (based on $n = 15$).

   a Compute Wherry's estimate of the population $\mathbf{R}^2$.

   b Compute the Lord-Nicholson estimate of R^2 in future samples.

   c Compare the amount of shrinkage in this problem with the amount of shrinkage in Problem 1. Based on our analysis of Table X.1, could we have predicted which of the problems would have had proportionately less shrinkage?

3 Suppose that researchers in your company's personnel department want to evaluate the effects of gender, undergraduate major (hard sciences, social sciences, liberal arts, other) and their interaction on subsequent job performance.

   a One researcher suggests that regression is needed; another researcher suggests that ANOVA is needed. What do you tell them?

   b Using indicator variables, set up a coding scheme that would enable the first researcher to use least squares regression. (*Hint*: For the two categorical predictors and their interaction, you should have a total of seven variables.)

4 In Chapter VIII, I referred to an article by Provan and Skinner (1989) that looked at opportunistic behavior (Y) of farm and power equipment dealers when these dealers engaged in relationships with their primary supplier. The two authors predicted opportunistic behavior from five X's. Two of the X's (say, X_1 and X_2) were measures of control the suppliers had over the dealers. The remaining three predictors were all somewhat different measures of the dealer's dependence upon the primary supplier (e.g., how many other suppliers the dealer had).

   Provan and Skinner found that the two measures of control significantly predicted opportunistic behavior ($R_{Y.12}^2 = .07$). When they placed all five predictors in the regression, they obtained $R_{Y.12345}^2 = .16$. Using $p = .05$, conduct a significance test to see if the set of three dependence predictors significantly increased the value of R^2. (*Hints*: I need to tell you the sample size. It was $n = 226$. Also, you may want to take a peek at Equation X.D. Also, in determining the critical value from the Appendix, use either 120 or infinity for the denominator degrees of freedom.)

REFERENCES

Aerospace Sciences, Inc. (1991). *Air traffic control specialist pretraining screen preliminary validation: Final report*. (Final report delivered to the Federal Aviation Administration under contract DTFA01-90-Y-01034). Washington, DC: FAA Office of the Deputy Administrator.

Anderson, T. (1958). *An introduction to multivariate statistical analysis*. New York: Wiley.

Aulakh, P., Kotabe, M., and Teegen, H. (2000). Export strategies and performance of firms from emerging economies: Evidence from Brazil, Chile, and Mexico. *Academy of Management Journal, 43*, 342–361.

Bartlett, C., and Green, C. (1966). Clinical prediction: Does one sometimes know too much? *Journal of Counseling Psychology, 13*, 267–270.

Bobko, P. (1990). Multivariate correlational data analysis. In M. Dunnette and L. Hough (Eds.), *Handbook of industrial & organizational psychology* (2nd. ed.), Vol. 1, pp. 637–686. Palo Alto, CA: Consulting Psychologists Press.

Browne, M. (1975). Predictive validity of a linear regression equation. *British Journal of Mathematical and Statistical Psychology, 28*, 79–87.

Cascio, W. (1998). *Applied psychology in human resource management* (5th ed.). Englewood Cliffs, NJ: Prentice-Hall.

Cattin, P. (1980). Estimation of the predictive power of a regression model. *Journal of Applied Psychology, 65*, 407–414.

Claudy, J. (1972). A comparison of five variable weighting procedures. *Educational and Psychological Measurement, 32*, 311–322.

Cohen, J. (1968). Multiple regression as a general data-analytic system. *Psychological Bulletin, 70*, 426–443.

Cohen, J., and Cohen, P. (1983). *Applied multiple regression/correlation analysis for the behavioral sciences* (2nd ed.), Hillsdale, NJ: Lawrence Erlbaum.

Conger, A. (1974). A revised definition for suppressor variables: A guide to their identification and interpretation. *Educational and Psychological Measurement, 34*, 35–46.

Cook, R., and Stewart, T. (1975). A comparison of seven methods for obtaining subjective descriptions of judgment policy. *Organizational Behavior and Human Performance, 13*, 31–45.

Darlington, R. (1978). Reduced-variance regression. *Psychological Bulletin, 85*, 1238–1255.

Dawes, R., and Corrigan, B. (1974). Linear models in decision making. *Psychological Bulletin, 81*, 95–106.

Dempster, A., Schatzoff, M., and Wermuth, N. (1977). A simulation study of alternatives to ordinary least squares. *Journal of the American Statistical Association, 72*, 77–91.

Dillon, W., and Goldstein, M. (1984). *Multivariate analysis: Methods and applications*. New York: Wiley.

Dorans, N., and Drasgow, F. (1978). Alternative weighting schemes for linear prediction. *Organizational Behavior and Human Performance, 21*, 316–345.

Dulebohn, J., and Ferris, G. (1999). The role of influence tactics in perceptions of performance evaluations' fairness. *Academy of Management Journal, 42*, 288–303.

Einhorn, H., and Hogarth, R. (1975). Unit weighting schemes for decision making. *Organizational Behavior and Human Performance, 13*, 171–192.

Evans, G., and Carrere, S. (1991). Traffic congestion, perceived control, and psycho-physiological stress among urban bus drivers. *Journal of Applied Psychology, 76*, 658–663.

Faden, V., and Bobko, P. (1982). Validity shrinkage in ridge regression: A simulation study. *Educational and Psychological Measurement, 42*, 73–86.

Ganzach, Y., Saporta, I., and Weber, Y. (2000). Interaction in linear versus logistic models: A substantive illustration using the relationship between motivation, ability, and performance. *Organizational Research Methods, 3*, 237–253.

Guilkey, D., and Murphy, J. (1975). Directed ridge regression techniques in cases of multi-collinearity. *Journal of the American Statistical Association, 70*, 767–775.

Gunst, R., and Mason, R. (1977). Biased estimation in regression: An evaluation using mean squared error. *Journal of the American Statistical Association, 72*, 616–628.

Hoerl, A., and Kennard, R. (1970). Ridge regression: Applications to nonorthogonal problems. *Technometrics, 12*, 69–82.

Huselid, M., and Day, N. (1991). Organizational commitment, job involvement, and turnover: A substantive and methodological analysis. *Journal of Applied Psychology, 76*, 380–391.

Johnson, N., Sambharya, R., and Bobko, P. (1989). The relationship between deregulation, business strategy, and wages in the airline industry. *Industrial Relations, 28*, 419–430.

Lautenschlager, G. (1990). Sources of imprecision in formula cross-validated multiple correlations. *Journal of Applied Psychology, 75*, 460–462.

Lord, F. (1950). *Efficiency of prediction when a regression equation from one sample is used in a new sample*. Research Bulletin 50–40. Princeton, NJ: Educational Testing Service.

Maddala, G. (1988). *Introduction to econometrics*. New York: Macmillan.

Montgomery, D., and Morrison, D. (1973). On note on adjusting R^2. *Journal of Finance, 28*, 1009–1013.

Morrison, D. (1976). *Multivariate statistical methods* (2nd ed.). New York: McGraw-Hill.

Nicholson, G. (1960). Prediction in future samples. In I. Olkin (Ed.), *Contributions to probability and statistics*, pp. 424–427. Stanford, CA: Stanford University Press.

Pedhazur, E. (1977). Coding subjects in repeated measures designs. *Psychological Bulletin, 84*, 298–305.

Pedhazur, E. (1982). *Multiple regression in behavioral research*. New York: Holt Rinehart.

Pinder, C. (1984). *Work and motivation: Theory, issues, and applications*. Glenview, IL: Scott, Foresman.

Price, B. (1977). Ridge regression: Application to nonexperimental data. *Psychological Bulletin, 84*, 759–766.

Provan, K., and Skinner, S. (1989). Interorganizational dependence and control as predictors of opportunism in dealer-supplier relations. *Academy of Management Journal, 32*, 202–212.

Raju, N., Bilgic, R., Edwards, J., and Fleer, P. (1997). Methodology review: Estimation of population validity and cross-validity, and the use of equal weights in prediction. *Applied Psychological Measurement, 21*, 291–306.

Rozeboom, W. (1978). The estimation of cross-validated multiple correlation: A clarification. *Psychological Bulletin, 85*, 1348–1351.

Rozeboom, W. (1979). Ridge regression: Bonanza or beguilement? *Psychological Bulletin, 86*, 242–249.

Schmidt, F. (1971). The reliability of differences between linear regression weights in applied differential psychology. *Educational and Psychological Measurement, 32*, 879–886.

Schmitt, N., Coyle, B., and Rauschenberger, J. (1977). A Monte Carlo evaluation of three formula estimates of cross-validated multiple correlation. *Psychological Bulletin, 84*, 751–758.

Thorndike, R. (1978). *Correlational procedures for research*. New York: Gardner Press.

Wainer, H. (1976). Estimating coefficients in linear models: It don't make no nevermind. *Psychological Bulletin, 83*, 213–217.

Wherry, R. (1931). A new formula for predicting shrinkage of the coefficient of multiple correlation. *Annals of Mathematical Statistics, 2*, 440–457.

TABLES OF CRITICAL VALUES

TABLE A.1   UPPER CRITICAL VALUES FOR THE *t*-DISTRIBUTION WITH GIVEN DEGREES OF FREEDOM†

	One-sided significance level			
	.05	.025	.01	.005
	Two-sided significance level			
df	.10	.05	.02	.01
1	6.314	12.706	31.821	63.657
2	2.920	4.303	6.965	9.925
3	2.353	3.182	4.541	5.841
4	2.132	2.776	3.747	4.604
5	2.015	2.571	3.365	4.032
6	1.943	2.447	3.143	3.707
7	1.895	2.365	2.998	3.499
8	1.860	2.306	2.896	3.355
9	1.833	2.262	2.821	3.250
10	1.812	2.228	2.764	3.169
11	1.796	2.201	2.718	3.106
12	1.782	2.179	2.681	3.055
13	1.771	2.160	2.650	3.012
14	1.761	2.145	2.624	2.977
15	1.753	2.131	2.602	2.947
16	1.746	2.120	2.583	2.921
17	1.740	2.110	2.567	2.898
18	1.734	2.101	2.552	2.878
19	1.729	2.093	2.539	2.861
20	1.725	2.086	2.528	2.845
21	1.721	2.080	2.518	2.831
22	1.717	2.074	2.508	2.819
23	1.714	2.069	2.500	2.807
24	1.711	2.064	2.492	2.797
25	1.708	2.060	2.485	2.787
26	1.706	2.056	2.479	2.779
27	1.703	2.052	2.473	2.771
28	1.701	2.048	2.467	2.763
29	1.699	2.045	2.462	2.756
30	1.697	2.042	2.457	2.750
40	1.684	2.021	2.423	2.704
60	1.671	2.000	2.390	2.660
100	1.660	1.984	2.364	2.626
120	1.658	1.980	2.358	2.617
(∞)‡	1.645	1.960	2.326	2.576

† Note that these are upper percentage points. For example, with a one-sided *t*-test with 4 df, the critical value of *t* for *p* = .05 will be 2.132. For a two-sided test with 4 df and *p* = .05, the critical *t* will be ±2.776.

‡ Note that as the degrees of freedom approaches infinity, the *t*-distribution becomes the standard normal distribution. Thus, the critical values for a *z*-test may be found in the last row of this table.

TABLE A.2 UPPER 5% CRITICAL VALUES OF THE *F*-DISTRIBUTION FOR SELECT
NUMERATOR DEGREES OF FREEDOM (n_1) AND DENOMINATOR DEGREES OF FREEDOM (n_2)

n_2	n_1							
	1	2	3	4	5	10	20	40
1	161.40	199.50	215.70	224.60	230.20	241.90	248.00	251.10
2	18.51	19.00	19.16	19.25	19.30	19.40	19.45	19.47
3	10.13	9.55	9.28	9.12	9.01	8.79	8.66	8.59
4	7.71	6.94	6.59	6.39	6.26	5.96	5.80	5.72
5	6.61	5.79	5.41	5.19	5.05	4.74	4.56	4.46
6	5.99	5.14	4.76	4.53	4.39	4.06	3.87	3.77
7	5.59	4.74	4.35	4.12	3.97	3.64	3.44	3.34
8	5.32	4.46	4.07	3.84	3.69	3.35	3.15	3.04
9	5.12	4.26	3.86	3.63	3.48	3.14	2.94	2.83
10	4.96	4.10	3.71	3.48	3.33	2.98	2.77	2.66
11	4.84	3.98	3.59	3.36	3.20	2.85	2.65	2.53
12	4.75	3.89	3.49	3.26	3.11	2.75	2.54	2.43
13	4.67	3.81	3.41	3.18	3.03	2.67	2.46	2.34
14	4.60	3.74	3.34	3.11	2.96	2.60	2.39	2.27
15	4.54	3.68	3.29	3.06	2.90	2.54	2.33	2.20
16	4.49	3.63	3.24	3.01	2.85	2.49	2.28	2.15
17	4.45	3.59	3.20	2.96	2.81	2.45	2.23	2.10
18	4.41	3.55	3.16	2.93	2.77	2.41	2.19	2.06
19	4.38	3.52	3.13	2.90	2.74	2.38	2.16	2.03
20	4.35	3.49	3.10	2.87	2.71	2.35	2.12	1.99
21	4.32	3.47	3.07	2.84	2.68	2.32	2.10	1.96
22	4.30	3.44	3.05	2.82	2.66	2.30	2.07	1.94
23	4.28	3.42	3.03	2.80	2.64	2.27	2.05	1.91
24	4.26	3.40	3.01	2.78	2.62	2.25	2.03	1.89
25	4.24	3.39	2.99	2.76	2.60	2.24	2.01	1.87
26	4.23	3.37	2.98	2.74	2.59	2.22	1.99	1.85
27	4.21	3.35	2.96	2.73	2.57	2.20	1.97	1.84
28	4.20	3.34	2.95	2.71	2.56	2.19	1.96	1.82
29	4.18	3.33	2.93	2.70	2.55	2.18	1.94	1.81
30	4.17	3.32	2.92	2.69	2.53	2.16	1.93	1.79
40	4.08	3.23	2.84	2.61	2.45	2.08	1.84	1.69
60	4.00	3.15	2.76	2.53	2.37	1.99	1.75	1.59
120	3.92	3.07	2.68	2.45	2.29	1.91	1.66	1.50
(∞)	3.84	3.00	2.60	2.37	2.21	1.83	1.57	1.39

Tables A.1 and A.2 have been adapted from tables 12 and 18 of the *Biometrika
Tables for Statisticians* (3rd ed.), Vol. 1, 1966, Cambridge University Press, E. S.
Pearson and H. O. Hartley (Eds.), with permission of the Trustees of *Biometrika*.

ANSWERS TO SELECTED PROBLEMS

Chapter II

1 Using Equation II.A (or the alternate formula immediately following that equation), one obtains $r = .674$.

2 The value of r remains at .674 because r is unchanged by linear transformations of the variables.

3 $r^2 = (.674)^2 = .454$. Thus, approximately 45% of the variation in performance ratings is associated with variation in test scores.

5 Using Equation II.C, one obtains phi $= -.327$. The negative sign means that females ($X_1 = 1$; i.e., the largest value on X_1) are more likely to be rated bad ($X_2 = 0$; i.e., the lowest value on X_2).

6 The values of d for the 15 subjects are, respectively, 5, -6.5, 5, -2, -7, -2, 0, -1, -2, 0, 4, -1, 4.5, 2, and 1. Since $n = 15$, Equation II.B yields $r_s = .649$.

7 Using the equation for Pearson r, the point-biserial is .088. The positive sign means that females ($X_1 = 1$; i.e., the largest value on X_1) are more likely to score higher on the test than males ($X_1 = 0$).

8 The completed correlation matrix is

	X_1	X_2	X_3	Y
X_1	1.000	$-.327$	.088	.206
X_2		1.000	.792	.261
X_3			1.000	.674
Y				1.000

Chapter III

1a Using Equation III.A, the sample t-value is 3.290. With a two-sided test, $p = .05$, and $df = 13$, the critical t is 2.160. Therefore, reject the null hypothesis that the population correlation is zero.

1b Assume the value of .60 is a population value. One must then convert each correlational value to a Fisher's z (.60 converts to .693; .674 converts to .818). The numerator of the test statistic is the difference between these two converted values. The denominator is the square root of $n - 3$ (i.e., the square root of 12). The test statistic is .433. With a one-sided test and $p = .05$, the critical z is 1.64. Therefore, .674 is not statistically significantly greater than .60 in these data.

2 From Equation III.A, the sample t-value is .319. As in Problem 1a, the critical t is 2.160. Therefore, the null hypothesis (that the point-biserial correlation is zero) is not rejected.

3 The sample chi-square value is $15(-.327)^2 = 1.604$. Therefore, the null hypothesis (that the correlation is zero) is not rejected.

5a Convert each r to a Fisher's z. Then, weight each value by $n_i - 3$. The average Fisher's z for the four values is .9086. Back-converting in Table III.1 implies that the average r is .72.

271

6 Convert each r to a Fisher's z. Using Equation III.D, the sample z-statistic is .785. With a two-sided test and $p = .05$, the critical z is 1.96. Therefore, there is no statistical support for the manager's conjecture.

7 Equation III.E yields a sample t of .443, which is less than either critical value (100 or 120 df). Therefore, the value of .20 is not statistically less than .15.

Chapter IV

3a Use Equation IV.G. The corrected r is then .785.

3b The correlation should be corrected for unreliability only in Y. The result is .710.

4 Use Equation IV.I by letting $r_{new, new} = .90$ and solving for k. The value of k is 1.98, so test length should be increased by a factor of almost 2. This means that the number of items in the new test should be 1.98×25 (i.e., about 50 items).

5 Use Equation IV.G again. The corrected correlation is .24.

Chapter V

1a Range restriction might occur because you have performance scores only for individuals hired using the selection test.

1b The restricted correlation is .614, and the restricted standard deviation for the selection test is 5.407. Use of Equation V.B results in $r_c = .907$.

2a Using the same logic and procedures as in Problem 1b, $r_c = .929$.

3 The population correlation is .40, and the population standard deviation of the gender variable is .50. The restricted standard deviation of the gender variable is .3571. Use of Equation V.A results in an estimated correlation of .298.

4a For the five lowest-scoring performers, $r = .438$.

4b The restricted correlation is .438, the restricted standard deviation for Y is 7.891, and the unrestricted standard deviation for Y is 2.702. Use of Equation V.B gives $r_c = .818$.

Chapter VI

1a Use Equation VI.D for b_1 and Equation VI.C for b_0. The result is $\hat{Y} = .920 + .977X_3$.

1b Using the hints in the statement of this problem, SSE is estimated as 475.5. Since $n = 15$, there are 13 error degrees of freedom and the mean squared error is 36.58. Then, use Equation VI.M to obtain a sample t-statistic of 3.29. With $p = .05$ and a two-sided test, the critical value is 2.160. Therefore, reject the null hypothesis (that the weight for X_3 is zero).

1c When $X_3 = 16$, $\hat{Y} = 16.552$. Use this predicted value and Equation VI.N. The equation says to add (and subtract) 13.505 to (and from) the value of 16.552. The confidence interval therefore ranges from 3.047 to 30.057.

2a $\hat{Y} = 3.732 + .896X_4$.

2b Mean squared error is 41.79. The sample t (from Equation VI.M) is 2.804. As in Problem 1b, the critical value is 2.160. Therefore, reject the null hypothesis. That is, the current aptitude test is a statistically significant predictor of Y.

2c The confidence interval ranges from 3.638 to 32.498.

3a The regression is: predicted value of $X_3 = 8.809 + .465Y$.

3b As in Problem 1b, the sample t-statistic is 3.29 and the null hypothesis is rejected.

5 The regression is: predicted value of $X_4 = 14.5 + 1.786X_1$.

Chapter VII

1a Using Equation VII.D gives $r_{Y1.3} = .199$.

1b Place the value of the partial correlation in Equation III.A. Replace the factor $n - 2$ with $n - 3$. The sample t-value is then .703. With $p = .05$, a two-sided test, and 12 df, the critical t is 2.179. Therefore, do not reject the null hypothesis.

2 Using Equation VII.E gives $r_{1Y_3} = .199$.

3 The partial correlation is $r_{Y2.1} = .744$.

4 The implied correlation is the semipartial correlation of $r_{Y3_4} = .430$.

Chapter VIII

1a Use Equations VIII.C through VIII.E. The resulting regression is $\hat{Y} = -2.993 + .713X_3 + .547X_4$.

1b $R^2_{Y.34} = .562$.

1c Consider the test of the weight for X_3 (i.e., the value .713). Since there are $15 - 2 - 1 = 12$ df for error, mean square error is 31.84. The standard deviation of X_3 is presented in the Chapter VI problem set as 5.444. Use of Equation VIII.K then provides $SD(b_{X3}) = .306$. The sample t-value is then $.713/.306 = 2.33$. With $p = .05$, a two-sided test, and 12 df, the critical t is 2.179. Therefore, the null hypothesis is rejected.

1d Use the squared semipartial correlation coefficient. This gives 18.5% and 10.7% for X_3 and X_4, respectively.

2a $\hat{Y} = .187 + 2.253X_1 + .958X_3$

2b $R^2_{Y.13} = .476$. From Equation VIII.I, the sample F-ratio is 5.45. With $p = .05$, the critical F-value with 2 numerator and 12 denominator degrees of freedom is 3.89. Therefore, reject the null hypothesis that $\mathbf{R}^2 = 0$ (i.e., folks would say that the value of R^2 is significant).

2c The value of b_{X3} is .958. Mean square error is 38.06. Using Equation VIII.K results in a standard deviation of .294. The sample t is 3.23. This value is greater than the critical value, the null hypothesis is rejected, and the salesperson's claim is upheld.

3a $\hat{Y} = -3.32 + 1.549X_1 + .712X_3 + .522X_4$

3b SSR is 498.351, and SST is 871.734. $R^2_{Y.134}$ is therefore .572.

3c For example, the weight for X_3 is .712, and the corresponding standard deviation is .327. The sample t-value is therefore $t = 2.176$ (see last column of the table presented at the beginning of Problem 3). With $p = .05$, a two-sided test, and 11 df, the critical t-value is 2.201. Therefore, do not reject the null hypothesis in this case (in fact, none of the b's are statistically significant).

3d Compute the difference in the R^2-values. The unique contribution is therefore $.572 - .562 = .010$.

3e Since the regression weight for gender is not statistically significant, neither is the corresponding unique contribution statistically significant.

Chapter IX

1a Use Equations VIII.C through VIII.E. The regression is $\hat{Y} = -4.506 + 1.976X_4 - .032X_4^2$.

1b The sample t-value is $-.032/.044 = -.727$. With a two-sided test and 12 df, the critical t is 2.179. Therefore, do not reject the null hypothesis (i.e., the variable X_4^2 does not have a unique contribution that is statistically significant).

2a The regression is: Predicted value of $Y_2 = -.669 + 1.257Y_1 + .014Y_1^2$.

2b The sample t-value is $.014/.006 = 2.333$. As in Problem 1b above, the critical t is 2.179. The null hypothesis (that the weight for Y_1^2 is zero) is therefore rejected. There is statistical evidence that Y_1^2 has a unique contribution to the prediction of Y_2, over and above the use of Y_1 alone.

3a Performance on $Y_2 = \mathbf{B}_0 + \mathbf{B}_1 X_1 + \mathbf{B}_2 Y_1 + \mathbf{B}_3 X_1 Y_1 + e$.

3b The sample equation is: Predicted value of $Y_2 = -4.889 + 1.926 X_1 + 1.790 Y_1 - .090 X_1 Y_1$. The sample t-value for the interaction term is $-.090/.098 = -.918$, which is not statistically significant.

4a Performance on $Y_1 = \mathbf{B}_0 + \mathbf{B}_1 X_1 + \mathbf{B}_2 X_4 + \mathbf{B}_3 X_1 X_4 + e$. The null hypothesis in question is $H_0: \mathbf{B}_3 = 0$.

5 The second researcher's sample regression equation would be: Prediction of $Y_1 = 8.596 - 11.135 X_1^* + .648 X_4 + .631 X_1^* X_4$. Notice that the signs of several weights change. However, the only weights whose magnitudes change are those of the constant term and the variable X_4.

Chapter X

1a Use Equation X.A. Wherry's estimate is .489.

1b Use Equation X.B. The Lord-Nicholson estimate is .459.

2a .993

2b .9925

2c The magnitude of the value of sample R^2 in Problem 2 is greater than the value of R^2 in Problem 1. Therefore, all else equal, one would have expected relatively less shrinkage in Problem 2.

4 Use Equation X.D. The value of R^2 is .16, $n = 226$, and $p = 5$. The difference in R^2-values is .09, and the difference in the number of predictors (p_{diff}) is 3. The sample F-ratio is then 7.857. With a .05 level of significance, 3 numerator degrees of freedom, and 120 denominator degrees of freedom, the critical F is 2.68. Therefore, reject the null hypothesis (i.e., there is statistical evidence that the three dependence variables uniquely add to the prediction of opportunistic behavior over and above the two control variables).

NAME INDEX

SUBJECT INDEX

ABOUT THE AUTHOR

Philip Bobko is currently Professor of Management and Psychology at Gettysburg College. He received his Bachelor of Science in Mathematics from M.I.T., his Master's in Educational Research from Bucknell University, and his Ph.D. in Economic and Social Statistics from Cornell University (School of Industrial and Labor Relations). Dr. Bobko has held prior faculty and administrative positions in the Management Departments at the University of Kentucky and Rutgers University, as well as in the Departments of Psychology at Virginia Tech and the University of Maryland. Dr. Bobko has won or been nominated for teaching awards at each of the state universities listed above. He is the author of over 60 publications in leading academic journals and book series in methodology, measurement, management, and industrial/organizational psychology. Content domains of his publications include test fairness, moderated regression analysis, validation methods, goal setting, decision making, utility analysis, and performance standard setting. He has authored two chapters in the most recent *Handbook of Industrial and Organizational Psychology*. Dr. Bobko has been scientific advisor or principal scientist for government contracts totaling approximately $50 million, and he was recently Principal Scientist on a multi-year project to revise the selection system for air traffic controllers in the United States. Dr. Bobko also served as the first elected chair of what is now the Academy of Management's Research Methods Division. In addition to service on many editorial boards, he was a Guest Co-Editor for a special issue of the *Academy of Management Journal*. He was appointed as Consulting Editor for that journal but stepped down from that role to become Editor of the *Journal of Applied Psychology*.